BEFORE THEY WERE TITANS

....

ESSAYS ON THE EARLY WORKS
OF DOSTOEVSKY
AND TOLSTOY

Ars Rossica

Series Editor – **David Bethea**
(University of Wisconsin–Madison)

BEFORE THEY WERE TITANS

....

ESSAYS ON THE EARLY WORKS
OF **DOSTOEVSKY**
AND **TOLSTOY**

Edited with an Introduction by
ELIZABETH
CHERESH ALLEN

BOSTON
2015

Library of Congress Cataloging-in-Publication Data:
A catalog record for this book is available
from the Library of Congress.

Copyright © 2015 Academic Studies Press
All rights reserved

ISBN 978-1-61811-815-8
ISBN 978-1-61811-431-0 (electronic)

Cover design by Ivan Grave

Published by Academic Studies Press in 2015
28 Montfern Avenue
Brighton, MA 02135, USA
press@academicstudiespress.com
www.academicstudiespress.com

To my beloved James

Table of Contents

Acknowledgements ix
Note on the Text xi
List of Contributors xiii
Introduction: Before They Were Titans
Elizabeth Cheresh Allen 1

Part I.
Dostoevsky: Works of the 1840s

I. **Agency, Desire, and Fate in *Poor Folk***
   Lewis Bagby 15

II. **Me and My Double: Selfhood, Consciousness, and Empathy in *The Double***
    Gary Saul Morson 43

III. **Husbands and Lovers: Vaudeville Conventions in "Another Man's Wife," "The Jealous Husband," and *The Eternal Husband***
     Susanne Fusso 61

IV. Dostoevsky's *White Nights:* Memoir of a Petersburg Pathology
Dale E. Peterson 93

V. Dostoevsky's Orphan Text: *Netochka Nezvanova*
Elizabeth Cheresh Allen 115

Part II.
Tolstoy: Works of the 1850s

VI. The Creative Impulse in *Childhood:* The Dangerous Beauty of Games, Lies, Betrayal, and Art
Robin Feuer Miller 153

VII. Fear and Loathing in the Caucasus: Tolstoy's "The Raid" and Russian Journalism
William Mills Todd III and Justin Weir 193

VIII. Tolstoy's *Sevastopol Tales*: Pathos, Sermon, Protest, and Stowe
Liza Knapp 211

IX. On Cultivating One's Own Garden with Other People's Labor: Serfdom in "A Landowner's Morning"
Anne Lounsbery 267

X. Tolstoy's Lessons: Pedagogy as Salvation
Ilya Vinitsky 299

An Afterword on the Wondrous Thickness of First Things
Caryl Emerson 317

Index 329

Acknowledgements

I have amassed great debts to many people in the course of completing this project. Above all, I want to thank the contributors to this volume for their exemplary professionalism, unflagging support, and limitless patience during the period of its assembly. It was truly a privilege, as well as a personal pleasure, to collaborate with each of them. I would single out Robin Feuer Miller for her sage advice, enduring faith, and unfailing encouragement at each step—I could not have compiled this collection without her—and Gary Saul Morson, who wisely gave me key advice at critical junctures, as he has done so often. William Mills Todd III, a steadfast supporter throughout my career, kept helpfully reminding me to "maintain a strict patience," and Caryl Emerson endorsed this volume at its inception and graced it with her elegant Afterword, for which I cannot thank her enough.

I am also grateful for the indulgence of my Bryn Mawr colleagues, Dan E. Davidson, Tim Harte, and Sharon Bain, as I worked on this volume—and over the years. Haverford College's inimitable Russian historian, Linda Gerstein, has my heartfelt thanks for her invaluable input into the introduction. Mikayla C. Holland, an exceptional reader and future scholar in her own right, surpassed all my expectations as a research and editorial assistant. Billie Jo Ember shared her technological expertise whenever it was needed. In addition, I thank the Myra T. Cooley Lectureship Fund and the Faculty Awards and Grants Committee, both of Bryn Mawr College, for their generous support of this project.

I want to acknowledge Igor Nemirovsky and Sharona Vedol of Academic Studies Press for their welcoming reception of the manuscript, and Meghan Vicks and Kira Nemirovsky for expertly shepherding it through the publication process. David Bethea was a model series editor, eminently cordial, generous with his time and counsel, sensitive to every concern. I am also indebted to Elizabeth F. Geballe, who copy-edited the manuscript with great skill, care, and collegiality.

And finally, I thank my husband, James Sloan Allen, for all his worldly wisdom and for keeping me going, literally and figuratively, these many years. I lovingly dedicate this book to him.

Note on the Text

Citations of Dostoevsky's Russian texts come from the *Complete Collected Works* [*Полное собрание сочинений (ПСС)*] in 30 volumes (1972-90) by volume and page number. Citations of Tolstoy's Russian texts come from one of two versions of the *Complete Collected Works*, either the 90-volume edition (1928-58), often known as the Jubilee edition, edited by V. G. Chertkov, or the 100-volume online edition, both cited by volume and page number—the author of each essay on Tolstoy will indicate which version was used. For the convenience of readers who do not know Russian, where there is a widely available translation in print (even if the essay's author did not rely on it), that translation is cited by page number after the Russian citation.

References to key secondary or additional primary sources are given in English, followed by the original titles in brackets. Endnotes, fashioned according to the University of Chicago style, can be found at the conclusion of each essay, followed by a bibliographic list of all the works cited in that essay. In the endnotes and works cited lists, Russian titles are rendered solely in Cyrillic, whereas authors' names are transliterated. In the body of the essays, except for the most commonly-used phrases, every term is translated into English, and then, if the author deems it important, the original term follows in the original language.

Transliteration of most Russian words adheres to the modified Library of Congress system, except for the names of individuals that have an established alternative spelling, including Dostoevsky and Tolstoy, in English. Unless otherwise noted, ellipses and emphases are the responsibility of each author.

List of Contributors

Elizabeth Cheresh Allen
Professor of Russian and Comparative Literature
Bryn Mawr College

Lewis Bagby
Professor (Emeritus) of Modern and Classical Languages
University of Wyoming

Caryl Emerson
A. Watson Armour III University Professor of Slavic Languages and Literatures
Princeton University

Susanne Fusso
Professor of Russian, East European, and Eurasian Studies
Wesleyan University

Liza Knapp
Associate Professor of Slavic Languages
Columbia University

Anne Lounsbery
Associate Professor of Russian Literature
New York University

Robin Feuer Miller
Edytha Macy Gross Professor of Humanities
Professor of Russian and Comparative Literature
Brandeis University

Gary Saul Morson
Frances Hooper Professor of the Arts and Humanities
Professor of Slavic Languages and Literatures
Northwestern University

Dale E. Peterson
Eliza J. Clark Folger Professor of English and Russian
Amherst College

William Mills Todd III
Harvard College Professor
Harry Tuchman Levin Professor of Literature
Harvard University

Ilya Vinitsky
Professor of Slavic Languages and Literatures
University of Pennsylvania

Justin Weir
Professor of Slavic Languages & Literatures
Harvard University

Introduction: Before They Were Titans

Elizabeth Cheresh Allen

Imagine nineteenth-century Russian literature without Dostoevsky and Tolstoy. Its stature would rest largely upon the poetry of Aleksandr Pushkin and Mikhail Lermontov; the short stories, plays, and one novel of Nikolai Gogol; the novels of Ivan Turgenev and Ivan Goncharov; and hundreds of stories and sketches by Anton Chekhov. However extraordinary many of those works are—and however many excellent second- and third-tier authors of nineteenth-century Russia there were—they would not elevate Russian literature to rank among the handful of the world's preeminent literary traditions. The great works of Fyodor Dostoevsky and Lev Tolstoy do that almost by themselves. Symbolist Andrei Bely dubbed the two of them "bogatyrs" ["богатыри"], larger-than-life warrior heroes of Slavic folklore.[1] Yet they rise even above that status. They are the Titans of Russian literature.

But they also in many ways differ dramatically from each other. As Caryl Emerson has observed, by the 1920s it had become "almost a cliché" in Russia to describe them as intellectual and artistic opposites. Dostoevsky, she says, was viewed as "a mystic, the apocalyptic poet of the underground, the celebrator of the trap of human consciousness" whose characters "live on the edge of perpetual crisis" and whose plots "rely heavily on madness, murder, and suicide."² By contrast, Tolstoy was seen as "the teacher of life. His is the sphere of *zhivaia zhizn'* ('living life'), an above-ground and exuberant immersion in nature, physicality, and organic process."³ This difference has become pretty much the common view of these two authors in the West as well, and any reader can see the reasons for it.

The eminent critic George Steiner exemplifies this perception in his emblematically entitled study *Tolstoy or Dostoevsky*. While acknowledging "the characteristic magnificence of the art of [both] Tolstoy and Dostoevsky" achieved through the imaginative scope of their greatest novels, Steiner sees the two "radically opposed" regarding the largest subjects they took on: human history, fate, and "the mystery of God."⁴ He identifies Dostoevsky with the dramatic depth, psychological penetration, and moral passion of Shakespeare, which gave rise in Dostoevsky to an intensive subjectivity, to an "assault" on order, and "a sense of nightmare" in human existence that pays "homage to the absurd."⁵ Steiner identifies Tolstoy with the epic breadth, psychological elevation, and moral dispassion of Homer, leading Tolstoy to a detached objectivity, a sense of harmonious order or "grand design," and an "essential sanity" rooted in an elemental humanism.⁶ Amidst many such critics contrasting the two authors, we can point to Dmitrii Merezhkovsky, who summarily asserted: "If in the literature of all ages and people we wished to find the artist who was the most opposite of Tolstoy, we would have to point to Dostoevsky."⁷

It is not difficult to find sources of the contrast between Dostoevsky and Tolstoy in their lives. Dostoevsky, born in 1821, seven years before Tolstoy, was the son of a strict Russian Orthodox doctor and a merchant's daughter. Although not impoverished as a child—his father had been awarded a small estate outside of Moscow that yielded some income—he lived an adult life marked by emotional upheavals, prolonged imprisonment and exile, chronic poverty, recurring bouts of epilepsy, and compulsive gambling, until he gained a measure of emotional stability and relative financial security only in the decade before he died in 1881, at the age of fifty-nine. In contrast, Tolstoy was born in 1828 into an aristocratic family, and he enjoyed good health and ample wealth throughout most of his life. He did suffer troubles, but these were largely troubles of his own making: he belonged to the elite and yet strove to live like a peasant; he was an innate sensualist and yet sought to behave like a monk; he preached universal brotherhood but emotionally tormented his wife; he fathered a large family but then died in isolation in 1910 at the age of eighty-two, having left his ancestral home to seek the spiritual peace he could never find.

And yet, as different as the lives of Dostoevsky and Tolstoy proved to be, their beginnings exhibit some striking similarities. Each author had lost both parents before his literary career began; each was unsure whether or not he wanted to devote his life to literature and flirted with a career as a journalist; each spent much of his early twenties in a large city—Dostoevsky in St. Petersburg, Tolstoy in Moscow—liberally indulging in the youthful urban male decadence of drinking, gambling, and prostitutes. In addition, each started by writing prose fiction in his early twenties and enjoyed widespread initial acclaim for his first published work, only to have the second work disappointingly received by critics and readers alike. Subsequently, they each experienced abrupt breaks in their literary careers, but then resumed them and rose to the pinnacle of literary greatness. The early writings preceding those breaks also show some provocative kinships, even while suggesting the divergent routes the two authors would eventually take on their way to literary greatness.

Still, why bother with the early works of any major author? For many reasons: how those authors started out, how they experimented with literary forms and contents, what they chose to adopt and what to reject, how they managed influences upon them, how they transmitted distinguishing characteristics of themselves, how they hinted at works to come and how they did not. But the early works of Dostoevsky and Tolstoy deserve attention for more than any or all of those reasons. They warrant reading and study for themselves as literature. Youthful creations as they are, they have much to say on their own. To encourage more attention to what they say is one principal purpose of the essays in this volume.

Yet in truth, it must be granted that if Dostoevsky and Tolstoy had ended their literary careers leaving only their early works, they would have remained relatively minor, if promising, authors. For it would be difficult to argue that the early works have the breadth and depth of the major novels. The early works are more inconstant in narrative style and tone, slighter in characterization, simpler in plot, and shallower in philosophy than the later works. They are, after all, the writings of young men and fledgling authors. But, that said, the early works are well worth exploring for several reasons. They played formative roles in the two writers' literary careers. They display Dostoevsky and Tolstoy experimenting with character types, literary genres, ideas, and narrative styles, drawing on their own experiences, and testing other authors' influence on them. Indeed, what William Mills Todd III and Justin Weir say in their essay on "The Raid" could be said of any of the early works treated here: they give "a remarkable account of the gestation of an artistic consciousness developing in response to both philosophical and narrative challenges," in which we can observe "some of the exciting chaos" caused by youthful experimentation with "aesthetic and professional decisions."[8]

Some of these experiments might be seen to typify any young author searching for a literary identity. Others might reflect the youth of the modern Russian literary tradition itself, barely half a century old, in which genres were still in flux—for instance, Pushkin would label his narrative poem *Eugene Onegin* a "novel in verse" and Gogol would dub his novel *Dead Souls* a "narrative poem." Still others may be said to contain seeds of the great authors that Dostoevsky and Tolstoy would become. The search for foreshadowing is probably the most common reason for reading the early works of any major author. Who could resist reading them with that in mind?

Nonetheless, the early works should not be reduced merely to "the laboratory in which the ideology and techniques of the great novels were worked out,"[9] which risks what Gary Saul Morson has labeled "backshadowing," as Caryl Emerson has pointed out in her perceptive Afterword, or "foreshadowing after the fact," that is, assuming that "the past contains legible signs of the future" that were "clearest in light of what happened later, but they were legible from the first."[10] In her essay included in this volume, Anne Lounsbery refers to that erroneous assumption applied to literature as the "already-always" fallacy. This fallacy induces readers to think they can detect with assurance in an author's immature works the shape of an author's mature thought and art, misperceiving future achievements as *faits accomplis*, as if, for instance, to say, "Look, there he is—it's Tolstoy! He's already *himself*!"[11] And as readers of *War and Peace* know, Tolstoy himself became openly hostile to such a linear, evolutionary view of events, past and present.

It could be more worthwhile to perceive early works in the light of what Morson has called "sideshadowing," which means "the sense that actual events might just as well not have happened" because *"something else* was possible." That "something else" "casts a shadow 'from the side,' that is, from the other possibilities" implicit in an early work that might have shaped later writings but did not. For literature, these "unrealized but realizable" possibilities can be experiments with narrative style or tone, plot, characterization, or theme that an author appeared to embark upon, but declined to follow, in whole or in part.[12] Hence Dostoevsky, for instance, could have sustained throughout his mature works the somewhat sentimental tone of *Poor Folk*, the comic style of "Another Man's Wife," or the female narrative voice of *Netochka Nezvanova*, but he did not. And Tolstoy could have carried throughout his mature works, say, the lyricism of *Childhood*, the reportorial style of *The Sevastopol Tales*, or the philosophical uncertainties of "A Landowner's Morning," but he did not.

Such roads not taken lend as distinctive an interest to early works as do any purported foreshadowing of things to come. For they point to what authors reject while seeking a literary identity with their own voice and vision. And that can say as much about them as does what they embrace. Later, literary maturation and life events set authors on the roads they will eventually take—although not necessarily to the end, as Tolstoy unpredictably proved in the last twenty-five years of his life. But who can tell what might have happened otherwise, given the circumstances of their beginnings?

In 1840, Dostoevsky found himself an orphan in St. Petersburg at age nineteen, enrolled in the Naval Military Engineering Institute, his father having died the previous year and his mother two years earlier. Promoted to the rank of ensign in 1841, he moved away from the Institute, continuing his military studies but devoting much of his time to attending the theater, ballet, opera, drinking, gambling, and generally leading the life of cosmopolitan *bon vivant*. And, as biographer Joseph Frank remarks, that life was expensive: "All of these amusements, of course, required a liberal supply of funds; and Dostoevsky was chronically short of cash. This was not so much poverty as a careless prodigality... . For Dostoevsky received his salary as an officer as well as a large share of the income from his family estate... . But he was always in debt" — a condition that would plague him almost throughout his life.[13] However, while carrying on this profligate life, he nonetheless appears to have nurtured fantasies, if not serious plans, of becoming a writer.

It was partly to earn money that Dostoevsky first acted on his amorphous literary ambitions. He took up the task of translating Balzac's *Eugenie Grandet*, and he tried writing historical dramas of his own—one he called *Mary Stuart*, another was his version of *Boris Godunov*—but these came to nothing. Then, in 1844, after resigning his military commission, he devoted himself to writing the epistolary novella *Poor Folk* (see Lewis Bagby's "Agency, Desire, and Fate in *Poor Folk*"), which was published in 1846. To his surprise, the most influential Russian literary critic of the day, Vissarion Belinsky, highly praised this debut work, befriended Dostoevsky, and drew him into Belinsky's own social circle. Dostoevsky thereupon resolved to dedicate himself to the literary life.

However, his next work, also published in 1846, the post-Gogolian, proto-absurdist novella *The Double* (see Gary Saul Morson's "Me and My Double: Selfhood, Consciousness, and Empathy in *The Double*"), was dismissed by Belinsky, who wrote a review article that, as Dostoevsky bitterly complained, "certified the total shipwreck of [my] literary reputation."[14] Discouraged, but not daunted, he took up journalism the next year as a necessary source of income, authoring several *feuilletons*, or short chatty essays on current cultural events. Yet, despite his literary discouragement, he continued to write and publish works of fiction, including the deceptively slight, humorous stories "A Jealous Husband" and "Another Man's Wife" (see Susanne Fusso's "Husbands and Lovers: Vaudeville Conventions in 'Another Man's Wife,' 'A Jealous Husband,' and *The Eternal Husband*") and the enigmatic novella *White Nights* (see Dale Peterson's "Dostoevsky's *White Nights*: Memoir of a Petersburg Pathology"), all in 1848. Although these works received at best mixed reviews, they kept him writing. Meanwhile, he also cultivated new circles of friends and acquaintances with whom he shared dinners and conversations on many subjects, such as literature and music, as well as social and political ideals, while falling further into a life of disarray and what had become consuming debt.

Unfortunately, the tsar at the time, Nikolai I (1825-55), psychologically scarred at the outset of his reign by the Decembrist Rebellion of young aristocrats and by the Revolution of 1830 in France, was fearful of anything that suggested political dissent. From the beginning of his reign, he had strengthened literary censorship and created a network of secret police and spies; when revolutions against monarchs erupted across Europe in 1848, he ordered the arrest of anyone even loosely associated with activities or groups that might be considered subversive.

Although Dostoevsky was no political revolutionary, he was something of an idealist and vehemently opposed serfdom. He had even discussed with like-minded friends setting up a clandestine printing press to disseminate literature condemning that dehumanizing practice. Such activities got him into trouble. Just as he was beginning to serially publish his first—very apolitical—novel, which retrospectively portrays early stages in the life of a young female opera singer (see my "Dostoevsky's Orphan Text: *Netochka Nezvanova*), he was arrested in 1849. Subjected to an emotionally shattering mock execution, he was subsequently sentenced to hard labor at a prison camp in Siberia, followed by mandated service in the Siberian army. He would return to St. Petersburg in 1859 a psychologically and spiritually changed man. That ten-year period of literary silence marked the end of the first phase of Dostoevsky's career as a writer.

The comparable formative period for Tolstoy commenced not long after Dostoevsky was sent to prison. The orphan Tolstoy, at age twenty-two, having dropped out of the University of Kazan, had returned in 1850 to the family estate to undertake its management. But his youthful self-indulgence soon induced him to shirk those responsibilities and to spend much of his time in Moscow and St. Petersburg drinking, gambling, and visiting prostitutes. As Andrew Wachtel has observed, "Although [Tolstoy] had harbored vague literary plans for years," in the early 1850s "there was as yet no sign that he would become a professional writer… . He had tried his hand at a number of occupations and had, in his own estimation and in that of his family, failed miserably at all of them. He had not gotten a university degree, his efforts to reorganize the family estate had produced no results, [and] he had accumulated gambling debts."[15]

So, like Dostoevsky in the early 1840s, Tolstoy, ten years later, at loose ends and in debt, also wound up in the military. But unlike Dostoevsky, he actually experienced the rigors of real military life. In 1851, he joined his brother Nikolai in the Russian Army stationed in the Caucasus. That same year, while recuperating in a military hospital in Tiflis, Tolstoy began to write what would become his first published work, the semi-autobiographical *Childhood* (see Robin Feuer Miller's "The Creative Impulse in *Childhood*: The Dangerous Beauty of Games, Lies, Betrayal, and Art").

Buoyed by the critical enthusiasm for *Childhood* when it was published in 1852, Tolstoy decided that he would write a series of "Caucasian sketches," which included the ambiguous and ambivalent portrayal of martial life in

"The Raid" (see William Mills Todd III's and Justin Weir's "Fear and Loathing in the Caucasus: Tolstoy's 'The Raid' and Russian Journalism"). Still unsure what type of writer to become, he considered working as a military journalist, but instead, in 1854-55, he published a series of fictionalized scenes based on his own experiences during the Crimean War, the openly anti-war *Sevastopol Tales* (see Liza Knapp's "Tolstoy's *Sevastopol Tales*: Pathos, Sermon, Protest, and Stowe"). However, although he had already envisioned writing long novels, including a three-part extension of *Childhood* and a novel about a Russian landowner, he did not produce one. He did publish two shorter sequels to *Childhood*, entitled *Boyhood* and *Youth*, as well as the novella *The Cossacks* and a handful of short stories—among them the thought-provoking tale of a conflicted serf owner "A Landowner's Morning" (see Anne Lounsbery's "On Cultivating One's Own Garden with Other People's Labor: Serfdom in 'A Landowner's Morning'")—over the course of the 1850s, but none of these works received the critical praise given to *Childhood*.

In late 1855, Tolstoy returned to St. Petersburg, but he remained uncommitted to the writer's life. As Boris Eikhenbaum points out, Tolstoy's writing was "constantly interrupted by other plans."[16] Besides that, Tolstoy felt insufficiently appreciated by readers and critics alike. He noted in his diary in 1857, "My reputation has fallen or barely squeaks and I was greatly distressed within."[17] In that dejected mood, he left Russia for Western Europe in 1858. Upon his return later that year, he wrote to his sister, "It seems I will never write again."[18] And he turned his prodigious energies from literature to what he had decided would be a more useful and rewarding enterprise—educating peasants.

Tolstoy had begun conjuring up his own pedagogical theories years earlier. Now he put those theories into practice, founding a school on his family estate in 1859, taking a second trip to Europe in 1860-61 in order to study European teaching models and methods, and publishing provocative pedagogical articles in the short-lived journal that he launched in 1862 (see Ilya Vinitsky's "Tolstoy's Lessons: Pedagogy as Salvation"). This fervent embrace of pedagogy might have ended Tolstoy's literary career, but it did not. Instead, it was more of a fruitful pause in that career, which he resumed in 1863.

The three-year hiatus between the uncertain first phase of Tolstoy's literary career and the mature writings that followed echoed, albeit it in a briefer, less tortured form, the ten-year break between Dostoevsky's early and mature careers. After those periods away from writing fiction, both authors started anew with more confidence in their intellectual and stylistic literary identities, and ready to give voice, in their own distinctive ways, to big, bold ideas, which they did in some of the biggest, boldest, most powerful novels the world has ever seen.

Arranged chronologically, in order of publication of the primary work examined, these essays offer insightful elucidations of works by Dostoevsky and Tolstoy written in first decade of the literary life of each author. For Dostoevsky, that decade was the 1840s; for Tolstoy, it was the 1850s. Some of these works are known and read outside scholarly circles; most are not. Some have received a fair amount of literary critical attention; most have not. None has received the attention from readers or critics that later works, especially the major novels, have attracted. But they all played formative roles in the two authors' lives on the paths to literary renown before the breaks in those lives that would give them surer footing.

On Dostoevsky's works of the 1840s: Lewis Bagby delves into the complex interplay of human desires and individual agency in *Poor Folk* to reveal the limits imposed on freedom and self-control by misperception and self-deception, as well as circumstances; Gary Saul Morson sets forth the existential quandaries and absurdities of *The Double* in uncovering vexing complexities of consciousness and empathy; Susanne Fusso exposes the unexpectedly dark and violent subtexts in "The Jealous Husband" and "Another Man's Wife" that underlie even these two seemingly slight comic short stories; Dale Peterson detects in the evocative novella *White Nights* a searing critique of urban dwellers' psychological disorders, nourished by a dreamlike city; and I elucidate the evolution of the moral imagination in the eponymous character of *Netochka Nezvanova* to show that Dostoevsky early on rooted morality in creativity, rather than in religion or rationality.

On Tolstoy's works of the 1850s: Robin Feuer Miller plumbs the intricate narrative *Childhood* to illustrate tensions between what she labels "the creative impulse" and the exigencies of actuality; William Mills Todd III and Justin Weir team up to highlight Tolstoy's uncertainties in "The Raid" about both military life and journalism as he searched for his own career; Liza Knapp probes Tolstoy's powerful rendering of human suffering in *The Sevastopol Tales*, exploring the ways Harriet Beecher Stowe's *Uncle Tom's Cabin* influenced that rendering; Anne Lounsbery discerns the deft intermingling of literary genres that subtly conveys the ambiguous view of serfdom in "A Landowner's Morning"; and Ilya Vinitsky maintains that founding a school for serf children was as much the result of Tolstoy's quest for personal salvation as his desire for social justice, as expressed chiefly in his contributions to the pedagogical journal he established.

I should note that these essays were not intended to be either comprehensive—that is, to provide a thoroughgoing survey of Dostoevsky's and Tolstoy's early works—or comparative—that is, to stress connections or contrasts between the two authors. Nor were these essays intended to advance theories about early literary writings or to explicate their debts to the past. The essays, each written by a leading specialist in nineteenth-century Russian literature, single out one early work (or, in one case, two, in one case, three works) by one of the two authors to give fresh, sophisticated readings, from the essayists' own critical perspectives, in their own distinctive voices, without any specified length, critical subject, or method of treatment—some favor close reading, others take a more interdisciplinary tack. But by the very eclecticism of their lengths, subjects, and critical methods, these essays almost uncannily mirror the eclecticism of the young Dostoevsky and Tolstoy, as they themselves tried their hands at different genres, subjects, and so on.

Individually, the essays demonstrate that these early works possess hitherto unexamined or insufficiently known literary riches rendering them worthy of appreciation for themselves alone. And together, the composite portraits of these two artists as young men yielded by the essays disclose unexpected similarities as well as expected differences, and unfamiliar qualities as well as familiar ones. Thus the sum of these essays is greater than its parts. Above all, the essays collected here illuminate in masterly fashion the searching curiosity and precocious literary skills that Dostoevsky and Tolstoy, from the beginnings of their careers, brought to subjects that would occupy them throughout their lives: the mysteries of human nature, the ambiguities of morality, and the yearnings of the human spirit. These essays therefore clearly show, with lucidity and grace, that the early works of Dostoevsky and Tolstoy can arrest our attention and win our admiration for many reasons, long before these authors became the Titans of Russian literature.

Endnotes

1 Bely, *Трагедия творчества*, 8.
2 Emerson, "Tolstoy Connection," 348.
3 Ibid., 346.
4 Steiner, *Tolstoy or Dostoevsky*, 18, 11.
5 Ibid., 229, 150, 229.
6 Ibid., 69, 75.
7 Quoted in Curtis, "Metaphor Is to Dostoevskii," 111.
8 Todd and Weir, "Fear and Loathing," 194.
9 Mochulsky, *Dostoevsky*, 113.
10 Emerson, "Tolstoy Connection," 234.
11 Lounsbery, "On Cultivating One's Own Garden," 294.
12 Morson, *Narrative and Freedom*, 118 (italics Morson's).
13 Frank, *Seeds of Revolt*, 115.
14 Ibid., 212.
15 Wachtel, *Battle for Childhood*, 7.
16 Eikhenbaum, *Young Tolstoy*, 120.
17 Tolstoy, *ПСС*, Chertkov edition, 47:161.
18 Ibid., 60:295.

Works Cited

Bely, Andrei. *Трагедия творчества. Достоевский и Толстой*. Letchworth: Prideaux Press, 1973.

Curtis, James M. "Metaphor Is to Dostoevskii as Metonymy Is to Tolstoi." *Slavic Review*, no. 1 (Spring 2002): 109-127.

Eikhenbaum, Boris. *The Young Tolstoy*. Translated by Gary Kern. Ann Arbor, MI.: Ardis Publishers, 1972.

Emerson, Caryl. "The Tolstoy Connection in Bakhtin." In *Leo Tolstoy. Tolstoy's Short Fiction*, edited by Michael R. Katz, 346-366. New York and London: W.W. Norton & Company, 1991.

Frank, Joseph. *Dostoevsky: The Seeds of Revolt (1821-1849)*. Princeton, NJ: Princeton University Press, 1976.

Lounsbery, Anne. "On Cultivating One's Own Garden with Other People's Labor: Serfdom in 'A Landowner's Morning.'" In *Before They Were Titans:*

Essays on the Early Works of Dostoevsky and Tolstoy. Edited by Elizabeth Cheresh Allen, 267-298. Boston: Academic Studies Press, 2015.

Mochulsky, Konstantin. *Dostoevsky: His Life and Work*. Translated by Michael A. Minihan. Princeton, NJ: Princeton University Press, 1967.

Morson, Gary Saul. *Narrative and Freedom: The Shadows of Time*. New Haven and London: Yale University Press, 1994.

Steiner, George. *Tolstoy or Dostoevsky: An essay in the old criticism*. New York: Knopf, 1959.

Todd, William Mills, III, and Justin Weir. "Fear and Loathing in the Caucasus: Tolstoy's 'The Raid' and Russian Journalism." In *Before They Were Titans: Essays in the Early Works of Dostoevsky and Tolstoy*, edited by Elizabeth Cheresh Allen, 193-210. Boston: Academic Studies Press, 2015.

Tolstoy, Lev. *Полное собрание сочинений*. 90 vols. Edited by V. G. Chertkov et al. Moscow: Gosudarstvennoe izdatel'stvo "Khudozhestvennaia literatura," 1928-1958.

Wachtel, Andrew. *The Battle for Childhood: Creation of a Russian Myth*. Stanford: Stanford University Press, 1990.

Dostoevsky: Works of the 1840s

Agency, Desire, and Fate in *Poor Folk*

Lewis Bagby

From the beginning of his literary career to its end, Dostoevsky explored how individuals can achieve empowerment and exercise their will, or agency, when their circumstances—economic, social, political, environmental, and psychological—would seem to thwart their every effort. Amidst these explorations, if not as openly, Dostoevsky also notably probed human aspirations, or desires.[1] In this essay I examine the subtle ways in which Dostoevsky engaged questions of agency and desire in his first published novel, *Poor Folk* [Бедные люди, 1846)], which shows us "poor folk"—whom Nikolai Dobroliubov, in a famous essay of 1861, labeled "downtrodden people" (301)—as they confront daunting, often crushing realities.[2]

Dostoevsky embarked on this initial exploration of agency and desire in *Poor Folk* at the age of twenty-four. In the fall of 1845, after nearly two years of drafting, revising, and then almost wholly rewriting this short novel, Dostoevsky took the advice of his apartment-mate and delivered the manuscript to the poet and publisher Nikolai Nekrasov for his reaction. Nekrasov gave it to the influential literary critic Vissarion Belinsky with great enthusiasm, and Dostoevsky's career was launched.[3]

In his first review of the novel, Belinsky praised the distinctiveness of Dostoevsky's style, asserting that "[Dostoevsky's] is a talent both unusual and unique. Just in this first work [that talent is] immediately and sharply distinguishable from the whole crowd of writers who are more or less dependent on [Nikolai] Gogol for the direction and character [of their fiction], and thus for their success."[4] To what we would now call popular literature Belinsky preferred literary works that stimulated serious thought. So his remark qualifies as high praise indeed. But he was even more explicit in concluding: "It is better that one read the novel in its entirety rather than enumerate just how much of it is superlative. And this is true for the simple reason that the entire novel, from beginning to end, is indeed superlative" (563).[5]

Despite Dostoevsky's subsequent dismissal of a Gogolian inspiration for *Poor Folk*, most contemporaneous readers affiliated Dostoevsky's novel with Gogol's works, and many twentieth-century critics followed suit, although differing on whether that affiliation constitutes imitation, homage, or parody.[6] And the differences of opinion among critics do not end there. Criticism of *Poor Folk* tends to fall into four categories: the literary-historical, the socio-economic, the structural or linguistic, and the psychological or thematic. Those critics who delve into the novel's literary-historical antecedents (such as Leonid Grossman, Emma Zhiliakova, and Viktor Vinogradov) focus on the influence of Sentimental and Romantic European and Russian literature. Critics who focus on the social and economic strains of the novel (such as Valerii Kirpotin, Georgii Fridlender, and V. I. Etov, among legions of Soviet commentators) stress Dostoevsky's moving depiction of social injustice against the background of tsarist Russia. A third group of critics who emphasize the structural and linguistic foundations of *Poor Folk* (Jane Altman, Gary Rosenshield, Mikhail Bakhtin, and V. P. Vladimirtsev) elucidate divergent aspects of the novel, including its epistolary form, its deployment of secondary and tertiary characters, its use of dialogic language, and its incorporation of folkloric speech. And a final group of critics (Robert Belknap, Susan McReynolds, Joe Andrew, and Carol Apollonio) addresses the psychological make-up of the novel's protagonists and the larger thematic implications of their characterizations.

Among critics, William Leatherbarrow alone touches on the issues of agency and desire, if only in passing. He finds much in *Poor Folk* that presages the treatment of the related issues of self and will (and their negation) in

The Double [Двойник, 1847)] and later in Notes from Underground [Записки из подполья, 1864] and Crime and Punishment [Преступление и наказание, 1867]. Leatherbarrow faults Belinsky for failing to recognize the innovations Dostoevsky incorporated in *Poor Folk*, largely because of Belinsky's focus on social concerns:

> Dostoevsky was groping towards a 'new causality,' a new logic and psychology of motivation that was already running against the grain of contemporary taste. He was tentatively immersing himself in the investigation of the psychological, rather than social, springs of man's behavior. In particular he was beginning to probe a problem which is of fundamental importance in his work as a whole—that of the individual's need to proclaim his freedom and self-will [своеволие] and the effects of this self-assertive impulse on the psychology of this individual.[7]

Even in the earliest works, Leatherbarrow concludes, Dostoevsky underscored the idea that "the human will in its search for total freedom of expression becomes a self-destructive impulse."[8] But, as I dwell on the interrelations of agency, desire, and fate in *Poor Folk*, I will draw conclusions different from Leatherbarrow, as well as those of other critics, arguing that Dostoevsky demonstrated subtle and nuanced conceptions of human desire and agency far earlier than is generally acknowledged.

I will begin by observing the remarkable aptness of the form of Dostoevsky's novel to my subject. He chose not to employ an omniscient narrator or any other authorial surrogate. Nor did he place a frame around his narrative to provide a context or to guide the reader's response (except for the work's title and an ambiguous epigraph).[9] Neither did he offer an epilogue or afterword to indicate what happens to his protagonists in the future. Instead, he turned to a narrative form favored by eighteenth-century European authors and readers alike, the epistolary novel. The narrative unfolds through a series of fifty-five letters exchanged by the two protagonists, a poor orphaned young woman named Varvara Alekseevna Dobroselova and a distant, increasingly impoverished relative of hers, a low-level bureaucrat named Makar Alekseevich Devushkin.[10]

However poor Varvara and Makar may be, and however outmoded the epistolary form Dostoevsky chose to depict their struggles, that form accords the protagonists a fundamental agency—they have the power to speak for themselves. They may have few possessions and fewer appealing prospects, but they can convey their thoughts, their emotions, and their experiences in their own words. Indeed, *Poor Folk* may constitute the earliest example in Dostoevsky's oeuvre of what Bakhtin calls polyphony, a narrative technique whereby each character in a fictional work articulates "a particular point of view on the world and on oneself," which is granted a legitimacy equal to any other point of view. The characters thus acquire the authority "to interpret and evaluate" themselves and their lives, seemingly without authorial intervention.[11]

Varvara's and Makar's letters reveal that they embody two different types of desire and two different senses of agency. Varvara's desires are pragmatic and delimited—she wants to rise up from poverty and to stabilize her social position—and she has a reduced sense of agency that she exercises in order to gratify those desires. By contrast, Makar's desires are idealistic and inchoate—he wants to form a romantic relationship with Varvara and to establish himself as a noteworthy member of society (he occasionally fantasizes about becoming an author)—and he initially succeeds in exercising his agency actively on Varvara's behalf, yet he descends into poverty as he grows increasingly passive. Hence their divergent plot trajectories—hers possibly upward, his probably downward. I will chart these divergent trajectories, first by highlighting the expression of Varvara's and Makar's desires at the outset of the novel, and then by tracing each one's sense of agency as measured by the quantity and quality of references throughout the novel to some higher power controlling the course of human affairs.

I will argue that *Poor Folk* does not portray Varvara and Makar as traditional star-crossed lovers, but as protagonists with desires at cross purposes and criss-crossed senses of agency. Through these portrayals, Dostoevsky suggests that individual efficacy does not derive solely from will or desire, but from a complex intermingling of desire and an individual's belief in a higher power controlling the course of human lives.

Desires at Cross Purposes

When we pick up the narrative thread, Makar's and Varvara's relationship has already taken shape and reached a point of fruition. Neither ever explicitly states how the two met and how long they have known each other.[12] When the narrative begins, however, we learn almost immediately that Makar has fairly recently gotten acquainted with this distant relative of his, having found her in near servitude to a procuress, Anna Fedorovna. Exercising his agency, he has extracted her from this dreadful situation.[13] Furthermore, we learn that Makar has found Varvara safe haven with one of his acquaintances, the seamstress Fedora, who provides a room and assists Varvara in securing honest work. He then moves into living quarters nearby.[14]

Makar desires one thing above all: Varvara's love. His first letter to her—or, more precisely, the first letter we see—is filled (more overtly than he may think) with his love for her:[15]

My precious [бесценная моя] Varvara Alekseevna!

> Yesterday I was happy—inordinately, impossibly happy! For once in your life, you stubborn girl, you have done as I asked. In the evening, at about eight, I woke up (you know, little mother, how I like to sleep for an hour or two after the completion of my duties). I had found a candle and some paper, and was sharpening my pen, when suddenly I happened to raise my eyes—and I will tell you that my heart fairly gave a leap! So you had guessed, after all, what it was my poor heart desired! I saw that one tiny corner of the curtain at your window had been pulled up and hitched onto the pot of balsams, precisely, oh, precisely in the way I had hinted you might do it when we met that time; I at once fancied that I saw your little face at the window for a moment, that you were looking at me from your little room, that you were thinking about me. And oh, my little dove, how disappointed I was when I simply could not discern your charming little face properly!"[16]

At the start of his letter, he lists what he has taken to be signs that she might reciprocate his love: "you have done as I asked," "you had guessed … what it was my poor heart desired," "you were looking at me," "you were thinking about me."[17] She has the power to fulfill his heart's desire.

In this first letter he also provides a reason to believe she reciprocates his feelings: "In my imagination your smile fairly shone [when I saw you in the window], my little angel—your kind, affectionate little smile and in my heart I had exactly the same sensation as that time I kissed you. Varenka, do you remember, my little angel?"[18] Makar feeds off this recollection, thrives on imagining her responses to his affections, and builds castles in the air.

It turns out that Makar has planned to win his heart's desire based on his reading of second-rate Sentimental and Romantic literature.[19] In his first letter, no sooner does he complete the description of his "curtain" fantasy than he embarks on a surprising description of the world about him. This description is the first of several comic passages linking the text to Gogol. But it is also touching. He intermittently borrows language from the literature he is reading because he feels inadequate to express his love. Thus two distinct voices—one matter-of-fact and prosaic and another stylized and literary (if somewhat antiquated)—alternate in his letter:

Prosaic Voice	**Literary Voice**
I am able to report to you, Varvara Alekseevna, my little mother, that last night, contrary to expectations, I slept in regular order and am accordingly most satisfied; it is always difficult to sleep in new lodgings one has just moved into; there is always something that is not quite right.	
	I rose this morning as fresh as a daisy— happy and cheerful! What a wonderful morning it was, my dear. Our window had been opened; the sun was shining, the birds were chirruping, the scents of spring were wafting on the air, and all nature was wakening to life—
well, and everything else was likewise in corresponding manner; everything was in order, spring-fashion. I even had some rather nice daydreams today, and they were all about you, Varenka—.	
	I compared you to a bird of the air, made for the delight of human beings and as an ornament for nature.
It suddenly occurred to me, Varenka,	

> well, and so on, and so forth; i.e., I continued to make similar far-fetched comparisons. I have a book here, Varenka, which says the same sort of thing—all described in the greatest detail.[20] *that we human beings who live in care and trouble ought to envy the carefree and innocent happiness of the birds of the air,*

Makar is not perturbed by borrowing words from books—he explicitly tells her he is doing so—for borrowing reflects his freedom to choose and hence some sense of agency in the pursuit of his own ends.[21] So he is not embarrassed in the least when he tells Varvara that he has taken passages straight from literature. Makar is too naïve and honest to attempt to deceive her. Most significantly, however, the sentimental words give him the means he evidently lacks to express his love. They become his.[22]

Whereas Makar's first letter makes clear his desire for romance, Varvara's first letter conveys her desires more ambiguously, in what she rejects, or in what she does not say:

> Makar Alekseevich, Sir!
>
> Do you know that I am at last forced entirely into quarreling with you? Upon my word, good Makar Alekseevich, I find it hard to accept your presents. I know what they cost you, what deprivations and denials to yourself of the very necessities of life they involve. How many times have I told you that I need nothing, nothing at all; that I have not the wherewithal to repay you for the good deeds with which you have showered me to date. And why these pots of flowers? I mean, the balsams are all right, but why the geranium? I have only to utter one unguarded word, as for example about that geranium, and immediately you go out and buy it; yet I am sure it was expensive, was it not? What wonderful flowers it has! Crimson, like little crosses. Wherever did you get such a pretty geranium....our room is now like paradise—so clean and bright! But listen—why sweets as well? ... [23]

For every expression of desire Makar makes, Varvara offers a gentle rebuff. She begins her letter with the formal salutation: "Makar Alekeevich, Sir"

["Милостивый государь, Макар Алексеевич"], in striking contrast to his letter's much more intimate "My precious Varvara Alekseevna," implicitly reproving him for excessive familiarity. She scolds him for the extravagance of his many gifts (all traditional symbols of love). She regrets that he used to have a much nicer residence than the new dwelling into which he has moved, evidently both to save money and to be closer to her: "You could live much better than this, judging by your salary. Fedora says the way you used to live was better by far. Have you really spent all your life in solitude, in hardship and joylessness, without a friendly word, renting corners from strangers?" She chides him for excessive sentimentality: "All those bits about paradise, and spring, and scents wafting, and birds chirping. What's this, I thought." She brushes aside their secret lovers' code of communication: "About the curtain, I never gave it any thought; I expect it must have got hitched up of itself when I was moving the pots of flowers; well I never!"[24] And she ignores his reference to a kiss they exchanged. Varvara dismisses every romantic gesture Makar makes and rebuts every romantic thought he utters. Apparently she does not desire a romantic relationship with him.[25]

Yet it would be misleading to suggest that Varvara does not desire anything from Makar. While attempting to rein in his excessive gifts and to tone down his discourse, in her first letter Varvara conveys genuine concern for Makar's well-being, shows that she appreciates his gifts, asks him to visit her, cautions him not to ruin his health, confesses to harboring doubts, to feelings of sadness and of anxiety about her future, and requests that he write to her again.[26] She evidently wants him to continue playing a role in her life, only on her terms. She wants him to be a friend, a confidant, an advisor—but not a lover.

So strongly does she wish to keep him in her life that she acquiesces to one of his romantic desires: "Write to me. Today I will hitch up a corner of the curtain intentionally. Go to bed a bit earlier; last night I saw your candle was lit until midnight."[27] Her precarious circumstances—she suffers from poverty, isolation, and ill health—may force her to succumb to his fantasy of romance a bit, but only a bit. These circumstances arguably transform Varvara's desires into needs for money, shelter, and protection, needs that at times cause her to strategically play upon Makar's desires for love.

But, as her subsequent letters reveal, Varvara has other desires for her future—for social stability, financial security, and psychological equilibrium.

These desires are rooted not only in her pressing needs of the present but also in her past, in cherished memories of her childhood. She frames these memories within the standard oppositions of the Sentimental canon—country/city; nature/culture; youthful love/loss; illiteracy/literacy; family/others; privation/privilege[28]—and collects them in what she labels her "memoir."[29] This memoir describes her early life, which was built around a happy home with a loving mother, the financial security of a simple existence in the countryside, and true love. She has gradually lost all of it as she has grown up, and her life of loss shapes her desires for the future. For Varvara longs to preserve something of her happy childhood: "And I should think that I should have been truly happy if it had been necessary for me to spend my entire life never leaving the village and staying in the same place."[30]

In hopes of fulfilling those desires, she eventually decides to accept a proposal of marriage from the man, Bykov, who, she hints, had despoiled her honor. Although she knows that "he's always in a bad temper and yesterday he administered a beating to the house manager, as a result of which he got into trouble with the police," she accepts his proposal as much because acceptance may restore what she has lost as because she desperately needs to have her needs met.[31] By marrying Bykov, she will return to her beloved countryside, she will raise and solidify her social position by becoming the wife of a landowner [помещица], and she may have children, since Bykov wants an heir. "Bykov is said to be a kind man," she tells Makar, although she may be trying to convince herself more than Makar of this lie. "He will respect me; perhaps I will respect him, too. What more can be expected of our marriage?" she asks rhetorically.[32]

In the same letter, however, where she tells Makar that she and Bykov may come to respect each other, she concludes on an ominous note: "Bykov has arrived; I am leaving this letter unfinished. There was much more which I wanted to tell you. Bykov is in the room!"[33] Clearly, she fears being caught writing to Makar. And later, she confesses that she is "afraid to look into the future. I have a certain premonition of what will happen, and am living in a kind of daze."[34] Rather than receiving respect, she has a premonition that she is choosing physical and emotional abuse.

Neither Makar nor Varvara has good reason to believe their desires will be fulfilled. Their basic needs may be met—Makar's through the generosity of his office superior, Varvara's through her marriage—but their desires for love and respectability, it appears, will not.[35]

Nonetheless, Varvara does act. She attempts to exercise her agency, as Makar does not. His will does not prevail in the world; by the end, he can only beg Varvara to write to him again. But she evidently falls silent, as their correspondence—and the novel—end. Why can Varvara actively seek to fulfill her desires while Makar cannot?

Critics have suggested a number of reasons for Makar's passivity: among them, social injustice, psychological instability, and moral weakness.[36] In my view, a crucial factor contributing to this passivity (in contrast to Varvara's activity) is the extent to which each believes in a higher power—be it God or fate or destiny—imposing order on human experience and controlling individual lives. I will now turn to the subtle way Dostoevsky conveys the differences between the two characters' references to a higher power as those references correlate with their divergent senses of agency.

Higher Powers

The bulk of *Poor Folk*—and of critical commentary on the novel—focuses on the major events that occur along the way toward Makar's failure to realize his desires, in contrast to Varvara's possible realization of hers. One way to explain Makar's and Varvara's divergent courses through the narrative comes by looking at the quantity and quality of their references to some higher power. Through these references we can see that, while Makar's fluctuate, Varvara's remain constant, thus suggesting that faith in an orderly universe may contribute to belief in oneself and to the assertion of one's agency.

Makar and Varvara refer to higher powers in *Poor Folk* slightly over one hundred times, which on average amounts to nearly two references per letter. Only 26 percent of these references occur in the first half of the narrative. They come in various guises, most often as manifestations of habitual speech (exclamations, formulaic blessings, phatic social gestures), and far less often as expressions of religious belief (invocations, confessions, and lamentations). 74 percent of those references appear in the novel's second half, where they most often express, if not authentic religious belief, at least faith in some superior force imparting order to human affairs.

Not surprisingly, Makar and Varvara make reference to higher powers differently, both quantitatively and qualitatively. The number of Varvara's

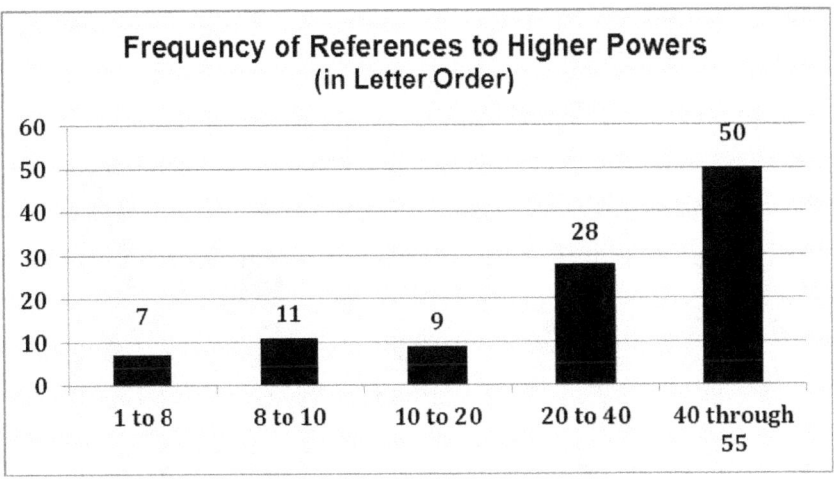

references is relatively constant—in the first twenty letters (that is, nearly halfway through the novel), she refers to God or fate or destiny in some form [бог, господь, рок, судьба, доля, жребий, etc.] twenty-two times; in the novel's second half, she refers to them twenty-six times, hardly a significant increase. By contrast, Makar refers to God or fate or destiny in some form only seven times in the novel's first half, mostly in habitual locutions. But his references increase dramatically in the novel's second half—to fifty-nine, approximately 90 percent of his total—growing in intensity, only to disappear in his final letter. Varvara's references tend to be fairly precise and pragmatic, whereas Makar's are more general, even idealistic.

Makar's first letter contains three references to God or the Lord typical of the first half of his letters, each reference seemingly a common set phrase rather than a reflection of religious belief. The first reference appears after his disquisition on the little birds of the air [небесные птицы] and his confession that he has copied out the flowery passages from a "little book": "There are various other thoughts in [the book], but God go with them" ["Там и еще есть разные мысли, да бог с ними"]. He immediately turns to other matters, suggesting that the expression "God go with them" is no more than a standard Russian turn of phrase that completes the preceding topic and enables the transition to a new one: "Now tell me, where were you going this morning, Varvara Alekseevna?"[37]

The second reference uses the same expression, but not as a transition to a new topic. It appears as something more akin to a blessing and is applied to

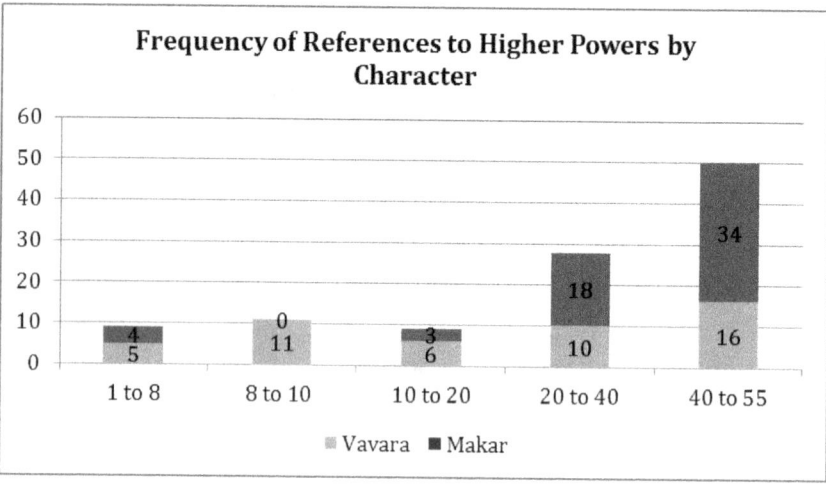

Fedora: "It's true that Fedora's a bit grumpy sometimes; but don't you pay any attention to that, Varenka. God be with her! She's such a kind one." This reference may have more substance than the previous one, conveying a positive attitude toward Varvara's servant. Makar similarly describes his servant, Teresa, invoking God a third time: "I have already written to you about the Teresa we have here—also a kind and reliable woman. And there I was getting so worried about our letters. How would they ever be delivered? And then, to our good fortune, the Lord sent Teresa. She is a kind, meek, gentle woman."[38] Whether Makar truly believes that the Lord sent Teresa or not remains moot, given the absence of other indications of his faith up to this point in the novel.

Throughout the first half of *Poor Folk* Makar uses a greater variety of expressions to refer to higher powers than Varvara, thereby suggesting a more imprecise feeling about them than she has.[39] His verbal habits seem drawn from a common fund of clichés, which themselves reflect largely unconscious, culturally acquired, unquestioned beliefs. And only Makar uses passive constructions like "written by God" ["написано богом"], both echoing and reinforcing his characteristic passivity.[40] In the second half, Makar's references to higher powers increase in number and intensity. For Makar, they seem to be accompanied by his growing loss of any sense of agency.

By the time Varvara announces her decision to marry Bykov and to move with him to Siberia, Makar responds in a letter of September 23 that makes more—and more substantive— references to higher power than in any other letter:

> I hasten to reply to you, little mother; I hasten to tell you, little mother, that I am amazed. This is somehow all wrong. . . . Yes, it is right, Varenka, it is right; Bykov has acted honourably; only you are agreeing to his proposal, my darling. Of course, God's will is in all things [конечно, во всем воля божия]; it is right, it must unquestionably be so [это так, это непременно должно быть так]—that is to say, God's will must be in this [то есть, тут воля-то божия непременно должна быть]; and the providence of the Heavenly Creator is, of course, blessed and unfathomable, and human fates, too—they are the same [и промысел творца небесного, конечно, и благ и неисповедим, и судьбы тоже, и они то же самое].[41]

Makar's letter, all searing emotion, is cast in the darkening shadow of permanent loss and the stark terror of meaninglessness. Any sense of agency has forsaken him. The letter is meant to change Varvara's mind—it does not—as well as to reassure himself that life still has some order and therefore potential meaning. He repeatedly attributes Varvara's decision to marry Bykov to variations of "God's will": "Of course, God's will is in all things"; "it is so, it must unquestionably be so—that is to say, God's will must be in this"; "and the providence of the Heavenly Creator is, of course, blessed and unfathomable, and human fates, too—they are the same."[42] In courting Varvara, Makar has sacrificed everything for her—his health, a modest degree of dignity, and financial security. He has maintained a minimal sense of agency, if only verbally, throughout the course of his correspondence with Varvara. Confronting the extinction of any hope of romance he had entertained over the past six months, Makar becomes almost completely passive. He feels powerless to change his fate, or, as he puts it here, to alter the Creator's "blessed and unfathomable" plan. Makar utterly submits to that plan, acting only to run pre-wedding errands for Varvara.

As an ironic sign of his submission, his final letter almost completely lacks reference to higher powers of any kind. Given that Varvara will be married to Bykov and thus likely to disappear from his life, higher powers, Makar seems to have concluded, do him no good.[43] They work only to exclude him. His fragile sense of agency, captured in his first letter, is completely shattered.

Varvara's sense of her own agency develops in the opposite direction. She is introduced as a recent victim with virtually no agency. Over the course of the narrative, however, she discovers that she *does* have some agency. For example, she manages her relationship with Makar, earns a modest, irregular, but honest income, and even—reversing roles—provides Makar with small amounts of money when he is most in need. As her sense of agency builds, she briefly entertains the possibility of employment as a governess. Then, within the limitations imposed by circumstances, she exercises what agency she can and decides to marry Bykov. We do not know whether that exercise succeeds.[44]

By contrast to Makar, who initially refers to higher powers only in passing and more as a habit of speech, in her first letter—when her sense of agency is presumably at its lowest ebb— Varvara mentions those powers seriously, without seeming either to blame them or to seek solace for her still-perilous circumstances. Lamenting those circumstances, she writes: "Oh, what is to become of me, what will be my fate? [Ах, что-то будет со мною, какова будет моя судьба!] The worst of it is that I am in a state of such uncertainty, that I have no future, that I cannot even guess what will become of me. I am afraid to look back, too. There is such misery there that its mere recollection is enough to make my heart tear apart. I shall grieve forever over the evil people who have destroyed me."[45] Notably, as she voices her fears here, Varvara refers to fate, not God or the Lord, as the impersonal force controlling her life—she does not hold God responsible.[46]

Yet in her subsequent letters, Varvara refers to God as a higher power over her life thirty-six of the forty-seven times she mentions such powers (in comparison, Makar refers to God only twenty-five out of fifty-eight times), and she uses fewer terms for higher powers than he does. Varvara's more precise, albeit more frequent, invocation of higher powers suggests that she mentally confines their influence to a narrower realm. She thus indicates that she has—or discovers—a greater sense of her own agency than Makar has. She displays this sense when she informs Makar that she has decided to marry Bykov: "I must agree to his proposal" ["я должна согласиться на его предложение"], not because she feels destined to do so, but because marrying Bykov is the most practical step she can take: "If there is anyone who can save me from my shame, restore to me my honorable reputation, and rescue me from poverty, deprivation and unhappiness, it is him, and him alone," she declares.[47] And she concludes, "God knows whether I will be happy, my fate is in His holy, ineffable power, but I have made up my mind" ["Знает бог, буду ли я счастлива, в его святой, неисповедимой власти судьбы мои, но я решилась"].⁴⁸ God may control her future, but Varvara can make her own decisions in the present. Her belief in God apparently goes beyond mere rhetoric. Yet she does not merely submit to divine authority. She retains a sense of agency sufficient to act even against great odds, and to hope that her actions might avail.

Nonetheless, Varvara's final letter contains more references to higher powers than any previous letter. Although she has chosen a future with Bykov, she knows she cannot control that future: "It is all done! My lot is cast [Выпал мой жребий]; I have no knowledge of what it is to be, but I am obedient to the Lord's will. . . . Don't grieve for me, live happily, remember me, and may God's blessing descend on you!"⁴⁹ Later in the letter she says, "God alone knows what may happen."⁵⁰ Dostoevsky leaves it to his readers to imagine what that future holds for Varvara.

Varvara's remark "My lot is cast" requires close scrutiny. On the surface, it may simply, even tritely, indicate that she will accept whatever comes her way. Beneath the surface, however, this remark may constitute something of a ruse on her part. Knowing that she has chosen to abandon Makar to pursue her desires, hence denying his, Varvara removes the implication of her own agency from her letter and attributes her fate to powers beyond her control. Then she attempts to assuage Makar's feelings of helplessness and isolation by proclaiming that she loves him deeply [крепко]. We must wonder, of course, whether this profession of love is even more torture for Makar than the prospect of her leaving and completely severing their relationship.

I do not mean to suggest that Varvara is insincere in her profession of love for Makar in her final letter. But she is expressing her guilt, too.⁵¹ He has given her everything—and she has taken it, and now is leaving him forever. This is no small matter. Varvara has become, in effect, the tragic "lot" that has befallen Makar. To be sure, she does what she can. She encourages him to exercise his agency on his own behalf. She tells him that she will remember him and will pray for him, and that she hopes "God's blessing descend[s]" upon him.⁵² But she has learned from her own experience that individuals, no matter how poor, can muster the agency to attempt to fulfill their deepest desires in an orderly universe. She herself desires wealth over penury, health over disease, hope over despair, life over premature death, and she pursues those desires. She will no longer be one of the poor folk. Makar must do the same.⁵³

In a postscript, she begs him to "remember, remember your poor Varvara."[54] What Makar should remember, however, is her moving example of agency, her courage. He will need it desperately now that she is gone.

Reading for (Dis)Closure

Dostoevsky subtly yet tellingly underscores the protagonists' differing desires and opposite senses of agency in their responses to what they read—most notably, Pushkin's "The Stationmaster" ["Станционный смотритель," 1830]. (Makar also reads Gogol's "The Overcoat" ["Шинель," 1842], which he strongly dislikes.[55]) As students of Russian literature know, the stationmaster of the title, Samson Vyrin, lives in a remote corner of Russia with his beautiful but bored daughter, Dunia. Dunia escapes the dull, unfulfilling life she leads with her meek, downtrodden father by running off with a young nobleman, Minsky. Pushkin leads readers to expect that the nobleman would ruin her and then leave her to return home in disgrace, only to be forgiven by her benevolent father, as in a gender-toppled parable of the Prodigal Son. Instead, Pushkin turns the parable on its head. Vyrin travels to the city to rescue Dunia, only to be repulsed by Minsky. Broken-hearted, Vyrin goes home alone, and within a few years he drinks himself to death. Dunia returns to visit after she is elegantly established, apparently married to Minsky, and living quite well, thank you, as the mother of their two children.

Pushkin's foiling of his readers' expectations is both serious and comic. But Makar takes the story quite seriously. Makar deems himself a Vyrin (a sweet, humble, if besotted man thoroughly dedicated to a female relative, actively seeking to rescue her from the consequences of poor choices). Makar so identifies with Vyrin's desire to save Dunia that he ignores the complete collapse of Vyrin's sense of agency and his utter failure to fulfill his desires and restore Dunia to their home. Makar misreads strength of desire for the successful exercise of agency.

Varvara's response to "The Stationmaster" is also a misreading, although for a different reason.[56] She likely finds a role model in Dunia, and secretly harbors desires for marriage and wealth similar to Dunia's. Moreover, Varvara discovers an inspiration to exercise her sense of agency in the success of Dunia's elopement. She misreads the exercise of agency for the assured satisfaction of desire.

Unfortunately, these misreadings do not bode well either for the fulfillment of their desires or the expansion of their senses of agency. For Makar and Varvara arguably misread themselves and their circumstances, as much as Pushkin's story. At the conclusion of the novel, Makar has prosaic options available to him. He remains employed at the novel's end and could return to living on the just adequate salary he continues to receive and that sustained him well enough prior to his meeting and falling in love with Varvara. He might again find quarters like those he enjoyed contentedly for twenty years in the bosom of a surrogate family. But his prospects do not look good because, in focusing so much on his desires and refusing to temper them, he forsakes his sense of agency, convinced that he has been victimized by an uncaring God and an unforgiving fate whose plan it is, he concludes, to subdue him.[57]

Varvara, by contrast, may accord her agency too much efficacy. Even the cautious optimism she voices about her future seems unjustified: "Bykov is said to be a kind man," she tells Makar. "He will respect me, perhaps I will respect him, too. What more can be expected of our marriage?"[58] But what we see of Bykov does not bespeak respect, for Varvara or anyone else. He appears arrogant, selfish, irritable, and insensitive. Moreover, in her penultimate letter, the exercise of her agency is reduced to attaining practical, even materialistic, goals. She sends Makar to her seamstress to ensure that the letters of the monograms on her handkerchiefs are embroidered correctly (*"tambour a broder"* and not "satin stitch"); that the leaves on her cape be sewn "in relief"; that the cape's collar be made of "lace or wide furbelows"; and—"the most important thing"— that the seamstress "must change the silk and match it with the pattern we chose yesterday." Her desires have been reduced to the size and shape of needlepoint stitches, her agency diminished to getting Makar to spend "the whole morning running around" performing these mundane tasks.[59] Still, she retains her faith in higher powers, as Makar does not, declaring in her last letter: "I am obedient to the Lord's will."[60]

Humans seem unwilling to alter their conception of higher powers, for that conception binds the universe and makes sense of what might otherwise be construed as randomness and meaninglessness. Few of us operate within an abiding consciousness of those powers—we take the order of the universe for granted until a crisis occurs, when we suddenly question the role of God or fate in our lives, suddenly doubting the validity of our desires and the extent of our agency. This is in its own way a form of misreading, and, like misreading literary texts, it delivers potentially erroneous conclusions about the nature of the universe. Makar, for one, concludes that losing Varvara is due to the workings of God and fate alone—he takes no responsibility for the loss.[61] Varvara has at least accepted a modicum of responsibility for her actions and, therefore, Dostoevsky suggests, has acquired a more realistic view of herself and her circumstances, as she sustains her faith in the cosmic order.

This last point raises questions about our relationship to the novel as readers. In this case the theme of reading reaches beyond the novel into our own lives. We are invited, if we are willing, to see ourselves in Makar's and Varvara's mold—as readers, if sometimes mistaken ones. The absence of closure in the novel opens up the possibility of taking responsibility for our own actions, even if only for the conclusions we draw from having exercised agency. As we envision what happens afterwards to Makar and Varvara (beyond the text we have in hand), we project our own desires, senses of agency, and the beliefs that undergird them, onto the characters. These conclusions can disclose us to ourselves. Moving readers to contemplate the weighty burden of self-knowledge and the dark-glassed complexity of individual responsibility is a remarkable achievement of Dostoevsky's in his first published fictional work, *Poor Folk*.

Endnotes

1 In this essay I will use the term "agency" in a narrow sense to signify the ability of the individual to act at will in the world. I will use the term "desire," in contrast to "need" or "want," to signify the subjective wishing for something that activates the quest for agency.

2 Dostoevsky may not have been prepared to fully depict the sources of his protagonists' desires. René Girard offers a provocative model in his theory of "mediated," or "triangular" desire (1-52), but applying that model to *Poor Folk* would require a good deal of conjecture about what takes place both before the narrative commences and after its conclusion.

3 *Poor Folk* appeared in *The Petersburg Almanac* [*Петербургский сборник*] in January 1846, but by then it was already widely known amongst literati. The history of Dostoevsky's work on *Poor Folk* is presented in Dostoevsky, *ПСС* 1: 464-80. See also Joseph Frank, *Seeds*, 127-156. Frank notes that Dostoevsky first mentions working on *Poor Folk* to his brother, Mikhail, in

the fall of 1844 (131). Commentary in *ПСС*, however, suggests that Dostoevsky began the novel as early as January 1844 (464-465). Iakubovich treats the biographical elements that appear in the novel (39-55). Vetlovskaia also discusses the genesis of the novel (5-10). Kirpotin assesses the immediate critical response to the novel (*Молодой*, 10-14).

4 Belinsky, "Петербургский сборник," 9:551.

5 Ibid., 563. A year later, in reviewing literary activity for the entirety of 1846, Belinsky's opinion had shifted from enthusiasm to only qualified support: "Almost all unanimously found in Mr. Dostoevsky's *Poor Folk* a capacity for wearying the reader even while it evoked his admiration, and attributed this, some to prolixity, others to excessive fecundity. Indeed, it must be admitted that if *Poor Folk* had appeared condensed by at least one-tenth and if the author had been judicious enough to expurgate needless repetitions of words and phrases his would have been an impeccably artistic work" ("A Survey," 409).

6 See Tynianov, 412-55; Bem, 127-36; Bakhtin, 204-11; Vetlovskaia, 125; Trubetskoi, 158-161; Terras, *Young Dostoevsky*, 15-19; and Frank, *Seeds*, 113-136. Jackson provides an intriguing synthetic reading of Gogol's significance by coupling the perspectives of Belinsky and Rozanov in *Dialogues*, 188-207.

7 Leatherbarrow, "The Rag with Ambition," 607-8.

8 Ibid., 617.

9 Peace alone treats both title and epigraph (56-57). He views the epigraph's antilogy, taken from Vladimir Odoevsky's short story "The Living Corpse" ["Живой мертвец," 1844], as a covert reference to Gogol. He maintains that the epigraph also reflects the influence of reading on the formation of Makar's desires (57). And Dostoevsky may have had yet another purpose in choosing as his epigraph the concluding lines of "The Living Corpse." For the epigraph Odoevsky affixed to his work presents in a dialogue format what Dostoevsky takes on as his challenge in writing *Poor Folk*— memorializing poor people. Odoevsky's epigraph reads: "'I wanted to give expression (in letters) to that psychological law by which not one word pronounced by a man, not one action, is forgotten . . . but without fail produces some kind of action; so that responsibility is connected with each word, with each apparently insignificant action, with each impulse of

a man's soul.' 'About that it would be necessary to write a whole book'" (66). Dostoevsky wrote that "whole book." See also Zhiliakova (20-21) and Vetlovskaia (55-56).

10 Dobroselova and Devushkin are characteronyms meaning, respectively, something like Goodtown and Younglady. These names have been much remarked in the critical literature for their associative and polemical qualities. The text is replete with characteronyms—e.g., Bykov (bull), Gorshkov (pot), Pokrovsky (intercessor). See Vinogradov, 187; Peace, 53; Vetlovskaia, 56-59.

11 Bakhtin, *Problems,* 47.

12 A number of critics have commented on the ambiguities of the novel's beginning. For instance, Robert Belknap remarks: "Dostoevsky plays a very different plotting game at the beginning of *Poor Folk*. The first five letters outline a situation obscurely, suggesting that the plot begins in the middle of things, but giving virtually no information on what [those] things are" (39). Peace expands on the point: "It is clear that [Varvara and Makar] meet in the intervals and silences between the literary exchanges. It is a form which, by its very nature, forces the reader to exercise his imagination, and his own analytic skills. It also allows Dostoevsky in this first of his literary works to display what will become basic features of his writing—hint, innuendo, allusion. Thus even here, typically, evil is shrouded in ambiguity: is Bykov Varvara's former seducer?; is he the father of Pokrovsky?; is his offer to marry her mere loveless calculation?; and what are Varvara's real feelings toward him?" (61). I think, however, that the initial letters provide fairly precise suggestions about the protagonists' relative desires and senses of agency in the period immediately preceding the events portrayed.

13 This traditional reading of the plot has been challenged recently by Apollonio, who suggests that Makar is a predator as much as is Bykov, that Bykov's attempts to seduce Varvara have been forestalled by her, and that Makar's failure (and Varvara's success) has cost Anna Fedorovna her investment in the girl. Anna Fedorovna then seeks to recoup her losses by encouraging Bykov to marry the object of his (sexual) desire (19-22). But seeing *Poor Folk* from this perspective does not account for (1) Makar's ineffectiveness and weakness, as well as his lineage from the Natural School that makes buffoons of humble clerks [чиновники] (Makar is no Bykov),

(2) Dostoevsky's insistence on the goodness and charity of Makar, Varvara, and other poor characters in the face of the evil represented by Anna Fedorovna and Bykov, and (3) suggestions about the nature of good and evil presented in Dostoevsky's other works of the 1840s. To re-evaluate the novel in this way is to isolate it from its social, historical, and literary contexts. Apollonio's interpretation nonetheless poses a valuable challenge to conventional thinking about *Poor Folk*.

14 Makar's third letter, dated April 12, sets forth in gruesome detail the indignities to which he is subjected in his new boarding house (1:19-21; 14-16). Apollonio comments (in reference to Ippolit's poverty in *The Idiot* [*Идиот*, 1869]): "He encounters the kind of squalor that often signals Dostoevsky's coded image of grace: a squalid garret with its impoverished family, the apparently drunk man on the bed, the rickety furniture piled with rags, the teapot, the crumbly black bread, the ever-present candle, the pale, sickly woman, the downtrodden husband, the toddler, *the newborn baby*" (34). This description perfectly fits the living quarters of a neighbor in Makar's boarding house.

15 Regarding the intimate tone of the letters exchanged between the two correspondents, Grossman maintains: "Dostoevsky's basic requirement [in using a novel in letters was] to reveal and reflect life not in its finished and polished forms, but in its ever-changing stages of formation, maturation and development" (62).

16 Dostoevsky, *ПСС*, 1:13; 3-4. Quotations of *Poor Folk* come from F. M. Dostoevsky, *Полное собрание сочинений* [*Complete Collected Works*], first cited by volume and page number, then followed by the page number in the translation of *Poor Folk* by McDuff.

17 Bakhtin finds in *Poor Folk* a more complex form of hidden dialogue than I present here. According to Bakhtin, the second voice must be inferred from the utterances of the first voice. Bakhtin fills in what he takes to be the missing half of the dialogue implied by Makar's utterances (207-11).

18 Dostoevsky, *ПСС*, 1:14; 4.

19 Fridlender, *Реализм*, 64-65.

20 Dostoevsky, *ПСС*, 1:14; 4-5 (italics mine).

21 Compare Makar's frankness with the duplicity of, for instance, Germann in Pushkin's "The Queen of Spades" ["Пиковая дама," 1834]. Germann

woos the naïve lady's companion Lizaveta with letters that he copies word for word from German Romantic literature. Germann does not disclose this fact to Lizaveta, and she falls for the ruse. Here Dostoevsky explicitly elevates Makar's moral stature above Germann's.

22 Gary Saul Morson reminds us that, once someone extracts a quotation from someone else, that quotation "belong[s] to the second speaker, who may or may not coincide with the historical first speaker of the extract" (155).

23 Dostoevsky, *ПСС*, 1:17-18; 7-8.

24 Ibid., 1:18; 8.

25 Arguing to the contrary, John Lyles in "Makar Devushkin as Eligible Bachelor?" asserts that, had Makar only proposed to Varvara, she would have accepted him (347-76). I am not persuaded by his arguments.

26 Dostoevsky, *ПСС*, 1:19; 9.

27 Ibid., 1:19; 9.

28 Karamzin's short story "Poor Liza" ["Бедная Лиза," 1792] provides the model here, which Varvara's memoir follows in spirit, if not to the letter.

29 Dostoevsky, *ПСС*, 1:27-45; 20-45.

30 Ibid., 1:27; 20.

31 Ibid., 1:103; 12.

32 Ibid., 1:101; 120.

33 Ibid.

34 Ibid., 1:103; 123

35 Zhiliakova predicts a more benign outcome for Makar: "Under the influence of love there flows a torturous, but unusual process of awakening in Makar Alekseevich's self-consciousness. It is love for Varen'ka that has raised him higher in his own eyes" (72).

36 Terras goes so far as to claim that in "An Honest Thief" ["Честный вор," 1848], it is suggested that Makar has died of drink (42).

37 Dostoevsky, *ПСС*, 1:14; 5.

38 Ibid., 1:14; 5.

39 There is no explicit reason provided in the first half of the novel to consider Makar's invocations of higher powers as anything other than common parlance.

40 Makar also uses "calculated by God" ["рассчитано богом"] and "arranged by God" ["устроено богом"] (1:61).

41 Dostoevsky, *ПСС*, 1:101-02; 120.
42 Another reading is possible here, due to a grammatical ambiguity (amphiboly). The word normally translated as "fates" ["судьбы"] (nominative plural) could also be translated as "of fate" (genitive singular). This would result in the translation: "The plan of the Heavenly Creator is, of course, blessed and unfathomable, and [the plan] of fate is too—they are the same." This translation would underscore Makar's inability to make even a modicum of sound theological sense.
43 As Leatherbarrow poignantly observes, "A man's position is ordained by the Almighty, but recognition of the will of God is for Devushkin tantamount to an act of self-effacement in that it calls for recognition and acceptance of his own insignificance" ("The Rag with Ambition," 608).
44 We may harbor some hope that Bykov's desires for sexual and emotional dominance will be thwarted. The basis for this hope comes from Pushkin's ironic conclusion to "The Queen of Spades," where Germann's once-naive victim, Lizaveta, now secure in a marriage that moves her socially upward (and overturns the model of Karamzin's "Poor Liza"), seems to have acquired from her cruel mistress and from her bitter encounter with Germann a sense of agency sufficient to hold her own with her husband, if not to dominate him.
45 Dostoevsky, *ПСС*, 1:18; 9.
46 In 2700 B.C.E. as he looked out over an empty, flood-washed world, Ziusudra of Sumer wrote a letter to the future. In it he reminds us that "fate, my dear friends, is like a wet bank. It is always going to make you slip" (http://ourlittleseal.wordpress.com/ entry for January 22, 2011). My thanks to Emily Rapp for providing this quotation. Buzina discusses the language of fate, destiny, lot, etc., as a function of social class and educational level (9-10).
47 Dostoevsky, *ПСС*, 1:101; 119.
48 Ibid., 1:101; 120. We must note that, for Varvara, God, fate, destiny, lot, etc. are not synonymous, as they seem to be for Makar. Varvara stands on more firm theological grounds. For her, God subsumes fate.
49 Ibid., 1:106; 126.
50 Ibid., 1:106; 127.

51 And more than guilt. Her utterance shows signs of an alien voice—Makar's. Yet what better way for her to express her love—or to convince him of it—than in his language? Makar's peculiar speech characteristics are well-known to her. His letters are suffused with his distinctive forms of repetition, affectionate forms of address, and epithet strings, which, if anything, have convinced her of how very much he loves her. Her use of Makar's style might in turn convince Makar of her love at the very moment that she reckons he needs it most. She calls him "precious" in the salutation (reminiscent of Makar's first letter). She repeats herself, in Makar's stylistic manner, to indicate the intensity of her feelings: "My soul is so full now, so full of tears...my tears are choking me....Remember, remember your poor Varenka." She strings epithets together: "I bid you goodbye for the last time, my precious one, my friend, my benefactor, my darling!" ["Прощаюсь с вами в последний раз, бесценый мой, друг мой, благодетель мой, родной мой!"] (1:106; 126-7).

52 Dostoevsky, *ПСС*, 1:106; 126.

53 "The total absence of sentimentality and the great restraint shown by Dostoevsky in passing judgment on [the hero's] pathetic figure are credentials of the mature, disciplined artist" (Terras, *Young Dostoevsky*, 117).

54 Dostoevsky, *ПСС*, 1:106; 127.

55 Makar's reaction to Gogol's story has elicited a great deal of critical commentary. See, for example, Leatherbarrow ("Pushkin," 368-85), Frank (*Seeds*, 101-56), Belknap (33-5), Fridlender (*Реализм*, 63-68), and the profound treatment in Jackson (*Dialogues*, 202-07). Makar misreads Gogol's famous short story "The Overcoat," which depicts an impoverished, self-effacing clerk, Akaky Akakyevich, who purchases a new, made-to-order overcoat, only to have the coat stolen. Akaky Akakyevich subsequently dies, and his ghost makes a brief return, only to be supplanted by a larger ghost. It is a tale of utter futility, redeemed only by a comic narrator and the absurdity of its conceit. Makar takes this story seriously, but to radically different effect. In fact, as numerous critics have remarked, he resembles Akaky too closely for comfort. Makar also identifies with Akaky, and he resents the comic treatment of his fellow clerk, yet he cannot admit the emotional connection. Jackson chalks this response up to Makar's denial of reality: "Devushkin's inability to find any

'verisimilitude' in 'The Overcoat,' though it attests to an acute awareness of his own inner human image, is nonetheless deceptive: ... it points with terrible truthfulness to an objective condition of despair and degradation, to a self-alienation that borders almost on a pathological ambivalence. Devushkin does not recognize himself. The truth is so terrible that the individual... refuses to recognize his own negation, his objective alienation from his own self-image" (*Dialogues*, 202).

56 Zhiliakova examines Dostoevsky's response to the Sentimental tradition, not Varvara's response to any specific text (see especially 60-72 and 82-93); Fridlender comments on Makar, but not Varvara, as a reader (68); the same can be said of Frank (*Between Religion*, 13-15).

57 In some ways, Makar resembles Maksim Maksimych, the old soldier whose friendship is rejected by the main protagonist in Lermontov's novel *A Hero of Our Time* [*Герой нашего времени*, 1840]. Dostoevsky's combination of the conventions of the Sentimental, Romantic, and Natural Schools recalls that novel too. See Eagle, 209-315.

58 Dostoevsky, *ПСС*, 1:101; 120.

59 Ibid., 1:102-3; 122-23.

60 Ibid., 1:106; 126.

61 As Jackson argues, like many a later Dostoevskian hero, Makar must now rail against that fate, or revolt against that God, and if not, then submit to chaos and nullity (*Dialogues*, 202).

Works Cited

Altman, Janet G. *Epistolarity: Approaches to a Form*. Columbus: Ohio State University Press, 1982.

Andrew, Joe. "The Seduction of the Daughter: Sexuality in the Early Dostoevsky & the Case of *Poor Folk*." In *Polyfunktion und Metaparodie: Aufsatze zum 175. Geburtstag von Fedor Michajlovic Dostojevskij*, edited by Rudolf Neuhauser, 173-88. Dresden and Munich: Dresden University Press, 1998.

Apollonio, Carol. *Dostoevsky's Secrets: Reading Against the Grain*. Evanston, Il: Northwestern University Press, 2009.

Bakhtin, Mikhail. *Problems of Dostoevsky's Poetics*. Edited and translated by Caryl Emerson. Minneapolis: University of Minnesota Press, 1984.

___. *Собрание сочинений в 7-и томах*. Vol. 2. Moscow: Russkie slovari, 2000.

Belinsky, V. G. "Петербургский сборник." In *Полное собрание сочинений*. 9:543-81. Moscow: Akademiia nauk, 1959.

___. "A Survey of Russian Literature for 1846." In *Selected Philosophical Works*, 370-420. Moscow: Foreign Languages Publishing House, 1956.

Belknap, Robert L. "The Didactic Plot: The Lesson about Suffering in *Poor Folk*." In *Critical Essays on Dostoevsky*, edited by Robin Feuer Miller, 30-39. Boston: G. K. Hall and Co., 1986.

Bem, Alfred L. "'Шинель' и *Бедные люди*.'" In *О Достоевском: сборник статей*, 3:127-136. Praga, 1936.

Buzina, Tatiana. *Dostoevsky and Social and Metaphysical Freedom*. Lewiston: The Edwin Mellen Press, 2003.

Dobroliubov, Nikolai A. "Забитые люди." In *Русские классики: избранные литературно-критические статьи*, edited by Iu. G. Oksman, 301-346. Moscow: Nauka, 1970.

Dostoevsky, Fyodor. *Полное собрание сочинений в тридцати томах*. 30 vols. Leningrad: Nauka, 1972-90.

___. *Poor Folk*. In *Poor Folk and Other Stories*. Translated by David McDuff. London: Penguin Books, 1988.

Eagle, Herbert. "Lermontov's 'Play' with Romantic Genre Expectations in *A Hero of Our Time*." In *Russian Literature Triquarterly*, 10:299-315. Ann Arbor: Ardis Press, 1974.

Frank, Joseph. "*Poor Folk* and *House of the Dead*." In *Between Religion and Rationality: Essays in Russian Literature and Culture*, 9-28. Princeton, NJ: Princeton University Press, 2010.

___. *Dostoevsky: The Seeds of Revolt: 1821-1849*. Princeton, NJ: Princeton University Press, 1976.

Fridlender, Georgii M. "*Бедные люди*." In *История русского романа*, 403-415. Leningrad: Nauka, 1962.

___. *Реализм Достоевского*. Moscow: Nauka, 1964.

Girard, René. *Deceit, Desire and the Novel: Self and Other in Literary Structure*. Translated by Yvonne Freccero. Baltimore: Johns Hopkins University Press, 1965.

Grossman, Leonid. *Balzac and Dostoevsky*. Ann Arbor: Ardis Press, 1973.

Iakubovich, I. D. "Достоевский в работе над романом *Бедные люди*." In *Достоевский: Материалы и исследования*, 9:39-55. Leningrad: Nauka, 1991.

Jackson, Robert Louis. *Dialogues with Dostoevsky: The Overwhelming Questions.* Stanford: Stanford University Press, 1993.

———. *Dostoevsky's Quest for Form: A Study of His Philosophy of Art.* New Haven, CT: Yale University Press, 1966.

Kirpotin, Valerii. *Избранные работы в трех томах.* Vol. 2. Moscow: Khudlit, 1978.

———. *Молодой Достоевский.* Moscow: OGIZ, 1947.

Leatherbarrow, William J. *Fedor Dostoevsky.* Boston: Twayne Publishers, 1981.

———. "The Rag with Ambition: The Problem of Self-Will in Dostoevsky's 'Bednye liudi' and 'Dvoynik.'" *Modern Language Review* 68, no. 3 (1973): 607-18.

———. "Pushkin and the Early Dostoevsky." *Modern Language Review* 74, no. 2 (1979): 368-85.

Lyles, John. "Makar Devushkin as Eligible Bachelor?—A Reexamination of Varenka's Relationship with Devushkin in Dostoevsky's *Poor Folk*." *Slavic and East European Review* 56, no. 3 (2012): 347-376.

Matveyev, Rebecca E. "Textuality and Intertextuality in Dostoevsky's *Poor Folk*." *Slavic and East European Journal* 39, no. 4 (1995): 535-51.

Morson, Gary Saul. *The Words of Others: From Quotations to Culture.* New Haven, CT: Yale University Press, 2011.

Odoevsky, Vladimir F. "Живой мертвец." In *Русская фантастическая повесть эпохи романтизма*, 191-214. Moscow: Sovetskaia Rossiia, 1987.

———. *The Salamander and Other Gothic Tales.* Translated by Neil Cornwell. London: Bristol Classical Press, 1992.

Peace, Richard. "The Analytical Genius: *Bednye liudi* and the Russian Prose Tradition." In *From Pushkin to Palisandriia*, edited by A. McMillin, 52-69. New York: St. Martin's Press, 1990.

Rosenshield, Gary. "Gorškov in 'Poor Folk': An Analysis of an Early Dostoevskian 'Double.'" *Slavic and East European Journal* 26, no. 2 (1982): 149-62.

———. "Old Pokrovskij: The Technique and Meaning in a Character Foil in Dostoevskij's *Poor Folk*." In *New Perspectives on Nineteenth-Century Russian*

Prose, edited by G. J. Gutsche and L. G. Leighton, 99-110. Columbus: Ohio State University Press, 1981.

———. "Varen'ka Dobroselova: An Experiment in Desentimentalization of the Sentimental Heroine in Dostoevskii's *Poor Folk*." *Slavic Review* 45, no. 3 (1986): 525-33.

Terras, Victor. "Шинель Гоголя в критике молодого Достоевского." *Записки Русско-Академической группы в США* 17 (1984): 75-81.

———. "The Young Dostoyevsky: An Assessment in the Light of Recent Scholarship." In *New Perspectives on Dostoyevsky*, edited by M. V. Jones and G. M. Terry, 21-40. Cambridge: Cambridge University Press, 1983.

———. *The Young Dostoevsky (1846-1949): A Critical Study*. The Hague: Mouton, 1969.

Trubeckoj, Nikolai S. "The Style of 'Poor Folk' and 'The Double.'" *Slavic Review* 7 (1948): 150-170.

Tynianov, Iurii. "Достоевский и Гоголь (К теории пародии)." In *Архаисты и новаторы*, 412-55. Leningrad: Priboi, 1929.

Vetlovskaia, Valentina E. *Роман Ф. М. Достоевского "Бедные люди."* Leningrad: Khudlit, 1988.

Vladimirtsev, V. P. "Опыт фольклаорно-этнографического комментария к роману '*Бедные люди.*'" In *Достоевский: Материалы и исследования*, edited by G. M. Fridlender, 5:74-89. Leningrad, Nauka, 1983.

Zhiliakova, Emma M. *Традиции сентиментализма в творчестве раннего Достоевского*. Tomsk: Izdatel'stvo Tomskogo universiteta, 1989.

II

Me and My Double: Selfhood, Consciousness, and Empathy in *The Double*

Gary Saul Morson

> Me and my shadow,
> Strolling down the avenue,
> Me and my shadow,
> Not a soul to tell our troubles to . . .
>
> And when it's twelve o'clock,
> We climb the stair,
> We never knock,
> For nobody's there . . .
>
> "Me and My Shadow," music and lyrics
> by Dave Dreyer, Billy Rose, and Al Jolson

Mysteries

How odd that consciousness should be located somewhere! Why should it require a particular place? And why must it be housed in a material body?

Consciousness seems to be private. I feel only my own, but must infer others'. Can that difference be overcome? Is there some way I can experience the experience of others? Does genuine *compassion* (co-suffering, сострадание in Russian) or empathy exist? When we empathize with others, do we sense, rather than just guess at, what they feel?

What happens when we identify with fictional characters? When men weep over the death of heroines, Catholics over the suffering of Protestants, or the rich over the degradation of the poor, are they really feeling the pain of people unlike themselves? And if authors can create believable characters, unlike themselves or other characters, does that mean authors can somehow escape the prison of their own point of view?

We usually think of empathy as an unqualifiedly good thing. From the perspective of the great realist novels, at any rate, it seems to be necessary, if not sufficient, for morality. But can it not be used for immoral purposes? Does every con-man not use it? Intrigues, plots, and deceptions apparently rely on such negative empathy.[1]

For that matter, do torture and sadistic cruelty not rely on a form of empathy? After all, people seem to love inflicting pain on each other but no one finds any point in abusing a stone. In *Notes from the House of the Dead* [*Записки из мертвого дома*, 1861], guards enjoy inflicting punishments only on the living.

We speak of torture as "dehumanizing," but, upon reflection, the very opposite seems true. Deliberately to cause pain to another necessarily acknowledges the victim's humanity and personhood. It is a way of *relating*, to use the current jargon.

Just as erotic love demands another person, so does torture. As Fyodor Pavlovich Karamazov likes to point out, the two are closely connected for just this reason. As we may inflict pain, we may inflict pleasure, if we reach deeply enough into the most private realm. The torturer and the lover use the body to expose another person's soul, stripping away all defenses and disguises to reveal the naked self.

All these "accursed questions" concerning the mystery of consciousness define the spirit of Russian literature. Dostoevsky wondered about them from his first works to his last. To be sure, his second published work, the novella *The Double* [*Двойник*, 1846; revised 1866], is not as overtly philosophical as his final novel, *The Brothers Karamazov* [*Братья Карамазовы*, 1880]— the main protagonist of *The Double*, Iakov Petrovich Goliadkin, can hardly think as abstractly as Ivan Karamazov—but this early work nevertheless sharpens our understanding of the uniqueness of selfhood, the imprisonment of consciousness in space and time, and the use or abuse of empathy.

Self is Here

"The eternal silence of these infinite spaces terrifies me," wrote Pascal.[2] The *I* that is my universe, and that looks out upon the immensity of the physical world, is somehow located at an infinitesimal point. Mentally I comprehend all of space, and physically it comprehends me. How can infinity be so compact?

In *War and Peace* [*Война и мир*, 1869], Pierre finds this mystery comic. Led away into captivity by the French, he finds himself seated by a campfire where he bursts into good-natured laughter. "They took me and shut me up... Who is 'me'?... Me—is my immortal soul! Ha, ha, ha! Ha, ha, ha!" He looks around at the fields, forest, "the bright shimmering horizon luring one on to infinity," and "the remote, receding, glimmering stars." He thinks: "And all that is within me, and is *me*!... And they caught all that and put it in a shed and barricaded it with planks!"[3]

It seems absurd that thought can be so confined. How can the infinite be locked in a shed? Pierre here expresses one of the ultimate mysteries of the universe. And for both Tolstoy and Dostoevsky, the important thing is to recognize that it *is* a mystery.

For the materialists of the intelligentsia, it was not. For them, as for today's "new atheists," selfhood and consciousness do not constitute anything radically different from all those other things explained by physical science. Physiologist and philosopher Jacob Moleschott is supposed to have said that the brain secretes thought the way the liver secretes bile. For Richard Dawkins and Daniel Dennett, as for Nikolai Chernyshevsky and Ivan Sechenov, *there is no mystery*.

In *The Brothers Karamazov*, Rakitin condescendingly explains the materialist view of consciousness to the imprisoned Dmitri. Only minor changes would be needed to make this explanation similar to the ones we so often read. Dmitri paraphrases what he has heard:

> Imagine: inside, in the nerves, in the head—that is, these nerves are there in the brain... (damn them!) there are these sort of tails, the little tails of these nerves, and as soon as they begin quivering... that is, you see, I look at something with my eyes and then they begin quivering, those little tails... and when they quiver an image appears... it doesn't appear at once, but an instant, a second, passes... and then something like a moment

appears; that is, not a moment—devil take the moment!—but an image; that is an object, or an action, damn it. That's why I see and then think, because of those tails, not at all because I've got a soul.[4]

"An image appears"—*to whom*? The explanation stops short just at the most important point, which is not how images can be created, but how they can appear *as* images *to me*, to a subjectivity.

Thought Experiments

One way to show that selfhood and subjectivity are real is to imagine accepting their absence. Philosophers have often constructed thought experiments to demonstrate or explore the consequences of ideas of personhood. These experiments often center on the unique subjectivity we presumably all experience. In a universe that in and of itself lacks point of view, each of us has one. There is no "to me" about Newton's laws, but there must be a "to me" to me.

One thing we all share is that we each have something we do not share. My consciousness is precisely mine. Typically, philosophical thought experiments about selfhood work by supposing the opposite and generating absurdity. Reduction to the absurd was one of Dostoevsky's favorite techniques. It contributes to the odd quality of his humor.

Consider: if I am nothing but how I appear to the outside, why could I not be copied? If I could be, would there be two of me? (This is sometimes called "the amoeba problem.") Would these two of me directly sense each other? If so, would they really be one of me in two bodies? As Siamese twins are two selves sharing part of a body, could there be Siamese selves sharing part of me? Or would me and copy-me each be a separate me, albeit absolutely identical to its counterpart, and each sensing only its own subjectivity?

Or imagine a new machine that could transport passengers instantly across thousands of miles. It seems to work as advertised, but someone discovers how the machine actually works: when a passenger steps into it, an exact duplicate is assembled at the destination point after the passenger is destroyed at the starting point. Would you travel that way? To others, the person who emerges would be just like you, but would it be *you*? Would there be any way of finding out, even in principle?

Is your double you? This is a core philosophical problem pertaining to stories about doubles in general and to Dostoevsky's in particular, and not just the one called *The Double* but also the later works in which doubles play a role. Our deep fascination with identical twins, still more with Siamese twins, comes in part from our sense that subjectivity must be unique. Goliadkin considers twinning as a sort of analogue to what he experiences when his precise double appears, but doubling goes a step further. *Ex hypothesi*, a person and his double are absolutely identical from the external standpoint. Identical twins do not have the same name, but the two Goliadkins do, and that is one reason our hero is especially horrified to learn that the other Goliadkin is also Iakov Petrovich! The story would not be nearly as funny if, for instance, the double were Foma Fomich, or Erast Erastovich, or even Akakii Akakievich.

"Both Together Is Impossible"

Dostoevsky creates humor from metaphysical quandary. Whenever the novella suggests that subjectivity is bifurcated or duplicated, we laugh at the absurdity. Our laughter testifies to our intuitive awareness that subjectivity must be unique.

If there were someone *exactly* like me, would it *be* me? For a materialist, that would have to be the case, since identical causes must produce identical results. Can there be a difference without any difference to produce it?

If someone *exactly* like me were to replace me, and no one could notice any change, would I still be there?

The identity of the Goliadkins' names is, if anything, weirder than mere identity of appearance. It cannot be the result of DNA. It suggests an identity of *persons* even where we see two *men*, and so creates a metaphysical comedy. If the two Goliadkins are objectively absolutely the same, perhaps they are also subjectively the same, but without knowing it? What would that be like?

Dostoevsky constantly plays on the identity of names suggesting an *identity of identity*. He milks the absurdity for all it is worth when Iakov Petrovich addresses a letter to Iakov Petrovich. Actually, in keeping with the theme of doubling, Iakov Petrovich addresses *two* such letters:

Dear Sir, Iakov Petrovich!

... Your obstinate desire to persist in your course of action, sir, and forcibly to enter the circle of my existence [насильственно войти в круг моего бытия], and all my relations in practical life, transgresses every limit imposed by the merest politeness ... I imagine there is no need, sir, for me to refer to . . . your taking away my good name. . . . I will not allude here to your strange, one may even say, incomprehensible behavior to me in the coffee house . . .

Your most humble servant,

Ia. Goliadkin[5]

Dear Sir, Iakov Petrovich!

Either you or I, but both together is impossible! [Либо вы, либо я, а вместе нам невозможно!] . . . However, I remain ready to oblige or to meet you with pistols.

Ia. Goliadkin[6]

The endlessly varying metaphysical joke is that the two who somehow *think* they are different people are indeed the same person. But how can one person think he is not himself? He might somehow forget or be brainwashed about his name and even his past, but how could he be wrong about his subjectivity? To cite a famous example from John Locke, if a prince's consciousness should change places with a cobbler's, the prince would still feel his own *me* even if he must repair shoes. Others could be mistaken because they must judge from the outside, but I *am* me, am I not?[7]

In the classic chapter on "Identity and Difference" of personhood in the *Essay on Human Understanding*, Locke supposes that two consciousnesses could alternate in the same body—or even in the same spiritual substance or soul!—but with no memory of having performed the other's actions. In that case, Locke argues, they would genuinely be two distinct persons. By much the same reasoning, if my soul could once have been Nestor or Socrates but did not remember having been so, I would not be Nestor or Socrates. Neither would I be responsible for Nestor's or Socrates' actions. But if I were conscious that I had been Socrates, even in a different soul as well as a different body, I would be the same person and responsible for Socrates' actions. Perhaps I could be charged with suicide. My consciousness—not my body nor my soul—makes me *me*, or so Locke contends.

"I know that in the ordinary way of speaking, the same person, and the same man, stand for one and the same thing," and in daily life, that way of speaking will do. But if we are really to understand "what makes the same spirit, man, or person," we must carefully distinguish these terms.[8] Personhood is neither soul, nor physical man, but precisely consciousness. And consciousness can be in only one place at a time. If we imagine a person whose finger is cut off, and further suppose that consciousness went with the finger—so that, in a sense, it was not the finger but the rest of the body that was cut off—we would see that personhood goes with consciousness. Wherever consciousness may be, Locke concludes, it must still be either here or there at any given moment.

Or as Goliadkin says: "Either you or I, but both together is impossible!" Of course, he has not read Locke or any other philosopher and he means something like "This town isn't big enough for the two of us!" But the reader also detects the literal sense of the words: either you are me or I am me, but not both. More than one me is "impossible"—not just in the sense of "unacceptable" but also in the sense of "logically incoherent." It is not taboo but senseless to say, except figuratively, that another person can "enter the circle of my existence." My existence as me cannot be in two persons, and two persons cannot be one me.

And yet: the very fact that Goliadkin has to protest so much, and tries to prove his point by threatening a duel, humorously suggests that he himself believes the opposite. He at least suspects that the supposedly impossible is not only possible but actually the case. He insists, without expecting to be believed: "He's another person, your Excellency, but I'm another person too; he's apart and I am also myself by myself [сам по себе]; I am really myself by myself" [or "separate"—I translate rather literally], he explains, as if he does needs convincing.[9]

Goliadkin's insistence that I am I, while he, Your Excellency, is he, and not at all the same as I, suggests the reverse: that I somehow am not at all "apart" ["особо"] or "separate"—whatever such an assertion might mean. Goliadkin constantly tells himself that he does not "intrigue," or "polish the floor with his boots," or "wear a mask," or practice deceit, like that other Goliadkin. But he says so deceitfully and wears a mask while saying it. On numerous occasions—say, when bribing Ostafiev for information—he speaks openly of laying his own plots and intrigues. And so he winds up saying of his double: "He is such a toady! Such a lickspittle! Such a Goliadkin!"[10] He is such a *me*! We laugh whenever Goliadkin verges on asserting that he *is* me.

This is not a case of resemblance or even congruence but of identity. It only resembles resemblance. The story's deep humor derives, in short, from

Goliadkin's recognition, and simultaneous refusal to recognize, that the double is not just like him but *is* him, and that *he is his own impersonator*. If anything, the double is more truly him (if comparatives have any meaning here) than he is.

One Step Further

And what if the matter is still more horrible? When Goliadkin encounters the double, "his hair stood on end, and he almost fell down with horror. And indeed there was good reason," the narrator explains. "He perfectly recognized his nocturnal visitor. The nocturnal visitor was no other than himself [не кто иной, как он сам]—Mr. Goliadkin himself, another Mr. Goliadkin, but perfectly the very same as he himself [совершенно такой же, как он сам]," a double in every respect.[11] An ellipsis consisting of a line and a half of dots concluding the chapter suggests both horror and wonder.

The real horror, which the hero constantly tries to ward off, is that while subjectivity is indeed unique and only one of a *me* can exist—the real me is not mine but his, and I am the one who does not have a *me*! I am the pretender! This possibility is hard even to state precisely because we all believe that a me is *directly* present to itself. I might, for instance, discover that a man people took to be a certain person is his twin, and, in fact, numerous murder mysteries have turned on this possibility of misidentification *from the outside*. But these "mysteries" are not at all mysterious in any fundamental way, as they would be if there were a misidentification of a subjectivity *from the inside*. The absurdity of such an idea suggests that we simply *know*, in the sense that we cannot sensibly doubt, that we have a subjectivity.

If that is the case, we cannot truly believe that a purely objective description of the world could ever be complete.[12] The materialists must be wrong precisely because for them the objective description is complete.

To believe that, you might as well—Descartes notwithstanding—doubt your own existence. Strangely enough, Goliadkin does: he "even began to doubt his own existence."[13] For that matter, so does the devil in *The Brothers Karamazov*, but there the philosophical comedy can be more explicit, since the devil himself deliberately plays the role of a metaphysical nihilist. Despite his status as a supernatural being, he is not sure whether he believes in the supernatural. He even knows he is Ivan's double, perhaps just a figment of Ivan's fevered imagination, and so might very well not exist at all. Dostoevsky never tired of varying this joke. He constantly found ways to refute any denial of subjectivity through laughter indicating recognition of an absurdity. Goliadkin is totally unaware of metaphysical quandaries, which he senses not as humorous but as terrifying and, above all, humiliating. But readers, at the same moments that they identify with Goliadkin's horror, also laugh at its incoherence. What he most fears is not just strange but "one may even say, incomprehensible."

Goliadkin uses expressions that can mean either "humiliation" or "nonbeing." He intends one, we hear both. Consider: "He recognized in an instant, that he had perished, was in a sense annihilated."[14] Goliadkin means, of course, that he has disgraced himself, but the reader can also hear the absurd literal meaning, that he knows he does not exist. By the same token, when Goliadkin challenges his double to a duel, he understands it as one man vindicating his honor by putting his life on the line, so that one of them will cease to be and the other will survive. But the reader also hears him as if it were selves, rather than lives, being shot at, and entertains the thought that a self, having been killed by itself, can know that it has made itself cease to be. So Goliadkin also says: "I'm my own murderer!"[15]

Siamese Noses

Dostoevsky adapts the comic technique Gogol uses in "The Nose" ["Нос," 1836], which depicts a nose acting for a time as an autonomous adult and plays endlessly on idioms with the word "nose" ("lead him by the nose," "as plain as your nose"; the devil in *The Brothers Karamazov* also offers such a nasal pun). We are constantly treated to assertions that, as we say today, do not pass the smell test. In *The Double* the puns concern not nose but self. In both Gogol and Dostoevsky, the character uses an expression in its figurative sense, but the reader hears it both ways. The literal meaning works by virtue of sheer nonsense.

The narrator of "The Nose" comes up with ostensibly rational attempts to prove that all the odd incidents depicted, though indeed strange, are perfectly explicable. They were all a "freak of nature," and the story ends by affirming that such things do happen—not often but they do happen. The joke is that the narrator treats an event as rare when it is patently self-contradictory. It is not "strange" but literally "incomprehensible." If it simply violated all human experience, it would still be comprehensible. But the adventures of the nose are impossible not because appropriate causes do not exist but in a quite a different way. It is as if someone explained that, to be sure, it is rare for triangles to have four sides, but, strange as it may seem, this one did.

The Double also offers such four-sided triangles. To explain his absurdly doubled subjectivity, Goliadkin appeals not only to Siamese twins, counterfeits, imposters, or pretenders to the throne (like Grisha Otrepev in Aleksandr Pushkin's *Boris Godunov* [Борис Годунов, 1825]), all of which do indeed exist. He tells us that somehow nature herself had a hand in all this. It is all quite natural, you see, so there is nothing to be ashamed of. But this sort of explanation is absurd: a me discovering it is not me, or that another person is really my me, makes no sense. Once we recognize the nature of the absurdity, we can no longer doubt the existence of unique selfhood. Subjectivity is mysterious, and perhaps we will never explain it, but its absence spells complete nonsense.

The Thinking Rag

The most famous aphorisms about the mystery of selfhood and of irreducible "me-ness" belong to Pascal, whose influence on Russian thought was immense. Pascal repeatedly evokes the sense of the radical difference between consciousness and the material world. "Out of all bodies together we could not succeed in creating one little thought. It is impossible and of a different order"[16] "All bodies, the firmament, the stars, the earth and its kingdoms are not worth the least of minds, for it knows them all and itself too, while bodies know nothing."[17]

"Are not worth": Pascal maintains that the difference is not just of kind but also of value. In fact, without thought there would be no value, which is a matter of judgment and preferences, both of which by their nature do not pertain to bodies. Nature does no ranking. The best known passage in Pascal's *Pensées* concerns the *nobility* of thought:

> Man is but a reed, the most feeble thing in nature, but he is a thinking reed. The entire universe need not arm itself to crush him. A vapour, a drop of water, suffices to kill him. But if the universe were to crush him, man would still be more noble than that which killed him, because he knows that he dies and the advantage the universe has over him; the universe knows nothing of this.[18]

The Double seems to rework these lines. Goliadkin tells himself he will not "allow himself to be insulted" since he is a man, not a thing. He stoutly insists he will not "be treated like a rag [ветошка] . . . I am not a rag. I am not a rag, sir!" As if paraphrasing Goliadkin's own uncertainties from within, the narrator mocks this statement:

> Possibly if someone wanted, if someone, for instance, actually insisted on turning Mr. Goliadkin into a rag, he might have done so, might have done so without opposition or punishment (Mr. Goliadkin himself felt this at times)—and there would have emerged a rag and not Goliadkin—yes, a nasty, filthy rag; but this rag would not have been a simple rag, this would have been a rag with self-esteem, this rag would have had animation [одушевление] and feelings, even though it would have been a timid pride and timid feelings, hidden far away and deep within the folds of this rag, but all the same they would have been feelings.[19]

I was forced to retranslate this passage to preserve the constant repetition of the word "rag," which seems to provoke a wince of pain in Goliadkin every time it is uttered, with every wince inspiring the narrator to say it again and again.

Since only a non-thing could say it either is or is not a thing, one would think that there would be no reason to insist on one's non-thing-ness. And yet, Goliadkin does insist, with every expectation of being successfully contradicted, that he is not a thing, that he is alive, that he has self-esteem and feelings. He has "ensoulment" [in Russian, о-душ-евление, anima-tion in the etymological sense]. For Pascal, man is a reed, but a thinking reed; for this narrator, the hero is a rag, but a feeling rag. Not just thinking, but feeling—because, for Dostoevsky, it is not consciousness, or even self-consciousness, but the particular sort of agonizing self-consciousness we call humiliation that makes us human. We have moved from man as *un roseau pensant* [a thinking reed] to man as *un chiffon tremblant* [a trembling rag].

The transformation is humorous because one hardly thinks of a rag as noble or dignified. And if the point were to show dignity and self-esteem, one would hardly have to add filth, or say that pride and feelings are timid (безответный, answerless), a sort of oxymoron. This is human dignity at its lowest, barely clinging to existence, ready, indeed, even to concede the right to exist if only it be allowed of its own free will to make that concession—or even to concede that right too, just so as to preserve the pretense of dignity, because, after all, only someone alive, only someone who is not a thing, can pretend!

Humiliation

The "rag" passage extends Pascal's logic. Pascal's thinking reed is overwhelmed only by the universe's physical force, but Dostoevsky's rag is also overwhelmed by society's moral force. Physical force at least leaves the self with nobility, but social force strips that away, too. Such *stripping* is unspeakably painful—Dostoevsky's underground man compares it to being flayed alive—and it seems to explain the etymology of the hero's name, Goliadkin (from *golyi*, naked). The narrator seems to revel in inflicting such pain. No wonder Dostoevsky was called "a cruel talent."

What is it to be a human, conscious, being? While Descartes pointed to thought, other philosophers have argued that pain proves consciousness still more clearly. When in pain, even a materialist who regards thought as analogous to bile *cannot doubt*, can barely pretend to doubt, that he is in pain. That is why, in his polemic against the materialists, Dostoevsky's underground man speaks of "an educated man of the nineteenth century who is suffering from toothache."[20] Just try to be a materialist with aching teeth! As there are no atheists in foxholes, there are no materialists in dental chairs.

But pain is not enough to make us human. Animals, after all, also suffer pain. Few of us would agree with Descartes's view that animals are unsouled automatons, but we also do not regard them as human. What is it they are missing?

In his earliest works Dostoevsky suggests that the answer is precisely *humiliation*. Pain proves we have a subjectivity, but humiliation proves we have a *social* subjectivity, and human subjectivity is essentially social. We are humiliated only in the eyes of others, in the awareness that others are watching us. I am humiliated, therefore I am human.

Goliadkin's inner discourse constantly reflects his awareness of being watched, spied on, evaluated, judged, regarded as strange. That is why he is constantly assuring himself that he is all right, he is just like everyone else, his position is like everyone else's, and why should it not be? When he leaves the doctor's office, he looks up and sees the doctor watching him from the window. It is a sort of early study in Stavrogin's resentment of Tikhon as a spy into his soul in Dostoevsky's novel *The Devils* [Бесы, 1872]. When Goliadkin sneaks into the party to which he is uninvited he makes a *spectacle* of himself. What most infuriates him about his double is that the double gets others to laugh at

Goliadkin. Everywhere Goliadkin faces "the witnesses of his ignominy."[21] They include us.

The "feeling rag" passage captures this sense of humiliation at its most vertiginous. Readers find it intensely painful. We wince when he suffers "agony upon agony, terror upon terror."[22] Terror, because the ultimate terror is threat to one's selfhood, as makers of horror movies know. Because of the narrator's taunting tone, readers simultaneously occupy the role of humiliator and humiliated, as they both identify with Goliadkin and laugh at him. In so doing, they are, of course, "laughing at themselves," like the spectators of Gogol's play *The Inspector General* [*Ревизор*, 1836].

The Bad Samaritan

So painful is the sense of Goliadkin's humiliation that readers cannot doubt that people are more than material objects, still less that they are essentially social. We are not monads that happened to be thrown together. In principle, selves cannot be isolated. No self is an island.

Goliadkin says he is "myself by myself too; I am really myself by myself."[23] But that is not how selves are. One is a self among others, or so Dostoevsky wants us to believe. *The Double* represents the first among many Dostoevskian demonstrations that the self is social. For Dostoevsky, this view of selfhood was essential to Christianity and its command to care for others, to be one's brother's keeper, and to love one's neighbor.

In the "Rebellion" ["Бунт"] chapter of *The Brothers Karamazov*, Ivan Karamazov tells Alyosha that one *cannot* love one's neighbor. "Suppose I, for instance, suffer intensely. Another can never know how much I suffer, because he is another and not I."[24] Here and elsewhere, Dostoevsky seems to echo La Rochefoucauld's famous comment that we all have sufficient fortitude to endure the misfortunes of others.[25] Ivan allows for human reactions that might look like genuine concern—or as he calls it, Christian love—for others, but these are all counterfeit. When John the Merciful took a frozen beggar in his arms and breathed into his mouth, loathsome with some putrid disease, he may have done it from "the self-laceration of falsity, for the sake of a charity imposed as a duty, as a penance laid upon him."[26] But these are not love; they are all forms of self-aggrandizement. We can affirm our love for "humanity," or for people in the abstract, or for those at a distance, but not for a specific person nearby, not for a *neighbor*. People in the abstract are ideas, *abstractions*, but a specific person is another self.

Ivan's point is not that we cannot acknowledge the *existence* of other selves. This is not the metaphysical problem of the existence of "other minds," and Ivan is no solipsist. On the contrary, he above all knows that we acknowledge others and can even empathize with them— but *negatively*. They are there *for us*, and their existence as other people is important for us in relation to our selves. We use other selves to show our nobility as charitable beings, like the "benefactress" who drove Ivan's mother to attempt suicide. And we also acknowledge other people as other selves so that we may enjoy torturing them, like the many torturers Ivan describes with such relish in "Rebellion." What Ivan denies is positive empathy, genuine concern for others as others. Ivan believes that we cannot acknowledge others as having value apart from their value for us.

Father Zosima recognizes the strength of Ivan's argument, but maintains that genuine empathy, though very difficult, is possible. "Father Zosima has talked of that more than once," Alyosha tells Ivan. "But yet there's a great deal of love in mankind, and almost Christ-like love." To overcome our natural limitation of interest to our own self, one has to be "practiced in love."[27]

Ivan breaks out of the circle of self he describes when he returns to help the drunken peasant freezing in the snow. The incident alludes to Jesus's story of the man who had "fallen among thieves" and been left naked and half-dead. A priest sees him and passes by "on the other side," as does a Levite. But a good Samaritan "had compassion on him."[28] This Samaritan stands as a model of kindness to someone who is unlike him and who can never repay his kindness. Jesus tells the story to explain what it means to "love thy neighbor," which, after caring for the peasant who will never know he has done so, Ivan now recognizes is indeed possible. For Ivan, the discovery comes too late, but for Goliadkin it does not come at all. That is why we sense there is hope for Ivan's, but not Goliadkin's, recovery from insanity.

I think the key incident in *The Double* has been overlooked. Let us call it "the bad Samaritan." When the double follows Goliadkin home, Goliadkin takes him in and, apparently, pities him. The new Goliadkin is a picture of humiliation as only Dostoevsky can describe it:

There was a downtrodden, crushed, scared look about all his gestures, so that—if the comparison might be allowed—he was at that moment rather like the man who, having lost his clothes, is dressed up in someone else's: the sleeves work up to the elbows, the waist is almost up to his neck, and he keeps every minute pulling down the short waistcoat; he wriggles sideways and turns away, tries to hide himself, or peeps into every face, and listens whether people are talking of his position, laughing at him or putting him to shame—and he is crimson with shame and overwhelmed with confusion and wounded vanity.[29]

This poor soul is fallen not among thieves but among Petersburgers, stripped not physically but morally, and left not naked but, still worse, in someone else's clothes that ostentatiously fail to fit. For a moment, Goliadkin is "genuinely touched" ["истинно тронут"].[30] If only he could continue being so!

Alas, almost immediately his mood takes on—if the phrase may be allowed—a Dostoevskian quality. "In short, Mr. Goliadkin was quite happy... because, so far from being afraid of his enemies, he was quite prepared now to challenge them all to mortal combat... [and] because he was now in the role of a patron."[31]

Goliadkin has the chance to show compassion and care for another person for the sake of the other person. But he treats the other as—well, as an extension of himself. He sees in his pitiful companion someone who will toady up to him as Goliadkin has toadied up to others; and, still worse, he values him as someone who will be his ally in intrigues against those others. "We shall be like brothers; we'll be cunning, my dear fellow, we'll work together; we'll get up an intrigue, too, to pay them out. To pay them out we'll get up an intrigue too."[32]

For Goliadkin, others exist either to intrigue against him or to be intrigued against. The only empathy he knows comes from recognizing another person as an object of pain or patronage. The next day, when the double treats Goliadkin with negative empathy, as someone to serve as an object of mockery and intrigue, he is only enacting Goliadkin's own intentions. It is, of course, because the double knows Goliadkin so intimately that he can touch his sore spots with such uncanny accuracy.

From this point on, the story unfolds with an inevitable logic of mounting humiliation leading to the madhouse. The story ends: "Our hero shrieked and clutched his head in his hands. Alas! For a long while he had been haunted by a presentiment of this!" ["он это давно уже предчувствовал"—literally, "he had long ago already fore-felt this"].³³ A presentiment, or fore-feeling, is a sort of temporal double. The sense of inevitability derives from the fact that the fore-felt event is a repetition of what was already long there.

And yet: for one moment, the moment when he felt genuine sympathy, Goliadkin could have escaped the self that extended no further than itself. He could have seen more in another than a reflection of his own needs. And he could have escaped the logic of doubling, leaving his own shadow behind.

Endnotes

1 Perhaps the most empathetic character in Russian literature is Porfiry Petrovich, the detective in *Crime and Punishment* [*Преступление и наказание*, 1867], who uses his amazing talent to send the novel's hero to prison.
2 Quoted in Shapiro, *Yale Book of Quotations*, 584.
3 Tolstoy, *War and Peace*, 1217. Quotations of Tolstoy's novel *War and Peace* come from the Dunnigan translation and are cited by page number. I have adjusted the translation where necessary.
4 Dostoevsky, *Brothers Karamazov*, 716-17. Quotations of Dostoevsky's novel *The Brothers Karamazov* come from the Garnett translation. I have adjusted the translation where necessary.
5 Dostoevsky, *ПСС*, 1:175; 218-19. Quotations of *The Double* are from Dostoevsky's 1866 revision of the novella as it appears in F. M. Dostoevsky, *Полное собрание сочинений* [*Complete Collected Works*], cited by volume and page number; the translations are from Garnett, cited second by page number, although I have often adjusted the translation, sometimes extensively.
6 Ibid., 1:188; 234.
7 See the chapter "Of Ideas of Identity and Diversity," Locke, 1:439-470.
8 Locke, *Essay Concerning Human Understanding*, I:457.
9 Dostoevsky, *ПСС*, 1:213; 264.
10 Ibid., 1:172; 215.
11 Ibid., 1:143; 179.
12 This is the formulation Thomas Nagel repeatedly uses in *The View from Nowhere*, to which I am indebted at several points in this essay.
13 Dostoevsky, *ПСС*, 1:147; 183.
14 Ibid., 1:167; 208.

15 Ibid., 1:180; 225.
16 Pascal, *Pensées*, 215.
17 Ibid., 125.
18 West, *Thinking Reed*. Here I cite the translation that serves as the epigraph to Rebecca West's novel, *The Thinking Reed*, facing title page.
19 Dostoevsky, *ПСС*, 1:168; 210. For a good version of this passage, see Evelyn Harden's interesting edition of the two versions of *The Double*, 100-101.
20 Dostoevsky, *Notes from Underground*, 274.
21 Dostoevsky, *ПСС*, 1:167; 208.
22 Ibid., 1:140; 174.
23 Ibid., 1:213; 264.
24 Dostoevsky, *Brothers Karamazov*, 281.
25 Quoted in Shapiro, *Yale Book of Quotations*, 443.
26 Dostoevsky, *Brothers Karamazov*, 281.
27 Ibid.
28 Luke 10:33.
29 Dostoevsky, *ПСС*, 1:153; 191.
30 Ibid., 1:156; 194.
31 Ibid., 1:157; 195.
32 Ibid., 1:157; 196.
33 Ibid., 1:229; 284.

Works Cited

Dostoevsky, Fyodor. *The Brothers Karamazov*. Translated by Constance Garnett. New York: Modern Library, 1950.

———. "The Double." In *The Eternal Husband and Other Stories*, translated by Constance Garnett, 138-284. New York: The Macmillian Company, 1956.

———. *The Double: Two Versions*. Edited and translated by Evelyn Harden. Ann Arbor: Ardis, 1985.

———. "Notes From Underground." In *Great Short Works of Fyodor Dostoevsky*, translated by David Magarshack, 263-377. New York: Harper Collins, 1968.

———. *Полное собрание сочинений в тридцати томах*. 30 vols. Leningrad: Nauka, 1972-90.

Locke, John. *An Essay Concerning Human Understanding*. Edited by Alexander Campbell Fraser. 2 vols. New York: Dover Publications, 1959.

Nagel, Thomas. *The View from Nowhere*. New York: Oxford University Press, 1986.

Pascal, Blaise. *Pensées*. Translated by A. J. Krailsheimer. Harmondsworth, UK: Penguin, 1987.

Shapiro, Fred, ed. *The Yale Book of Quotations*. New Haven, CT: Yale University Press, 2006.

Tolstoy, Leo. *War and Peace*. Translated by Ann Dunnigan. New York: Signet, 1968.

West, Rebecca. *The Thinking Reed*. New York: Viking, 1936.

III

Husbands and Lovers: Vaudeville Conventions in "Another Man's Wife," "The Jealous Husband," and *The Eternal Husband*

Susanne Fusso

In 1848 Dostoevsky published two stories in two different issues of *Notes of the Fatherland* [*Отечественные записки*]: "Another Man's Wife. (Street Scene)" ["Чужая жена. (Уличная сцена)"] and "The Jealous Husband. (An Unusual Occurrence)" ["Ревнивый муж. (Происшествие необыкновенное)"].[1] The stories are closely connected: they share a protagonist, and they both take as their subject the humiliation of a cuckolded husband. In 1860, for a two-volume collection of his works, Dostoevsky lightly revised and combined them into one story with the title "Another Man's Wife and the Husband under the Bed. (An Unusual Occurrence)" ["Чужая жена и муж под кроватью. (Происшествие необыкновенное)"].[2]

These stories have attracted little attention from readers or critics, and are generally considered weak attempts to reproduce in prose the devices of vaudeville, a theatrical genre that had been imported from France to the Russian stage in the early decades of the nineteenth century.[3] But, as Joseph Frank points out in his discussion, "the very triviality and conventionality of these stories allows us to catch one of the outstanding features of his art in—as it were—a pure state."[4] Frank is referring here to Dostoevsky's subtle use of dialogue, and he quotes Bakhtin's discussion of the way in which each of two characters becomes intimately connected to the "interior voice" of the other.⁵ Following Frank's lead, in this essay I will examine in more detail how Dostoevsky manages even in seemingly trivial works to begin to explore the psychological depths he later became famous for capturing in his art. I will then suggest ways in which the "purely Dostoevskian" quality of these not entirely conventional stories later appears, transformed but still recognizable, in Dostoevsky's masterly novella of 1870 *The Eternal Husband* [*Вечный муж*].

Because these stories are not widely read, I will summarize them in some detail. And because they were initially published separately, I will discuss them as two distinct but related works. Dostoevsky's subsequent creation of a single work out of the two stories obscured their connection to two of his other works of the time, the feuilleton "A Petersburg Chronicle" ["Петербургская летопись"] for 27 April 1847 and another story of 1848, "A Christmas Party and a Wedding. (From the Notes of an Unknown Person)" ["Елка и свадьба. (Из записок неизвестного)"], a connection I will address below. But, given the stories' indebtedness to vaudeville, I will begin with an outline of the conventions of that genre.

The origins of Russian vaudeville are entirely French; many Russian vaudeville plays are either translations or re-workings of French originals. Vissarion Belinsky went so far as to assert that "vaudeville is a beautiful thing only in French, on the French stage, with French actors playing it. To imitate it is just as impossible as to translate it."⁶ So we are justified in looking at the conventions of French vaudeville for an understanding of Russian vaudeville.⁷ Jennifer Terni has provided a comprehensive discussion of the genre of vaudeville in its heyday in France from 1830 to 1848, which can serve as a guide for our consideration of Dostoevsky's use of vaudeville conventions in the works of 1848 mentioned above, as well as in *The Eternal Husband*. Unlike Anglo-American vaudeville, which tended to be presented as revues made up of disparate "acts," "turns," or "numbers," French vaudeville took the form of plays with coherent narratives, although those narratives would be punctuated by sung musical interludes, much like modern musical comedy.⁸ Terni sees the closest parallel in the twentieth-century television situation comedy, based, like vaudeville, on "stereotypes, situation-based plots, reversals of fortune, mistaken identities, and, of course, happy endings."⁹ Among the standard devices of vaudeville are physical comedy, disguises, hiding behind curtains and under furniture, and a language rich in wordplay, puns, and dialect. Terni argues, "One way to describe vaudeville—and much situation comedy—might be as a protracted foray into disaster control. . . . The contained panic of the intrigue multiplies possible disasters and thus possible outcomes, deepening the momentousness of each comment, each situation."[10] Vaudeville characters are not well-rounded, but adhere to stock formulas: the young lovers, the rival, the schemer, the father or guardian, and most apposite to Dostoevsky, the deceived husband. According to Belinsky, vaudeville roles are "doll-like" and "marionette-like," and there is "no originality, no life, no verisimilitude and truth" in them.[11]

Yet within the seemingly narrow characterological boundaries of vaudeville, the devices of impersonation, disguise, and verbal dissimulation give rise to a sense of the ambiguity of identity. Central to many vaudeville plots, Terni observes, is "the anxiety felt when one is asked to perform a new social script or try on a new persona in unfamiliar social settings. . . . Vaudeville's obsession with display, substitutions, and appearances can be read as the expression of a deep-seated apprehension about the essential contingency, and thus falseness, of identity as such. Vaudevilles implied that identity was not grounded by stable categories, that it was always to some extent strategically deployed or performed."[12] Vaudeville often deals with situations involving infidelity, but, Terni notes, "sexual lapses . . . are inevitably suppressed or forgiven . . . Although the plays invariably gesture to the conventional wisdom that would counsel moderation before the finale, vaudeville's happy endings almost always represent the victory of (usually masculine) excess."[13]

"Another Man's Wife" reads more as a scene from a vaudeville play than a complete vaudeville (as the subtitle "street scene" implies), but, like its companion story, it includes many of the standard devices of vaudeville: stock characters, wordplay, "disaster control," light treatment of sexual infidelity, and most centrally, the instability of identity. The theatrical source is reflected in the narrative form: the narrator's role of "storytelling" is kept to a minimum, as almost the entire story unfolds in dialogue, to the point that we can become confused about who is speaking. Toward the end of the story we learn that the two main characters are named Ivan Andreevich Shabrin and Ivan Ilich Tvorogov, but for most of the story they are referred to as "the gentleman in raccoon furs" and "the young man in a fur-trimmed winter coat," respectively.

(I will use their names for ease of reference, although much of the disorienting effect of the story lies in their lack of clear identification. Dostoevsky seems to be trying to evoke anxiety in the reader as he muddles the individuality of the characters.)

One evening toward eight o'clock Ivan Andreevich approaches Tvorogov on a street in St. Petersburg, in front of a tall apartment building.[14] Despite the outward marks of his respectability (his expensive fur coat, the wrinkles that betray his age, and the "highly significant ornaments," i.e. service medals, on his tail-coat), Ivan Andreevich seems agitated and timid about approaching the young man.[15] After many false starts, Ivan Andreevich manages to ask the young man whether he has seen a lady in a fox-fur coat. After receiving a negative reply, Ivan Andreevich retreats, only to keep coming back, to the great annoyance of Tvorogov. The reader becomes aware that Tvorogov is also waiting for a lady—probably the same lady—to emerge from the building. As Ivan Andreevich says, "Circumstances sometimes bind together people of completely heterogeneous characters;"[16] both the distinguished, middle-aged civil servant and the young man are being betrayed somewhere in that building by the same woman. With brutal frankness, Tvorogov says, "In essence I do not know the reason for your state of mind, but probably you've been betrayed, won't you say so directly?"[17] Ivan Andreevich admits that this is a case of betrayal, but he refuses to identify himself as the husband of the lady he is trying to catch in the act. He claims that "it's another man's wife" ["это чужая жена"], and that the actual husband is waiting on the Voznesensky Bridge for his friend, Ivan Andreevich, to help him out. Just as Tvorogov surmises that Ivan Andreevich is a betrayed husband, Ivan Andreevich surmises that Tvorogov is "a lover." Tvorogov says, "Yes, fine, to be honest, I'm a lover, only not of your wife; otherwise I wouldn't be on the street, but would be together with her now!" Ivan Andreevich responds by again disclaiming the title of husband: "Wife? Who said wife to you, young man? I'm a bachelor, that is, I myself am a lover."[18] Tvorogov then plays on the double meaning of the phrase "your wife," which could mean "the wife you are married to" or "the wife you were talking about," as he says, "You said there was a husband…on the Voznesensky Bridge."[19] In the course of their extended dialogue, Ivan Andreevich blurts out part of the name of "the other man's wife," Glafira.

Finally, the two men enter the building and ascend the dark staircase. A man and a woman begin to emerge from one of the apartments, and Ivan

Andreevich believes he has determined from the voices that "it's not her;"[20] he retreats to the street. As the lady waits on the staircase for the man accompanying her to summon a sleigh, Tvorogov approaches her with the words, "Glafira! Where are your vows?"[21] Ivan Andreevich was apparently engaging in wishful thinking when he determined that it was "not her," for this is indeed the Glafira for whom both men have been lying in wait. She claims that the man she was with was her husband, but Tvorogov quickly shows her that her actual husband, Ivan Andreevich, is standing a few feet away. Glibly lying as she tries to juggle two lovers and a husband, Glafira manages to placate Ivan Andreevich with an implausible story of a street accident, while surreptitiously arranging a later *rendezvous* with Tvorogov. Only the third man, Bobynitsyn, fails to be drawn into her net and leaves in a huff. The story ends on a strange note, as Tvorogov displays a kind of sympathy for Ivan Andreevich over the loss of one of his galoshes as he and his wife drive away.

What lifts this story above the standard vaudeville is that Dostoevsky here elevates Ivan Andreevich's anxiety of identity, a comic convention in vaudeville, to a degree of seriousness approaching the tragic. This anxiety is reflected in his repeated claims that "I am not a husband." Ivan Andreevich is not simply a vaudeville character, but a character aware of vaudeville conventions and rebelling against them. Russian has borrowed from French the word *emploi* [in Russian, амплуа], meaning an actor's specialty, such as ingénue, father figure, leading man, etc. Ivan Andreevich, who we learn in the second story is a theatergoer, knows well the significance of the emploi of "husband" on the vaudeville stage. While in life the role of "husband" can mean many things, including "beloved companion," on the vaudeville stage it means only one thing: a deceived, humiliated, ridiculous buffoon. Ivan Andreevich realizes, with a self-consciousness that would be out of place in an actual vaudeville character, that his dignity is not compatible with the role of husband: "I am not doing this for myself; don't even think that—it's another man's wife! The husband is standing over there, on the Voznesensky Bridge; he wants to catch her, but he can't resolve to do it—he still doesn't believe, like any husband . . . (here the gentleman in raccoon furs tried to smile), I'm his friend; you have to agree, *I am a man who enjoys a certain respect—I cannot be the person you take me for.*"[22] Ivan Andreevich tries to escape the fate of the husband and embrace the more attractive emploi of the lover.

As the two men stand in the darkness on the stairway, Ivan Andreevich reproaches Tvorogov for his stereotyping, as if he were addressing the very foundations of vaudeville: "It's simply immoral. . . . In your opinion, every offended husband is a simpleton [колпак]!"[23] Tvorogov responds by calling Ivan Andreevich a simpleton, to which Ivan Andreevich replies, "'That is, you mean to say that I am a husband!' . . . stepping back as if he had had boiling water poured over him"[24] Soon afterwards, in an attempt at reconciliation, he concedes the young man's (and vaudeville's) point, while at the same time protesting the injustice: "Of course, I agree with your idea that a husband in such a situation is a simpleton . . . But why such embittered persecution of the unfortunate husband?"[25]

As the voices of the man and woman in the apartment become audible, and Tvorogov identifies the woman as "her," i.e., the Glafira in whom they are both interested, Ivan Andreevich launches into a last desperate aria of denial:

> "My dear sir, my dear sir!" muttered the gentleman in raccoon furs, turning pale and whimpering. "I, of course, am in an upset state . . . you have seen enough of my humiliation; but it's night now, of course, but tomorrow . . . but we will probably not meet tomorrow, although I am not afraid to meet you—and by the way, it is not I, it's my friend on the Voznesensky Bridge, indeed, it's him! It's his wife, it's another man's wife! Unfortunate man! I assure you. I know him well; if you like, I'll tell you all about it. I'm a friend of his, as you can see . . .; I said to him several times: why are you getting married, dear friend? You have rank, you're well off, you're a respected man, why exchange all that for the whim of coquetry! You must agree! No, I'm getting married, he says: family happiness . . . There's your family happiness! Before, he deceived husbands himself, and now he drinks the cup . . . You'll excuse me, but this explanation was forced by necessity—he's drinking the cup now! He's an unfortunate man and is drinking the cup—there!" Here the gentleman in the raccoon furs whimpered in such a way that he seemed to be sobbing in earnest [не на шутку].[26]

The Russian phrase for "in earnest," "не на шутку," literally means "not as a joke." In this moment of true despair Dostoevsky takes Ivan Andreevich's story beyond the bounds of the vaudeville joke and introduces it into the realm of the tragic.[27]

The first section of the second story, "The Jealous Husband," is presented in a more conventional fashion than "Another Man's Wife," with interpolations and asides by the narrator; only about five pages into the narrative does it become the same sort of dialogue-rich vaudeville scene as "Another Man's Wife," complete with the role of a wheezing old husband that would be perfect for a comic actor. The story begins with a narrator's introduction (omitted in the 1860 version) that reminds the reader of Ivan Andreevich's situation and sets up the moral message of the story (to be discussed below). In the first scene, Ivan Andreevich bursts "like a bomb" into a performance at the Italian Opera, again in search of his wife, who had told him she was not planning to attend. In fact, he sees her in a loge, accompanied by a general and his family, as well as the general's adjutant, "an extraordinarily adroit young man," and also a civilian who cannot be identified because he is standing behind the adjutant (the implication may be that it is Tvorogov, although this is never confirmed in the story).[28] Unlike in "Another Man's Wife," where the reader has to infer Ivan Andreevich's mental state from his dialogue, here the narrator tells us that "the duplicity that [his wife] Glafira Petrovna had recently been manifesting at every step was killing Ivan Andreevich," and that he has been unable to sleep at night.[29]

His humiliation continues at the opera, as something falls onto his head: "Onto the respected and bared head (that is, partly deprived of hair) of the jealous and irritated Ivan Andreevich flew such an immoral object as, for example, a scented little love note."[30] The note, which arranges a rendezvous, could have fallen from any one of the five tiers of boxes above, but Ivan Andreevich in his jealousy jumps to the conclusion that his wife has written it. Ivan Andreevich rushes to the address indicated in the note. A fop in an overcoat overtakes him and runs up the stairs ahead of him. Ivan Andreevich hears a door being opened overhead to admit the fop; when Ivan Andreevich follows him up he sees that the door has been left open. Although he would like to stop for a moment and make a plan, Ivan Andreevich panics when he hears a carriage drive up to the building and someone treading heavily up the stairs while wheezing and coughing. With no time to waste, Ivan Andreevich rushes into the apartment, past the servants and into the bedroom, where he is met by a young, beautiful woman whom he doesn't know. As the man with the heavy steps also enters the apartment, the woman cries, "My God! It's my husband!"[31] In her fright, she does not try to stop Ivan Andreevich as he hides under the bed, where he finds yet another man already lying. Apparently, the man who ascended the stairs before Ivan Andreevich had been instructed by the woman to dive under the bed.

Now begins the truly vaudevillian part of the story, in which the two men under the bed conduct a furious, whispered conversation at the same time as we hear the old, wheezing husband and his terrified wife talking to each other. Much comic confusion ensues as the old husband interprets the noise under the bed as coming from the housecat chasing mice. Ivan Andreevich and his companion under the bed learn from the old husband's conversation with his wife that they have entered the wrong apartment; the old man has seen a flirtatious woman and a "little fop with a little mustache"[32] ascending to an upper floor of the building. It appears that the situation of "Another Man's Wife," in which a wife betrays both a husband and a lover with a third man, is being repeated. Finally, the lady's lapdog, Amishka, begins barking and biting Ivan Andreevich's nose. Ivan Andreevich strangles the dog "in a fit of self-preservation."[33] The other man manages to slip out while the husband is looking under the bed on the other side. Upon seeing the other man emerge, the wife exclaims, "My God! Who are you? And I thought . . . " thus revealing that she too has a lover, who she thought was the man she had told to dive under the bed.[34] Ivan Andreevich is left to face the angry husband, who first takes him for a thief. After Ivan Andreevich dissolves into humiliating explanations, the married couple, indignant at first, finally collapses into uncontrollable laughter. Ivan Andreevich rushes home, only to have his wife reproach him for not being there when she came home from the opera. His final humiliation comes when, as he reaches for a handkerchief, out falls the lifeless corpse of Amishka, and Ivan Andreevich is left to come up with an explanation for his angry wife.

In "The Jealous Husband," Ivan Andreevich's anxiety of identity again figures prominently. Again he is brought into close contact with someone he considers to be beneath him. Lying under the bed, pressed up against the other man, Ivan Andreevich says, "My dear sir! I am a little older than you, I tell you . . ." The man replies, "My dear sir! You should know that here we are on the same level" (literally "we are on the same board" ["мы здесь на одной доске"], a pun on the floorboards they lie on).[35] In his explanations to the married couple, Ivan Andreevich again denies that he is a husband: "It's all the wife, that is not my wife, but another man's wife—I am not married, I'm just . . . It's my friend and childhood companion."[36] A turning point comes when the wife and husband ask him, "Just who are you?" and he replies, "I cannot say."[37] For a moment Ivan Andreevich comes to terms with what he has become:

"'It's nothing that I sat for a while under the bed ... I didn't lose my importance thereby. It's the most comic story, Your Excellency!' Ivan Andreevich exclaimed, turning to the spouse with a pleading look. 'You especially, Your Excellency, will laugh! *You see on the stage a jealous husband.* You see, I am abasing myself, I myself am voluntarily abasing myself ... *I'm only an insulted husband, nothing more!* Do not think, Your Excellency, that I am a lover: I am not a lover!'"[38] Ivan Andreevich has utterly failed to escape the emploi of the insulted husband.

Despite all this, the question of identity is less central to "The Jealous Husband" than to "Another Man's Wife." The second story's main focus is the question of morality, but that question appears in an unexpected light. The narrator's introduction specifically sets forth the moral significance of the story: "I affirm that my story is completely moral and that its moral is the definitive triumph of virtue and the complete defeat of the jealous husband. At the same time I prove that jealousy in general, and principally jealousy that suspects even innocence itself, is a vice, a ridiculous and absurd vice that destroys family happiness and causes even an intelligent and learned man to fall often into the most ticklish situations."[39] The reader might be surprised to find that the villain of these stories is not the wife who is carrying on affairs with at least three if not four lovers (depending on whether the "civilian" at the opera and the man under the bed with Ivan Andreevich is or is not Tvorogov). Rather the villain, according to the narrator, is the husband she has betrayed. Certainly the endless humiliations to which Ivan Andreevich is subjected in the two narratives support the narrator's assertion that the aim of the works is to defeat the "jealous husband."

Not coincidentally, one of the first critics to devote sustained attention to "Another Man's Wife and the Husband under the Bed" was N. K. Mikhailovsky in his famous 1882 essay "A Cruel Talent," in which he argued that Dostoevsky's whole aesthetic was based on the enjoyment of the contemplation of suffering. After summarizing "Another Man's Wife and the Husband under the Bed," Mikhailovsky concludes, "I have on purpose recounted all this triviality in order for the reader to better appreciate all the superfluity of this abundance of misfortunes of Ivan Andreevich. . . . Isn't this a bullfight, undertaken solely for unnecessary cruelty? We'll admit that Ivan Andreevich is a very funny bull, but all the more inappropriate is this whole arsenal of misfortunes directed against him, all this personnel of banderilleros, picadors, and matadors who irritate, stab and kill him."[40] For Mikhailovsky, it is precisely the extended torture of Ivan Andreevich that distinguishes the story from "the most ordinary vaudeville by the most talentless producer of that kind of work."[41]

The narrator's introduction speaks of "jealousy that suspects even innocence itself."[42] The narrator seems to be invoking the kind of tragic situation that obtains in Shakespeare's *Othello*, where the wife is unjustly suspected by the jealous husband, and jealousy truly becomes a kind of madness that does not take reality into account.[43] By contrast, we have seen in "Another Man's Wife" that Glafira Petrovna is indeed betraying her husband, Ivan Andreevich. Her guilt is somewhat less clear-cut in "The Jealous Husband": the note that falls onto Ivan Andreevich's head could have come from any of several tiers of loges; Ivan Andreevich does not recognize the handwriting (although this could be taken as the same kind of wishful thinking that caused him not to recognize his wife's voice in "Another Man's Wife"); the narrator refers to him as someone who "considered himself" an insulted husband;[44] we never see Glafira Petrovna at the site of the rendezvous; and she is already home when her husband returns. Nevertheless, the narrator reminds us in his introduction that the events of "The Jealous Husband" occurred the very next day after those of "Another Man's Wife." This makes it harder to credit the "innocence" of Glafira Petrovna in the second story.

So why is the husband, who is not suspecting "innocence itself" but a wife clearly guilty of adultery, subjected to the extended tortures of these two stories (with future torments promised in the final paragraph of the second story)? As Mikhailovsky noted, the length and severity of Ivan Andreevich's humiliation exceeds the usual norm for vaudeville, which usually ends on a note of happy reconciliation. The explanation may lie in the connection between these stories and two other works by Dostoevsky, the feuilleton "A Petersburg Chronicle" for 27 April 1847 and another story of 1848, "A Christmas Party and a Wedding."[45] The latter story begins with the line, "A few days ago I saw a wedding" ["На днях я видел свадьбу"];[46] "The Jealous Husband" begins, "I saw a certain wedding" ["Я еще видел одну свадьбу"].[47] The use of nearly the same words to begin each story implies that the wedding or weddings referred to share a kinship. In "The Jealous Husband," the wedding in question is that of Ivan Andreevich and Glafira Petrovna, whose courtship is not depicted, and the stories of adultery tell us what happened "exactly one year after the wedding."[48]

The wedding mentioned at the beginning of "A Christmas Party and a Wedding" is not explained until the very end of the story. Most of that story concerns a Christmas party, at which a respectable and imposing man, Iulian Mastakovich, learns that one of the children at the party, an eleven-year-old girl, is going to inherit 300,000 rubles. He resolves on the spot to marry her when she turns sixteen. The story mostly concerns Iulian Mastakovich's interference in children's play in the interests of his own future plans; the wedding is depicted only on the last page. Robert Louis Jackson provides a detailed analysis of Iulian Mastakovich's "rapacious and voluptuous feelings" toward the girl, which are rewarded with the marriage alluded to in the first sentence of the story.[49] At the end of the story, the narrator describes the wedding, focusing on the bride: "The beauty was pale and sad. She looked around absent-mindedly; it even seemed to me that her eyes were red from recent tears. The classical severity of each feature of her face lent a kind of significance and solemnity to her beauty. But through that severity and significance, through that sadness there still glimmered the first childish, innocent image; one could see something extremely naïve, not yet formed, youthful, and, it seemed, praying for mercy for itself without making any open requests."[50] Given what we have seen of Iulian Mastakovich in the rest of the story, this bride appears as a lamb to the slaughter.

As several critics have noted, Iulian Mastakovich also appears in two other works by Dostoevsky, "A Faint Heart" ["Слабое сердце," 1848], and, more apposite to my discussion, the feuilleton "Petersburg Chronicle" for 27 April 1847. In "A Faint Heart," there is no reference to Iulian Mastakovich's lecherous tendencies, but in "Petersburg Chronicle," a marriage similar to the pedophilic union described at the end of "A Christmas Party and a Wedding" is discussed:

> My good friend, former well-wisher and even a bit of a patron of mine, Iulian Mastakovich, plans to get married. To tell the truth, it is hard to get married when one is of a more prudent age. He hasn't yet gotten married, there are still three weeks for him to wait until the wedding; but every evening he puts on his white waistcoat, wig, the whole regalia, buys a bouquet and some candy and rides off to be pleasing to Glafira Petrovna, his fiancée, a girl of seventeen, full of innocence and the utter ignorance of evil. Just the mere thought of the latter circumstance brings the most puff-pastry-like smile to the sugary lips of Iulian Mastakovich. No, it's even pleasant to get married at such an age! In my opinion, if one is to fully express it, it's even unseemly to do it in youth, that is before the age of thirty-five. Such passion passes so

quickly! But here, when a man is nearing fifty—he's settled, he has decorum, good tone, a physical and moral roundedness—it's good, indeed it's good!⁵¹

The narrator goes on to describe Iulian Mastakovich's efforts to maintain relations with his mistress, the young widow Sofia Ivanovna, even after his marriage to Glafira Petrovna.

Obviously, this Glafira Petrovna is not identical to the Glafira Petrovna to whom Ivan Andreevich is married; she is not even identical to the girl in the story "A Christmas Party and a Wedding," since that girl is only sixteen at the time of her marriage.⁵² It is also somewhat risky to identify the Iulian Mastakovich of the three stories as the same Iulian Mastakovich, since his fairly benevolent behavior in "A Faint Heart" does not jibe with his character in "A Christmas Party and a Wedding."⁵³ But, perhaps taking his cue from the practice of stereotyping in vaudeville, Dostoevsky seems to be interested in types rather than individuals: the type of the young, innocent girl and the type of the much older man with a weighty position in society who is allowed to marry her, thanks to the norms of society, and contrary to what would seem natural. (The fact that in "Petersburg Chronicle" even a man of thirty-five, i.e., twice as old as Glafira Petrovna, is considered too young for her says something chilling about those norms.) Significantly, in both "Petersburg Chronicle" and "A Christmas Party and a Wedding," the bride's innocence is stressed; as the narrator of "Petersburg Chronicle" says, Glafira Petrovna is "full of innocence and the utter ignorance of evil" ["полной невинности и совершенного неведенья зла"].⁵⁴

Given that the narrator of "The Jealous Husband" begins with the same words about "a wedding" that the narrator of "A Christmas Party and a Wedding" does, we are invited to imagine that the pale, sad, innocent young bride described in such detail at the end of "A Christmas Party and a Wedding" represents what Ivan Andreevich's wife might have looked like on her wedding day one year earlier. When the narrator of "The Jealous Husband" speaks of "jealousy that suspects even innocence itself," he seems to be referring to this aspect of Glafira Petrovna—Glafira Petrovna as the victim of the pedophilic marriage whose sacrifice lies a year in the past, not the adulterous wife we see in the story.

V. S. Nechaeva warns against identifying the Glafira Petrovna of "Petersburg Chronicle" with the Glafira Petrovna of "Another Man's Wife" and

"The Jealous Husband": "Dostoevsky could not in ['Another Man's Wife and the Husband under the Bed'] have lowered the image we cited earlier, the deeply tragic image of the young bride, to the level of a vulgar society lady who adroitly deceives her husband."[55] But one cannot just dismiss the parallel suggested by Dostoevsky. In the narrator's introduction to "The Jealous Husband," he links Ivan Andreevich's story to that of Iulian Mastakovich with the words "I saw a wedding," as well as with the name Glafira Petrovna and his assertion of her innocence. Glafira Petrovna may be "innocent," in that Ivan Andreevich's sin has absolved her in advance: the situation of the pedophilic marriage leads almost inevitably to the situation of the adulterous wife.[56] (The situation is reproduced as a story-within-a-story in "The Jealous Husband" by the married couple in whose bedroom Ivan Andreevich is stuck; the husband is much older than the wife, as Ivan Andreevich notes, and the wife is carrying on an affair, as her surprise upon seeing the wrong man come out from under the bed indicates.) In this light, the torments visited upon Ivan Andreevich in the two stories, what the narrator calls "the definitive triumph of virtue and the complete defeat of the jealous husband," no longer seem as inexplicable and needlessly sadistic as they did at first. The differential between the comic humiliations visited upon the cuckolded husband in vaudeville and the extended torture of Ivan Andreevich is accounted for by the deeper moral dimension Dostoevsky introduces through the web of references to the pedophilic impulse that lies behind the socially approved marriage of a couple like Ivan Andreevich and Glafira Petrovna.

The architect Robert Venturi has lucidly described the way an artist uses convention in the attempt to create something new: "You need a norm to vary as well as a functional basis for contradiction.... To me the main strength is not the canons of historical architecture, but the fact that canons allow you to divert and to go off from them.... You have to refer to a norm in the first place before you break the rules."[57] Earlier he had asserted: "The architect's main work is the organization of a unique whole through conventional parts and the judicious introduction of new parts when the old won't do."[58] We can see the young Dostoevsky organizing "a unique whole through conventional parts and the judicious introduction of new parts" in the way he uses well-worn vaudeville conventions in "Another Man's Wife" and "The Jealous Husband" while complicating vaudeville lightness and simplicity with darker currents. He makes the convention strange by forcing us to look closely at what lies behind the "humor" of the cuckolded husband.

Much later in his career, Dostoevsky again placed the cuckolded husband at the center of a story, in the novella *The Eternal Husband* [*Вечный муж*], published in the journal *Dawn* [*Заря*] in 1870.[59] Unlike "Another Man's Wife" and "The Jealous Husband," *The Eternal Husband* is widely recognized as one of Dostoevsky's finest works. Yet the use he makes of vaudeville conventions in the later work, long after vaudeville's heyday in Russia had passed, demonstrates that the artistic energy inspiring the earlier stories had not been exhausted, and that Dostoevsky found the questions raised in them still worth revisiting and extending.

The Eternal Husband is narrated from the point of view (although not in the voice) of Aleksei Ivanovich Velchaninov, a man of good society who has fallen on hard times due to his own profligacy.[60] As he lingers in St. Petersburg during the hot summer months pursuing a lawsuit over an inheritance, he is tormented by memories of his past misdeeds. He comes to realize that these memories have been triggered by seeing a mysterious "gentleman with mourning crape on his hat" several times on the street. Eventually this gentleman appears at his apartment in the middle of the night, and Velchaninov finally recognizes him as Pavel Pavlovich Trusotsky, a civil servant with whose wife Velchaninov had had a year-long affair nine years previously while visiting their province. The wife, Natalia Vasilevna, has recently died, and after her death, Pavel Pavlovich, who had suspected nothing during her lifetime, has read her love letters and discovered her "constant and innumerable betrayals"[61] Yet Velchaninov, who never wrote her any compromising letters, remains uncertain for a long time, throughout a series of cat-and-mouse conversations with Pavel Pavlovich, whether the husband knows about Velchaninov's own affair with her or not.

Pavel Pavlovich has brought with him to St. Petersburg his daughter Liza, whom Velchaninov instantly recognizes as being his own daughter. Although she had earlier been cherished by Pavel Pavlovich, his realization after her mother's death that she is not his biological daughter causes him to abuse and neglect her. Seizing upon the child as his hope for renewal, Velchaninov takes her from Pavel Pavlovich to the dacha of friends in the country, where she soon dies of grief and anxiety. The child Liza is barely cold in the ground before Pavel

Pavlovich and Velchaninov begin a sexual competition over another child, Nadia Zakhlebinina, a fifteen-year-old girl whom Pavel Pavlovich plans to marry. Nadia openly scorns Pavel Pavlovich, but she is charmed by the experienced seducer Velchaninov, although she is in love with a young man named Aleksandr Lobov.

In the novella's climactic episode, Pavel Pavlovich spends the night at Velchaninov's apartment, nurses him through a severe attack of liver disease, and then, after Velchaninov falls asleep, attempts to kill him with a straight razor that Velchaninov has happened to leave out in the open. Having warded off Pavel Pavlovich's murderous attack, Velchaninov considers that they are "quits"; Pavel Pavlovich, instead of killing himself as Velchaninov expects, leaves St. Petersburg, conveying to Velchaninov through Lobov a key document: a letter written by Natalia Vasilevna to Velchaninov but never sent, in which she tells him she is pregnant with his child.

An epilogue takes place two years later, in a chapter entitled "The Eternal Husband." Velchaninov, having won his lawsuit and thus improved his financial and social situation, is on his way to visit "an extraordinarily interesting woman."[62] At a stopover at a provincial train station, he encounters Pavel Pavlovich, who is now married to a young, beautiful, but tastelessly dressed woman who has in tow a drunken young "distant relative" with whom she appears to be on intimate terms. Instantly charmed by Velchaninov, she invites him to visit them in the country. Velchaninov and Pavel Pavlovich have one last *tête-à-tête*, in which Velchaninov promises not to visit him and his wife. When Velchaninov extends his hand to say goodbye, Pavel Pavlovich refuses to take it. Velchaninov shows him the scar from the wound inflicted by Pavel Pavlovich's murder weapon, and says, "If I, *I*, extend to you this hand, then you could certainly take it!" Pavel Pavlovich responds with his own trump card: "And Liza?"[63] They are not "quits" at all.

There are numerous connections between *The Eternal Husband* and Dostoevsky's stories of 1848, beyond the basic theme of adultery. In the early part of the novella, Pavel Pavlovich is referred to not by name but as "the gentleman with mourning crape on his hat" ["господин с крепом на шляпе"], much like Ivan Andreevich, "the gentleman in raccoon furs" ["господин в енотах"]. His speech, like that of Ivan Andreevich, is marked by the constant use of the suffix "-с," a contraction for "sir" that is a marker of pretentious obsequiousness.

His adulterous wife, who considered herself "completely innocent,"[64] exerts the same absolute authority over him that Glafira Petrovna has over Ivan Andreevich at the end of "The Jealous Husband."[65] When confronted by Lobov, his rival for Nadia, Pavel Pavlovich addresses him as "young man," recalling the "young man" with whom Ivan Andreevich converses on the street in "Another Man's Wife." Like that earlier "young man," Lobov turns this supposed disadvantage in social position into an advantage in sexual attractiveness: "At any other time I of course would forbid you to call me 'young man,' but now you'll agree yourself that my youth is my main advantage over you, and you would really like . . . to be just a tiny bit younger."[66] In the final scene, there is a specific reference to "The Jealous Husband," when Pavel Pavlovich's young male relative says, "Under the bed . . . [Pavel Pavlovich] looks for lovers . . . under the bed."[67]

The anxiety of identity that pervades "Another Man's Wife" is also a strong theme in *The Eternal Husband*, whose very title refers to the emploi that Velchaninov has assigned to Pavel Pavlovich:

> Velchaninov was convinced that there actually existed such a type as [women born to be unfaithful]; but he was also convinced that there existed a type of husband corresponding to these women, whose sole purpose consisted in corresponding to that female type. In his opinion, the essence of such husbands consisted in being, so to speak, "eternal husbands" or, to put it more precisely, to be in life *only* husbands and nothing more. "Such a man is born and develops solely in order to get married, and having gotten married, to immediately turn into an appendage to his wife, even when he happens to have his own peculiar, indisputable character. The main sign of such a husband is a well-known adornment [a cuckold's horns]. He can't help but be a cuckold, just as the sun can't help but shine; but he not only never knows about this, but can never find out, according to the very laws of nature."[68]

Velchaninov has a harder time recognizing that he too is stuck in the emploi of the seducer, the "eternal Don Juan," or what Branwen E. B. Pratt calls the "comfortable, conscienceless exploiter of the other."[69]

Tetsuo Motidzuki has demonstrated that the first section of *The Eternal Husband* represents an exchange of roles between Pavel Pavlovich and Velchaninov. After his wife's death, Pavel Pavlovich has discovered "that instead of the familiar roles of 'kind husband,' 'faithful friend,' and 'good father,' he has in fact played the role of 'deceived husband,' 'stupid nice guy,' and 'nominal father.' Having become widowed and deprived of his emploi not only in the domestic theater but also in real life, he seems to intentionally play roles that are inappropriate for him (tormenter of an orphan, debauchee, suitor of a fifteen-year-old girl)."[70] He and Velchaninov exchange roles: "The eternal husband behaves like a St. Petersburg debauchee-drunkard, tasteless joker, and irresponsible father, and the eternal Don Juan behaves like an upright, kind citizen, taking pains about the fate of a little orphan (that is, his daughter)."[71]

This attempt to escape one's emploi may remind us of Ivan Andreevich, desperately announcing that he is "a lover, not a husband," and diving under the bed of a lady, "as if he considered himself a Don Juan or a Lovelace!"[72] Like Ivan Andreevich, Pavel Pavlovich and Velchaninov are destined to return to their "eternal" roles at the end of the novella. Dostoevsky takes us on a much more complex psychological journey in *The Eternal Husband* than he does in "Another Man's Wife" and "The Jealous Husband," and the departures from emploi represented by Pavel Pavlovich and Velchaninov make them far more multifaceted, mysterious characters than Ivan Andreevich. Yet Dostoevsky chooses to end the novella with the two men settling back compulsively into their seemingly fated conventional roles.[73]

Motidzuki analyzes in detail the theatricality of *The Eternal Husband*, going so far as to refer to Velchaninov and Pavel Pavlovich as "failed actors who have been deprived of their usual roles."[74] I would add that the particular kind of theater most meaningfully evoked in *The Eternal Husband* is vaudeville, although the height of its popularity in Russia lay in the past, in the 1840s. The first specific allusion to vaudeville comes in the title of chapter 4, "The Wife, the Husband, and the Lover." The notes to Dostoevsky's complete works identify this as the title of Paul de Kock's novel of 1830, *The Wife, the Husband, and the Lover* [*La femme, le mari et l'amant*].[75] But given the theatrical atmosphere that pervades the novella, as demonstrated by Motidzuki, the more apposite reference is probably to the "comédie vaudeville en quatre actes" ["a vaudeville comedy in four acts"] adapted by de Kock (with Charles Dupeuty) from his novel, performed at the Palais-Royal theater in Paris in 1834.[76] The works of de Kock are often referred to in Dostoevsky as the quintessence of frivolity and salaciousness; for example, Ivan Andreevich's wife "eternally has Paul de Kock under the pillow."[77]

Clearly the reference in *The Eternal Husband* to "The Wife, the Husband, and the Lover" is meant to evoke an atmosphere of vaudeville mockery of the clichéd love- triangle situation. But perhaps appropriately, in light of Pavel Pavlovich's and Velchaninov's attempts to shake up the standard vaudeville roles, de Kock's play does not present "the wife, the husband, and the lover" in the ways one might expect. The husband is a wastrel who has rejected his faithful wife and is spending his fortune on mistresses and gambling; the wife is a virtuous woman who continues to love him after two years of separation; and the lover is a young man who has fallen in love with her at first sight and who accedes to her demand that their relationship remain chaste. In de Kock's play, it is the wife who is accused of jealousy by the husband: "I thought she was good natured, but we had been married not even a year when I perceived that she was surly, sulky . . . jealous . . . horribly jealous" ["Je lui croyais un bon caractère, mais il n'y avait pas un an que nous étions mariés, quand je me suis aperçu qu'elle était maussade, boudeuse . . . jalouse . . . horriblement jalouse"].[78] Uncharacteristically for a vaudeville, despite its abundance of comic business, *The Wife, the Husband, and the Lover* does not have a happy ending: the husband is killed in a duel with a man who has swindled him, and the lover vows to the grieving widow that he will avenge him.[79] In this play, de Kock almost resembles Dostoevsky in his willingness to disrupt convention.

Besides the specific allusion to de Kock, vaudeville appears in *The Eternal Husband* through the use of certain conventions: wordplay and puns, physical comedy—like Pavel Pavlovich's miming of horns or his anticlimactic request for a chamber pot after scaring Velchaninov as an apparition in the middle of the night—and the "unexpected meeting between enemies" that Terni sees as one of the engines of reconciliation in vaudeville.[80] But most striking in this regard are the events portrayed in chapter 12, "At the Zakhlebinins," especially the episode in which Pavel Pavlovich brings Velchaninov to meet his fifteen-year-old intended bride, Nadia Zakhlebinina, at her family's dacha.

This chapter is by far the longest one in *The Eternal Husband*, and, as several critics have noted, its tone and atmosphere are distinctive. Frank, for example, says it is "written in a Turgenevian tonality unusual for Dostoevsky."[81] Both Frank and Motidzuki refer to the episode as a "play within a play."[82] I would add that the type of play this episode represents is vaudeville, but in a disguised form. In his 1845 essay "The Aleksandrinsky Theater," Belinsky described the standard vaudeville plot as follows: "Some foolish parents have a sweet, educated little daughter; she is in love with a charming young man, but a poor one—usually an officer, or now and then, for the sake of variety, a civil servant, and they want to marry her off to some sort of fool, an eccentric, a scoundrel, or all three together.... But toward the end virtue is rewarded, vice is punished: the lovers get married, the dear parents give them their blessing, the interfering party is left looking foolish [разлучник с носом]—the gallery laughs at him."[83] This could be an outline of the plot setup of the scene at the Zakhlebinins': Nadia's fond but somewhat foolish parents are planning to marry her off to Pavel Pavlovich, who at various times can be seen as a fool, an eccentric, and a scoundrel; she is already in love with the impoverished Aleksandr Lobov, whose abortive civil service career is just getting started. Lobov, who speaks in the stilted language of a Chernyshevsky character, describes the situation to Pavel Pavlovich in a subsequent chapter whose title might be a good one for a vaudeville, "Sashenka and Nadenka": "We, that is Nadezhda Fedoseevna [Nadia] and I, have loved each other for a long time and have given each other our word. You are now an obstacle between us ... You want to take a girl by force, you're buying her from senile people who as a result of social barbarism preserve power over her."[84]

The scene at the Zakhlebinins' dacha displays many of the features of vaudeville. The main characters are surrounded by a chorus of young girls (Nadia's sisters and neighbors), reminiscent of vaudeville choruses that break into song, as does the crowd of pretty young seamstresses who provide several musical interludes in *The Wife, the Husband, and the Lover*. Velchaninov displays his verbal gifts like a trained actor and attracts the undivided attention of his audience: "He had magnificently mastered the art of chattering in high society, that is, the art of seeming completely ingenuous and at the same time pretending that he considered his audience to be people just as ingenuous as he.... He also knew how to interject into his words a witty and provocative *bon mot*, a cheerful hint, a funny pun, but completely as if by chance, as if not even noticing, even though the witticism, the pun, and the conversation itself, perhaps, had long ago been prepared and learned by heart and had been used more than once."[85] The girls play a number of games, the object of which is to humiliate Pavel Pavlovich; his embarrassment is displayed for all to see, as if on a stage. When the young people play "theater," the role of the "young man" goes to the eternal lover, Velchaninov.[86] There are musical interludes; Nadia's sister plays Haydn, Nadia herself sings for Velchaninov, and, most strikingly, a page and a half is devoted to Velchaninov's singing of a romance by Glinka, complete with a detailed analysis of his artistic performance technique.[87]

In general Velchaninov plays a role described by Terni as characteristic of French vaudeville, that of the "stabilizer," the character "who masters the arts of plotting, verbal manipulation, and imposture." This character "tends to be interested in outcomes only obliquely and is therefore the one who maintains the necessary distance to help produce happy endings."[88] Fittingly, "Nadenka and Sashenka" (Nadia and Lobov) choose Velchaninov as their mediator, the one to return Pavel Pavlovich's embarrassing gift of a diamond bracelet and to explain to him the impossibility of his plan to marry Nadia. We do not get to see the happy ending for these star-crossed lovers, who have in classic vaudeville fashion been exchanging their vows of love through a gap in the fence.[89] But we do see the retreat of the "obstacle," the eccentric fool Pavel Pavlovich, to whom Nadia's parents had planned to marry her off.

When Lobov comes to Velchaninov's apartment to have it out with Pavel Pavlovich, he addresses head-on the same problematic that emerges in Dostoevsky's stories of 1847 and 1848: the way in which the pedophilic marriage leads inevitably to the cuckolded husband. Pavel Pavlovich plans to go away for nine months, until Nadia has turned sixteen, and only then to make the betrothal public.[90] Of course "nine months" had a different significance for Pavel Petrovich when he calculated the time between the departure of Velchaninov and the birth of Liza.[91] Now Lobov, in what Pavel Pavlovich terms a "nasty hint," makes the connection clear: "'Watch out!' the youth pointed at him threateningly with a haughty smile. 'Don't make a mistake in your calculations! Do you know what such a mistake in one's calculations leads to? Well, I'm warning you that in nine months, when you've already spent all your money and worn yourself out, and you return here, you yourself will be forced to give up Nadezhda Fedoseevna, and if you don't give her up—it will be the worse for you; that's what you'll bring yourself to!'"[92]

Certainly Dostoevsky does not leave the vaudeville substratum of his novella untransformed by the atmosphere of the 1860s or by his own artistic development since the 1840s. Lobov and Nadia differ from the standard vaudeville couple by clothing their planned union in nihilist ideology. No doubt inspired by the "woman question" and the familial experiments of Nikolai Chernyshevsky, Lobov explains that he will provide Nadia with documents that will make it possible for her to dissolve their marriage at any time: "That way everything is guaranteed, and I am not risking anyone's future."[93] And unlike vaudeville or Dostoevsky's stories of 1848, *The Eternal Husband* directs attention to the inconvenient topic of children. Neither the frivolous world of vaudeville adultery nor the convention-breaking ideology of nihilist youth takes into account the element that lends *The Eternal Husband* its truly tragic dimension: the potential ruin of the life of a child as adults pursue their sexual or ideological desires.[94]

For Pavel Pavlovich and Velchaninov, *The Eternal Husband* ends with vaudeville. Pavel Pavlovich is once again in the emploi of the deceived husband; as Velchaninov thinks when he hears about the family arrangements consisting of young wife, old husband, and young lover, "Well, all right, everything's in order—the whole setup [полная обстановка]!"[95] Velchaninov too ends his story in a vaudevillian way. As Terni points out, vaudeville "portray[s] desire in a positive light," and its happy endings "almost always represent the victory of (usually masculine) excess."[96] This is a good description of the ending of *The Eternal Husband*, as, after the encounter with Pavel Pavlovich, Velchaninov goes on his way to visit an "interesting woman." In the last line of the novella we see him consumed by regret, not for the death of Liza, but for his failure to take a detour where he could have seduced yet another woman. Unlike most of Dostoevsky's works of the time, *The Eternal Husband* has very little discussion of God. The closest it comes to invoking God is at the beginning, when Velchaninov, tormented by his memories, thinks, "So someone out there [кто-то там] is worrying about the correction of my morality and is sending me these damned recollections and 'tears of repentance.'"[97] That "someone," possibly the divine, is not with Velchaninov at the end of the novella. Instead he seems to be watched over by "the providence of all decent and respectable people" ["провидение всех порядочных и приличных людей"].[98] This is a lesser god, possibly the god of vaudeville itself.

In December 1879, Dostoevsky received a letter from the actor V. V. Samoilov (1812-1887) in which Samoilov wrote, "I have always been struck by the subtlety of your powers of observation, and in each of the psychologically heterogeneous characters you have created, I have seen living people with their weaknesses and virtues, and I became sad that over the course of my work on the stage I did not have the opportunity to reproduce a single one of your personalities for the reason that you, while possessing such truthful talent, did not wish to leave a memory of yourself on the stage, which I greatly regret both for the public and for myself, since I might have added one of the best roles to my repertoire."[99] In a letter of 17 December, Dostoevsky replied, "Your opinion of me is *dearer* than all the opinions and judgments of my works that I have had the opportunity to read. I hear this opinion from one who is also a great psychologist, who produced rapture in me in my youth and adolescence, when you were just beginning your artistic exploits. With your brilliant talent you, no doubt and *certainly*, had a great deal of influence on my soul and mind. At the end of my days it is pleasant to attest this to you."[100]

Perhaps bowing to Soviet pieties, A. Gozenpud hypothesizes that Dostoevsky could not have been speaking of Samoilov's famous roles in vaudeville, in which his skill at disguise demonstrated his virtuosic art of transformation, but must have been thinking of his later work in the plays of the "natural school" or possibly some of the more "psychological" roles in the vaudevilles of F. Koni and Nekrasov.[101] But Dostoevsky could not have been clearer about the time he had in mind: "… in my youth and adolescence, when you were just beginning your artistic exploits." Samoilov's earliest triumphs were precisely his roles in vaudevilles, beginning in 1839. (The "natural school" play mentioned by Gozenpud was performed in 1846, when the 25-year-old Dostoevsky could hardly have been called a youth or adolescent.) This is the Samoilov whom Dostoevsky praises as "a great psychologist," who "had a great deal of influence on my soul and mind." S. S. Danilov's description of Samoilov's working method can give us some insight into precisely what Dostoevsky learned from him at the beginning of his own career. Trained in painting at the Mining Cadet School, Samoilov would first create a finished drawing of each of his characters, deciding in this way how to present a multitude of personae, including women and men of various ages and ethnicities. As Danilov writes,

> In all these transformations there was something more than the usual vaudeville transformation. The 'typicality' [типичность] of Samoilov's images is what critics, including Belinsky himself, began to speak of right away. The skill of capturing in the image the most characteristic features, of emphasizing them through expressive details of costume and makeup, the subtle 'genrism' of imitating representatives of different nationalities—that is what was distinctly marked out already in Samoilov's vaudeville images. . . .

From the external to the internal—that is the method with which Samoilov works from the first steps in his stage activity.[102]

In his stories "Another Man's Wife" and "The Jealous Husband," we see Dostoevsky working with seemingly obvious vaudeville types: the adulterous wife, the jealous husband, the young lover. Yet, like Samoilov, he works "from the external to the internal"—from the distinctly outlined conventional figure of the deceived husband to the emotional depths of a man tormented by this stereotypical identity and bearing the sinful load of the pedophilic marriage. Dostoevsky returns in *The Eternal Husband* to the lessons he learned from vaudeville, exploring with great psychological and moral insight the roles—the eternal husband, the eternal lover—that help people live their lives, but that often imprison them, whether like Pavel Pavlovich, in an adulterous marriage, or like Velchaninov, in a meaningless "happy ending."

Endnotes

1 "Another Man's Wife. (Street Scene)" was originally published in *Notes of the Fatherland* in 1848, no. 1, otd. VIII, pp. 50-58, approved by censor 31 December 1847; "The Jealous Husband. (An Unusual Occurrence)" was originally published in *Notes of the Fatherland* in 1848, no. 11, otd. VIII, pp. 158-175, approved by censor 31 October 1848. See F. M. Dostoevsky, *Полное собрание сочинений* [*Complete Collected Works*], 2:479 (hereafter cited as *ПСС* by volume and page number).

2 The combined story first appeared in F. M. Dostoevsky, *Сочинения*, 2 vols. (Moscow: N. A. Osnovsky, 1860). See *ПСС* 2:479-80.

3 See the discussions in *ПСС* 2:480; Nechaeva, *Ранний Достоевский*, 228-30; Terras, *Young Dostoevsky*, 46-47; and Frank, *Seeds of Revolt*, 330-331. Gozenpud briefly discusses Dostoevsky's "rethinking" ["переосмысление"] of vaudeville conventions in the stories (*Достоевский и музыкально-театральное искусство*, 42). One of Dostoevsky's first works after he emerged from Siberian exile, "Uncle's Dream" ["Дядюшкин сон," 1859], was heavily influenced by vaudeville and was later staged under the title *An Enchanting Dream* [*Очаровательный сон*]. See Dmitriev et al., *История театра*, 5:107, 491.

4 Frank, *Seeds of Revolt*, 330. Compare N. K. Mikhailovsky on "Another Man's Wife and the Husband under the Bed": "For our aim this insignificant story may turn out to be very useful and important. In these trifles, Dostoevsky all the same remains Dostoevsky, with all the particular strengths and weaknesses of his talent and his thought. In them, in these old trifles, one can find the rudiments of all the subsequent images, pictures, ideas, and artistic and logical devices of Dostoevsky" ("Жестокий талант," 185).

5 Frank, *Seeds of Revolt*, 331.

6 Belinsky, "Александринский театр (1845)," *ПСС*, 8: 544.

7 For more on Russian vaudeville, see Danilov, *Очерки по истории*, 262-77; Dmitriev et al., *История театра*, 3:62-70, 144-45; and 4:46-7, 82-9; and Karlinsky, *Russian Drama*, 269-77.

8 See Terni's discussion of the origins of the term "vaudeville" in a fifteenth-century Norman group of poet-songwriters, the "Vau de Vire" ("Genre for Early Mass Culture," 248n7).

9 Terni, "Genre for Early Mass Culture," 222.

10 Ibid., 234.

11 Belinsky, "Александринский театр (1845)," *ПСС*, 8: 552.

12 Terni, "Genre for Early Mass Culture," 246.

13 Ibid., 242-43.

14 The main character is called "Ivan Andreevich" later in the stories. In order to avoid confusion with Ivan Ilich Tvorogov, I will refer to this character as "Tvorogov."

15 Dostoevsky, *ПСС*, 2:49. I am citing the stories according to the original texts as published in *Notes of the Fatherland* (original variants are found in 2:416-21).

16 Ibid., 2:51.

17 Ibid., 2:52.

18 Ibid., 2:53.

19 Ibid.

20 Ibid., 2:59.

21 Ibid., 2:60.

22 Ibid., 2:52 (italics mine).

23 Ibid., 2:57.

24 Ibid., 2:58.
25 Ibid.
26 Ibid., 2:58, 417.
27 Dostoevsky had dealt in detail with the anxiety of identity in his earlier novella *The Double* [*Двойник*, 1846]. In that work, however, the basic generic framework was the German Romantic double tale, in which questions of identity were a standard component. As a result, *The Double* lacks the sense of formal surprise that Dostoevsky creates in "Another Man's Wife" by combining the light and comic (vaudeville conventions) with the serious (Ivan Andreevich's torment over his identity).
28 Dostoevsky, *ПСС*, 2:62.
29 Ibid., 2:62, 61.
30 Ibid., 2:63, 418.
31 Ibid., 2:65.
32 Ibid., 2:73.
33 Ibid., 2:76.
34 Ibid.
35 Ibid., 2:67.
36 Ibid., 2:77.
37 Ibid., 2:78.
38 Ibid. (italics mine).
39 Ibid., 2:417.
40 Mikhailovsky, "Жестокий талант," 225.
41 Ibid., 226.
42 Dostoevsky, *ПСС*, 2:417.
43 A. Gozenpud surmises that the opera being performed when Ivan Andreevich bursts into the theater at the beginning of "The Jealous Husband" is Rossini's *Otello* (1816), although he does not adduce any textual evidence other than the fact that the soprano Erminia Frezzolini is mentioned (her debut role was Desdemona in that opera). He goes on to speculate that the aria that used to lull Ivan Andreevich to sleep as he sat at the opera was Desdemona's "Willow Song" (*Достоевский и музыка*, 32).
44 Dostoevsky, *ПСС*, 2:66.
45 "A Petersburg Chronicle" was originally published in the *Saint Petersburg News* [*Санктпетербургские ведомости*] in 1847 on 27 April, no. 93;

"A Christmas Party and a Wedding" was originally published in *Notes of the Fatherland* in 1848, no. 9, otd. VIII, pp. 44-49. Dostoevsky originally planned a cycle called "From the Notes of an Unknown Person" that was to include "Another Man's Wife," "The Jealous Husband," and "A Christmas Party and a Wedding." See *ПСС* 2:479, 484, and 18:216.

46 Dostoevsky, *ПСС*, 2:95.
47 Ibid., 2:417.
48 Ibid.
49 Jackson, "Dostoevsky in Chekhov's Garden of Eden," 96.
50 Dostoevsky, *ПСС*, 2:100-101.
51 Ibid., 2:14.
52 Terras goes so far as to refer to the girl in "A Christmas Party and a Wedding" as Glafira Petrovna, although her name is never given in that story (*Young Dostoevsky*, 93-94).
53 See "A Faint Heart," *ПСС*, 2:16-48. Nechaeva regards Iulian Mastakovich as the same person in all three works and tries to reconcile the seeming discrepancies (*Ранний Достоевский*, 230-37).
54 Dostoevsky, *ПСС*, 18:14.
55 Nechaeva, *Ранний Достоевский*, 233.
56 I briefly discussed the idea of the pedophilic marriage in my article "Maidens in Childbirth" (268).
57 Jencks, "An Interview," 50-51.
58 Venturi, *Complexity*, 43.
59 First published in *Dawn*, 1870, no. 1, otd. I, pp. 1-79; no. 2, otd. I, pp. 3-82; separate publication 1871. See *ПСС*, 9:469.
60 On the complex use of narrative voice in the novella, see Woodward, "Transferred Speech," and Parts, "Polyphonic Plot Structure."
61 Dostoevsky, *ПСС*, 9:26.
62 Ibid., 9:106.
63 Ibid., 9:112.
64 Ibid., 9:27.
65 Ibid., 2:81.
66 Ibid., 9:90.
67 Ibid., 9:110. The phrase "чужая жена" ["another man's wife"] appears in the drafts for *The Eternal Husband* as well (9:294).

68 Ibid., 9:27. In the drafts, this theory is first assigned to the husband himself, and the label is not "eternal husband" but the more readily understandable "lawful husband" ["законный муж"] (9:294). V. Ia. Kirpotin convincingly argues that the term "eternal husband" was inspired by Balzac's labeling of Père Goriot as "the eternal father" (*Мир Достоевского*, 173). One of the inhabitants of Goriot's boarding house, a medical student who dabbles in phrenology, says, "That's what he was cut out for. I examined his head: there's just one bump, the one meaning paternity. He'll be an Eternal Father" (Balzac, *Père Goriot*, 76). In Dostoevsky, the pun on "God the Father" is lost, and the term "eternal husband" retains an aura of mysterious incomprehensibility.

69 Pratt, "Role of the Unconscious," 22. See also Parts, "Polyphonic Plot Structure," 614.

70 Motidzuki, "*Вечный муж*," 138.

71 Ibid., 139.

72 Dostoevsky, *ПСС*, 2:66.

73 Velchaninov is particularly prone to slapping labels on other people, especially Pavel Pavlovich, whom he calls "drunken buffoon," "Quasimodo," "monster," and "murderer," among a host of other unflattering appellations. As Woodward points out, Velchaninov has a "predilection for classifying or categorizing which underlies his conspicuous weakness for clichés" ("Transferred Speech," 405). Thus Dostoevsky is to some extent able to shift the responsibility for stereotyping onto his hero, something he was unable to do in the 1848 stories. For a discussion of the use of the terms "rapacious type" and "gentle type" in the novella and their origins in contemporaneous literary polemics, see Peace, "Dostoyevsky's 'The Eternal Husband.'"

74 Motidzuki, "*Вечный муж*," 138.

75 Dostoevsky, *ПСС*, 9:477.

76 Another vaudeville referred to specifically in the text of *The Eternal Husband* is Ivan Turgenev's *Провинциалка* [*A Provincial Lady*] (1851). See Serman, "*Провинциалка* Тургенева"; Turner, "Eternal Husband."

77 Dostoevsky, *ПСС*, 2:53. For a summary of the references to Paul de Kock in Dostoevsky's works, see Anisimov, *Литературное наследство*, 502-3.

78 de Kock, *La Femme, le mari, et l'amant*, 35.

79 Ibid., 37. The novel, on the other hand, does end happily: the lover, Deligny, learns that the husband's killer has died of natural causes, and the wife, Augustine, comes to love him and agrees to marry him.
80 Terni, "Genre for Early Mass Culture," 235n49.
81 Frank, *Miraculous Years*, 390.
82 Ibid., 389; Motidzuki, "Вечный муж," 138.
83 Belinsky, "Александринский театр (1845)," *ПСС*, 8: 545.
84 Dostoevsky, *ПСС*, 9:89-90.
85 Ibid., 9:72.
86 Ibid., 9:79.
87 Ibid., 9:81-82.
88 Terni, "Genre for Early Mass Culture," 234.
89 Dostoevsky, *ПСС*, 9:93.
90 Ibid., 9:67, 81.
91 Ibid., 9:33.
92 Ibid., 9:94.
93 Ibid., 9:92.
94 See Parts for a particularly eloquent analysis of "the tragedy of Liza's situation" ("Polyphonic Plot Structure," 617-18). For a discussion of Chernyshevsky's efforts in life and in art to transform familial conventions and structures, see Paperno, *Chernyshevsky*.
95 Dostoevsky, *ПСС*, 9:111.
96 Terni, "Genre for Early Mass Culture," 242, 243.
97 Dostoevsky, *ПСС*, 9:9.
98 Ibid., 9:104.
99 Quoted in Dostoevsky, *ПСС*, 30,1:320.
100 Ibid., 30, 1:135-36.
101 Gozenpud, *Достоевский и музыка*, 18. N. A. Nekrasov wrote several vaudevilles in the 1840s (sometimes under the pseudonym Perepelsky), including *Feoklist Onufrich Bob, or the Husband Who's Not Quite Himself* [*Феоклист Онуфрич Боб, или Муж не в своей тарелке*, 1841] and *The Actor* [*Актер*, 1841], in which Samoilov had one of his most successful roles. In his later study, *Достоевский и музыкально-театральное искусство*, Gozenpud raises the possibility that Dostoevsky saw Samoilov perform earlier (37). He also

points out the possible influence of Samoilov's art of transformation on the figure of the Prince in "Uncle's Dream" (an old man masquerading as a young man, 42).

102 Danilov, *Очерки по истории*, 309. See also Belinsky, "Александринский театр (1840)," *ПСС*, 4:281-84; and Dmitriev et al., *История театра*, 4:201-5. Incidentally, Samoilov played Count Liubin (the "lover") in Turgenev's *Provincial Lady*, which is prominently featured in *The Eternal Husband*. See Serman, "*Провинциалка* Тургенева"; Turner, "Eternal Husband"; Danilov, *Очерки по истории*, 310. Gozenpud believes that Dostoevsky may have seen Samoilov in the role of Liubin in 1875 (*Достоевский и музыкально-театральное искусство*, 133).

Works Cited

Anisimov, I. I., et al., eds. *Литературное наследство*, vol. 77: *Достоевский в работе над романом "Подросток," творческие рукописи*. Moscow: Nauka, 1965.

Balzac, Honoré de. *Père Goriot*. Translated by A. J. Krailsheimer. Oxford: Oxford University Press, 1991.

Belinsky, Vissarion. *Полное собрание сочинений*. 13 vols. Moscow: AN SSSR, 1953-59.

Danilov, S. S. *Очерки по истории русского драматического театра*. Moscow, Leningrad: Iskusstvo, 1948.

Dmitriev, Iu. A., et al. *История русского драматического театра в семи томах*. Moscow: Iskusstvo, 1977-87.

Dostoevsky, Fyodor. *Полное собрание сочинений в тридцати томах*. 30 vols. Leningrad: Nauka, 1972-90.

Frank, Joseph. *Dostoevsky: The Seeds of Revolt, 1821-1849*. Princeton, NJ: Princeton University Press, 1976.

―――. *Dostoevsky: The Miraculous Years 1865-1871*. Princeton, NJ: Princeton University Press, 1995.

Fusso, Susanne. "Maidens in Childbirth: The Sistine Madonna in Dostoevskii's *Devils*." *Slavic Review* 54, no. 2 (Summer 1995): 261-75.

Gozenpud, A. *Достоевский и музыка*. Leningrad: Muzyka, 1971.

―――. *Достоевский и музыкально-театральное искусство*. Leningrad: Sovetskii kompozitor, 1981.

Jackson, Robert Louis. "Dostoevsky in Chekhov's Garden of Eden: 'Because of Little Apples.'" In *Dialogues with Dostoevsky: The Overwhelming Questions*, 83-103. Stanford: Stanford University Press, 1993.

Jencks, Charles, ed. "National Gallery—Sainsbury Wing: Robert Venturi, David Vaughan & Charles Jencks, an Interview." *Architectural Design* 61, 5-6 (1991): 48-57.

Karlinsky, Simon. *Russian Drama from Its Beginnings to the Age of Pushkin*. Berkeley: University of California Press, 1985.

Kirpotin, V. Ia. *Мир Достоевского: Этюды и исследования*. Moscow: Sovetskii pisatel', 1980.

Kock, Paul de. *La femme, le mari et l'amant, comédie vaudeville en quatre actes, par mm. Paul de Kock et Ch. Dupeuty; représentée, pour la reprise, sur le Théatre du Palais-Royal, le 1er février 1834*. Paris: Barba, libraire, Palais-Royal, 1834.

Mikhailovsky, N. K. "Жестокий талант (*Полное собрание сочинений Ф. М. Достоевского*. Том II и III. СПб.)." In *Литературно-критические статьи*, edited by G. A. Bialyi, 181-263. Moscow: Gosudarstvennoe izdatel'stvo "Khudozhestvennaia literatura," 1957.

Motidzuki [Mochizuki], Tetsuo. "*Вечный муж* как театр катарсиса." *Русская литература*, no. 1 (2002): 135-40.

Nechaeva, V. S. *Ранний Достоевский 1821-1849*. Moscow: Nauka, 1979.

Paperno, Irina. *Chernyshevsky and the Age of Realism: A Study in the Semiotics of Behavior*. Stanford: Stanford University Press, 1988.

Parts, Lyudmila. "Polyphonic Plot Structure in Dostoevsky's *The Eternal Husband*." *Slavic and East European Journal* 50, no. 4 (2006): 607-20.

Peace, Richard. "Dostoyevsky's 'The Eternal Husband' and Literary Polemics." *Essays in Poetics* 3, no. 2 (1978): 22-40.

Pratt, Branwen E. B. "The Role of the Unconscious in *The Eternal Husband*." *Literature and Psychology* 23, no. 1 (1972): 13-25.

Serman, I. Z. "*Провинциалка* Тургенева и 'Вечный муж' Достоевского." In *Тургеневский сборник: Материалы к полному собранию сочинений и писем И. С. Тургенева*, edited by A. S. Bushmin, et al. 4 vols, 2:109-11. Moscow-Leningrad: Nauka, 1966.

Terni, Jennifer. "A Genre for Early Mass Culture: French Vaudeville and the City, 1830-1848." *Theatre Journal* 58 (2006): 221-48.

Terras, Victor. *The Young Dostoevsky (1846-1849): A Critical Study*. The Hague: Mouton, 1969.

Turner, C. J. G. "*The Eternal Husband*: Bagautov and Stupend'ev." *Russian Literature* 38 (1995): 97-110.

Venturi, Robert. *Complexity and Contradiction in Architecture* (1966). New York: The Museum of Modern Art, 1977.

Woodward, James B. "'Transferred Speech' in Dostoevskii's *Vechnyi muzh*." *Canadian-American Slavic Studies* 8, fasc. 3 (Fall 1974): 398-407.

IV

Dostoevsky's *White Nights:* Memoir of a Petersburg Pathology

Dale E. Peterson

> I write my reveries only for myself . . . and decrepit, I will live with myself in another age as if I were living with a younger friend.
>
> Jean-Jacques Rousseau, *The Reveries of a Solitary Walker*

Toward the end of his life, disenchanted with worldly engagement and public controversy, Rousseau withdrew into the consolations of the mind, composing a last, ostensibly private addendum to his lifelong confessional discourse that he entitled *The Reveries of a Solitary Walker* [*Les Rêveries du Promeneur Solitaire*, 1776-78]. These *Reveries* comprise ten "walks" or rambling essays in which Rousseau, struggling to accept his isolation and involuntary status as an outsider to society, devotes himself to recording philosophical reflections and botanical observations without regard for public utility or personal repute. In the *Reveries*, Rousseau offered readers an influential eighteenth-century rural prototype of the nineteenth-century *flâneur*, that detached urban spectator and speculator who emerged at the edge of the Parisian crowd in the 1830s and who, like Rousseau, was an idler "out of circulation," abstaining from social relations in order to secure a space for private reflection.[1]

As it happens, the Russian translation of *Reveries of a Solitary Walker*, published by Ivan Martynov in 1802, was cleverly advertised as Rousseau's final, most authentic act of self-revelation, surpassing his earlier renowned *Confessions* [*Les Confessions*, 1782].[2] Although we cannot know when, or even if, Dostoevsky read this later, most extreme of Rousseau's experiments in self-exploration and self-justification, numerous literary historians and critics have noted Dostoevsky's long-standing interest in Rousseau's thought and art. They have a tendency to affiliate the young, politically-minded Dostoevsky before his Siberian exile with the progressive Rousseau of the *Social Contract* [*Du contrat social ou Principes du droit politique*, 1762] or the sentimentalist Rousseau of *The New Heloise* [*Julie, ou la nouvelle Héloïse*, 1761], whereas a critical divergence from Rousseau can be clearly noted in the older, more conservative Dostoevsky after his exile.[3] In any event, Dostoevsky was well aware of the intellectual revolution that the *Confessions* had brought about by virtue of Rousseau's adamant quest to assert the self's inimitable individuality. Even before his mature influential experiments in confessional narration, the young Dostoevsky instilled in his protagonists a Rousseau-esque fascination with the effort to write oneself into existence and to affirm one's subjective truth.

This fascination is nowhere more on display than in *White Nights* [*Белые ночи*, 1848], a gentle, though rueful, evocation of a thwarted high-minded dreamer. Like Rousseau in *The Reveries*, the first-person anonymous narrator of *White Nights* complains bitterly of suffering from solitude, abandonment, and friendless isolation. Moreover, both that anonymous narrator and Rousseau fill the present moment's total lack of social interaction with the fullness of a mind's sovereign reveries. Significantly, the impetus for recording and minutely reconstructing past sensations and interior states of mind is provided by an increasing sense of desperation that overtakes both Rousseau and Dostoevsky's narrator *fifteen years* after experiencing one blissful, transient moment of self-fulfillment.[4] And each of these rhetorical exhibitions of willed introspection raises the question of whether the act of self-composition can actually engender true self-sufficiency and mental composure.

Rousseau's *Reveries* would have us believe that his act of composition can achieve and sustain the bliss of withdrawal into the abode of the mind's autonomous meditations without regard for others or self-regarding *amour propre* [literally, self-love; egotism]. Rousseau celebrates his capacity to abstain from, rather than engage with, the world's distractions from self-contemplation:

> ... I write my reveries only for myself. If in my later days as the moment of departure approaches, I continue—as I hope—to have the same disposition as I now have, reading them will recall the delight I enjoy in writing them and causing the past to be born again for me will, so to speak, double my existence ... and decrepit, I will live with myself in another age as if I were living with a younger friend.[5]

His claim, as announced at the beginning of "The First Walk," invites comparison with the dramatized experiment in self-redemption attempted by Dostoevsky's nostalgic narrator. In this essay I will suggest that the young author of *White Nights* was initiating a prolonged polemic with Rousseau by critiquing, sometimes harshly, Rousseau's cult of self and sentiment as manifest in *The Reveries of a Solitary Walker*. In contrast to critics who find in *White Nights* a tender romantic pathos for the narrator's poetic dreaminess, I will argue here that Dostoevsky was illustrating a Petersburg pathology—specifically, a compulsion to memorialize moments of imaginative perception and to revel in reverie rather than to acknowledge the demands and risks of human relations in the real world.[6]

One of the few revelations of Dostoevsky's state of mind at the moment when he was giving imaginative embodiment to the Petersburg flâneur and sentimental dreamer of *White Nights*—he hardly mentions this narrative in his correspondence—appears in a letter to his brother in early 1847. It confirms his precocious anxiety about the perilous relationship between intellectual refinement and solitary confinement as exemplified by Rousseau's narrator: "The external ought to be equivalent in force to the internal. Otherwise, in the absence of exterior phenomena the internal will take the upper hand to a dangerous degree. Nerves and fantasy will occupy too large a place in existence."[7]

In the spring of that same year, Dostoevsky made a brief appearance as a peripatetic commentator on urban life in the *Saint Petersburg Gazette*. These pieces, collectively entitled *The Petersburg Chronicle* [Петербургская летопись], clearly anticipate his later fictional embodiment of a representative Petersburg voice in *White Nights*. In four journalistic segments Dostoevsky impersonated the manner and mode of a contemporary *feuilletonist* or columnist. As the French name implies, the feuilleton was originally a separate newspaper enclosure or "leaflet" conveying information and observations about cultural events. By the time this mass-market medium had become the rage in Petersburg in the 1840s, the form implied not only particular content but a particular authorial persona and perspective as well, that of the flâneur. Both spectator and idler, the feuilletonist positions himself as a chatty, erratic perambulator of city sites whose ostentatious inactivity enables him to be a privileged interpreter of the urban system of signs, "a semiologist *avant la lettre*."[8] Under the guise of informality and randomness, the feuilletonist's rambling observations purport to decode the hieroglyphic spectacle that is the parade of metropolitan life. In his feuilletons, Dostoevsky embraced this narrative figure, employing the witty, half-ironic voice of the chronicler to conduct a withering commentary on the self-censorship of meaningful speech and action in Petersburg, the imperial city of private "circles" ["кружки"] and public silences. Especially in Dostoevsky's fourth and final column (June 15, 1847), he memorably diagnosed what, along with other progressives of his generation, he identified as the endemic malady of Petersburg's meteorological and societal climate—dreaminess [мечтательность] or reverie:

> Are there many among us who have found their real vocation? . . . Then, little by little, there arises what is known as dreaminess in types who are avid for activity, avid for spontaneous living, avid for authenticity but who are weak, feminine, and tender; and finally a man is no longer recognizable as a man but a kind of strange entity of neuter gender—*a dreamer*. And do you know, gentlemen, what this phenomenon called a dreamer is? It is a Petersburg nightmare, the personification of sin, a mute, mysterious, gloomy and wild tragedy… and we say this not at all in jest.[9]

In his journalistic role as rival "physiologist" of Petersburg's denizens, Dostoevsky exposed with cutting precision the anatomy of the contemporary body of the Russian urban intelligentsia, stifling in fear, frustration and avoidance. It is precisely this theme—the "nightmare" of dreaminess—though without the sermonizing, that is transposed into the agitated reminiscence penned by the protagonist of *White Nights*. As an author of fiction, however, Dostoevsky functioned more as a psychologist, laying bare the inner workings of the affliction of dreaminess as a Petersburg pathology.

Originally printed in the last number of *Notes of the Fatherland* [*Отечественные записки*] in 1848, Dostoevsky's novella bore a tripartite title in three different fonts: **WHITE NIGHTS**/A Sentimental Novel/(*From the Memoirs of a Dreamer*) [**БЕЛЫЕ НОЧИ**/Сентименталный роман/ (*Из воспоминаний мечтателя*)], providing, so it seems, a typographical image of the text's mixed genres and messages.[10] From the very beginning, the title alludes to Petersburg's atmospheric confusion of boundaries—between day and night and between the imagined and the actual. The text was also preceded by an epigraph, a truncated final quatrain from a Turgenev poem of 1843, "The Flower" ["Цветок"]: "... Or, was it only fated / To exist for but a moment / As companion to your heart?"[11] It is worth noting that Dostoevsky changed the syntax of the poem from a statement to a question, raising some doubt about the durability of gathered rosebuds, as it were.

What follows is a rather simple story told at length in a highly elaborate and self-conscious literary manner. The opening sentence indicates that the narrator knows he is writing to an educated, mature audience: "It was a marvelous night, such a night as can only really occur when we are young, dear reader."[12] It is apparent, then, that whatever tale *White Nights* unfolds will be in the form of an autobiographical narrative told by its narrator from a temporal distance and with a degree of cautious embarrassment. From the outset, the narrative voice betrays a nervous blend of apology and nostalgia. Appropriately so, for the reader will learn that this extraordinary night is the first of four nights *fifteen* years in the past, when the narrator's younger self, a twenty-six-year-old Petersburg "dreamer," imagined a romantic affair with a pert young woman named Nastenka whom, by sheer chance, he had rescued from molestation and rendered apparently receptive to his pursuit. On the night of their fourth *rendezvous*, however, Nastenka's tardy fiancé returns to Petersburg and sweeps her away. Crushed, the dreamer retreats to his dingy room and dreary daily rounds until he finally decides to pen the confessional memoir that reveals who he is, as well as who he was.

The retrospective narrator—who remains nameless throughout—is, inevitably, characterizing his younger self while also exposing his present cast of mind. Much is at stake in this delicate balancing act as the narrator seeks both to re-embody and keep distant his callow youthful self. With gentle irony, the older writer recreates the sensibility of a young dreamer who acts as a Petersburg parody of a Parisian flâneur. After eight years in residence, this stroller of streets boasts of his intimate acquaintance with Petersburg, yet he flees actual contact with its citizens, preferring instead to converse with its buildings.

As the older memoirist retraces the steps of the solitary walker before his fateful encounter with young Nastenka, the flights of fancy he once entertained are indulgently (and revealingly) rehearsed. Surveying various architectural features of Petersburg's streets, the young stroller projects a feminine allure onto his favorite objects of attention. For instance, he anthropomorphically recollects the "very cute rosy-pink cottage" who looked so welcomingly at him and glared so proudly at her ungainly neighbors. Her imaginary story ends melodramatically with a sudden shriek—"They are painting me all in yellow!"—that results in an attack of bile directed by the horrified observer against the "villains, barbarians" who have defiled her—no doubt because in Petersburg a "yellow house" [желтый дом] signified a lunatic asylum.[13] It is not difficult to see in this fantasy male anxiety about seduction and corruption.

A similar feminized fantasy takes the form of an extended conceit comparing the brief efflorescence of a Petersburg spring to the attractive flush of excitement that temporarily lends color to the features of a consumptive girl. Dostoevsky borrowed this passage nearly verbatim from his fourth "Petersburg Chronicle," but he fitted it effectively into the psychological plot of *White Nights*. This recycled version of springtime in Petersburg ends, significantly, with a bitter foretaste of disenchantment:

> But the moment passes, and tomorrow, perhaps, you will see again that same brooding, distracted gaze, the same pallid face . . . and even traces of remorse and the numbing ache of vexation over a momentary rapture . . . And you will regret how quickly and irretrievably an instant's beauty has faded and how seductively and vainly it glimmered before you—and regret, too, that there was barely time even to fall in love . . .[14]

Here the features of the frail girl and the depressed male voyeur merge indistinguishably; both show the sickly traces of prematurely withered youthfulness. In this passage, the former Petersburg feuilletonist sounds very much like a fatigued flâneur.

The ensuing reminiscence of the first night's unexpected encounter with a weeping Nastenka is depicted with a light touch that obscures the true import of the event. By and large, the narrator's initial account of his former self is winsome and comic, well befitting a sentimental recollection. The ridiculously shy stroller dares not cross the street to address a then-unknown pensive maiden, a brunette in a "coquettish" black mantilla staring into the murky waters of the canal, although he realizes that "no matter how timid I am with women, this really was quite an opportunity!"[15] Yet despite ostensible concern for her plight, the dreamy young man is too self-consciously literary to know how to talk to her and is only able to overcome his constraint when he instinctively rushes to protect her from pursuit by a drunken lout.

What follows is a witty dialogue in which Nastenka calms the inexperienced suitor's nervous jitters and slyly keeps him interested, drawing out of him an embarrassing confession of his loneliness and ineptitude. Reassured by his benevolent, bumbling manner, she allows herself to be accompanied by the stranger, and even agrees to meet him at the same hour the following evening: "For now, let it be a secret—so much the better for you; anticipation will make it seem more like a romance."[16] She admits that she has a private reason for appearing again on the embankment and, without revealing it, insists that, although she, too, appreciates having a confidant, he must not fall in love with her! Much as their bodies take turns trembling with nervous excitement, their situations, too, seem parallel: both are wary of engagement and feel alone and abandoned in a city that is for them vacant and silent. The reader might well begin to think they are well-matched.

There are, however, darker strains suggesting otherwise in the tentative relationship that comes into being on that first white night in Petersburg. The narrator's fortuitous meeting with Nastenka has been preceded by three days of aimless wandering in a desperate panic; all the men of substance have scampered off to their country dachas, leaving the rootless dreamer a voyeur utterly deserted, alone and insignificant. Every day he has been cruelly reminded of his lack of status and stature in the eyes of those he observes. The would-be carefree stroller of streets begins to resemble an alienated disaffected intellectual, "a half-sick townsman, practically suffocating within the city walls."[17] No wonder, then, that the first sight of an apparently bereft woman induces in him a nervous crisis of manhood. The older narrator's sentimental reminiscence does not entirely delete traces of suppressed masculine urges; despite the pretense of overt solicitude, he had set out to follow the dark-haired beauty covertly and she had responded by avoiding him. Yet when the unwelcome stalker, his "double," intrudes on the scene and enables the narrator to intervene, that narrator oddly disclaims his own agency: "I bless fate for the excellent knobby stick that just happened to be in my right hand at that time."[18] This reluctance to assume conscious ownership of predatory or aggressive impulses is symptomatic of his profound ambivalence toward replacing furtive imaginings with realized aspirations.

That ambivalence is displayed during his first conversation with Nastenka, which contains some odd locutions revealing anxieties over the sort of man he is. When she recognizes his fluttered state in approaching her, an unknown woman, and allows him to accompany her home, he responds breathlessly: "You will make me stop being shy all at once . . . and, then, goodbye to all my devices."[19] She is nonplussed by this remark; what, after all, is he struggling to protect himself from? He is eager to impress upon her that he is a dreamer "out of the habit of women": "True, one can't avoid coming across two or three women, but what sort of women? They're all such landladies [хозяйки] . . . but I'm making you laugh."[20] This defensive remark about his own fastidiousness even as he ecstatically converses with a real woman elicits her laughter here, but there is a strange mixture of reluctance and impetuousness in the dreamer's wary approach to Nastenka.

It is he, not she, who first clamors for a second meeting; indeed, he announces he will return to "this place, at this hour" and explains: "I cannot not come here tomorrow. I am a dreamer; I am so inexperienced with real life that moments like this are so precious I cannot not repeat them in my reveries."[21] The syntax here (emphatic affirmation by double negation: "не могу не прийти . . . не могу не повторять") testifies to the awkwardness of an involuntary compulsion. At the end of the first night, the lonely young man is overjoyed to be behaving like a suitor, but we also learn that he has a habit of ritualizing visits to sites of intense emotion: "I will be happy bringing what has occurred to mind. Already this place is dear to me. And I already have two or three such places in Petersburg."[22] As one shrewd observer of Dostoevsky's mapping of topography and gender in *White Nights* has noted, even at its beginning, the relationship with Nastenka is haunted by the narrator's terror of confinement and his compulsion to run in circles, to fall into "repetitious stasis."[23] Initially, though, the narrator's "two minutes" with her cause him to gush with hope: "Who knows, perhaps you have reconciled me to myself and resolved all my doubts . . . "[24] He relies on her to allay any insecurity about his manhood.

On the second night, a shared torrent of words and tears is unloosed as the newly-met couple agrees to begin again by describing their lives. Although the two accounts seem to lead to a giddy moment of mutual recognition and understanding, the dreamer narrates his life as an interminable character sketch, while her account is truly a narrative of development and action. The reader, in comparing their stories, has an opportunity to measure what is compatible and what is discordant in the Petersburg relationship Dostoevsky has staged. Most obviously, the theme of confinement links the two lives. In the testimonials provided by the older narrator's memoir, however, his youthful isolation is self-inflicted, while Nastenka is literally "pinned" to her grandmother's skirt and strict guardianship. The young male who is free to walk city streets retreats into solitude, whereas the young female who is actively constrained boldly seeks new human contact.

Even as he begins his autobiographical account, the narrator in the role of Nastenka's new suitor is painfully self-conscious and calculatedly aware of his auditor: "I seated myself next to her, adopted a pedantically pompous posture and began to recite as if following a script" ["словно по-писаному"].[25] What he recites is a cunning apologia for his life as a dreamer [мечтатель]. His apologia at first protectively cloaks itself as an impersonal physiological sketch of an original Petersburg "type," but it soon collapses into a tortured personal appeal that reaches out uncertainly both for judgment and compassion. Although it is he who accosted Nastenka on the street, he describes himself as a pathetic creature who lives self-enclosed, like a snail or tortoise, in retreat from worldly banter and conversation about the fair sex. He imagines he looks to others like a tormented kitten huddled under a chair in the dark, "where for a whole hour it can at leisure bristle and hiss and wash its aggrieved mug."[26] No aspect of *White Nights* more closely anticipates *Notes from the Underground* [*Записки из подполья*, 1864] than the young dreamer's prolix self-analysis with its paradoxical blend of vulnerability, defensiveness, and resentment.

Nastenka, meanwhile, understands perfectly well that his extravagant metaphors are a half-serious means of telling the truth, and that her new acquaintance suffers a strange compulsion to "speak like a book." Unfortunately, her shrewd reading between the lines only intensifies the keen anxiety of his confessional performance. He solemnly begs her not to interrupt the floodgate of his pent-up words as he speaks freely, in a mixture of shame and pride, of his richly fanciful existence of solitary refinement. In one breath, he upbraids the dreamer type of individual for being a "sensuous idler" removed from mundane life, but then boasts that "he desires nothing because he is above all desires, is everything to himself and is the artist of his own life, creating it by the hour with each new whim."[27]

When the dreamer finally exhausts the stream of his own rhetoric and realizes how pathetic he must appear, the older memoirist interrupts the reported speech and allows us to glimpse an ugly recoil from this moment of embarrassment: "I remember how desperately I wanted in spite of myself to laugh out loud because I already felt stirring within me a malevolent little demon . . . and I already was regretting that I had gone too far, uselessly spilling what had for so long been festering in my heart...."[28] Here surfaces a nasty impulse of self-mockery to hold at bay the compulsion to confess his hidden inner torment.

At this explosive moment, Nastenka presses his hand and expresses tender concern for the life he has led. Here, in this early work, the reader is spared the furious spite and cruel rejection with which Dostoevsky's Underground Man responds to Liza's profound empathy. Instead, buoyed by Nastenka's tears and her sensible rejection of a life of imaginary gratification, the dreamer voices (with apparent sincerity) penitence for his wasted life of all-consuming reverie. He does admit, however, that he remains the sort of man who has a sentimental penchant for commemorating the dates and revisiting the places of his peak emotional experiences.

Nastenka's story, by contrast, is told with refreshing directness and wily self-awareness. We are told that when her lessons ended at age fifteen she became restless and was protectively pinned to her blind grandmother to prevent unsupervised wandering. But, at seventeen, she learned, with the collusion of a male lodger upstairs and his offer of tickets to Rossini's opera *The Barber of Seville*, to slip out from grandmother's control under the guise of cultural enrichment. Although Grandmother had banned racy European sentimental novels in which young ladies are seductively courted and abandoned, she allows the lodger to alleviate her boredom by reading aloud from reputable works by Scott and Pushkin. Gradually, the book traffic between upstairs and downstairs leads to an intimate connection; it is on the staircase that the blushing girl and the cultivated lodger begin their romance. In Dostoevsky's construction of Nastenka's story, we perhaps can glimpse an allusion to art's power to liberate, as well as confine, the imagination. In any case, when the obviously infatuated lodger mysteriously ceases to pay attention to her and suddenly announces his departure for Moscow on "business," she summons the boldness of Pushkin's Tatiana in *Eugene Onegin* [*Евгений Онегин*, 1823-31]; she climbs the stairs to offer her heart and suggest an elopement. At the time she is relating this story, her fate still seems precarious and the reader will probably, along with Grandmother, anticipate the worst. Nastenka has her suitor's pledge to return in a year with the intention to marry her, if she agrees. But as she finishes her story, he is already days late and has sent no letter for her.

Nastenka's awkward situation is revealed in her testimony on the second night, and her enigmatic behavior adds a new level of intrigue. Having offered her moral support to rehabilitate the dreaming narrator, she seeks reciprocal aid from him. At the end of her tale, she lowers her head and rather prettily bursts into tears, evoking in her distress an offer of rescue. It turns out, however, that she does not need a romantic hero to rush into confrontation with her laggard lover; instead she wants a literary advisor, an educated ally to give counsel regarding an effective appeal she might write. With her wits about her, Nastenka explains she need not lose time composing a letter, for, like Rosina in *The Barber of Seville*, she has already prepared one. Conveniently, she has also found in her new companion a Figaro substitute to deliver it in her stead! Dostoevsky thus engineers a comic temporary resolution to the heroine's dilemma and, in the process, demonstrates how, in an alert mind, a fictional prototype can promote worldly action as well as induce unworldly reveries.

But the giddy conspiracy hatched on the second night leads directly to the psychological complexity and moral complications that overtake the retrospective narrator's "sentimental novel." Both the weather and the narration abruptly turn murky. The description of the "third night" begins oddly with a depressing evocation:

> Today was dreary and rainy, without a ray of hope, like my impending old age. Such strange thoughts oppress me, such dark sensations, such vague questions crowd in my head, and I have neither the strength nor the will to resolve them.... Today we shall not meet.[29]

Disruptively, the narrative technique of using the present tense thrusts the reader into a strangely intense recollection. This obfuscation of temporal borders is soon matched, in the account of the delayed third night, by suddenly permeable emotional boundaries in the narrator's account of his renewed encounter with Nastenka. Even as he fondly recollects her childish effusion of joy in finding a heartfelt sympathizer, unseemly notes of grievance intrude: "How she made up to me, lavished attention on me and inspired and soothed my heart! How coquettish was her happiness! And I . . . I took it all at face value."[30] A freshly felt resentment impinges on this long past sentimental recollection. And no wonder. The longer the co-conspirators are forced to sustain their mutual dependency without a resolution of Nastenka's suspended love affair, the higher the sexual tension mounts. Unaccountably, the missing suitor is neither heard from nor seen and his absence provides a harsh test of the romantic altruism—or voyeurism—in which the dreamer indulges.

As for Nastenka, her gratitude for the "brotherly" sentiments she has aroused in the narrator soon yields to more complicated feelings of guilt and yearning. She cleverly deduces the self-sacrificial nature of the dreamer's chivalry and clearly both desires and fears more openness in his protestations of fidelity to her. But he suddenly becomes self-protective and even a bit sadistic, reminding her that the arranged rendezvous hour with her lover has struck and passed, although he immediately regrets his cruelty: "I right away repented that I had frightened her, had forced her to count the hours and I cursed myself for this attack of malice."[31] Nastenka, for her part, struggles with pride and humiliation, wishing to show off her acquisition of a devoted friend and expose her tardy lover as the less deserving of the two suitors: "Why isn't he you?"[32] Things become more and more curious as the reticent admirer continues to encourage her faith in her lover's return, even as she is striving to bring the dreamer closer to a recognition of his emotional investment in her.

A dreadful rain-soaked day passes without a meeting, though the dreamer, despite being forewarned of Nastenka's absence, ritually observes the hour of their first and ensuing appointments. The "fourth" and final night thus occurs on the fifth day, subtly reinforcing the structural repetition of mismatched expectations in the text. Significantly, the fourth meeting begins with a symmetrical recurrence of the initial encounter. Nastenka hangs despondent in a flood of tears on the railing of the embankment, providing a final opportunity for heroic rescue. Before long, the young narrator is awash in tears in response to her cruel sense of abandonment. With excruciating slowness, both seem on the verge of acknowledging a new attachment beyond mutual commiseration. Although she never forswore her love for the former lodger, the moment seems opportune for an evolving relationship based on a sense of kinship and compassion. And, astonishingly, the narrator's suppressed emotions overflow, as he finds himself in an ironic reversal: "At first it was simple, Nastenka, but now, now I'm exactly like you when you went to him with your little bundle, but worse because he didn't love anyone then, but you do."[33] Yet this admission of susceptibility to romance is inauthentic, because the narrator quickly withdraws from the prospect of entanglement in a burst of ludicrous apologies and evasions. He assures Nastenka that his protestation of love is impossible, inadmissible because she only pities him, and even if she were not to drive him off, he would go away voluntarily. What he prefers to being a supplicant, a genuine suitor, is the fantasy of being a phantom lover:

> Listen, my friend, for you are after all my friend . . . what matters is that I'd love you so well, so well that even if you loved him and continued to love him whom I don't know, my love would not be noticed as a burden. You'd only be aware of feeling every minute that next to you there beats a very grateful, ardent heart . . .[34]

The incorrigible dreamer imagines a virtual future as a spectral bridegroom haunting the chambers of his true love's heart.[35]

Despite these indications of an unsustainable romance, Nastenka and her reluctant suitor permit themselves the illusion of a fresh start. They begin to act out a repetition fantasy in which the dreamer will replace the lodger in Grandmother's attic. But when he dares suggest they go see *The Barber of Seville*, she refuses, seeming to recognize the folly of replaying her initial romance with an understudy.

While accompanying her home, reality intrudes in the form of an *eros ex machina* denouement. The delayed lover returns and Nastenka reverses her previous opinion of the dreamer: "If only *you* were he!"[36] With this final twist of the plot, Dostoevsky plays fast and loose with literary expectations and performs a quick *volte face* that aborts the developing sentimental affair and, in the spirit of Pushkin's "The Stationmaster" ["Станционный смотритель," 1830], parodies the standard female seduction plot by making a male dreamer the true victim of delusion.[37]

White Nights concludes with a dismal morning's awakening that lingers on for fifteen years as a lifetime hangover. The narrator reproduces her plangent farewell letter, in which she regrets the injury of their mutual delusion, begs forgiveness, and vows to remember gratefully the "sweet dream" of their open-hearted affection. Innocently, she imagines their compassionate friendship will be everlasting. But the narrator offers no response to her plea. Instead, he recalls how, in the dim prospect of that distant morning, "I saw myself as I am now, fifteen years on, growing old, in the same room, just as lonely."[38] His valedictory message to Nastenka is hardly a benediction. Dostoevsky scripts final words that give us a true measure of the character and his pathology:

> As if I would recall my resentment, Nastenka! Or would cast a dark cloud across your bright untroubled happiness, or would inflict misery on your heart with my bitter reproaches, stinging it with hidden pangs, making it beat anxiously in your moment of bliss. That I would crush even one of those tender blossoms which you wove into your dark curls as you approached the altar with him . . . oh, never, never! May your sky always be bright, and your sweet smile always be radiant and serene, yes, and may you be blessed for the moment of bliss and happiness you gave to another lonely, grateful heart! My God! One whole moment of bliss! Is that not sufficient for a man's entire life?[39]

Surely, given the sheer intensity of this rhetorical flourish, the jilted narrator protests too much; he imagines too vividly fantasies of revenge and cannot successfully exorcise his lasting resentment or recover from the enduring grievance he nurtures. Dostoevsky's *White Nights*, the Petersburg memoir of a "sentimental affair," is finally a confessional monologue that stagnates in its own pathos; it is a precursor text that anticipates the dire solipsism of later Dostoevskian antiheroes.

Yet the text's final paragraph does pose an intriguing question. It reminds the reader of the ephemeral bliss of the epigraph's plucked flower, and it also looks ahead to one of those eternal questions that Dostoevsky spent a lifetime contemplating: Can a single cherished memory of something noble and good suffice to resist the temptation of despair?[40]

Not surprisingly, there are many conflicting critical interpretations of *White Nights*. It is commonly regarded as a somewhat anomalous early work, reflecting a kinder, gentler, more charming and more sentimental example of the young Dostoevsky's socially-aware portraits of Gogolian losers and "poor folk."[41] Other readers, however, are more attuned to Dostoevsky's critical perspective on мечтательность and the work's formal resemblance to *Notes from Underground*.[42] It is, indeed, remarkable how early in his career Dostoevsky employs the form of the literary monologue to implicate lofty rhetorical posturing in a humiliating confessional reminiscence.

How does one manage to separate the sensibility of the older narrator from the mentality of the young dreamer, let alone detect the implicit perspective of Dostoevsky himself? Attentive readers agree that the primary narrator's reminiscence fabricates in diary form a chronological reproduction of his younger self's encounter with the one meaningful relationship of his life. But that act of reminiscence is retrospectively composed for publication and the perspective of the mature writer is always implicit and at times made explicit. Readers are given the formidable task of locating the boundary between these two temporally distinct experiential selves and mapping their relationship to one another. One recent interpretation holds that the mature memoirist depicts his younger self's ludicrous sentimental affair and records the dreamer's embarrassed attack on imaginative fancy in order "paradoxically to depict himself as the positive hero of his own story" by virtue of writing's "power to sublimate the adversities of everyday life into art."[43] In this reading, Dostoevsky simultaneously enables the narrator's artistic transcendence of an early disenchantment and anchors it solidly in mundane "real life" experience. In the reading I have offered, I argue that the older narrator is more like his former self in stubbornly adhering to ritual returns to *lieux de mémoire*, to sites of imaginative fulfillment—a congenital malady, it could be argued, of Petersburg intellectuals, those dreamy denizens of the "most abstract and premeditated city in the world" that incubated Dostoevsky's Underground Man.[44]

Like the Rousseau of the *Reveries*, Dostoevsky's solitary unattached dreamer and memoirist has willfully retreated from engagement with others and the world but, unlike Rousseau's flâneur, Dostoevsky's narrator makes a futile attempt to exist contentedly in a prolonged soliloquy with himself. In this regard, *White Nights* may be read as a premonitory sign of Dostoevsky's mature critique of Rousseau's influential cult of sensibility, as well as a preliminary sketch for Dostoevsky's later novel-length portraits of the tragic pathology of interminable self-consciousness.

Endnotes

1 The full range and richness of the flâneur character type is best surveyed in the compilation of essays edited by Tester. Derived from the verb *flâner* (to ramble), the noun originally carried the taint of a malingerer, but as a literary referent it came to denote a strolling spectator of the modern metropolis. In Baudelaire's later variant, in such works as *Les Fleurs du Mal* [*The Flowers of Evil*, 1857], inspired by Edgar Allan Poe's "The Man of the Crowd" (1840), the flâneur is a poet-journalist who seeks to merge his solitary self into the transitory spectacle of urban life. Unlike the introspective, intensely self-analytical narrator of Rousseau's *Reveries*, Baudelaire's street-walking poet is "a *kaleidoscope* equipped with consciousness," acutely aware of the constant shock of novel sensations while immersed in, but separate from, the crowd (Benjamin, "Some Motifs in Baudelaire," 175).

2 Barran points out that Martynov's prolix title, *Philosophical Solitary Walks of Jean-Jacques Rousseau, or His Final Confession, Written by Himself . . . in which Are Portrayed the True Character and Authentic Motives for the Deeds of This Famed Genevan Philosopher*, gave prominence to Rousseau's latter-day withdrawal into self-sufficient introspection (227).

3 Fink offers a succinct and judicious review of this extensive literature, drawing attention to Dostoevsky's much-noted animus toward the deceitful rhetoric of Rousseau's *Confessions*, as well as Dostoevsky's attraction to Rousseau the social visionary and proponent of an innate "natural goodness" corrupted by societal inequalities and the resentments they breed. Any neatly chronological account of Dostoevsky's disenchantment with Rousseau is belied by the resurgence of utopian strains in as late a work as "Dream of a Ridiculous Man" ["Сон смешного человека," 1876].

4 Rousseau writes, in part, to reconstitute the serenity he enjoyed while exiled in Switzerland on St. Peter's Isle in the middle of Lake Bienne. He strives fifteen years later to recreate in writing the mental freedom of uninterrupted introspection and precise observation unconstrained by compelling duties or desires. Huet captures well the radical extent of Rousseau's willed abstention from reciprocal relations in order to achieve the sovereignty of solitary subjectivity. As she explains, "when the love of

self is no longer moderated by the opposite movement of pity, Rousseau can at last feel liberated from any impulsive move toward the other" (126).

5 Rousseau, *Reveries of the Solitary Walker*, 8. Quotations of Rousseau come from the Butterworth translation. I have adjusted the translation where necessary.

6 See, for instance, the defense of Romantic мечтательность [dreaminess] and incorruptible idealism present in the readings of *White Nights* by Mochulsky (93-98) and Frank (343-47). For Proskurina, Dostoevsky's primary aim is to depict a chastened sentimental idealist, but without repudiating the ennobling value of reverie: "Thus the verdict against foolish futile dreaminess is combined with delight and astonishment aroused by the creation of an invented world at the whim of the imagination" (133).

7 Dostoevsky, *Полное собрание сочинений*, 28 (1):138; 1:148. Quotations from the *Complete Collected Works* are cited by volume and page number. The additional reference here is to the Ardis English language edition of Dostoevsky's letters; subsequent additional references are to comparable pages in Magarshack's English translation for the convenience of readers who do not know Russian, but all the translations here are mine.

8 Burton, *The Flaneur and his City*, 2. See Fanger, 135-37, for an account of Dostoevsky's attraction toward the popular, garrulous form of the feuilleton.

9 Dostoevsky, *ПСС*, 18:32. The ideological thrust of Dostoevsky's feuilletons is best summed up by Frank: "The Petersburg chronicler, throughout his seemingly casual *causerie*, conveys all the smoldering frustration undoubtedly felt by the progressive intelligentsia of the mid-1840s at their social-political helplessness" (237).

10 Little has been made of this curiously hydra-headed title. Translators have a difficult time capturing the ambiguity latent in the word роман, which signifies both a novel and a love affair; the border between what is literary and what is experiential being, of course, permeable. In an 1860 reprint Dostoevsky removed some of the narrator's vapid lachrymose phrases and added a virtual catalogue of his reading in sentimental and romantic European writing (see 2:485), thus underlining the literary origins of the dreamer's imaginative life.

11 Turgenev, *Полное собрание сочинений и писем*, I:29. My translation is literal, but refers to the masculine gender of "flower" ["цветок"] as "it."
12 Dostoevsky, *ПСС*, 2:102: 147.
13 Ibid., 2:103; 148.
14 Ibid., 2:105; 151-2.
15 Ibid., 2:106; 152.
16 Ibid., 2:109; 158.
17 Ibid., 2:105; 151.
18 Ibid., 2:106; 153.
19 Ibid., 2:107; 154.
20 Ibid., 2:107; 155. The term "landlady" is, indeed, peculiar, for хозяйка covers a range of meanings from housewife to hostess, and one translator (Magarshack, 1968) even refers to these ladies as "mercenary" (155). Later, Nastenka teases the narrator by asking how he knew she was worthy of a relationship and not just another *khoziaika*. Apparently, strictly contractual relations with ladies do not count as actual relationships.
21 Ibid., 2:108; 156.
22 Ibid., 2:109; 159.
23 Andrew, *Narrative, Space and Gender*, 45.
24 Dostoevsky, *ПСС*, 2:110; 160.
25 Ibid., 2:112; 161.
26 Ibid., 2:113; 163.
27 Ibid., 2:116; 167.
28 Ibid., 2:117; 169.
29 Ibid., 2:127; 182-3.
30 Ibid., 2:128; 183.
31 Ibid., 2:130.
32 Ibid., 2:131; 187.
33 Ibid., 2:134; 192.
34 Ibid., 2:135-6; 193-4.
35 Surely there is an ironic evocation here of Pushkin's well-known double-edged love lyric of 1829, "Я вас любил" ["I loved you"], when, bidding adieu, the poet declaims less than sincerely, "I would not have you feel the least regret . . . I loved you with such purity, such passion / As may God grant you to be loved once more" (Translation from Arndt, 94-5).

36 Dostoevsky, *ПСС*, 2:140; 188.

37 In this respect, "White Nights" is both dissimilar and similar to the melodramatic ending of Dostoevsky's *Poor Folk* [*Бедные люди*, 1846]. The beloved woman rests comfortably in the arms of a devoted lover, unlike poor Varvara in the grasp of Bykov, yet the pathos of Devushkin, who has lost his one and only correspondent, is similar to the plight of the abandoned dreamer who has only his reiterated "romance" for company.

38 Dostoevsky, *ПСС*, 2:141; 201.

39 Ibid.

40 To leap far ahead in Dostoevsky's career, the redemptive potential of a remembered moment of self-overcoming is invoked prayerfully in Alyosha's sermon to the boys at the conclusion of *The Brothers Karamazov* [*Братья Карамазовы*, 1880], yet its efficacy is called into question at the end of "Dream of a Ridiculous Man."

41 Both Passage (73-81) and Terras (30-39) see Dostoevsky's narrator as the literary offspring of E.T.A. Hoffmann's self-ironizing dreamers, but emphasize that Dostoevsky's eulogy to romantic daydreaming is performed with a warm pathos that Hoffmann and Gogol lack. Frank, too, perceives a note of redemption in the elegiac tenderness with which the brief moment of romantic bliss is cherished (346-47) and Fanger (169) agrees that the dreamer is portrayed in the most sympathetic of lights.

42 Holquist elucidates the work's generic relationship to the *roman-feuilleton* and the "physiological sketch," while also illuminating rhetorical and structural similarities to the later *Notes from Underground* (37-43).

43 Rosenshield, "Point of View and the Imagination," 195.

44 5:101. See Nora: "A *lieu de mémoire* is any significant entity, whether material or non-material in nature, which by dint of human will or the work of time becomes a symbolic element of the memorial heritage of a community" (I:xvii). Dostoevsky's Petersburg dreamer fabricates a private site of memory around the embankment bridge to which he ritually returns at the ten o'clock hour; for him, the city of his solitary promenades contains innumerable markers of recollected emotion and recurring fantasy.

Works Cited

Andrew, Joe. *Narrative, Space and Gender in Russian Fiction: 1846-1903*. Amsterdam: Rodopi, 2007.

Arndt, Walter. *Pushkin Threefold: Narrative, Lyric, Polemic and Ribald Verse*. New York: E. P. Dutton & Co., 1972.

Barran, Thomas. *Russia Reads Rousseau, 1762-1825*. Evanston, IL: Northwestern UP, 2002.

Benjamin, Walter. "Some Motifs in Baudelaire." In *Illuminations*, 155-200. New York: Shocken Books, 1969.

Burton, Richard D. E. *The Flaneur and His City: Patterns of Daily Life in Paris 1815-1851*. Durham, UK: University of Durham Press, 1994.

Dostoevsky, Fyodor. Полное собрание сочинений в тридцати томах. 30 vols. Leningrad: Nauka, 1972-90.

____. *Complete Letters: 1832-1859*. 2 vols. Edited by David Lowe and Ronald Meyer. Ann Arbor: Ardis, 1988.

____. "White Nights." In *Great Short Works of Dostoevsky*, translated by David Magarshack, 145-201. New York: Harper & Row, 1968.

Fanger, Donald. *Dostoevsky and Romantic Realism: A Study of Dostoevsky in Relation to Balzac, Dickens, and Gogol*. Chicago: University of Chicago Press, 1967.

Fink, Hilary. "Dostoevsky, Rousseau, and the Natural Goodness of Man." *Canadian American Slavic Studies* 38 (2004): 273-87.

Frank, Joseph. *Dostoevsky: The Seeds of Revolt, 1821-1849*. Princeton, NJ: Princeton University Press, 1976.

Holquist, Michael. *Dostoevsky and the Novel*. Princeton, NJ: Princeton University Press, 1977.

Huet, Marie-Hélène. "Altered States." In *Approaches to Teaching Rousseau's Confessions and Reveries of the Solitary Walker*, edited by John C. O'Neal and Ourida Mostefai, 121-26. New York: MLA, 2003.

Mochulsky, Konstantin. *Dostoevsky: His Life and Work*. Translated by Michael A. Minihan. Princeton, NJ: Princeton University Press, 1967.

Nora, Pierre. "From *lieux de mémoire* to realms of memory." In *Realms of Memory: Rethinking the French Past*, translated by Arthur Goldhammer, xv-xxiv. New York: Columbia University Press, 1996.

Passage, Charles E. *Dostoevsky the Adapter: A Study in Dostoevski's Use of the Tales of Hoffmann*. Chapel Hill: University of North Carolina Press, 1954.

Proskurina, Iu. M. "Повествователь-рассказчик в романе Ф. М. Достоевского *Белые Ночи*." *Филологические науки* 2 (1966): 123-35.

Rosenshield, Gary. "Point of View and the Imagination in Dostoevskij's 'White Nights.'" *Slavic and East European Journal* 21 (1977): 191-203.

Rousseau, Jean-Jacques. *Les Rêveries du Promeneur Solitaire*. Edited by Marcel Raymond. Geneva: Librairie Droz, 1948.

———. *The Reveries of the Solitary Walker*. In *Collected Writings of Rousseau* vol 8, translated by Charles E. Butterworth, 1-90. Hanover, NH: University Press of New England, 2000.

Terras, Victor. *The Young Dostoevsky (1846-1849): A Critical Study*. The Hague: Mouton & Company, 1969.

Tester, Keith, ed. *The Flâneur*. London: Routledge, 1994.

Turgenev, Ivan Sergeevich. *Полное собрание сочинений и писем в двадцати восьми томах*. Leningrad: Nauka, 1960.

Dostoevsky's Orphan Text: *Netochka Nezvanova*

Elizabeth Cheresh Allen

As every student of Dostoevsky knows well, he portrays orphans and near-orphans throughout his literary career, from the early "A Christmas Tree and a Wedding" ["Елка и свадьба," 1848], to *The Insulted and Injured* [*Униженные и искорбленные*, 1861], to *The Brothers Karamazov* [*Братья Карамазовы*, 1880]. Yet it seems particularly fitting to dub Dostoevsky's unfinished novel of 1849, *Netochka Nezvanova* [*Неточка Незванова*], his distinctively orphan text for several reasons. The most obvious is that it—or what we have of it—centers on the first phases in the life of an orphan, the eponymous Netochka, whose father had died when she was two years old, before the narrative begins, and whose mother and stepfather die when she is ten, leaving her to be sent from one new home to another.[1] But not only does Netochka lose her parents as a child, Dostoevsky abandoned her too, albeit not entirely by choice, leaving her story an orphan.

Dostoevsky's arrest in St. Petersburg for political subversion in late 1849, followed by his imprisonment in Siberia, interrupted work on the novel, which he had begun in 1846. And although he did correct proofs of the second installment of the novel while still incarcerated in St. Petersburg—it was being published serially in *Notes of the Fatherland* [*Отечественные записки*] during 1848 and 1849—and he did revise what he had written of the novel in 1860 for inclusion in a collection of his works, he did not add anything substantive to it then, or ever. Instead he left it unfinished, breaking off abruptly with the promise of an encounter between Netochka and a minor character "tomorrow," despite his original plan to carry the narrative on through to Netochka's success as a performing artist.

Netochka Nezvanova qualifies as Dostoevsky's orphan novel in several formal ways as well. For one, Dostoevsky never again used a character's name as a title; for another, he never again wrote a *Bildungsroman* [novel of education], the subgenre to which this novel arguably belongs; and for yet another, he never again employed a female character as a narrator—*Netochka Nezvanova* is couched in the first person as a memoir.[2] Thus in these ways too *Netochka Nezvanova* stands alone among Dostoevsky's works, an orphan in form as well as content.

One additional reason for viewing *Netochka Nezvanova* as Dostoevsky's orphan text is the sparse attention the work has received from literary historians and critics. With a few exceptions, most notably an essay by Elena Krasnostchekova in a study of violence in Russian literature, the novel has garnered only passing critical interest.[3] Even in a study that takes Dostoevsky's depiction of children as its subject, *Dostoevsky: Child and Man in His Works*, William Rowe devotes only a few pages to this novel, and Andrew Wachtel does not mention it at all in his literary historical study *The Battle for Childhood: Creation of a Russian Myth*, maintaining that "the advent of a specifically Russian conception of childhood can be dated to September 1852, when Tolstoy's *Childhood* appeared anonymously in the journal *The Contemporary*."[4] For most historians and critics, *Netochka Nezvanova* has significance only as a harbinger of what was to come. As Konstantin Mochulsky puts it, the novel was "the laboratory in which the ideology and technique of the great novels were worked out."[5]

The few commentators who explore the novel's substance have tended to focus on specific themes. Robert Louis Jackson and Thomas Marullo, for instance, have concentrated on the fatal self-aggrandizing delusions of musical genius held by Netochka's violinist stepfather.[6] Joe Andrew and Victor Terras, among others, have dwelt on the sexual precocity and, at times, perversity of various characters, including Netochka herself. Leonid Grossman and Konstantin Mochulsky have highlighted the types of female characters represented or, more broadly, the novel's relation to the "woman question" in Russia at the time, as does Nina Pelikan Straus.

As intriguing as these subjects are, I would like to illuminate an aspect of *Netochka Nezvanova* that has not been sufficiently examined and yet that fundamentally marks the novel and reflects Dostoevsky's aesthetic and ethical vision early in his career. This is the role of stories. Although a number of critics have remarked Netochka's tendency to fantasize for its own sake—William Rowe, for one, notes Netochka's frequent "precarious journeys across the borderland between illusion and reality"[7]—I will consider that tendency differently. For I see stories and the fantasies they fuel shaping Netochka's imagination and much of her behavior.

In what follows, I will define "imagination" as the mental capacity to evoke sensations without immediate sensory stimuli. To be sure, sensory stimuli—a taste, a smell, a touch, a sound, or a sight, alone or in combination—may be re-created by the imagination from pieces of the past, or they may be newly created from a notion of what the present or future might hold. Derived from the Latin word *"imaginatio"*—imag(e) + in + noun suffix [the Russian воображение is rooted in the same segments, в(о)/in + образ(ж)/image + ение/noun suffix]—the etymology makes clear that, of all the senses, vision provides the core of the imagination.[8] It is the "mind's eye," as Hamlet famously puts it, which conjures up images that may stimulate an individual's thoughts, emotions, and even actions, often powerfully.[9]

In his entry on "imagination" in *A Companion to Aesthetics*, Roger Scruton stresses "the voluntary nature of imaginative acts," arguing that images produced by the imagination belong to "the domain of the will."[10] He explains:

> When I stand before a horse it involves no act of creative imagination to entertain the image of a horse—for this image is implanted in me by my experience, and is *no doing of mine*.... When, however, I summon the image of a horse in the absence of a real horse, or invent the description of a battle which I have heard about from no other source, my image and my thought go *beyond* what is given to me, and lie within the province of my will. Such inventive acts are paradigm cases of imagination.[11]

Calling up images by the imagination requires an act of will; exercising the imagination is a conscious, deliberate activity, Scruton affirms. Otherwise, if involuntary, the images that the mind engenders constitute false beliefs or illusions.

Imagination is, to quote William Hazlitt, "that faculty which represents objects not as they are in themselves, but as they are moulded by other thoughts and feelings into an infinite variety of shapes and combinations,"[12] even if those "shapes and combinations" may not exist in reality and may inspire bad—hostile, vicious, harmful—thoughts or actions.[13] Such a sense of the imagination, for example, led Joseph Warren in 1753 to extol Shakespeare's play *The Tempest* as "the most striking instance of his creative power," adding, "[Shakespeare] has there given the reins to his boundless imagination, and has carried the romantic, the wonderful, and the wild to the most pleasing extravagance."[14] Warren prizes the limitless potential of artistic creativity; he does not take any moral implications of *The Tempest* into consideration.[15]

Ethicist John Kekes identifies four particularly significant functions of the imagination: 1) re-creative (e.g., recalling "the face of an absent friend"); 2) inventive (e.g., "non-linear thinking"); 3) falsely creative (e.g., fantasizing "the facts [as] other than they are"); and 4) moral (e.g., envisioning "possibilities" as "good or evil").[16] In this essay, I will focus on the "creative" and "moral" functions of the imagination, following the convention of referring to them as distinct types of imagination—the "creative imagination" and the "moral imagination." I will also adapt Kekes's definition of the imagination's creative function in a specific way. I will use the term "creative imagination" to refer to any image or idea invented by the mind without regard for the moral consequences of that invention.

The goal of exercising the creative imagination is creation, whether with the intention to escape, to entertain, or to produce high art, regardless of the moral effects that this creation will have. I will thus contrast the "creative imagination" to the "moral imagination." By "moral imagination" I mean the capacity to envision the potential for good or ill not only of an imaginative invention itself, but of a real action, emotion, or idea. In its capacity to gauge such potential, the moral imagination is, in the words of Lionel Trilling, the "essential imagination of variousness and possibility, which implies the awareness of complexity and difficulty."[17] Kekes amplifies his understanding of this concept by asserting that it has "both an exploratory and a corrective function" through which "agents are trying to envisage and evaluate their own possibilities by asking whether it would be morally good or evil to live and act according to them."[18] Or, as Martin Price more succinctly defines it, the moral imagination is the quality of "a mind that has stretch and reach, an unconstricted consciousness that can make significant choices" regarding right and wrong.[19]

Of course, to most philosophers, intellectuals, and artists of the Romantic era in the late eighteenth and early nineteenth centuries, the creative imagination and the moral imagination are one and the same. To William Wordsworth, for example, the creative imagination, particularly the imagination that creates poetry, arises from a fusion of ideas and emotions into what he terms in *The Prelude* a "feeling intellect."[20] As he describes this kind of intellect in the Preface to *Lyrical Ballads* (1799), it yields an imagination that can give form to "truth, not individual and local, but general." This truth consists of what is "the most important" to human beings, the truth "that binds together by passion and knowledge the vast empire of human society, as it is spread over the whole earth, and over all time."[21] This is a moral truth, the product of unified creative and moral imaginations. And to Percy Bysshe Shelley, "the great instrument of moral good is the imagination," because "to be greatly good," an individual "must imagine intensely and comprehensively; he must put himself in the place of another and of many others; the pains and pleasures of his species must become his own."[22] Such imaginative empathy enables moral value judgments and actions.

However, as cultural historian James Sloan Allen observes, "a long tradition from Plato (whose idealism Shelley much admired) to many contemporary moralists has accused the imagination and its artistic inventions of warring with morality."[23] Plato attributed that war chiefly to the persuasive deceptions that artists create. Prior to the Romantic era in Western culture, philosophers and artists generally conceived of the imagination, to use M.H. Abrams's terms, as a "mirror" re-creating or imitating, with varying degree of fidelity, images from the external world, whereas the Romantics viewed the imagination as a "lamp," radiating a light of visionary invention.[24] In *The Republic* Plato condemns the imitative imagination he deems most artists to possess because they "have no grasp of the truth," and merely reproduce "appearances," which are themselves only imperfect representations of pure ideal forms that exist in their own abstract realm.[25] These imitations are "easy to produce without any knowledge of the truth," and some artists are so skilled that they "can persuade people who are as ignorant as [they are]" that the imitations of appearances are real, when, in fact, imitations [*mimesis*] are at "a third remove" from reality and truth.[26]

Plato bans most artists and craftsmen from his ideal republic not only because their works are "quite untrue" but because these works can deceive their audience.[27] And to Plato, as Allen remarks, "this is the Great Lie of Art," for "when art deceptively imitates life, people gullibly imitate art."[28]

The deception becomes all the more insidious through art's appeal to what Plato judges the basest part of human beings, the part given over to instinctive desires that render us "irrational and lazy and inclined to cowardice."[29] When art "gratifies and indulges the instinctive desires," he says, "it waters [those desires] when they ought to be left to wither, and makes them control us when we ought . . . to control them."[30] Art thereby "strengthens the lower elements in the mind to the detriment of reason, which is like giving political control to the worst elements in a state and ruining the better elements."[31] Then "pleasure and pain become your rulers instead of law and the rational principles commonly accepted as best," thus allowing "disorder" to undermine "morals and manners."[32]

Plato singles out storytellers—he names Homer and Hesiod—because of their appeal to the lower instincts of impressionable young people with portrayals of gods and heroes alike as driven by emotions and lacking restraint. No good can come of this. Instead, he says, given the influential power of art, storytellers should depict gods and heroes as moral models of virtue and goodness, thereby encouraging "the highest excellence of character."[33] Therefore, Plato recommends that the state would do well "to supervise the production of stories," and to "compel our poets" to compose only "suitable" stories to tell to both children and adults.[34] Harmful as art can be, Plato recognizes its capacity for good as well.

In *Netochka Nezvanova* Dostoevsky suggests that he holds much the same divided view of the imagination, art, and stories as Plato.[35] I am not arguing that Dostoevsky was directly influenced by Plato—we have no evidence showing that Dostoevsky read Plato in his early days—but I am arguing that the similarity of their views of stories, art, and imagination is striking, and that this similarity betokens Dostoevsky's youthful Platonic idealism, or, in Jackson's words, the "Platonist character" of his thought.[36] For Dostoevsky shows Netochka's imagination being distinctively shaped by stories that she either encounters or invents as she goes through the phases of her early life. In her childhood and girlhood, Netochka acquires largely a creative imagination, displaying only glimmers of any moral sensibilities. And she is corrupted first by tendentious stories she is told and then by stories she tells herself, deceptively satisfied by their seductive images of self-gratification while remaining indifferent to their moral consequences. Only as an adolescent encountering the stories of heroes and heroines that she reads in novels does she grow to couple that creative imagination with a moral imagination sensitive to the moral world. We see this growth occurring as Netochka passes from childhood narcissism through girlish romanticism to adolescent altruism. This passage reveals Dostoevsky's own early creative and moral imaginations at work as he contemplates both the dangers and benefits of stories, a subject that recurs throughout his works.

Netochka's love of stories and her creative imagination appear in different ways, with different moral consequences, at each of the three stages of her life recounted in the seven chapters we have of *Netochka Nezvanova*. Dostoevsky originally subtitled the three chapters devoted to the first stage of her life "Childhood," and, anticipating Tolstoy's early published works, the novellas *Childhood, Boyhood,* and *Youth* [Детство, 1851; Отрочество, 1854; Юность, 1857], he could have called the two chapters covering the next stage "Girlhood," since they treat Netochka at the ages of ten or eleven, and he might have labeled the last two chapters dealing with the third stage "Youth," since they depict Netochka as an adolescent.[37] But her young life follows a very different course from that of the main protagonist Nikolenka in Tolstoy's novellas. Nikolenka was born into rural comfort and a supportive family (although his mother dies), and he winds up secure in his role as a university student. Dostoevsky's Netochka begins her life in urban squalor and familial strife, which she escapes only when her parents both die and she becomes an insecure orphan dependent on the whims of unreliable if wealthy strangers.

She remembers the sixth-floor, "dirty grey," impoverished one-room attic where she lived amidst "a disordered mess" of "brushes, rags, wooden bowls, a broken bottle, and God knows what else," furnished only with "an oilcloth sofa with the stuffing coming out covered in dust, a simple white table, two chairs, my mother's bed, a little corner cupboard with something in it, a chest of drawers that always tilted to the side, and a torn paper screen."[38] And Netochka hates her poverty: "I loathed our miserable lodgings and the rags I had to wear."[39]

What is more, her earliest memories brim with terrible arguments between her mother and the man whom Netochka takes to be her father but who, she learns later, is actually her stepfather, Efimov.[40] "Watching [my parents] together," she says, "I realized that there was a vague but permanent antagonism between them, which produced an atmosphere of grief and disorder that permeated our life"[41]—an atmosphere that Krasnostchekova maintains "verg[es] on physical abuse" of Netochka[42]—and that often engendered explosive quarrels, presumably over Efimov's conviction that he is a musical genius unwilling to accept a menial job and thereby contribute to the family upkeep. One evening, for instance, Netochka recalls, Efimov "made some sarcastic remark that enraged [my mother] more than ever, and then the brushes and bowls began to fly."[43] And when her parents were not arguing, Netochka reports, "sometimes there was a death-like silence in our attic weeks on end," instilling an "everlasting, unbearable sorrow in our attic room."[44]

These squalid and sad beginnings render Netochka no sheltered innocent, but prompt her to grow up fast, if not altogether well. Identifying herself around the age of eight-and-a-half as "someone who, already at an early age, had experienced so much good and evil," she explains: "My development began with incomprehensible and exhausting rapidity . . . I began to think, to reason, to observe. But these faculties were put to use at such an unnaturally early age that my mind could not really interpret things properly and I found myself living in a world of my own" ["в каком-то особенном мире"][45]—a world invented by her creative imagination.

Netochka stresses how active that imagination was during childhood, repeatedly remarking her games, fantasies, and other imaginative inventions. She recollects that "for a whole year I lived an interior life, always thinking, daydreaming, and secretly tormented by unintelligible and obscure impulses that were developing inside me."[46] And she says that everything "became twisted and refashioned in my mind," so that "in my inflamed imagination [в моем пораженном воображении] were born the most incredible thoughts and suppositions," and that, when she did not understand something, "fantasy [фантазия] came to my assistance."[47] This is her creative imagination at work, unconstrained by moral judgments.

Her "fantasy" fixates on a handsome house with crimson red curtains across the street from her apartment to which Efimov has drawn her attention.

Through her attic window she had long watched with fascination the "sumptuous carriages, drawn by handsome proud horses, [that] were continually driving up to the door" and the resultant "clamor and commotion at the entrance, the different-colored lamps of the carriages, and the lavishly dressed women who drove up in them. In my child's imagination [в моем детстком воображении]," Netochka remembers, "all this assumed an image of regal magnificence and fairy-tale enchantment." And not only that—this house becomes her idea of heaven: "I soon conjectured everything in terms of moving to that house and enjoying uninterrupted peace and comfort . . . I imagined the harmonious strains of music drifting through the windows and I watched the shadows flitting across the curtains, always trying to guess what was going on there and always convinced that this was the realm of paradise and eternal joy."[48] Her creative imagination soars into infinity.

We learn that Netochka's creative imagination has actually been stirred by her stepfather, on whom it comes to focus: "I got it into my head that my father was a martyr and the unhappiest man in the world." In fact, she declares that she loves him with a "boundless," "strange sort of love, not a childlike feeling." Indeed, Netochka asserts that her stepfather always seemed "so pitiful, so unbearably tormented, such a crushed creature, and so horribly full of suffering," it would have been "horribly unnatural for me not to have loved him passionately."[49] Although Netochka at one point describes this love for her stepfather as something "more like a compassionate *motherly* [материнское] feeling," she later confesses, "I had only one true pleasure, which was dreaming and thinking about him. I had only one true desire, which was to do anything that might please him."[50] She recalls, "I used to become almost delirious with joy whenever he offered me the slightest caress." Over time, she concedes, "my love, or perhaps I should say my passion (for I do not know a word strong enough to express fully my overwhelming, anguished feelings for my father), reached a kind of morbid anxiety."[51]

As several critics have remarked, Netochka's intense attachment to her stepfather bespeaks an almost textbook Freudian Electra complex, according to which Netochka develops a love for her stepfather and an antagonism toward her mother, eventually to the point of implicitly wishing for her death. But, in addition to her psychosexuality, this love for her father likely has several other causes. For one, she gets the first "parental caress" she can remember from

Efimov, recalling one evening when "he called me to him, kissed me, stroked my hair, put me on his knee and let me nestle close to him."[52] In line with his psychoanalytic interpretation of *Netochka Nezvanova*, Joe Andrew asserts that this scene marks the beginning of Efimov's "seduction of his step-daughter," and even alleges that scenes like this one "teeter on the brink of child pornography."[53] But, starved as she was for the comfort of physical contact, his caresses alone would probably have won Netochka's allegiance. Another cause of her attraction is that he speaks with her at length, something no one else does: "Sometimes," she reports, "we talked for hours, never growing weary," even though she admits that "I frequently failed to understand a word of what he said to me."[54] At that time, understanding was unimportant to Netochka—human communication was all that mattered.

However, the main reason that Netochka is so drawn to her stepfather, I would argue, is that he fuels her creative imagination with stories. It is Efimov who teaches Netochka to read, and then one day after a lesson, she says, "he told me a fairy tale. It was the first tale I had ever heard. I sat spellbound. I followed the story with great excitement and found myself drifting off into another world.... I was quite ecstatic."[55] Although we do not know the name of this fairy tale, it was likely in the vein of those portraying children in peril who are rescued as good triumphs over evil, a storyline that would strongly appeal to the needy Netochka and her creative imagination, while possibly planting the seeds of a moral imagination.

But fairy tales are not the only stories Efimov tells Netochka. He also tells her a beguiling story about his own future. "The time will come," he affirms, "when I shall no longer live in poverty, when I shall be a gentleman. When your mother dies, I shall be born again."[56] This is his Life Lie, as playwright Henrik Ibsen would label the notion in *The Wild Duck* [*Vildanden*, 1884]—the story of his eventual financial success and professional renown—that he tells himself and Netochka in order to imagine escaping from his present poverty and ignominy, for which he irrationally holds his wife responsible.[57] His creative imagination has been taken over by illusions, untempered by any moral considerations.

Netochka comes close to that condition, too. Although initially upset by the reference to her mother's death, she quickly and creatively turns Efimov's fantasy into a captivating daydream of her own: "I fastened onto the idea that when my mother died my father would leave this miserable attic room and go away somewhere, taking me with him. . . . It seemed to me that we would soon be rich. . . . I resolved, daydreaming, that my father would immediately dress himself well and we would move into a magnificent house"[58]—the house with crimson red curtains, in fact. She then conflates this tale of future riches with a story he is reading to her, as a result of which "somehow my father appeared as a character in the story (goodness knows how, since he was reading it), and my mother was there too, doing something or other in order to prevent my father and me going off together; and I too was participating, with my brain brimming with the wildest and most impossible phantoms."[59] She persuades herself that "at any moment my father might give a furtive wink . . . and then we would run away together and never see mother again."[60] Enthralled by the stories Efimov tells her and the fantasies of luxury and love they inspire, Netochka almost succumbs to her father's illusion, finding herself increasingly alienated from her mother until Netochka all but wishes her dead. This cold-bloodedness betrays Netochka's unleashed creative imagination, as she narcissistically fantasizes about a virtual elopement with her stepfather. At this moment, Netochka displays no signs of a moral imagination that could constrain her creative fantasies.

Indeed, Netochka's lack of moral imagination is displayed most fully in her antagonism toward her mother. Even as an adult narrator looking back on her childhood, she expresses surprise and remorse over—but total incomprehension of—her own lack of sympathy for her mother. "I blamed my mother and I saw her as my father's evil genius," she grants early on, but, she adds naively, "I have no idea how such a monstrous image developed."[61] Later, she wonders, "How did I develop such cruel feelings towards a creature who suffered so eternally as my mother? . . . For some reason," she observes, "we were estranged from one another and I cannot remember feeling affectionate toward her."[62] As Joe Andrew points out, Netochka's memories favor her stepfather by devoting the entire first chapter to his history and only one page to her mother's life. Therefore, Andrew concludes, "Netochka's mother remains a shadowy, dull figure, completely overshadowed (in the narrator's presentation of the 'facts') by her sadistic husband."[63] I would suggest that the difference in length between the treatments of these two characters reflects how lopsided were the impressions made by Netochka's stepfather on her memories, and how little her mother ignited Netochka's creative imagination.

For her mother does not lead her creative imagination into the fantasy-rich world of stories as Efimov does. She has no time for stories—she is consumed by the demands of reality. Her mother loves Netochka but is beleaguered by illness and the burden of supporting the household. Although seriously ill herself, she has to worry about feeding and sheltering her family; she assigns Netochka chores and other responsibilities and scolds Netochka when she fails to do as she is told. Netochka's mother is therefore the voice of misery, sacrifice, and constraint—the voice of an unappealing reality.[64]

So tight are those constraints that on the few occasions when her mother has the time and strength to display her genuine affection for Netochka, she cannot formulate sentences, much less stories. On one such occasion, for instance, Netochka reports: "The poor woman continued to stroke my hair almost mechanically, hardly knowing what she was doing and repeating: 'My child, Annetta, Netochka.'"[65] The burdens of reality weigh on Netochka's mother too heavily to allow her to narrate or even to imagine a tale in which she and Netochka might live happily ever after.

Netochka does acknowledge some emotional conflict over her divided feelings. "Pangs of conscience and self-reproach rose up within me," she admits, "and I was deeply distressed that I was so obstinately cold towards my poor mother, and at moments I was torn to shreds with pity and misery as I looked at her."[66] And these feelings suggest the beginnings of a moral imagination.[67] But, "tainted by my fantastic, exclusive love for my father," she goes on, "I had to side with one or the other [of my parents]."[68] And so, "I took the side of [Efimov] because he seemed to me so pitiful, so humiliated, and because he aroused my fantasy [моею фантазию]."[69] Just so—Efimov is the source of stories that gratify Netochka's creative fantasies of a love enabling escape from a life of deprivation and despair, leaving the seeds of her moral imagination on fallow ground.

Thus Netochka's first phase of life is filled with her creative imagination feeding her childish narcissism. Her moral imagination barely awakens. But a new jolt of harsh reality thrusts her into an uncertain future that would change her thereafter. Her childhood ends when her mother finally does die and, instead of living out her fantasies of love and security with Efimov, she finds herself abandoned by him on the street. He too dies shortly thereafter.

Had Dostoevsky ended *Netochka Nezvanova* at this point, implicitly blaming stories for Netochka's cold-hearted rejection of her mother in favor of the delusional Efimov, we would have to conclude that he attributed solely pernicious moral value to stories. But Dostoevsky did not end *Netochka Nezvanova* there. He described two more phases of Netochka's life, in which Netochka again embraces stories and exercises her creative imagination, but also shows signs of a developing moral imagination as well, along with her growing maturity.

In the next phase of her life, Netochka transforms her creative imagination from childish narcissism and fantasies of paternal love to a girlish romance with another girl, again nurtured by stories. After her mother and stepfather have both died, leaving her a full-fledged orphan, Netochka is taken into the home of a wealthy prince who had been acquainted with Efimov and who had learned of Netochka's plight. In his home she meets a girl her own age, the prince's daughter Katya, with whom Netochka becomes enamored.

Before she meets Katya, though, in the version of 1849, Dostoevsky introduced the figure of *another* orphan, the sentimentally pathetic eleven-year-old boy, Laria—an additional reason to dub this work Dostoevsky's "orphan text"—who appeals to Netochka's creative imagination, albeit in unhealthy ways. First encountering Laria hiding in a corner of a room in the prince's house, Netochka asks him, "Who are you?" to which he replies, "I'm an unhappy boy," which proves to be something of an understatement.[70] She later remembers him well: "I see Laria before me as if it were now—a poor little boy trembling at the least sound, at every voice, with a tear running down from his little red eyelashes."[71] He was unhappy and cried so much, Netochka learns, because his father, a poor clerk, had recently died from a stroke, and his mother had succumbed to "despair" a week later.[72] Added to that, a distant relative of Laria who took the boy in after his parents' deaths had repeatedly psychologically tortured him, telling him that "he was unfeeling, that he was a tyrant, that he was depriving [the relative's] children of food, that he and no one else had driven his feckless parents to their grave."[73]

Unlike Netochka, for whom stories of escape and happiness had fired a wayward creative imagination, Laria suffers from a wayward moral imagination, which is manipulated by his relative's distorted stories of Laria's life that turn loss into guilt. "He imagined to himself [вообразил себе] that he was partially responsible for his parents' death!" Netochka exclaims, adding, "according to some strange idea, some unfortunate conviction, Laria imagined [вообразил] that, aside from bitterness, they died due to the fact that he did not love them." Thus, from the time they died, Netochka reports, "the poor little orphan tortured himself . . . with remorse, reproaches," and "worst of all was that he kept this conviction secret and that there was no one to disabuse him of it for a whole year."[74] Instead of using his moral imagination to envision a moral life for himself in the present and the future, Laria finds this imagination turned against him over invented events in the past.

Not surprisingly, Netochka tries to cheer Laria up by stimulating an escapist creative imagination with "one of those magical fairy tales that I had heard from my father."[75] But, when she interrupts this story to talk about her parents, Laria turns their conversation back to his imaginary crime against *his* parents and its consequences. He complains that everyone is always looking at him because he is an orphan—a condition he believes he has brought upon himself. And when Netochka asks him what he means by the term "orphan," noting that "this word was somehow familiar to me . . . but until that time, I hadn't completely understood what it meant," he replies, "It's a person . . . who doesn't have a father or a mother, Netochka, who has been left utterly alone and lives in someone else's house, where everyone gets angry at him and scolds him."[76] Projecting his self-contempt onto the people who have taken him in, Laria perceives hostility everywhere. Netochka realizes that, "from everything that Laria told me, I understood that the heart of a child who was mature not in years, but abnormally mature, mature emotionally, had been deeply pierced, at the same time as his mind was more and more darkened by daydreams [and] fantasies, and that some sort of fatalism loomed over his head."[77] His perverted moral imagination overwhelms his creative imagination and becomes a curse, dooming Laria to misery.

We never learn whether his fatalism was justified—the prince sends Laria away to school a week after Netochka meets him.[78] But we do see the damage that a "darkened mind" can do, in Dostoevsky's view, not only to the hapless Laria but to Netochka herself as she falls under the shadow of Laria's darkness and makes it her own. As she recalls: "I completely assimilated [Laria's] mode of thought"[79]—that is, his way of envisioning and understanding the world. Moreover, she has assimilated his woes as her own: "It was Laria's fate to explain to me my misery with his story."[80] That story and others about Laria's past affect Netochka as deeply as Efimov's stories had, but with the opposite effect.

Whereas Efimov entranced her creative imagination, Laria oppresses it. She recollects:

> Of course, at that time, I couldn't understand Laria precisely, but, listening to him, I reconsidered my entire past. I myself was in some sort of frenzy from grief, from horror, from everything that so suddenly arose in my heart but that had already been accumulating for so long. I finally began to understand my poor mother and my conscience rose up against me! I reproached myself, I was tormented by remorse, I felt I had been inhumanly unjust, when I recalled that not one drop of love had poured forth from my heart—which had desired, had thirsted after justice and love in its turn—into her wounded heart…. I myself was under the same impression as the one that had ruined the poor boy, and some sort of burst of enthusiastic sympathy filled my soul.[81]

To be sure, Netochka had not bestowed much sympathy on her mother. But her identification with Laria is based on the false "impression," fostered by a "burst of enthusiastic sympathy" and a nascent moral imagination infected by his, that she bears some responsibility for her mother's death. The adults in the prince's household sense Laria's negative influence on Netochka, and "they tried to separate us."[82] Then "one morning, he disappeared from the house"—and, ultimately, from the revised text of *Netochka Nezvanova*.

We do not know why Dostoevsky first included, then excluded, this second orphan from his first attempt at a novel, but we can detect the effects of his inclusion and then his removal. By including Laria and the influence of his dark moral imagination on Netochka, Dostoevsky shifted the focus away from Netochka's own maturation. By removing Laria, Dostoevsky kept the focus strictly on Netochka as she enters a stage of life when she begins to truly develop a moral imagination. Retaining Laria would have diluted Netochka's story, rendering her a more generic orphan than Dostoevsky perhaps intended.

Setting aside the episode of Laria, Dostoevsky shows Netochka in her girlhood falling in love with the prince's proud, capricious daughter, Katya, and he depicts that love's consequences. Netochka proclaims, "It was love, real love with all its ups and downs, real passionate love" that she felt for Katya.[83] And it was love at first sight: "From the moment I saw her, a feeling of happiness filled my soul. Try to imagine [представьте себе] a face of idyllic charm and stunning, dazzling beauty, one of those before which you stop, transfixed in sweet confusion, trembling with delight, a face that makes you grateful for its existence, for allowing your eyes to fall upon it, for passing you by."[84] Katya captures Netochka's heart by appealing to her incipient aesthetic and erotic sensibilities. And, as had happened with her previous, more childlike, illusory attraction to Efimov, she feeds her feelings with her imagination, dreaming of attachment. "While she was with me I could not take my eyes off her," Netochka confesses, and

> after she left, I would continue to gaze, spellbound, at the spot where she had been standing. I started to dream of her and, when I was awake, invented lengthy conversations with her in her absence: I would be her friend, playing all sorts of pranks with her and weeping with her when we were scolded. In short, I dreamt of her like someone in love.[85]

Katya gives Netochka much happier and more substantial material for her creative imagination to build on than Efimov—or Laria—ever had.

In striking contrast to Efimov, and after some initial resistance, which Frank attributes to "the unwillingness of [Katya's] prideful ego to surrender its own autonomy to the infringement represented by the temptation of love," Katya comes to fully reciprocate Netochka's affections, and the two girls develop a prepubescent but dramatically open homoerotic relationship.[86] Once Katya admits to an equal passion—"She sprang up from the sofa ... [and] began kissing me wildly: my face, eyes, lips, neck, and hands"[87]—the two begin to share a bed at night. Then, "crying and laughing," Netochka recalls, "we kissed each other until our lips were swollen."[88]

Terras detects here all the characteristics of "an adult love story."[89] Yet the girls are still young. And they enhance the pleasure of this precocious physical intimacy with what else but stories, which they tell each other. These revolve around fantasies of their future life together, colored by a tinge of sadomasochistic role-playing. Netochka reports:

> We talked about what we might do the next day, and the day after, and all in all we settled everything for the next twenty years. Katya decided how we should live: one day she would give the orders for me to obey, and the next day I would give them to her and she would obey me unquestioningly. After this, we would take turns giving the orders, and if it happened that one of us refused to obey, we would argue about it just for the sake of appearance, and then quickly make it up. In short, we looked forward to eternal happiness.[90]

By contrast to Laria, to whom the future had seemed so bleak, Netochka and Katya can imagine only a future of endless shared bliss.

The bliss of this storied future—another version of the "eternal joy" that Netochka had imagined for the inhabitants of the house with crimson red curtains of her childhood—is short-lived, however. Suspecting what she deems an inappropriate intimacy between them, Katya's mother decides to separate the girls, and Netochka is sent to live with Katya's grown half-sister, Aleksandra Mikhailovna, and her husband, Petr Alexandrovich. Despite the pain caused by this separation, Netochka nevertheless treasures her connection to Katya: "Our stories are inseparable," she affirms.[91] The stories they tell to one another, as well as the stories of their lives, continue the development of Netochka's creative and moral imaginations. Those stories have become more complex as Netochka enfolds first Laria's nightmares and then Katya's and her daydreams into visions of her past and future. Both visions may have been unrealistic, but both expand her emotional compass, and thus help to prepare her for the creative and moral actions that she will undertake in the reality of the next phase of her life.

The final chapters of *Netochka Nezvanova* portray Netochka's adolescent years at the home of Aleksandra Mikhailovna and Petr Aleksandrovich.[92] During these years, Netochka becomes engrossed anew in stories and her creative imagination takes flight again. At the same time, she comes to display for the first time a mature moral imagination. This is the moral imagination of altruism, courage, and action.

The emotionally needy Netochka quickly forms a new attachment to the kindly Aleksandra Mikhailovna, whom she comes to regard as a surrogate mother. Aleksandra Mikhailovna treats her, Netochka recalls, "as if I had been her own daughter," as a result of which, "I threw myself eagerly into the maternal embrace of my benefactress."[93] This benefactress also becomes Netochka's favorite teacher, eclipsing Netochka's hired tutors, "from whom I would have learned nothing," and securing her devotion by doing what Netochka's own mother could not do—telling Netochka stories.[94] But these are not fictional stories, whose potentially wayward effects Aleksandra Mikhailovna and her husband try to guard Netochka against. The stories Aleksandra Mikhailovna tells, or rather reads, to Netochka are rooted in the realities of geography and history. And yet they captivate Netochka's imagination. "We set off on such voyages," Netochka recollects, mentally "visiting such countries, seeing so many marvelous sights and experiencing so many magical and fantastic hours," that she was utterly enthralled. Aleksandra Mikhailovna would read from historical works "deep into the night," Netochka says, noting, "I have never felt as enthusiastic as after those readings."[95] But Aleksandra Mikhailovna does not move Netochka's imagination with reading alone. She shares in this experience. The two become companions in the imaginative evocation of narratives about the past and its heroes. "We were both excited," Netochka exults, "as if we ourselves were the heroes."[96] Identifying with the heroic actors of history and their noble, self-sacrificing, and courageous deeds, Netochka encounters a new type of human being and a new realm of human activity as her creative imagination fosters her moral sensibilities.

So aroused is Netochka's creative imagination, along with her developing moral imagination, by these readings that she decides to read on her own. But she wants to read fiction, as well as the facts of history, despite the household prohibition against her doing so. Stealing the key to Petr Aleksandrovich's library, Netochka goes in one night, and there she discovers novels, which she "began reading avidly," wholly losing herself in the rich fantasy world they provide her. "Soon my heart and my mind were so enchanted and my imagination [моя фантазия] was developing so wildly," Netochka confides, "that I seemed to forget the whole world that had surrounded me until then." These novels—also unidentified, but probably historical novels, particularly those of Walter Scott—heighten Netochka's imaginative sense of the past and her identification with its heroes and heroines. "Almost every page I read," she exclaims, "seemed already familiar, as if I had lived this all long ago: the passions, the enchanting pictures, life portrayed in such unfamiliar forms, was already familiar to me."[97]

But these novels do not just take her into the past. They also give her new fantasies of the future. "Every day," Netochka says, "hope grew stronger in my heart, and my yearnings, too, grew greater; yearnings for that future, for that sort of life about which I read every day, and which struck me with such artistic force and poetic fascination."[98] These fantasies of the future are not those of her childhood, when she imagined being transported from hardship to happiness by her stepfather. Nor are they the fantasies of her girlhood, when she imagined a life of joy with her beloved Katya. These new fantasies, born of both historical fact and fiction, are fantasies of noble heroics. Krasnostchekova detects a conscious moral goal inspiring Netochka's reading, remarking that Netochka "searched in books for 'the correct path.'"⁹⁹ I would argue that it is her creative imagination, rather than her moral imagination, that first inspired her in this search. "I imagined myself the heroine of every novel I read," she confesses, although she also concedes that "it was only in daydreams that I was so bold, while in reality I was instinctively nervous of the future." Such nervousness is natural, given Netochka's dependence on the good will of others for her sustenance. After three years of daydreaming—of living a "life of the imagination" ["жизнь фантазии"]—however, her nervousness notwithstanding, her fantasies of heroism become reality.¹⁰⁰

This happens when she courageously risks the security of that sustenance in order to protect Aleksandra Mikhailovna from Petr Aleksandrovich's emotional abuse. For Petr Aleksandrovich has long been an unloving husband, treating his wife with disdain and an air of icy, if subtle, moral superiority. As Netochka learns, this superiority arises from Petr Aleksandrovich's knowledge that Aleksandra Mikhailovna had once fallen in love with another man, albeit chastely. These circumstances set the stage for Netochka's heroic actions.

While leafing through Walter Scott's *St. Ronan's Well* (1824)—the only novel of his, she says, she has not previously read¹⁰¹—Netochka discovers an impassioned and embittered letter from Aleksandra Mikhailovna's erstwhile lover folded into its pages. Netochka happens to be furtively re-reading it one day when Petr Aleksandrovich observes her and demands to see the letter. Netochka refuses and flees to Aleksandra Mikhailovna. When Petr Aleksandrovich follows Netochka and angrily accuses her of having a secret lover, Aleksandra Mikhailovna defends Netochka but becomes overwhelmed with the guilty memory of her own lover. Acting to spare Aleksandra Mikhailovna more abuse and suffering, Netochka herself creates—a story. This one is an outright lie, albeit one with a moral purpose. She fabricates the claim that the letter is actually from a lover with whom she herself is having "an affair." Although Netochka confides to the reader that she acted "hardly knowing what I was doing," she is clearly attempting to shield Aleksandra Mikhailovna, who not only fears her husband's wrath but is in an "agony" of guilt and shame over her emotional betrayal of her husband.¹⁰²

In fact, this is not the first time that Netochka has fabricated a lie to defend someone. In each of her previous phases of life, she invented and told lies, but those lies clearly arose more from self-interest than selflessness.[103] In her childhood, she lied to her mother in order to ingratiate herself with her stepfather: Netochka gave the change from a shopping errand to Efimov at his request and then lied about it, telling her mother she had lost the money in the snow. That lie took some courage to utter, because Netochka "expected at least a beating" from her mother.[104] Yet, knowing "the thing that most frequently vexed [Efimov] was not having any money and therefore being unable to get a drink," Netochka persevered.[105] Although her mother "was genuinely beside herself with grief," Netochka recalls, and "started to shout at me," then, unexpectedly "she stopped scolding me and started telling me what a careless and clumsy girl I was and that obviously I did not love her much if I could be so negligent with her money." This reaction "hurt me more than any beating would have done,"[106] Netochka states, adding "I had never before suffered such excruciating torment and heartbreak."[107] Nonetheless, Netochka refused to confess that the lie, as a result of which, she recalls, Efimov "kissed me until I reached a kind of hysterical ecstasy, laughing and crying at the same time."[108] Her lie won her stepfather's momentary affection, even at the expense of her relationship with her mother. Her creative imagination in childhood clearly trumped her moral imagination.

The same pattern appears during Netochka's girlhood—before she and Katya have become intimate. Then she invents a lie to protect Katya, whom she already loves, accepting the punishment Katya should have undergone for misbehavior in order to win her affections. Intensely disliking a curmudgeonly old aunt who resides in rooms on the second floor of the prince's house, Katya allowed the huge family bulldog, Falstaff, through a door leading to those rooms, although she was forbidden to do that, because her aunt hated and feared the dog. Upon being questioned about the incident, Katya was "prepared to tell the whole truth" when, Netochka recalls, "seeing Katya's deathly pallor, I stepped forward and firmly declared to Katya's mother: 'I let Falstaff go up.'" This was another absolute fabrication—Netochka had had no inkling of Katya's scheme. Although she immediately qualified her confession, adding that she did it "by accident," she never sets the record straight. And she received the punishment—four hours locked alone in an empty room—gladly. Indeed, "I went into my dungeon dizzy with joy," she exults, "I knew that I had scored a victory" in quest of Katya's love.[109] She was right, too—her intimate relationship with Katya commenced the following evening. Netochka's moral imagination could not stand on its own at this time. Self-interest and her creative imagination conquered all.[110]

In striking contrast to these earlier incidents, by creating a lie to tell to save Aleksandra Mikhailovna from Petr Aleksandrovich, Netochka potentially sacrifices her self-interest in order to act on the moral principle of helping someone else for their sake alone. Hence when Petr Aleksandrovich contemptuously alludes to his wife's earlier betrayal, causing Aleksandra Mikhailovna to collapse in hysteria and eventual unconsciousness—an early Dostoevskian scandal scene—Netochka further ratchets up her courage and changes her moral strategy. She tells Petr Aleksandrovich the truth about the letter, and then she lashes out at him for his consistent mistreatment of Aleksandra Mikhailovna. Accusing him of imperiously seeking to prove to her that she has erred and that he is "more sinless than she," Netochka proclaims with moral indignation: "Your vanity and your jealous egocentricity have been merciless." Next she threatens him, "I can see through you, don't forget that!"[111] Though utterly dependent on Petr Aleksandrovich, Netochka here boldly and selflessly rises to defend the emotionally fragile woman who has been so good to her. In so doing, Netochka exerts her moral imagination and will, proving her superiority over Petr Aleksandrovich. Leaving her threatening words echoing, Netochka storms out of the room, where she encounters Petr Aleksandrovich's secretary, who asks "to have a word" with her. Exhausted, she promises to meet him "tomorrow."[112] And there Dostoevsky lets her story end. He wrote no more of it.

Netochka's final acts of moral courage were not intended by Dostoevsky to be the concluding and climatic acts of the book—he had planned to end it with Netochka's triumph some years later as an opera singer.[113] But I think these final acts give us grounds for drawing some suggestive conclusions about the literary import of this orphan novel, in which we see Dostoevsky's early creative and moral imaginations engaged in explorations of story-telling. For I would say that Netochka's ultimate act of selfless courage came from the moral imagination she developed out of her creative imagination through the historical stories of noble heroics, fact and fiction, that she had absorbed during the preceding years. Whatever these stories were—we know that she values the stories told by Walter Scott—they had a different effect on her than did Efimov's stories, which had previously fed her narcissistic childish daydreams, or did Katya's and her shared stories, which had aroused her precociously erotic girlish fantasies.

They also had a markedly different effect on her than, say, the works of sentimental and Romantic literature had on Pushkin's Tatiana in *Eugene Onegin* [*Евгений Онегин*, 1824-31] and on Flaubert's Emma Bovary [*Madame Bovary*, 1857], both of whom let themselves be led astray by these works into fantasies of romance—from which Tatiana later saved herself by rejecting fantasy for reality, as Emma never could.

By contrast, the histories that Aleksandra Mikhailovna introduced to Netochka and the novels that Netochka read to herself not only induced her to imagine a heroic life, they eventually inspired her—as nothing else in her often sad, sometimes sordid, past could have done—to act imaginatively and heroically, with moral courage and altruistic selflessness, on her own.

My interpretation of Netochka's selflessness and burgeoning capacity to love might be seen to jibe with Joseph Frank's claim that Netochka's heroic behavior arises from "the emotive-experiential basis of Christianity" with her "free self-sacrifice of love" (360). This interpretation might also seem to support James Scanlan's broader claim that Dostoevsky never finds "altruism in man's purely material makeup" because he believed that "love of others is a spiritual ability that enters human nature only through its participation in the divine."[114] But, however selfless and loving Netochka's courageous defense of Aleksandra Mikhailovna may be, it derives not from Christianity or any "participation in the divine"—virtually no trace of religion or spirituality can be found in *Netochka Nezvanova*. Her self-sacrificing love of Aleksandra Mikhailovna derives from her identification with the heroes of history and fiction. She identifies with and emulates those heroes imaginatively, without weighing the rational consequences or moral implications of her actions. Dostoevsky thus largely dissociates morality from rationality—by contrast to Plato—and makes morality more the province of the imagination. Indeed, throughout his works, Dostoevsky harbored deep suspicions about rationality, perhaps most explicitly expressed in *Notes from Underground* [*Записки из подполья*, 1864].

Yet, like Plato, Dostoevsky at once condemns stories promoting self-indulgence and escapism—the sort that at first seduce Netochka—and he lauds stories commending the virtues and valor of heroes—the kind that later inspire Netochka's emulation. In *Netochka Nezvanova*, Dostoevsky shows stories educating Netochka, ushering her from identification to identity, from a creative to a moral imagination, as she grows to maturity. Once she reached that maturity, perhaps Dostoevsky lost interest in developing the character of his eponymous orphan, and in continuing the novel that portrayed her.

But whatever his reasons for abandoning this novel, Dostoevsky never abandoned his belief in the power of stories, and of stories within stories, to reveal the exigencies, ambiguities, and conflicts of the moral imagination. That belief should offer sufficient reason for students of Dostoevsky to adopt the orphan text *Netochka Nezvanova* and give it a suitable home among Dostoevsky's other works as a pivotal foray into his vision of story-telling and the vexed relationship between creativity and morality.

Endnotes

1 Leonid Grossman succinctly summarizes the standard critical view of Dostoevsky's intention in writing *Netochka Nezvanova*: "The principle idea that Dostoevsky was trying to express in the novel was apparently that of the emancipatory mission of a great artist in the corrupt society of the day which is unexpectedly regenerated by the radiant power of the heroine's art" (126). Joseph Frank similarly asserts that Dostoevsky wanted "to portray a character who unites a dedication to art with an equally firm commitment to the highest moral-social ideals," thereby "endeavoring to steer a middle way between the discredited Romantic glorification of art on the one hand, and the temptation to discard the values of art entirely in favor of the utilitarian and the practical on the other" (350). Such views might therefore lead us to consider the extant portion of the novel *Netochka Nezvanova* as Dostoevsky's *A Portrait of the Artist as a Young Woman*.

2 Varvara Pavlovna in *Poor Folk* [Бедные люди, 1846] constitutes an obvious forerunner, but Dostoevsky does not formally make her the narrator, except for the pages from her journal that she incorporates into her letter of June 1. In Dostoevsky's experimental use of a female narrator, many commentators detect the influence of a number of European novels, most notably, the novels of George Sand, Eugène Sue's *Mathilde. Memoirs of a Young Woman* [*Mathilde. Memoires d'une jeune femme*, 1841] and Charlotte Brontë's *Jane Eyre* (1847), which Dostoevsky was reportedly reading in prison.

3 Those critics who do address *Netochka Nezvanova* vary in their assessments of its merits. Contemporaneous criticism was decidedly mixed.

Nikolai Chernyshevsky, for example, writes that "although I did not like the contents... this [novel] was written by a person with talent." Another critic, L.B. Brant, complained that Dostoevsky had offered too many "monological digressions, boring summaries, monotony, [and] oppressive analysis of inner sensations." However, Brant also finds "a dramatic and even tragic effect" on some pages bespeaking "the originality and independence of the author's talent." And A. V. Druzhinin finds that Dostoevsky "*visibly* tries to astonish, to mystify his reader with the depth of his observations.... This, together with the lack of restraint... makes an unpleasant impression. It is as if Mr. Dostoevsky does not know that it is better to say too little than to say too much, as if he is afraid that he will not be understood." Yet he concludes that, "if you consider the whole novel as a series of separate scenes, you read it with pleasure" (all quotations from Fridlender, 66).

Critics in the twentieth century followed suit. Mochulsky criticizes it on the grounds that "the author failed in his desire to achieve either compositional or stylistic unity," and that "Netochka is too pale a figure, too much the narrator and not the heroine" to hold the novel together (101, 108); in other words, he deems this first attempt at a novel an artistic failure. Terras maintains that Dostoevsky unoriginally "followed the example of George Sand, imitated her stylistic mannerisms, even adopted some of her patterns of thought." Nonetheless, "the image of the little girl who emerges from the narrative... is drawn as boldly and surehandedly as that of any of the countless girls whose confessions fill the French, English, and Russian journals of the 1840s" (102, 103). Grossman likewise perceives the influence of George Sand, but specifies that it is the influence wielded "not by the George Sand who was a socialist and a herald of future phalansteries, but by the George Sand of her first [i.e., Romantic] period, with its ... graphic expression of the omnipotence of love ... [and] the beauty of creative art, songs and poetry" (130). However, little of adult love or beautiful art is explicitly described in *Netochka Nezvanova*. Grossman nonetheless concludes that Dostoevsky "combined profound psychological insight with nobility of theme" (132) in this novel, unfinished as it is.

4 Wachtel, *Battle for Childhood*, 2. Of course, Wachtel may not consider Netochka "specifically Russian," but he could at least have acknowledged

her. More notable critical attention does await Netochka in the future. Liza Knapp, for instance, devotes a chapter to *Netochka Nezvanova* in her forthcoming book *Dostoevsky and the Novel of the Accidental Family*, and Thomas Marullo has written an entire book on the novel.

5   Mochulsky, *Dostoevsky*, 113. This assertion is, of course, true, as far as it goes. For example, in her essay "Dostoevskii and the Family," Susanne Fusso notes that by the 1870s Dostoevsky had produced "a grim kaleidoscope of family disintegration: a boy sits in a juvenile penal colony and dreams of being rescued by his relatives (whom he imagines as princes and counts); a man kills his wife in front of his nine-year-old son, who helps him hide the body under the floor; a father, who has learned after his wife's death that their son is not biologically his, abandons the boy on the street in the freezing cold" (175-76). Variations on all these images can be found, thirty years earlier, in *Netochka Nezvanova*.

6   In a review of Ann Dunnigan's translation of *Netochka Nezvanova*, Jackson claims that "the work is a crystal in which may be viewed in shifting focus the elements of his art in the first period of his work and many of the elements of his later postexile period" and that he finds the novel "a particularly engaging work" (657). Unfortunately, aside from the few pages on Efimov (see especially *Quest*, 162-63, 181-82), Jackson has not engaged with it extensively in print—as yet.

7   Rowe, *Dostoevsky*, 62.

8   Like many other authors, Dostoevsky also interchangeably uses the term "fantasy" [фантазия in Russian; *phantasia* in Greek and Latin] for "imagination." In doing so, he is following a well-established tradition. As Penelope Murray points out, that tradition traces back to Augustine,

> who used both the transliterated word *phantasia* and the translated word *imaginatio*. This dual usage continued in all the vernaculars of Europe. And already before Augustine there was a tendency to distinguish two aspects or uses of imagination. Images can correspond to truth or falsity; they can be seriously or lightly entertained. As time went on, this duality of meaning tended to correspond to Augustine's dual vocabulary . . . imagination became the important activity, and fancy the light, airy, playful activity of the mind in its freedom.

But this distinction was never fixed, and rarely observed in the language of philosophy ... (quoted in Murray, xiii)

9 Shakespeare, *Hamlet*, 937 (Act I, scene ii, line 85). Hamlet, whose father has died before the play begins, utters this phrase to his friend Horatio, lamenting what he takes to be his mother's precipitous re-marriage:

> Hamlet: My father—methinks I see my father—
> Horatio: Where, my lord?
> Hamlet: In my mind's eye, Horatio. (937)

10 Scruton, "Imagination," 213.
11 Ibid., 214 (italics Scruton's).
12 Hazlitt, *Complete Works*, 5: 4-5.
13 Ibid.
14 Quoted in Abrams, *Mirror and the Lamp*, 275.
15 For provocative contemporary discussions of the concept of imagination, see e.g., Richard Kearney, *The Wake of Imagination* (Minneapolis, MN.: University of Minnesota Press, 1988); Alan White, *The Language of Imagination* (Oxford and New York: B. Blackwell, 1990); Richard Mathews, *Fantasy: The Liberation of Imagination* (New York and London: Twayne Publishers, 1997); Richard Kearney, *Poetics of Imagination: Modern and Postmodern* (New York: Fordham University Press, 1998).
16 Kekes, "Moral Imagination," 101.
17 Trilling, *Liberal Imagination*, xii.
18 Kekes, "Moral Imagination," 101.
19 Price, *Forms of Life*, 70.
20 Wordsworth, *The Prelude*, Book. XIV, line 226 (1850).
21 Wordsworth, "Preface to *Lyrical Ballads*," 420, 423, 422.
22 Shelley, "Defense of Poetry," 425.
23 Allen, "Morality and Immorality of Art," 442. Another tradition, of course, ignores or dismisses any relationship between imagination and morality—J. Hillis Miller and other so-called deconstructionists are renowned for this (see, most recently, his *Reading for Our Time: Adam Bede and Middlemarch Revisited*, Edinburgh: Edinburgh University Press, 2012), but even the thoroughgoing Scruton does not raise any moral considerations in regard to the imagination.

24 See Abrams, especially 57-69, for discussion of these metaphors for the mind and imagination. Abrams credits Plato as "the main source of the philosophical archetype of the reflector," and Plotinus as "the chief begetter of the archetype of the projector" (59).
25 Plato, *Republic*, 429, 427.
26 Ibid., 427, 429, 425.
27 Ibid., 132.
28 Allen, "Morality and Immorality of Art," 349.
29 Plato, *Republic*, 435.
30 Ibid., 436, 437.
31 Ibid., 435.
32 Ibid., 437, 192.
33 Ibid., 133. In his magisterial history of the idea of the Western imagination, J.M. Cocking claims: "For art [Plato] can be made to provide some support; for imagination none" (1). This claim is somewhat contradicted by Plato's call for artists to depict gods and heroes as ideal role models, which would seem to entail the exercise of something like imagination. Cocking more plausibly maintains that, in regard to art, Plato's attitude "is perhaps not so much ambiguous as ambivalent" (2).
34 Plato, *Republic*, 131, 133.
35 Jackson, for one, offers general support for this assertion with his suggestion, "If it is the romantics of D's higher aesthetic that one seeks, one can point to Plato" (*Quest*, 187). And Jackson reminds us that in Russia of the 1840s, "one did not have to read [particular authors] in the original or even in translation to be imbued with their ideas," that Dostoevsky "drew freely and unsystematically from all sources," and that "the [critics'] quest" must be "not for 'influences,' for the direct or devious paths of acquaintance with [Western] philosophers, but for correspondences" (186).
36 Jackson, *Quest*, 187. As J. M. Cocking has observed, "Plato has been . . . an inspiration for those idealists in a less philosophical sense who, seeing certain things as good, dream dreams of those same things as even better, projecting images toward some notion of perfection" (1). Jackson has affirmed that, despite his eclecticism, Dostoevsky was fundamentally one of those idealists: "The notion of beauty and the ideal—as it has migrated from Plato through medieval Christian aesthetics down to the romantic

aesthetics of Schiller and Chateaubriand, Schelling and Hegel—structures and dominates Dostoevsky's entire world outlook; it is the controlling center of his views about art" (*Quest*, xv). In its treatment of stories, art, and imagination, *Netochka Nezvanova* may be placed at the core of that center.

37   In fact, Dostoevsky did initially divide the extant chapters into three parts: Chapters One through Three he called "Childhood," Chapters Four and Five he named "A New Life," and Chapters Six and Seven he dubbed "A Secret." He deleted these part titles, as well as the subtitle for the work as a whole—"The History of a Certain Woman" ["История одной женщины"]—when he revised the parts for inclusion in his collected works in 1860-61.

38   Dostoevsky, *ПСС*, 2:169; 30, 31. The first citation comes from Dostoevsky, *Complete Collected Works* [*Полное собрание сочинений*] (hereafter *ПСС*), cited by volume and page number. The second citation, for the convenience of readers who do not know Russian, is from the translation of *Netochka Nezvanova* by Jane Kentish. When necessary, I have amended the translation.

39   Ibid., 2:163; 36.

40   Andrew astutely points out that Netochka's real father is mentioned at the beginning—indeed, "father" is the first word of the narrative ["Отца моего я не помню," (translated literally as "Father my I don't remember")]—and thus he "is the first person to be spoken of, but then [he] disappears" and is never mentioned again. Nonetheless, Andrew observes, the real father's "death is of significance, in that this event has led to Netochka becoming fatherless and this in turn led to the initiation of the action" involving her stepfather [отчим], Efimov (218).

41   Dostoevsky, *ПСС*, 2:164; 38.

42   Krasnostchekova, "Wounded Young Heart," 73.

43   Dostoevsky, *ПСС*, 2:159; 31.

44   Ibid., 2:164, 161; 37, 33. Dostoevsky will pick up this motif of silence decades later in "The Gentle Creature" ["Кроткая," 1876], suggesting that long-maintained periods of silence between spouses can have fatal effects.

45   Ibid., 2:179, 160; 57, 32.

46   Ibid., 2:165; 38.

47 Ibid., 2:160,162; 32, 34, 35. Rowe emphasizes how greatly Netochka's imagination affects her perceptions, rendering her, in his view, "adult-like" (62).
48 Ibid., 2:162, 163; 34, 35-36.
49 Ibid., 2:160; 32.
50 Ibid., 2:160, 172; 32, 48. Terras goes so far as to claim that "the story of this strange romance bears most of the features of Dostoevsky's subsequent treatments of the love theme"—I would not go that far—and, more plausibly, that "Netochka's love, like any great Dostoevskian love, is really inexplicable and very complex" (103).
51 Ibid., 2:172; 48.
52 Ibid., 2:159-60; 31.
53 Andrew, "Law of the Father," 221.
54 Dostoevsky, *ПСС*, 2:165; 38-39. Admissions like this one render dubious Terras's assertion that "Dostoevsky de-emphasizes the daughter-father relationship and lets Efimov and Netochka meet as two PERSONS" (105; emphasis Terras's), that is, as equals. The relationship appears to be much more of a power struggle, in which Efimov mostly holds the upper hand.
55 Ibid., 2:165; 39.
56 Ibid., 2:162; 35.
57 Netochka never understands precisely why he views his wife as an obstacle that must be overcome in order to make his "story" come true, only that "there was a vague but permanent antagonism between them" (2:164; 38).
58 Dostoevsky, *ПСС*, 2:162-63; 35.
59 Ibid., 2:165; 39.
60 Ibid., 2:166; 39-40.
61 Ibid., 2:161; 33.
62 Ibid., 2:163; 36. Frank provocatively suggests that Netochka's antipathy towards her mother "can well be seen as a barely disguised transposition of Dostoevsky's own resentment against his father for having insisted that he become a military engineer and for having forbidden any thought of a career as a writer" and that "Netochka's terrible sense of guilt for having hated her poor, long-suffering and hard-working mother . . . can also be interpreted as a reflection of Dostoevsky's own guilt-feelings connected

with his father's murder." If these autobiographical elements are valid, then, Frank concludes, "*Netochka Nezvanova* would be truly a 'confession'—and perhaps to a greater extent than even Dostoevsky himself was fully aware" (351).

63 Andrew, "Law of the Father," 220. Here Andrew resorts to a psychoanalytic interpretation: "In this way the text is structured in classically Oedipal terms in that the girl identifies with and privileges the phallus, at the expense of the mother's body" (220). This interpretation seems to me stretched.

64 Andrew attributes Netochka's narrative neglect of her mother to "the power of the paternal seduction, and the consequent repression" of memories of her (223).

65 Dostoevsky, *ПСС*, 2:164; 37.

66 Ibid., 2:163, 172; 36, 48.

67 In retrospect, the adult Netochka insists, "I do not believe that this kind of cruelty was natural to me, or that her severity could have turned me against her," but I would argue that Dostoevsky suggests otherwise, on both counts (2:164; 37).

68 Dostoevsky, *ПСС*, 2:164, 172; 37, 48.

69 Ibid., 2:172-73; 48.

70 All translations of the excised passage treating Laria in *Netochka Nezvanova* are mine. The original maybe found online in Fridlender's Commentary on the novel at: http://az.lib.ru/d/dostoewskij_f_m/text_0240.shtml, 60-63.

71 Dostoevsky, Lib.ru, 60.

72 Ibid., 61.

73 Ibid., 62.

74 Ibid., 61.

75 Ibid., 60.

76 Ibid., 61. In the revised version of the novel, the task of emphasizing Netochka's status as an orphan falls to the prince:

> "'Poor little orphan,' he said, patting me on the head.
> 'No, no, not an orphan, no!' I said…. 'No, no, not an orphan, no!'"

Netochka here resists the thought that her mother is dead, imploring the prince to take her to her "darling mother" (2:194; 77). Days later, though,

Netochka replies to Katya's questioning why Netochka has come to live with Katya's family by saying, "Because I'm an orphan" (2:203; 90), so Netochka does finally acknowledge both her mother's and Efimov's deaths.

77 Ibid., 63.
78 Although Netochka dubs Laria "the future hero of my story" (60), he does not reappear in the existing text.
79 Ibid., 63.
80 Ibid., 61.
81 Ibid., 63.
82 Ibid.
83 Dostoevsky, *ПСС*, 2:207; 94.
84 Ibid., 2:197; 81.
85 Ibid., 2:197; 82. Citing the same passage, Rowe argues that Netochka's "world of fancy is both factually resourceful and emotionally self-sufficient" (64), and thus declares, "Of equal or even greater import than sexual feeling is the imagination" (61) in this relationship. I agree that the imagination is more important here, but I consider Netochka's "world of fancy" more emotionally dependent on external resources than Rowe does.
86 Frank, *Dostoevsky*, 360. Grossman detects "an early study of the 'meek' and the 'proud'" character types in the portrayal of their relationship, concluding that, in consequence, "this part of the book is one of the finest in Dostoevsky's early work" (128). Similarly, Mochulsky views the differences between Netochka and Katya the reflection of "a psychological format to which [Dostoevsky] would forever remain faithful," "meek" female characters versus "proud" ones (109). Note that, despite their temperamental differences, their creative imaginations run in identical veins.
87 Dostoevsky, *ПСС*, 2:217; 108.
88 Ibid., 2:220; 112.
89 Terras, *Young Dostoevsky*, 105.
90 Dostoevsky, 2:221; 112-13. Compare this scene to the one in *Jane Eyre* at the orphanage where the prepubescent Jane has been sent, when she gets in bed with her one true friend, Helen Burns. Knowing only that Helen is seriously ill, Jane makes her way to the room of a beloved teacher, Miss

Temple, where Helen has been taken. Their subsequent conversation addresses the future, as do Netochka and Katya, but from a very different perspective. Helen invites Jane into her bed, saying, "Jane, your little feet are bare; lie down and cover yourself with my quilt." Helen tells Jane she is going to her "last home"—Helen knows that she is dying—and Jane poses a series of metaphysical questions to which Helen provides answers that would never occur to Netochka and Katya:

> "But where are you going to, Helen? Can you see? Do you know?
> "I believe; I have faith: I am going to God."
> "Where is God? What is God?"
> "My Maker and yours, who will never destroy what he has created. . . ."
> "You are sure, then, Helen, that there is such a place as heaven; and that our souls can get to it when we die?"
> "I am sure there is a future state; I believe God is good . . . I love him; I believe he loves me."
> "And shall I see you again, Helen, when I die?"
> "You will come to the same region of happiness . . . no doubt, dear Jane."

The narrator then shifts the narrative to a more sentimental vein as the girls prepare to sleep and Jane promises, "I'll stay with you, *dear* Helen: no one shall take me away."

The adult Jane who narrates recalls the near-Gothic denouement: "When I awoke it was day . . . the nurse held me; she was carrying me . . . back to the dormitory. . . . A day or two afterward I learned that Miss Temple, on returning to her own room at dawn, had found me laid in a little crib, my face against Helen Burns's shoulder, my arms round her neck. I was asleep, and Helen was—dead" (69-70). This image of innocent amicability, however morbid, only highlights by contrast the passionate affection displayed by Netochka and Katya.

91 Dostoevsky, *ПСС*, 2:223; 116.
92 Mochulsky finds this third section the weakest, arguing that "Netochka's new friend and benefactress is, like herself, a 'meek' type. The end result is a duplication of one and the same psychological tonality" that imparts only "monotony" to this segment of the narrative, until the end (111).

93 Dostoevsky, *ПСС*, 2:225; 118.
94 Ibid., 2:231; 126.
95 Ibid., 2 231; 126-27.
96 Ibid., 2: 231; 127.
97 Ibid., 2: 233-34; 130.
98 Ibid., 2:234; 131.
99 Krasnostchekova, "Wounded Young Heart," 78.
100 Dostoevsky, *ПСС*, 2: 234; 131.
101 *St. Ronan's Well* is an apt choice, given that its plot revolves around a young woman, Clara Mowbray, who is falsely accused of infidelity. And the physical resemblance between Clara and Aleksandra Mikhailovna is striking, although Clara's description is presented by a female acquaintance of hers in much more dramatic—even melodramatic—terms than Aleksandra Mikhailovna's. Clara is said to have "eyes something hollowed—care has dug caves for them, but they are caves of the most beautiful marble, etched with jet—a straight nose, and absolutely the Grecian mouth and chin—a profusion of long straight black hair, with the whitest skin you ever saw—as white as the whitest parchment—and not a trace of colour in her cheek—none whatever" (89). Compare this image to Netochka's recollection of Aleksandra Mikhailovna's appearance: "Her features have never faded from my memory. They were symmetrical, and their thinness and pallor only accentuated the austere charm of her beauty. Her thick black hair, combed smoothly down, framed her cheeks in sharp, severe outline. Her large, childishly clear blue eyes at times . . . seemed defenseless, as if fearful of every sensation, every outburst of emotion, every momentary joy and frequent quiet sorrow" (2:229; 123-24).
102 Dostoevsky, *ПСС*, 2:264; 163.
103 Dostoevsky devoted the equivalent of at least three printed pages to each of these incidents, thus, I think, signaling their significance.
104 Dostoevsky, *ПСС*, 2:170; 45.
105 Ibid., 2:169; 44.
106 Ibid., 2: 170; 45.
107 Ibid., 2;171; 47.
108 Ibid.
109 Ibid., 2: 215;105.

110 These lies at the very least call into question the view expressed by S. Iu. Nikolaeva that Netochka, among other female protagonists of Dostoevsky's early works, "approach[es] the image of an ideal person," because "purity of thought, whole-hearted devotion, the absence of egoism, sincerity, and trust, which the author so valued in his positive heroes, are characteristic of the heroines in the highest degree" (200).

111 Dostoevsky, *ПСС*, 2:66; 173

112 Ibid.

113 Krastnostchekova stands virtually alone in declaring that "the novel *Netochka Nezvanova* may be considered to be complete in its revised version of 1860," because, "in keeping with the tradition of the bildungsroman, this version of Dostoevsky's novel . . . ends on the brink of adult life" (80).

114 Scanlan, *Dostoevsky the Thinker*, 84.

Works Cited

Abrams, M. H. *The Mirror and the Lamp: Romantic Theory and the Critical Tradition*. London and New York: Oxford University Press, 1953.

Allen, James Sloan. "The Morality and Immorality of Art." In *Worldly Wisdom: Great Books and the Meanings of Life*, 345-70. Savannah: Frederic C. Beil Publishers, Ltd., 2008.

Andrew, Joe. "The Law of the Father and *Netochka Nezvanova*." In *Narrative and Desire in Russian Literature, 1822-49: the Feminine and the Masculine*, 214-226. New York: St. Martin's Press, 1993.

Brontë, Charlotte. *Jane Eyre*. Garden City: Literary Guild of America, 1954.

Cocking, J. M. *Imagination: A Study in the History of Ideas*. London and New York: Routledge, 1991.

Dostoevsky, Fyodor. *Полное собрание сочинений в тридцати томах*. 30 vols. Leningrad: Nauka, 1972-90.

____. *Netochka Nezvanova*. Translated by Jane Kentish. Harmondsworth, UK: Penguin Books, 1985.

Fridlender, Georgii. "*Комментарии: Неточка Незванова*." http://az.lib.ru/d/dostoewskij_f_m/text_0240.shtml. 59-67. 2012.

Frank, Joseph. *Dostoevsky: The Seeds of Revolt, 1821-1849*. Princeton, NJ: Princeton University Press, 1976.

Fusso, Susanne. "Dostoevskii and the family." In *The Cambridge Companion to Dostoevskii*, edited by William J. Leatherbarrow, 175-192. Cambridge, UK: Cambridge University Press, 2002.

Grossman, Leonid. *Dostoevsky: A Biography*. Translated by Mary Mackley. Indianapolis: Bobbs-Merrill Co., 1975.

Hazlitt, William. *The Complete Works of William Hazlitt*. 21 vols. London and Toronto: J. M. Dent and Sons, Ltd., 1930.

Jackson, Robert Louis. *Dostoevsky's Quest for Form: A Study of his Philosophy of Art*. New Haven, CT: Yale University Press, 1966.

___. Review of *Netochka Nezvanova* by Fyodor Dostoyevsky. Translated by Ann Dunnigan. *Slavic Review* 32, no. 3 (Spring, 1973): 657-58.

Kekes, John. "Moral Imagination, Freedom, and the Humanities." *American Philosophical Quarterly* 2, no. 2 (April 1991): 101-11.

Krasnostchekova, Elena. "The Wounded Young Heart: Dostoevsky's *Netochka Nezvanova* as Bildungsroman." In *Times of Trouble: Violence in Russian Literature*, edited by Marcus C. Leavitt and Tatyana Novikov, 70-91. Madison: University of Wisconsin Press, 2007.

Marullo, Thomas. "Pointing to the Man-God: Efimov as Artist-Hero in Dostoevkij's 'Netocka Nezvanova.'" *Russian, Croatian and Serbian, Czech and Slovak, Polish Literature* 30, no. 2 (1991): 231-52.

Mochulsky, Konstantin. *Dostoevsky: His Life and Work*. Translated by Michael A. Minihan. Princeton, NJ: Princeton University Press, 1967.

Murray, Penelope. Editor's Introduction to *Imagination: A Study in the History of Ideas*, by J. M. Cocking, vii-xvi. London and New York: Routledge, 1991.

Nikolaeva, S. Iu. "Проявление нравственного идеала в ранних произведениях Ф. М. Достоевского." *Мир романтизма* 7 no. 31 (2002): 193-200.

Plato. *The Republic*. Translated by Desmond Lee. Harmondsworth, UK: Penguin Books, 1955.

Price, Martin. *Forms of Life: Character and Moral Imagination in the Novel*. New Haven, CT: Yale University Press, 1983.

Rowe, William W. *Dostoevsky: Child and Man in his Works*. New York: New York University Press, 1968.

Scanlan, James P. *Dostoevsky the Thinker*. Ithaca and London: Cornell University Press, 2002.

Scott, Walter. *St. Ronan's Well*. N.p.: BiblioBazaar, 2007.

Scruton, Roger. "Imagination." In *A Companion to Aesthetics*, edited by David E. Cooper, 212-17, Oxford and Cambridge: Blackwell Publishers, 1992.

Shakespeare, William. *Hamlet*. In *William Shakespeare: Complete Collected Works,* edited by Andrew Harbage, 933-974. Baltimore: Penguin Books, 1969.

Shelley, Percy Bysshe. "A Defense of Poetry." In *The Selected Poetry and Prose of Shelley*, edited by Harold Bloom, 415-448. New York: Signet Classics, 1966.

Straus, Nina Pelikan. "Introduction: Dostoevsky and 'the Feminine.'" In *Dostoevsky and the Woman Question: Rereadings at the End of a Century*, 1-18. New York: St. Martin's Press, 1994.

Terras, Victor. *The Young Dostoevsky (1846-1849): A Critical Study*. The Hague: Mouton, 1969.

Trilling, Lionel. *The Liberal Imagination*. Garden City: Doubleday & Co., 1953.

Wachtel, Andrew. *The Battle for Childhood: Creation of a Russian Myth*. Stanford: Stanford University Press, 1990.

Wasiolek, Edward. *Dostoevsky: The Major Fiction*. Cambridge: The MIT Press, 1964.

Wordsworth, William. "Preface to *Lyrical Ballads*." In *The Selected Poetry and Prose Of William Wordsworth*, edited by Geoffrey H. Hartman, 410-424. New York: Signet Classics, 1970.

____. *The Prelude: The Four Texts: 1798, 1799, 1805, 1850*, edited by Jonathan Wordsworth. Harmondsworth, UK: Penguin Books, 1995.

Tolstoy: Works of the 1850s

VI

The Creative Impulse in *Childhood*: The Dangerous Beauty of Games, Lies, Betrayal, and Art

Robin Feuer Miller

> The heart has reasons which reason knows nothing of.
> Pascal, *Penseés*

> When you read Tolstoy, you feel that the world is writing, the world in all its variety.
> Isaac Babel, "Babel Answers Questions about His Work"

> 'Betrayal . . . We betray to be loyal. Betrayal is like imagining when the reality isn't good enough.' He wrote that. Betrayal as hope and compensation. As the making of a better land. Betrayal as love. As a tribute to our unlived lives. On and on, these ponderous aphorisms about betrayal. Betrayal as escape. As a constructive act. As a statement of ideals. Worship. As an adventure of the soul. Betrayal as travel: how can we discover new places if we never leave home? 'You were my Promised Land, Poppy. You gave my lies a reason.'
> John Le Carré, *The Perfect Spy*

> I taught them to love the beauty of a lie.
> Dostoevsky, "The Dream of a Ridiculous Man"

> Without my Iasnaia Poliana I can hardly imagine Russia or my relationship to her. Without Iasnaia I could perhaps see more clearly the general laws necessary for my country, but I could not love my country so passionately.
>
> Lev Tolstoy, *Summer in the Country*

For both Tolstoy and Dostoevsky, the rudiments and foundations of the creative impulse emanated from a complex compound of the real and the imagined, the remembered and the invented. Their descriptions of this process were remarkably similar, but, for Tolstoy, from his earliest fiction this impulse was marked with ambivalence—euphoria and moral guilt—whereas for Dostoevsky the creative impulse and the process ensuing from that impulse were affirmative, even when the undertones were dark. The real, the remembered, and the imagined combine in protean ways. In 1876 Dostoevsky wrote:

> All through my four years in prison I continually thought of all my past days, and I think I relived the whole of my former life in my memories. These memories arose in my mind of themselves; rarely did I summon them up consciously. They would begin from a certain point, some little thing that was often barely perceptible, and then bit by bit they would grow into a finished picture, some strong and complete impression. I would analyze these impressions, adding new touches to things experienced long ago; and the main thing was that I would refine them, continually refine them, and in this consisted my entire entertainment.[1]

This may be as close as Dostoevsky ever came to describing his actual creative process, although he wrote frequently about his fundamental ideas about art—about the importance of embodying ideas within characters, about his fantastic realism, about not showing his own "ugly mug" to the reader.

Art, for Dostoevsky, could express human and spiritual truths that other forms of discourse could not. Certain lies—the fictions—at the heart of the creative endeavor could operate in service of the truth and not really be lies at all. Other kinds of lies were clearly and unambiguously morally corrupt. But even in such instances, Dostoevsky could usually find a diamond amongst the filth. For example, those newly fallen people in "The Dream of a Ridiculous Man" ["Сон смешного человека," 1876], fictional products of the ridiculous man's dream, who had learned "to love the beauty of a lie," become more precious to the ridiculous man (and by extension to his author, Dostoevsky) than when they were innocent, before he had corrupted them.² All of Dostoevsky's fictional works explore, in some way, the uneasy borders between lies and truths and how each can serve the other.

Tolstoy's stance toward the creative process, with its unavoidable mixture in art of the real and the imaginary, or put more starkly, truth and lies—and his attitude toward that complex compound—could not have been more different, even though the process itself was, in his description of it, similar. Where Dostoevsky embraced these intertwinings and variations on truth, lies, and fictions, Tolstoy wrestled with the nuanced tension between art and truth, the fictive and the real, games and betrayals, throughout his entire life. John Updike expresses a paradox about the tension between actual life and the rendering of it into art that was also operative for Tolstoy. In an essay appraising Updike's oeuvre, the novelist Ian McEwan wrote, "The plain facts of life were 'unbearably heavy, weighted as they are with our personal death. Writing, in making the world light—in codifying, distorting, prettifying, verbalizing it—approaches blasphemy.'"³

Tolstoy's first published work of fiction, the semi-autobiographical novel *Childhood* [*Детство*, 1852], is drenched in death, blasphemy, and betrayal.⁴ It is his first meditation on "what is art?" It is a novel that also timelessly encapsulates the sunshine and magic of childhood. Most important, it renders numerous explorations of the creative impulse widely experienced by children and, with luck, by the adults they quickly become. In this essay I explore how Tolstoy, in this early work, hauntingly portrays the falsehoods and betrayals that art, play, and dreams can lead to.

Before Tolstoy settled on the version of the novel that he eventually submitted to Nikolai Nekrasov's journal *The Contemporary* [*Современник*], where *Childhood* was first published, he had written four separate drafts. In the second version, there is a chapter he subsequently omitted, but it contains a telling observation by the narrator about his creative process that bears a marked resemblance to Dostoevsky's description:

> It is possible to write from the head and from the heart. When you write from the head, the words fall into place on the paper in an obedient and well ordered manner. But when you write from the heart, there are so many thoughts in your head, so many images in your imagination, so many

memories in your heart, that their expression is incomplete, inadequate, halting and crude. Perhaps I was mistaken, but I always used to stop when I began writing from the head and tried to write only from the heart."[5]

Tolstoy describes the same crowding of images, the same mixing of memory and imagination, the same emphasis on the impressionistic over the rational that Dostoevsky had expressed. Chernyshevsky, whom Tolstoy was to ridicule later as "a gentleman stinking of bedbugs,"[6] wrote the earliest and still most astute descriptions of the process emanating from Tolstoy's creative impulse. In one of the first reviews of *Childhood* and several other early works of Tolstoy, not only did Chernyshevsky coin the important term "interior monologue," but he wrote in minute detail of how he understood Tolstoy's particular brand of artistic creation:

> He is interested in observing how a feeling immediately arising out of a given circumstance or impression and then, subjected to the influence of memory and the powers of association in the imagination, turns into different feelings.... how a thought, born of an original sensation, leads to other thoughts, is carried further and further away, blends reverie with real sensations, dreams of the future with reflections on the present.... Count Tolstoy is most of all concerned with the psychic process itself, its forms, its laws, with, to express it precisely, the dialectic of the soul.[7]

Emphasizing words like "feeling," "impression," "imagination," "sensation," "dreams," and "reverie," Chernyshevsky comes close to duplicating both Tolstoy's own idea about writing from the heart and Dostoevsky's description of analyzing impressions and memories and then adding new touches to them. How doubly ironic that Chernyshevsky was to become, for both authors, an object of derision and a focus of ideological rage.

At the heart of the creative impulse we can consistently recognize elements of wonder, observation, and play. Before speculating about the creative impulse in Tolstoy's *Childhood*, it is worthwhile to focus on the creative impulse, as distinct from the more elaborate creative process, in its most general, elemental contours. It is no surprise that scientists and those from other disciplines have learned from works of fiction (including in great abundance from Tolstoy and Dostoevsky) because the same elements of wonder, observation, and play lie at the heart of creativity for both the artist and the scientist.

Wonder, Observation, Play, and the Creative Impulse in General

The humanist and the scientist are not the proverbial farmer and cowman from the musical *Oklahoma* who cannot be friends. They are wandering the same precious terrain, observing it, playing in it, trying to understand and communicate it through conversation, discourse, and writing—whether through the language of words or of numbers. For both the humanist and the scientist, however deeply they seek knowledge, an ongoing sense of wonder and an acknowledgment that mystery constantly outpaces solution contribute to our joint awareness that all knowledge is provisional. Recently Freeman Dyson wrote about the ways in which "the information flood" and technology have brought enormous benefits to science. But, he goes on, "the public has a distorted view of science, because children are taught in school that science is a collection of firmly established truths. In fact, science is not a collection of truths. It is a continuing exploration of mysteries. Wherever we go exploring in the world around us, we find mysteries.... Science is the sum total of a great multitude of mysteries. It is an unending argument between a great multitude of voices. It resembles *Wikipedia* much more than it resembles the *Encyclopedia Britannica*."[8]

Certainly for Tolstoy all knowledge was provisional; mysteries always outstripped solutions, the question of how to live and how to die could never quite be answered. Tolstoy frequently resorted to similes and analogies, that is, to artistic devices, to express the provisional quality of both knowledge and wisdom. Instances of this abound: remember, for example, Prince Andrei and the oak in *War and Peace* [*Война и мир*, 1869], Levin and the clouds in *Anna Karenina* [*Анна Каренина*, 1877], the narrator's parable of the mice in *Confession* [*Исповедь*, 1882], and Ivan Ilych and the syllogism about Caius in *The Death of Ivan Ilych* [*Смерть Ивана Ильича*, 1886]. Indeed, similes and analogies are fundamental to Tolstoy's way of understanding the world, his existence in it, and God. They are primary markers of his style.

As William Wordsworth has told us in the well-known poem "My heart leaps up when I behold" (1802), "the Child is father of the Man."[9] Adult scientists and artists frequently bump up against experiences reminiscent of childhood wonder. Samuel Taylor Coleridge wrote in his *Biographia Literaria* (1834): "To carry on the feelings of childhood into the powers of manhood; to combine the child's sense of wonder and novelty with the appearances which every day for perhaps forty years had rendered familiar... this is the character and privilege of genius."[10] The rare ability for an adult to be able to continue to see familiar things as new constitutes the experience of wonder. For an artist to be able to inspire that feeling in his or her audience is to successfully use the technique of "defamiliarization" or "making strange" ["остранение"] as defined by Viktor Shklovsky in his seminal essay, "Art as Technique" (1917).[11]

This wonder has often been born of spontaneous, close observation of the natural world in childhood. Biographer Janet Browne describes how Darwin pursued natural history "with total absorption" from a very early age.[12] His passion for observing the natural world, especially beetles, led him to create "entirely imaginary achievements": "He often told lies about seeing rare birds. Other times, more complicated stories emerged." He admits lying "for the pure pleasure of exciting attention & surprise," and Browne tells us, "to lie, and to make secret places and languages, was to construct a new world order. Natural history, even at such an early age, was for him inseparably linked with the heady power of games and creative speculation."[13]

Browne could have been writing about Tolstoy, who as a young child was also preoccupied with observation of the natural world, with the telling of lies, and with playing games.[14] In *Childhood* Tolstoy's ten-year-old alter ego Nikolai scrutinizes the ants: "They hurried one after another along the smooth tracks they had made for themselves, some carrying burdens, others un-laden. I picked up a twig and barred their way. It was a sight to see how some of them, despising the danger, crawled underneath and others climbed over it."[15] He is then suddenly distracted by the beauty of a butterfly and the appearance of a hare. Later that day he tries, unsuccessfully, with blue paint to transmit his wonder, his emotion about the day, his raw experience into art. He is ashamed and disgusted by his failure. But his efforts to transmit that wonder nevertheless continue.

E. O. Wilson describes how, as a teenager, "I had schooled myself in natural history... during solitary excursions... [in] my native state. I saw science, by which I meant (and in my heart I still mean) the study of ants, frogs, and snakes, as a wonderful way to stay outdoors."[16] Soon afterward, Wilson's professor at Cornell, having listened to him "natter for a while about [his] lofty goal of classifying all the ants of Alabama," hands him a copy of Ernst Mayr's *Systematics and the Origin of Species* (1942). Wilson undergoes what he describes as an "epiphany." Sounding almost like Tolstoy, he uses the language of religious conversion: "I saw the world in a wholly new way."[17] Observation of the natural world and meditations upon it spark innumerable epiphanies and religious conversions in Tolstoy's fictional and non-fictional writings.

Annie Dillard describes her creative impulses as resembling the motions of an inchworm and goes on to imagine the creative process of the writer through an extended analogy: "The line of words is a fiber optic, flexible as wire; it illumines the path just before its fragile tip. You probe with it, delicate as a worm. Few sights are so absurd as that of an inchworm leading its dimwit life.... It is a skinny bright green thing, pale and thin as a vein, an inch long, and apparently totally unfit for life in this world. It wears out its days in constant panic. Every inchworm I have seen was stuck in long grasses." Yet Dillard goes on to describe the inchworm's precarious, often panic-stricken, progress up the blade of grass—"every step brings it to the universe's rim."[18] Cannot one easily imagine the mighty, weighty Tolstoy as an inchworm, stuck in long grasses and seeking to measure, with every step, the rim of his universe? Such is the creative process: the primary impulse of unpremeditated, sudden wonder through observation—"measuring the marigold"[19]—followed by the perseverance in this activity despite the heavy odds of failure.

This raw experience of wonder through observation seems nearly identical for the scientist and the creative artist. In his play *Arcadia*, Tom Stoppard's young heroine, Thomasina, who invents statistical mechanics fifty years before Boltzmann, is an ardent lover of poetry, mathematics, and nature. She tells her tutor Septimus: "Each week I plot your equations dot for dot, xs against ys in all manner of algebraical relation, and every week they draw themselves as commonplace geometry, as if the world of forms were nothing but arcs and angles. God's truth, Septimus, if there is an equation for a curve like a bell, there must be an equation for one like a bluebell, and if a bluebell, why not a rose?"[20] And in *Boyhood* [*Отрочество*, 1854] young Nikolai muses about symmetry:

> Another time, standing before the blackboard and drawing various figures on it with chalk, the thought suddenly struck me: "Why does symmetry please the eye? What is symmetry?"—"It is an innate feeling," I answered myself. "What is it based on? Is there symmetry in everything in life? On the

contrary, this is life"—and I drew an oval on the board. "When life ends the soul passes into eternity—here is eternity" and I drew a line from one side of the oval figure right to the edge of the board. "Why is there no corresponding line on the other side? And yes, indeed, how can eternity be only on one side? We must have existed before this life, though we have lost the recollection of it." This argument, which seemed to me exceedingly novel and clear and whose logic I can now perceive only with difficulty, pleased me mightily.[21]

This passage is also significant in the evolution of Tolstoy's literary style, for it may be the earliest instance in his fiction of a "reported dialogue" between two different aspects of a character (a common technique of Tolstoy's). Interestingly, in this particular excerpt there is a third version of the self, for the dialogue is being reported by the adult that the child has become. This layered narrative is a consistent feature (which Tolstoy eventually found limiting) of the narrative texture of the trilogy as a whole: the child narrator, the adult narrator—a young man of twenty-four—are orchestrated by the author, Tolstoy, who allows himself occasional aphoristic intrusions into the text.[22]

These children, fictional and real, school us in the nature of the creative impulse and its frequent fascination with the natural world, closely observed, played with, and then eventually transfigured into science or art.

In *Wonder and Science* Mary Baine Campbell is careful to distinguish the experience of wonder from the experience of the sublime. She describes wonder as something that "arrests the gaze, the intellect, the emotions, because (consciously at least) it leads nowhere, reminds us of nothing. It has no value. As a result, wonder is a form of perception now mostly associated with innocence. . . . And of course artists."[23] In the wide-ranging passages I have drawn upon here, it is the complete openness to experience—most precisely the experience of wonder, the willingness to let observation lead where it will, whether to scientific pursuit, to lies, or to making art—that constitutes part of what is essential to the creative impulse. Tolstoy's intense experiences of wonder, evident throughout his fiction and formally articulated first in *Childhood*, and his willingness to follow the tracks and implications of his own observations in his diaries, his fiction, his non-fictional writings, and, indeed, in his life—wherever they might lead—have alternately invoked joy and despair in Tolstoy himself and in his readers.

But what about play? The creative impulse in any discipline is more akin to play than to method. The scientific method, the sonnet form—these may indicate the important rules of a game, but they are always provisional, as is knowledge in any discipline or innovative expression in art. Without play there would be no actual creation. The scientist and the artist are always at play with both their subject matter and the standard methods or forms for its expression. The much discussed "eureka moment," as satisfying as it must be, is always transitory. The structure of a gene may be elaborated, a poem or a short story completed, but the creative impulse to play continues. Indeed, the rise of modern science may emanate not from a Puritan or Protestant ethic, as is so often claimed, but rather from a fully hedonist impulse and an uninhibited courage in the formation of hypotheses.[24] Richard Feynman tells us that it was through "*play* with physics" that he "ultimately worked out what the motion of the mass particles is." He describes being in a cafeteria and seeing "some guy, fooling around, throw a plate in the air. As the plate went up in the air I saw it wobble . . . I had nothing to do, so I start[ed] to figure out the motion of the rotating plate . . . for the fun of it. . . . It was effortless. It was easy to play with these things. It was like uncorking a bottle."[25]

It is always dangerous, however, to try to render the reality of play into a theory of play, a discourse of play, or a dictum that one must play.

To return to Tolstoy—we know that the games that he played, both positive and negative, were vital to his subsequent artistic work. Indeed, one can understand much about Tolstoy's moral views through his depictions of games—whether "Robinson," "robbers," cards (especially the card game "Happy Families"), egg-rolling, horse-racing, hunting, or war. Most often recalled by critics is the story of the green stick. Tolstoy's older brother formed with the younger boys an "Ant Brotherhood," which became an elaborate game they played throughout childhood. The name of their brotherhood may well have been a misunderstanding of "Моравские братья" ("*Moravskie bratia*," "Moravian Brothers"), which the brothers probably "transformed" into "Муравейные братья" ("*Muraveinye bratia*," "Ant Brothers"). The latter name certainly made more sense for Tolstoy who, as a child, was so interested in the world of nature around him, especially the ants and the bees. These creatures, as I have written elsewhere, "exist enmeshed in a brotherhood that transcends the life of the individual, yet where individual choices and desires exist.

Entry into the Tolstoy children's 'brotherhood' had impossible but wonderful requirements such as to 'stand in a corner and not think of a white bear.'"[26] Somewhere, Tolstoy's brother told them, he had buried a green stick the discovery of which could make all men good and happy. Of course the children never found it, but at the end of his long and tumultuous life, Tolstoy asked to be buried in its vicinity. The game, freely embraced, endured a lifetime.

But such spontaneous, positive, creative play cannot be mandated. Think of poor Pip in Charles Dickens' *Great Expectations* when he is first brought to Miss Havisham's "to play." "'I am tired,' said Miss Havisham. 'I want diversion, and I have done with men and women. Play . . . play, play, play!'" The adult narrator Pip then comments, "I think it will be conceded by my most disputatious reader that she could hardly have directed an unfortunate boy to do anything in the wide world more difficult to be done under the circumstances."[27]

The creative impulse in each of these broad areas—science and art—is virtually identical. It is no accident that Albert Einstein is reported to have said that Dostoevsky had influenced his thinking about the theory of relativity more than anyone, even the German mathematician and scientist Carl Friedrich Gauss. Tolstoy used his practical and scientific fascination with bees and swarm intelligence to try to understand in history the chaos of individual choices and acts, the potent mixtures of freedom of choice with determinism.[28] Had he been alive today, he would likely have had a profound interest in chaos theory. James Gleick writes in his book *Chaos*:

> Watch two bits of foam flowing side by side at the bottom of a waterfall. What can you guess about how close they were at the top? Nothing. . . . Traditionally when physicists saw complex results, they looked for complex causes . . . The modern study of chaos began with the creeping realization in the 1960s that quite simple mathematical equations could model systems every bit as violent as a waterfall. Tiny differences in input could quickly become overwhelming differences in output. . . . In weather for example, this translates into what is only half-jokingly known as the Butterfly Effect.[29]

As I have suggested elsewhere, Sophocles, Shakespeare, Honoré de Balzac, Dickens, Dostoevsky, Henry James, Virginia Woolf—many literary artists—have experimented for centuries with creative fractals, with small changes of input that result in vast differences of outcome, not unlike those of chaos theory.³⁰ One could argue that this may be the primary focus of both *The Brothers Karamazov* [*Братья Карамазовы*, 1880] and especially *War and Peace*, but that is the subject for a different essay. At any rate, the creative impulse of the scientist and the artist is as one.

A Return to Childhood

It is illuminating to read Tolstoy's trilogy *Childhood, Boyhood, Youth* [*Юность*, 1857] with broad considerations like these in mind. Tolstoy's preoccupation with his own childhood, with the depiction of childhood in fiction, and with actual childhood in general (both as he observed it in the world and through the works of writers like Laurence Sterne, Jean-Jacques Rousseau, Rodolphe Toepffer, and, to my mind, especially Dickens, as well as Charlotte Brontë, to the extent that her novel *Jane Eyre* [1847] is refracted through *David Copperfield* [1850]), suggests that he would have engaged in contemporary conversations about the creative impulse and the child.³¹

The entire trilogy *Childhood, Boyhood, Youth* offers an uncanny medley of the questions, locales, and narrative techniques that were to engross, inspire, and trouble Tolstoy throughout his life. The trilogy constitutes a virtual workbook for his future written output. *Childhood* alone has important scenes of *ostranenie* [making strange], descriptions of a holy fool, close observations of animals in nature, a hunt, a death, a "first love," a rivalry, a ball, and many other such elements that were to become touchstones of Tolstoy's later work. How do wonder, observation, and play figure in the world of lies, betrayal, and art with which the ten-year-old hero of *Childhood* grapples in the course of his moral and aesthetic growth?

Despite Tolstoy's later dismissal of this work as sentimental, *Childhood, Boyhood, Youth* forms a seamless piece with his entire oeuvre; indeed, such a late work as *What is Art?* [*Что такое искусство?*, 1892] can be read in part as a companion to this earliest of works. In 1903 Tolstoy was asked to write his reminiscences of childhood. At that time, he reread the trilogy. He deemed it so dishonest and sentimental that he regretted having written it: "It is so bad, so literary, so insincerely written."³² But a few years later, in 1910, shortly before his death, Tolstoy is said to have told V. Bulgakov: "When I was writing *Childhood*, it seemed to me that prior to me no one had ever felt or expressed all the poetry and wonder of childhood."³³ This statement implies a deep affection for his early work. Clearly the old Tolstoy was ambivalent about this work, in part because in later life he emphasized its autobiographical aspects, which were of course inaccurate, and minimized the novelistic, since by then he had largely repudiated the novel as a genre.

Although as a young man Tolstoy had, on the contrary, insisted on the fictionality of his work, his own family, as well as Nekrasov, had all gravitated toward reading it as autobiography, even though the author's name was only given as L. N., which in itself argues, as Wachtel trenchantly points out, for its fictive essence. Wachtel observes: "There is evidence showing that the final version of *Childhood* contained enough autobiographical material for Tolstoy's immediate family to recognize themselves."[34] A.V. Goldenveizer describes the moment of recognition quite dramatically. It seems that I.S. Turgenev read *Childhood* aloud to Tolstoy's sister and brother before the identity of the author had been revealed: "From the very first lines Mariia Nikolaevna and Sergei Nikolaevich were stunned: 'But that's us he described! Who is this? At first we just couldn't think about Lyovochka,' continued Mariia Nikolaevna. 'He had gotten into debt and been taken off to the Caucasus. In all probability we thought about brother Nikolai.'"[35]

In general, the reception of *Childhood* in Russia was positive. Russians all along the political spectrum, from Chernyshevsky to the Tsar, admired the work. Dostoevsky wrote to Maikov from Siberia in 1856, "I like L.T. very much, but in my opinion he won't write much (perhaps I'm mistaken however)."[36] Tolstoy himself writes to his brother in December of 1856: "I learned the other day that the Emperor read my *Childhood* to his wife and wept."[37]

It is amusing, in contrast, against this backdrop of universal praise, to read the first review of *Childhood* in English (based on a poor translation). The reviewer seems to have missed entirely the point of the novel. An unsigned *Saturday Review* article characterized the "whole production" as "insipid," as a work whose "merits" are "mostly negative." The reviewer reads the work as purely autobiographical and chastises the author (Nikolai Tolstoy!) "for describing the shortcomings of his father to the world."[38]

There is another layer of irony in the fact that, against Tolstoy's wishes, Nekrasov had entitled the work *The History of My Childhood* [*История моего детства*], instead of simply *Childhood*, as Tolstoy had wished. We know that Tolstoy considered the work fiction and maintained that Nekrasov's title erroneously and without his permission implied that it was an autobiography. Tolstoy's later removal of the word "history" from Nekrasov's version of the title may also suggest that even at this early stage in his career he believed that the writing of true histories was impossible. Certainly, the other work that Tolstoy was laboring over at the same time, "The History of Yesterday" ["История вчерашнего дня"] is also an exploration of the impossibility of writing history, even a history of something as simple as one day—yesterday. *Childhood* explores the ways in which lies, self-interest, imagination, and the haze of memory distort any attempts to render an accurate account of any event, no matter how simple. From the outset of the novel, events, its "real events," are shaped and conditioned by lies—by false accounts—of events that never happened, and the ensuing chains of causality—real in the world of this novel—are forged from the combination of the real and the non-real or imaginary. This models the way Tolstoy later presents the workings of "history" writ large in works such as *The Sevastopol Tales* [*Севастопольские рассказы*, 1854-57)] and *War and Peace*.

The opening of the novel, with Nikolai awakening from sleep, illustrates this point: the young Nikolai wakes up because his tutor, Karl Ivanych, has swatted at a fly just over his head. The dead fly drops onto his head, and, still pretending to be asleep, Nikolai peeks out from under the bedclothes to knock the dead fly to the floor.

This incident precipitates a flurry of emotion in Nikolai: a sense of indignity, injustice, jealousy, and a belief that Karl Ivanych is being deliberately nasty to him. He finds everything about Karl Ivanych "disgusting" ["противный"], down to the tassel on Karl Ivanych's skull cap. Through this angry haze Nikolai is simultaneously aware of his love for Karl Ivanych, who starts to tickle his heels. Alarmed that he could have had such horrid thoughts and now annoyed with himself, he starts to laugh and cry at the same time. Nikolai reports, "I felt ashamed and could not understand how only a moment before I had hated Karl Ivanych."[39] In the meantime, Karl Ivanych becomes alarmed by Nikolai's tears. Nikolai, who has experienced at least ten different emotions within the space of a second or two, is suddenly overcome by affection for all the things about Karl Ivanych he has just hated; "even the tassel" seems a testament to Karl Ivanych's goodness. The result? Nikolai instinctively, without premeditation, tells a lie: he tells Karl Ivanych that he has been crying because he had dreamed that his mother had died. The lie works to good effect—Karl Ivanych tenderly tries to comfort him.

It then seems to Nikolai that he actually had had the dream, and his tears become genuine. The imaginary dream—the lie—becomes powerful and takes its important place amongst the real events of the day. Nikolai's false account becomes entwined with the real and completely inseparable from it. Moreover, he uses the language of creativity rather than moral censure to describe his self-serving lie: "I invented [выдумал] all this."[40] The coexisting feelings of vexation and affection for KarI Ivanych, who has utterly failed to realize the range of emotions his swatting of the fly has provoked, and the fact of the dead fly unceremoniously dropping on the child's head, provoke Nikolai's lie—a lie told instinctively to mask these genuine feelings. The lie instantly earns him attention and sympathy; it also becomes more real to him than the initial event that inspired him to lie (the killing of the fly), which is almost forgotten. Instead, "the melancholy thoughts occasioned by the dream I had invented still haunted me."[41]

Most interesting perhaps, Nikolai has twice used the word "invention" for his lie. In his ten-year-old mind, he did not lie; he *invented* a dream, although the adult narrator (who is twenty-four) presents this account as a lie. His lie was an instinctive, unpremeditated creative impulse, a literary invention that worked successfully on both himself and his audience, and, once invented, it became somehow true. This first page of Tolstoy's first work thus radiates precisely the ambivalences about the making of fictions and the attempts at historical accounts that were to remain with him until his death.[42] The lie also turns out to have predictive value.

This last real day of Nikolai's childhood before he departs to Moscow with his father marks both an example of a perfect typical day from childhood and the end of such days.[43] (This technique, in which a very particular day stands for many such days but is also the last of them, is reminiscent of the way in which Dickens in *David Copperfield* has his first-person narrator portray his idyllic childhood and its abrupt end when his mother marries Mr. Murdstone, although the periodic "reverie retrospectives" that Dickens inserts in the voice of his adult narrator David are far more sentimental than the comparable passages in *Childhood*.)

Even as this lie becomes real to him, it is necessary, almost immediately, to hide it in the same way as he had hidden by means of this very lie his initial, genuine, complicated emotions precipitated by the dropping of the dead fly. The lie about the dream, which converges with a kind of truth, is dangerous. In the opening of the second chapter, "Mamma," the adult narrator's retrospective tone alerts the reader immediately that Nikolai's mother is dead, although we do not yet know how soon she will die. The adult narrator tells us that "so many memories of the past arise when one recalls the features of somebody we love that one sees those features dimly through the memories, as though through tears."[44] Here, in an early Tolstoyan simile—a primary hallmark of his later writing—memories are likened to abundant and free-flowing tears, but because there are so many of them, they dim the primary thing which the speaker wishes to remember. The mist of tears provokes a synecdoche of recollection, where the dear remembered parts must stand in for the whole: he remembers her brown eyes, the mole on her neck just below the place where the short hairs grow, her embroidered white collar, and the delicate dry hand that so often caressed him and that he would cover with kisses. But "the complete image" escapes him. Are the recollected parts more evocative than a complete description would be? Here the reader witnesses Tolstoy developing his technique for physical description: we remember each of his characters in his many subsequent works of fiction precisely through such vivid, living descriptions of a few features. The part is greater than the whole.

His mother asks him if he has been crying. And then, "What were you crying about?"[45] Instinctively, instantly, he lies again, this time to shield her from the dream he never had. "'I cried in my sleep, mamma,' I said, remembering my invented [again, the language of creativity, not of falsehood] dream in all its details and involuntarily shuddering at the recollection."[46]

The lie—the invention—continues to exert force and becomes ever more real. By the next chapter, "Papa," the lie has become, simply, true. Nikolai and his brother learn that they will travel with their father to Moscow that night to live with their grandmother. This news is a "terrible shock." Nikolai's instant reaction is to find predictive value in his lie: "So this is what my dream forboded? ... God grant there may be nothing worse to follow."[47] His lie, within a short time, first earns him comfort and attention to soothe his bruised ego about the fly-swatting incident; it quickly precipitates the necessity for its own cover-up ("I cried in my sleep," also a lie), and, as it gains authoritative force, it is validated by the news that the boys are to leave their mother and move to

Moscow. Of course, the worst—his mother's death—is yet to come. By the time she does die, Nikolai's lie, his predictive dream, has been temporarily forgotten.

The next significant instance of Nikolai's creative impulse—his inventiveness whether in lies or vivid imaginings—occurs a few hours later during the hunt. He is assigned to wait and watch in a particular glade for the hare. He lies in the grass at the foot of an oak with the dog Zhiran, and he recollects: "My imagination as usual on such occasions far outstripped reality."[48] He imagines himself pursuing "at least" his third hare. Then, lulled by the noise of the actual hunt that grows fainter, he begins to observe a swarm of ants. As I have noted elsewhere, he becomes intrigued by their purposeful social activity, by how they respond, individually and as a group, to the danger he poses to them by endeavoring to bar their way with a twig. In sum, the ants act in various ways as individuals, but all of them work toward the aim of fulfilling a larger purpose for the anthill.[49] Then his "attention" becomes "diverted from these interesting observations" by a "butterfly with yellow wings fluttering most alluringly." Thoughts about social order give way to aesthetic considerations, to "the delight" of gazing at a butterfly. Suddenly the hare appears, and he releases the dog too soon. His reveries give way to shame and mortification—his mistake has been observed by the expert peasant hunter Turka. "For a long time I stood where I was in deep despair... only repeating as I slapped my thighs, 'Heavens, what have I done!'"[50] There is no overt lie here, but his creative impulses—his imagining of himself as the hero of a successful hunt and his dreamy observations of the ants and the butterfly—have distracted him from the actual hunt and resulted in another instance of mortification. Imagination and observation collide with efficient performance in the moment. As with the lie (the invented dream), once again the course of events is effected by the processes occurring in his mind. Here the outcome of the hunt for Nikolai has been altered not by concrete events but by the results of his own imaginings and reveries: the ants, the butterfly, and the fictive hares help the real hare to escape.

Next comes a foray into the imaginary world of games. After the hunt Nikolai's sister Liuba proposes that they play a favorite game, "Robinson," which consists in the children's enactment of scenes from the novel *The Swiss Family Robinson* [*Der Schweitzerische Robinson*, 1812] by Johann David Wyss. The creative impulse shifts here from the individual (lies, imaginings, reveries) to the group and the goal is, simply, to have fun through the collective exercise of imagination. This goal can be thwarted, however, if a single member of the group refuses to join in. Nikolai's older brother, Volodia, destroys "all the fun of the game" by his "lazy bored look." Volodia engages in a kind of reverse *ostranenie*, where, instead of something familiar being rendered strange by describing it in a new, elemental way, something playful and imaginary is rendered commonplace and boring. "When we sat on the ground, and pretending we were going fishing, began to row with all our might, Volodia sat with folded arms in an attitude which had nothing in common with the attitude of a fisherman.... Such talk and behavior had a damping effect on the game and were extremely distasteful, the more so because in one's secret heart one had to admit that Volodia was right."[51] Nikolai remembers other such games—of hunting birds with a stick, of driving on chairs, of turning an arm-chair into a carriage on long winter nights. He exclaims: "And what adventures we used to meet on the way, and how gaily and swiftly those winter evenings passed! ... If you only go by what's real there won't be any games. And if there are no games, what is left?"[52] To play a game and know that it is not real but still to engage in it is to take a collective leap of faith, to play in the moment, to share and to have fun. This may be the ideal expression of the creative impulse.

Negative variations of game playing exist as well. Later in the novel, in Moscow, the younger Nikolai develops a kind of crush on the handsome, but morally compromised, Seriozha (who resembles the brave and handsome but immoral Steerforth whom the young David Copperfield so idolizes). He admires Seriozha's physical bravery for playing "Robbers" after having been injured: "I cannot express how impressed and enthralled I was by this heroic behavior: in spite of terrible pain he not only did not cry—he did not even show that he was hurt, or for a moment forget the game." (The analogy to war as a game is clear.)[53] Shortly afterwards, the poor and less attractive Ilinka Grap arrives, and when the boys go upstairs to show off their gymnastic prowess to each other, the act of playing turns ugly. Led by Seriozha, who increasingly resembles Steerforth in his combination of social snobbery, cruelty, bullying, and seductive power over the young narrator, Nikolai and the other boys force the unwilling Ilinka to stand on his head. The "cries of despair" of "the unfortunate victim," Nikolai admits, "encouraged us the more." The narrator depicts an incident of pure bullying in a game. Ilinka, endeavoring to right himself, inadvertently kicks Seriozha in the eye. Heroic no longer, he pushes Ilinka "with all his might." Ilinka crashes to the floor yet again and mutters through his tears, "Why do you bully [тираните] me?"⁵⁴ Nikolai knows that his participation in this game has been wrong; he feels compassion for Ilinka but continues to admire Seriozha.

The adult narrator realizes what the child Nikolai does not—that Ilinka was crying not from pain but from being rejected for no reason by five boys whom he probably liked. The adult Nikolai asks himself why he had engaged in such cruel behavior: "Where was my tender heart which often caused me to sob wildly at the sight of a young jackdaw pushed out of its nest, or a puppy being thrown over a fence, or a chicken the cook was going to make soup of?"⁵⁵ He realizes that these instincts had been stifled by his affection for Seriozha and his desire to be attractive to him. The chapter closes with one of the only false notes in the novel, a sentimental outburst that is Rousseauian in its self-exoneration and dishonesty. "Contemptible then were both the affection and my wish to be a fine fellow, for they left *the only dark spots* on the pages of my childhood's recollections!"⁵⁶ Why the narrator chooses to ignore other such dark spots in his novel, spots that he has delineated for us in such detail but does not explicitly name as "dark spots," the reader can only conjecture. Indeed, most of the episodes described in any detail in *Childhood* constitute precisely such dark spots. Is it because these other dark episodes had something to do with creativity in some way? Nor does he seem to dwell upon this disturbing episode with Ilinka with particular shame. He seems deliberately to endeavor to cast a significant episode into a more minor key.

To return to the countryside and the day of the hunt—that evening the children gather with paper, pencils, and paints and their mother sits down to play the piano. Nikolai sets out to recreate the experience of his day through artistic representation of it: "I only had blue paint; but for all that I took it into my head to draw a picture of the hunt. After representing in very lively style a blue boy on a blue horse, and some blue dogs, I stopped, uncertain whether one could paint a blue hare, and ran into Papa's study to consult him."⁵⁷ The creative impulses of the child are in full swing at this point; his artistic vision can easily encompass a blue boy, fence, horse, and dog but it stops short at a blue hare. Why? Could it be that the hare and his shame at not catching it were the sources of genuine feeling for him in this episode, and thus its color must somehow be differentiated from the others?

He goes to consult his father: "Papa was reading something and in answer to my question 'Are there blue hares?' replied without lifting his head, 'Yes, my dear, there are.'"[58] Nikolai returns to the table, paints a blue hare, but "finds it necessary to turn it into a bush." He does "not like" the bush either and makes it into a tree, "then the tree into a hayrick, and the hayrick into a cloud, until finally I had so smeared my whole sheet of paper with blue paint that I tore it up in vexation and went off to meditate in the high-backed arm-chair."[59] What has happened?

The reader has witnessed a child engaged in acting upon a series of creative impulses. But impulse quickly gives way to process and to product. The child asks an adult for advice and guidance ("Are there blue hares?"). When the preoccupied adult gives an automatic, untrue answer, the consequences for the child are significant.[60] It is one thing to draw a blue hare from the pleasure of imagination; it is another to ask an authority if such a creature exists and to be told it does. Reality, an untruth about it, and an artistic impulse collide in an unsatisfactory way. Nikolai's attempt at authentic artistic creation—rendering his day's experience directly into art—fails, although such direct transformation of the real into art is the ideal way for artistic creation to work, as Tolstoy himself was to argue eloquently both in later fictional works like *Anna Karenina* in the scenes with the painter Mikhailov, and in the non-fictional "What is Art?" Here, toward the end of his life, Tolstoy writes:

> To evoke in oneself a feeling one has once experienced, and having evoked it in oneself, then, by means of movements, lines, colors, sounds, or forms expressed in words, so to transmit that feeling that others may experience the same feeling—that is the activity of art. . . . Art is a human activity consisting in this, that one man consciously, by means of certain external signs, hands on to others feelings he has lived through, and that other people are infected by these feelings and also experience them.[61]

Young Nikolai has been engaging fully in that "activity of art." Although his ten-year-old self may have failed to pass on through the external signs of his blue paint what he has lived through, his twenty-four-year-old self has, without question, succeeded in infecting his readers.

Meanwhile, in the drawing room, Nikolai's mother is playing the piano—the second concerto of Field and then Beethoven's *Sonata pathétique*. The music affects Nikolai's memory powerfully: "My memories became sad, oppressive and gloomy. Mamma often played those two pieces and so I well remember the feelings they aroused in me. They resembled memories—but memories of what? It almost seemed as if I were remembering something that had never been."⁶² Not only does this passage clearly prefigure what was to become Tolstoy's stance toward music at the end of his life, it also grafts powerfully onto the range of associations connected with the lie Nikolai had told earlier that day. The lie—the undreamed dream of his mother's death—had affected Nikolai in ways similar to music. By the end of the day Nikolai is haunted by both a dream he never dreamt and by memories he never had. Yet these non-events are central to the later depiction of his childhood, and they are thus in some ways as real as anything else. As with the false dream, the lie—the false recollection—can become real and thus functions disturbingly as a kind of truth.

Correspondingly, "the truth" can also be a kind of lie. Right after Nikolai listens to his mother play the piano, he wanders to the door of his father's study where his father has been meeting privately with Karl Ivanych. The adult narrator reproduces an actual document: a detailed "expense account" that Karl Ivanych had presented his father for costs beyond his salary. "Reading this note, in which Karl Ivanych demanded payment of all the money he had spent on presents, and even the price of a present promised to himself, anyone would conclude that Karl Ivanych was nothing but an unfeeling mercenary egoist—and everyone would be wrong."⁶³ The accurate, detailed list of expenses misrepresents the essence of its author; it constitutes a kind of false evidence. Lies can express truth; a truthful list of facts can be a drastic distortion of what the list is actually seeking to convey. Although he never explores this dichotomy further, this paradox is what Nikolai learns on this last day of his childhood in the country.

Nikolai's day ends much as it had begun—with a flurry of emotion in which feelings of having been insulted by a social inferior, anger, and shame give way to love. The day had begun with the dead fly dropping on his head; it ends with another undignified assault to his head, this time the memory of such an event. Nikolai recalls how once, when he had stained the tablecloth with some *kvass* (a lightly fermented beverage), Natalya Savishna had sprung out at him after dinner. He remembers that she "caught hold of me and despite desperate resistance on my part began rubbing my face with the wet cloth, 'Don't thee go dirtying tablecloths, don't thee go dirtying tablecloths.'" I was so offended that I howled with rage."⁶⁴ As with Karl Ivanych, his fury gives way to love and shame when, a few minutes later, she asks his forgiveness ("Forgive an old fool") and gives him two caramels and a grape wrapped in red paper. The experience of shame infuses all the important moments of *Childhood* in one way or another—the hunt, his painting, his poem, his bullying of Ilinka, his mother's death. Curiously, Tolstoy later maintained that it can be a good thing for a child to witness an adult's shame when that adult has made a mistake. In an 1865 letter to Countess A. A. Tolstaya, Tolstoy writes:

> But you can't deceive children—they are wiser than us. We want to prove to them that we're intelligent, but they aren't at all interested in this, but want to know whether we're honest, truthful, good, and compassionate, whether we have a conscience, and unfortunately they see that beyond our efforts to appear infallibly intelligent, there's nothing else at all. To make a mistake in front of a child, to be carried away, to do something stupid, humanly stupid, even to behave badly and blush in front of a child and admit it, has far more educational value than to make a child blush 100 times in front of you, and to be infallible. A child knows that we are more resolute, more experienced than he is, and we are always able to retain this halo of infallibility in front of him, but he knows that this doesn't require much, and he doesn't value such cleverness, but values the flush of shame appearing on my face against my will, telling him about all that is most secret and best in my soul. I remember how Karl Ivanych once blushed in front of me.⁶⁵

For all of Dostoevsky's preoccupation with shame and its ramifications, he never depicted the positive aspects of a child witnessing an adult's shame. Ilyusha Snegirov perhaps comes closest in his attempt to gain retribution on behalf of his shamed father (after he witnesses Dmitri Karamazov pull at his father's beard in public), but his attempts, while deeply moving, do not have any positive outcome.

The end of these childhood days in the country is marked by a retrospective chapter that seems modeled on the several similar chapters the narrator in *David Copperfield* employs to demarcate various stages in his autobiography—his childhood, boyhood, and youth. Like Dickens, Tolstoy creates a narrative that mixes the general with the specific, in which the latter becomes the former. Likewise, there is experimentation with perspective. The little David, overcome with drowsiness, is sitting by the fire with his beloved Peggotty (the literary model for Natalya Savishna): "I had reached the stage of sleepiness when

Peggotty seemed to swell and grow immensely large. I propped my eyelids open with my two forefingers, and looked perseveringly at her as she sat at work."[66] Tolstoy reverses the equation—his mother grows tiny, and instead of propping his eyes open like David, Nikolai squints them mostly shut. Gazing with adoration at his mamma, "with eyes drowsy with slumber . . . all at once she becomes quite, quite little, her face no bigger than a button; but I see it just as plainly still . . . I like seeing her so tiny. I screw my eyes tighter still, and now she is no bigger than a little boy reflected in the pupil of an eye, but I move and the spell is broken."[67] Here the creative impulse of the child mingles with a near dreamlike state: "Vague sweet visions fill your mind, the healthy sleep of childhood weighs your eyelids down."[68]

The opening of the novel, in which Nikolai told the lie about dreaming that his mother had died, now takes on frightening overtones by the end of this chapter, also entitled "Childhood." The adult narrator, with extreme tenderness, lays bare the passionate force of his love for his dead mother and his living memories of her. His creative reverie transports him to the past. She brings the drowsing child up to bed: "There are no onlookers to restrain her and she is not afraid to pour out all her tenderness and love on me. I do not move but kiss and kiss her hand. . . . She puts her other hand round the back of my head and her slender fingers run over my neck, tickling me. . . . I feel all quivery with being tickled and roused from sleep; mamma is sitting close beside me; she touches me; I am aware of her scent and her voice. . . . 'Oh, dear dear mamma, I do love you so!'"[69] Her reply brings us firmly back to the beginning of the novel, "If mamma was no longer here, you would not forget her? You would not forget her, little Nikolai?" Tears stream from his cheeks, and the chapter ends with the narrator's retrospective, sentimental celebration of those tears—"the finest gift of all—the pure tears of emotion."[70] This scene (besides being drawn from *David Copperfield*) recuperates in an unsettling way the opening of the novel: Nikolai is again tickled and caressed in bed, the theme of the loss of the mother is sounded, tears abound. But where the first scene reflected the emotional complexities of childhood with its anger, shame, lies, love, and creativity, the second—composed of nearly identical elements—renders them in the language of aching, intimate, sentimental love for a lost mother. Both are the product of the creative impulses and processes of a child; both are works of art.

In Moscow Volodia and Nikolai must each produce an artistic creation on demand: something for their grandmother's name day. Volodia, under the strict direction of the drawing master, executes in black crayon the head of a Turk in a turban. Nikolai decides to write a poem. The first two verses come to him easily, complete with rhymes. Then, "try as I would I could not produce any more."[71] The would-be poet searches for inspiration from books, not from his own direct experience, "but neither Dmitriev nor Derzhavin helped me at all—far from it, they convinced me still more of my own inability."[72] He snoops amidst Karl Ivanych's private papers for inspiration and finds, amongst transcriptions of German poems, one written by Karl Ivanych himself in Russian—a love poem. The child Nikolai in his prying does not acknowledge his betrayal of Karl Ivanych by this act. Moved by the poem (a very poor one), he memorizes it to use as a model.

Once his own poem is completed, he copies it (after several attempts) onto good paper. It concludes, he tells us, "thus: To comfort thee we shall endeavour, / And love thee like our own dear mother" ["Стараться будем утешать / И любим, как родною мать"]. Nikolai thinks to himself that the lines sound "quite fine" but acknowledges that "in a strange way the last line offended my ear."[73] He had chosen the last word "mother" for purely formal reasons—to rhyme with the last word of the previous line. He rereads the poem to himself (complete with gestures) up in his room, and although he recognizes other flaws in the poem, he is not overly concerned with them. "The last line, however," he recollects, "struck me even more forcibly and disagreeably than before."[74] He finally realizes that he had allowed the need for a rhyme to lead him to a lie: "Why did I put that? Why did I write a lie? Of course it's only poetry but I needn't have done *that*!"[75] Only poetry! He has committed an act of betrayal. Filled with dread, he joins the others in the drawing room to present their gifts. He has imagined his "good-for-nothing verses would be read out in front of everybody, and the words *like our own dear mother* would clearly prove that I had never loved her and had forgotten her."[76] He expects his father, when confronted with such "plain proof of want of feeling," to rap him on the nose— another insult to his face—and say, "You horrid boy, you are not to forget your mother . . . take that!"[77]

This lie, this artistic invention, however, proves even more successful than his lie about the dream. The poem is a wild success; his father is proud; his grandmother calls it "*charmant*" ["charming"] and kisses him on the forehead—again, his head—and he continues to be praised for it throughout his grandmother's party. The germs of Tolstoy's later guilt about and repudiation of his artistic work glimmer here with fleeting, firefly clarity. Art leads to artifice and a betrayal of the truth. "Why did I write a lie?" Nikolai's question has no easy answer.

The question arises again in a slightly different form when Nikolai is flirting with Sonia at the children's ball. Managing to escape ridicule over the torn dirty glove of Karl Ivanych's that he had stolen in an effort to find a glove to wear at the dance, Nikolai instinctively turns her playful question, "Where did you find such a funny glove?" to good artistic effect. He offers up an ironic description of Karl Ivanych about "how once in his green overcoat he had fallen off his horse right into a puddle."[78] Afterwards he asks himself: "But why did I ridicule Karl Ivanych?"[79] He realizes he would not have forfeited Sonya's good opinion if he had simply told her the truth about the glove. His humorous rendering of Karl Ivanych's character constitutes both a lie (because it does not convey his real feelings about him) and a betrayal of him. As "author," Nikolai experiences both the pride of success and the pangs of guilt.

On the one hand, it might have been preferable, according to the rules Tolstoy seems to set here at the outset of his literary career, as well as elsewhere throughout his life, if Nikolai had composed his poem in direct response to his experience (like his attempt to draw the hare after the hunt) instead of using literary crutches and models. On the other hand, as Nikolai has told us, to the extent that the creative impulse is also play, a spontaneous game, it makes life worth living. "If you only go by what's real, there won't be any games. And if there are no games, what is left?" Perhaps Tolstoy himself was so critical of *Childhood* in later years because it was so redolent of his own readings of Rousseau, Sterne, Toepffer, and especially Dickens, although Tolstoy does not cite Dickens as an influence at this point. Moreover, Dickens drew heavily on the early chapters of *Jane Eyre* in composing some of the early chapters of *David Copperfield*, and those are the same chapters that hover clearly over *Childhood*. From the retrospective chapters, to the experimentations with perspective, to the depiction of the passionate love of the little boy for his mother (soon to be lost), to the pairing of the mother with the devoted, faithful servant who had also raised the mother and is beloved by the child (Peggotty/Natalya Savishna), to the dark world of male sexuality, betrayal, and rivalry hinted at in both Mr. Murdstone and Nikolai's father, and, most compelling of all, the death of the mother and the layers of grief, both false and genuine, experienced by the child—all these elements and many more find their way from *David Copperfield* to *Childhood*. We do know that Tolstoy was reading *David Copperfield* serially in Russian translation around this time, and in 1853 he asked Count S. N. Tolstoy to get it for him in English. He amusingly alludes to Mr. Micawber in an even earlier letter to his brother Nikolai, teasing him that Nikolai's recent letter to him is like one of Mr. Micawber's—"a long epistle on one sheet of notepaper, two words to a line."[80] And he reportedly named his dog Dora.[81] Most important, late in life, Tolstoy did include *David Copperfield* on the list of books that had most influenced him between the ages of sixteen and twenty. His diaries, letters, and notebooks praise the novel over a period of more than fifty years. "If you sift the world's prose literature, Dickens will remain; sift Dickens and *David Copperfield* will remain."[82]

Seven months after their arrival in Moscow, Nikolai, his brother, and his father rush back to the countryside where mamma is dying. She dies in terrible agony. Later, Nikolai's reaction to the sight of his mother's dead face offers the first extended passage of Tolstoy's later trademark technique of *ostranenie*, described so succinctly by Viktor Shklovsky:

> The purpose of art is to impart the sensation of things as they are perceived and not as they are known. The technique of art is to make objects "unfamiliar," to make forms difficult, to increase the difficulty and length of perception because the process of perception is an aesthetic end in itself and must be prolonged. Art is a way of experiencing the artfulness of an object; the object is not important. . . .The narrator of "Kholstomer" ["Strider"], for example, is a horse, and it is the horse's point of view (rather than a person's) that makes the content of the story seem unfamiliar.[83]

His mother's face had been the dearest, most familiar thing in the world for Nikolai. Now it becomes the least familiar. Gone are the brown eyes, the mole on her neck just below the place where the short hairs grow, her delicate dry hand—all the elements of the loving synecdoche that had constituted his earlier description of mother. Instead a new and frightening synecdoche presents itself to him, a familiarity suddenly bedecked with something too terrible and unknown to name takes over: "I stopped at the door and looked but my eyes were so swollen with weeping and my nerves so unstrung that I could distinguish nothing. The light, the gold brocade, the velvet, the tall candlesticks, the pink lace-trimmed pillow, the frontlet, the cap with ribbons, and something else of a transparent wax-like color—all ran together in a strange blur. I climbed on to a chair to look at her face but there in its lace I again saw the same pale-yellow translucent object."[84] The passage, with its strongly marked similarities to the experience young David Copperfield has beside his mother's body, continues in this vein.[85] This instance in Tolstoy's oeuvre of "making strange" is a making strange and terrifying of the dearest, most familiar thing in the world to Nikolai, *his mother's face.*

Nikolai also describes his shame when he remembers the elements of "self-love" in his grief—"now a desire to show that I prayed more than anyone else, now concern about the impression I was producing on others."[86] He feels even deeper shame when he observes the genuine grief of Natalya Savishna, who continues to perform her duties amidst her own terrible sense of loss.

All of these elements—the manner of describing the beloved dead mother's body and the encroachments on that description of something completely unfamiliar and initially unnamable—the physical decay wrought by death (that is, the *ostranenie*)—the acute sense the child has of the pleasure of enacting his grief in front of others while not yet feeling it acutely, the observation of one whose grief is powerful, authentic, and modest—all these elements are imported wholesale into *Childhood* directly from *David Copperfield*.[87] Yet each of these elements becomes a hallmark of Tolstoy's artistic vision. He replays each of them again and again in other works, whereas, oddly enough, Dickens does not. Tolstoy's first use of *ostranenie* and his first primer on grief may emerge straight out of *David Copperfield*, but they are purely Tolstoyan for all that. A couple of passing scenes written by one author becomes emblematic, a quiddity, for another author. The sentiment, variously attributed to T. S. Eliot and Pablo Picasso, that minor artists borrow whereas great ones steal, proves true.

Observation, play, the experience of wonder, the telling of lies, the act of betrayal, the rendering of experience through art are as entangled *en masse* in the creative impulses of children as they are in those of adults.[88] Our most vivid realities and memories are always composed of mixtures of the real with the imagined. No one has portrayed these potent mixtures as compellingly as has Tolstoy, and perhaps no one has experienced such ambivalence over the fact that this is the way things are or has struggled so hard to strip away artifice from the essential.

Endnotes

1 Dostoevsky, *ПСС*, 22:46. Quotations from Dostoevsky's fictional works are from F.M. Dostoevsky, *Полное собрание сочинений*, hereafter cited by volume and page number in parentheses. This quotation of Dostoevsky's *A Writer's Diary* [*Дневник писателя*, 1876-78] comes from the translation by Kenneth Lanz, 1:352. See also Robin Feuer Miller, *Unfinished Journey*, 76-77.

2 Ibid., 22:43. See Dostoevsky, *A Writer's Diary*, 1:347. See also Miller, *Unfinished Journey*, 19.

3 McEwan, "On John Updike," 4. McEwan is quoting from Updike's autobiography, *Self-Consciousness* (New York: Fawcett, 1990).

4 Many critics read *Childhood* as a largely cheerful, sentimental hymn to the happy memories of childhood. Andrew Wachtel, for example, writes: "If there is a simple overarching message in *Childhood*, it is that childhood is an essentially happy period" of "joyous innocence" (44). His primary interest is in how this novel set the standard for future representations of childhood in Russian fiction, and he analyzes at length the tension between Tolstoy's early descriptions of the work as a novel and his later harsh judgment of it as a failed autobiography. Wachtel also focuses on the three layers of narration present in the novel. Wachtel revisits some of these observations, placing them in a larger context in his rich and interesting *Russian Literature*, co-authored with Ilya Vinitsky, 147-151. Where Wachtel emphasizes the sentimental aspects of Tolstoy's *Childhood*, Donna Orwin argues that it was precisely Tolstoy's "realism in his depiction of children" that "affected Dostoevsky's sentimentalism. It is after the appearance of Tolstoy's trilogy that Dostoevsky ... begins his more radical exploration of the damaged psyche of the abused child. This same novel also contains his first critique of childhood as Tolstoy portrayed it" (148). Nevertheless, Orwin, like Wachtel, argues for a generally optimistic, Rousseauian, and sentimental reading of this work and the trilogy as a whole, maintaining: "The following argument emerges from the trilogy. As long as we are children, conscience is not needed, and this is happiness.

Innocence keeps children both happy and virtuous" (140). My reading discerns little happiness and even less innocence in Nikolai's experience, although the adult narrator may wish to smooth out his recollections with a patina of both. The present essay argues for a much darker reading of the work than either Wachtel or Orwin describe, in which the primary tensions are not between autobiography and fiction, but between truth and artifice, morality and play, honesty and betrayal. Justin Weir, in his excellent *Leo Tolstoy & the Alibi of Narrative*, engages, as I do here, with the theme of false memory in this novel. He labels Nikolai's account of the dream of his mother's death variously as a "false memory," "a memory that recapitulates an event that never happened," "a non-existent dream," and a "fake dream" (64, 49). My reading is grounded in a more stark and dire sense of this dream as a lie, for my focus here is on the uneasy boundaries among lies and art, betrayal and games—boundaries that confound and confuse a child's deepest sensibilities even as they help to shape them.

5 Tolstoi, *ПСС*, Chertkov edition, 1:208; quoted in Christian, *Critical Introduction*, 23. Quotations of Tolstoy's works in this essay, unless otherwise noted, come from one of two sources: the online *Полное сабрание сочинений* [*Complete Collected Works*] in 100 volumes, hereafter cited by volume and page number in parentheses, or the hardcover *Полное собрание сочинений* in 90 volumes, hereafter cited as Chertkov edition, followed by volume and page number in parentheses. See also Note 15 below.

6 Tolstoi, *ПСС*, Chertkov edition, 60:74. See the fine essay by Anne Hruska, 64.

7 Quoted in Knowles, *Tolstoy*, 59-61.

8 Dyson, "Information Flood," 10.

9 In "My heart leaps up when I behold" Wordsworth was, in part, writing about the creative impulse through his observation of nature: "My heart leaps up when I behold / A rainbow in the sky," an impulse first experienced in childhood and then throughout life.

10 Coleridge, *Biographia Literaria*, 55. In this passage, Coleridge is writing about Wordsworth.

11 "Art as Technique" ["Искусство как прием"] became the first chapter in Shklovsky's influential *Theory of Prose* [*О теории прозы*], published in 1925.

12 Browne, *Charles Darwin*, 13.
13 Ibid., 13, 15.
14 The correspondences between Darwin's and Tolstoy's experiences of childhood wonder are particularly interesting in the light of Tolstoy's growing antipathy toward Darwin's writings, even when he agreed with them. In fact, Darwin was to join the pantheon of writers of whom Tolstoy was suspicious, whom he disliked, of whom he was probably jealous, and by whom he was undoubtedly influenced: Dante, William Shakespeare, Friedrich Nietzsche, and others. Readers interested in Tolstoy and Darwin should read the outstanding chapter by Hugh McLean, "Claws on the Behind: Tolstoy and Darwin," in his *In Quest of Tolstoy*, 159-181. Tolstoy's resistance to Darwin is epitomized by the following: "When the ordinary person asks, how should I live, how [should I] relate to my family, to my neighbors, and to foreigners, how can I control my passions, what should I believe and not believe, and much else, what does our science answer him? It triumphantly tells him how many miles separate the earth from the sun, how many millions of vibrations per second in the ether constitute light, how many vibrations in the air make sound. It will tell about the chemical composition of the Milky Way, about a new element called helium, about microorganisms and their excreta . . . about X-rays and so forth. 'But I don't need any of that,' says the ordinary man. 'I need to know how to live'" (Tolstoi, *ПСС*, Chertkov edition, 31:89-90, cited in McLean, 164-65). Tolstoy's somewhat disingenuous rant also shows how carefully he kept up with developments in science.
15 Tolstoi, *ПСС*, online edition, 1:30; 34. All quotations from *Childhood, Boyhood,* and *Youth* are from volume 1 (2000-) of the online *Полное собрание сочинений* [*Complete Collected Works*] in 100 volumes, hereafter cited by volume and page number, followed by page numbers from the English translation of *Childhood, Boyhood, Youth* by Rosemary Edmonds, all in parentheses.
16 Wilson, *Consilience*, 3.
17 Ibid., 4.
18 Dillard, *Writing Life*, 7-8.
19 In an email of March, 2011, Judith Shapiro has reminded me of an old favorite, the inchworm song sung by Danny Kaye "in the movie where he

plays Hans Christian Andersen. He sings it to a group of children outside playing hooky in order to hear his stories as the other children are heard from inside the school reciting their math lesson":

(Two and two are four
Four and four are eight
Eight and eight are sixteen
Sixteen and sixteen are thirty-two.)
Inchworm, inchworm
Measuring the marigold

You and your arithmetic
You'll probably go far
Inchworm, inchworm,
Measuring the marigold
Seems to me you'd stop and see
How beautiful they are.

20 Stoppard, *Arcadia*, 37. The lovely Thomasina from Stoppard's play does indeed both measure the marigold and see its beauty. The two pursuits are simply one, facets of each other.
21 Tolstoi, *ПСС*, online edition, 165-66; 158.
22 Wachtel describes this strategy of layered narrative at length in his chapter on *Childhood* (1-57). Interestingly, Tolstoy complained that he found the narrative technique he had devised for the trilogy quite burdensome and was tempted not to complete it. He wrote to Nekrasov, "The autobiographical form that I chose and the obligatory link between the following parts and the preceding one so constrain me that I often feel the desire to abandon them and leave the first part without a continuations" (Tolstoi, *ПСС*, Chertkov edition, 1:330). This passage is cited by Wachtel in *The Battle for Childhood*, 11.
23 Campbell, *Wonder and Science*, 3-4.
24 See Lewis S. Feuer, especially p. xi.
25 Feynman, "Dignified Professor," 67.
26 Miller, "Tolstoy's Peaceable Kingdom," 58. The account Simmons gives is the most vivid in English. He states that Tolstoy's brother Nikolai told the

other boys that he possessed a wonderful secret. If it became known, a Golden Age would exist on earth—the earth would be without disease, misery, and anger. All would become "Ant Brothers" and love one another. The children, as in *Childhood*, would huddle under chairs or boxes covered with shawls. Nikolai devised conditions under which he would show them a secret place: "The first was to stand in a corner and not think of a white bear. The second was to walk along a crack in the floor without wavering; and the third was to keep from seeing a hare, alive or dead or cooked, for a whole year" (23). Nikolai also invited them to share one wish that would come true: "Seriozha wished to be able to model a horse and a hen out of wax; Mitenka wished to be able to draw everything in life size, like a real artist; and the five-year-old Liovochka, clearly puzzled, lamely wished to be able to draw things in miniature" (24). For another account of the significance of this childhood game, see Miller, "Tolstoy's Peaceable Kingdom," 58.

27 Dickens, *Great Expectations*, 88.
28 See Miller, "Tolstoy's Peaceable Kingdom," 58, 65-66. See also Thomas Newlin's excellent recent article.
29 Gleick, *Chaos*, 8.
30 See Miller, *Unfinished Journey*, 186-188, 229.
31 All of the modern critics I have already cited take these influences into account. See also the landmark work by Boris Eikhenbaum, *The Young Tolstoi*, 48-67.
32 Tolstoi, *ПСС*, Chertkov edition, 34:348-349. Wachtel discusses this passage in *The Battle for Childhood*, 14. Weir does not take this comment of Tolstoy's at face value, however. He asserts, "Wachtel's interpretation of *Childhood* may have been influenced by Tolstoy's later statements on his early fiction, especially his *Reminiscences*, a particularly untrustworthy work, which was written for a favorite biographer, Pavel Biriukov. In that work, Tolstoy accuses himself of writing *Childhood* too literally and insincerely [Tolstoi, *ПСС*, Chertkov edition, 34:348], suggesting, among other things, that he will now write 'the veritable truth' [Tolstoi, *ПСС*, Chertkov edition, 34: 345]. Eikhenbaum, who notes his lack of access to Tolstoy's archives, also relies on Biriukov, and he says much the same thing" (Weir, 247-48). Nevertheless, it still seems safe to postulate that the old Tolstoy was ambivalent about this early work.

33 Quoted in Wachtel, *Battle for Childhood,* 211.
34 Ibid., 12.
35 Ibid., 52-53.
36 Dostoevsky, *ПСС*, 28(1): 210.
37 Tolstoi, *ПСС*, Chertkov edition, 60:137. This translation comes from Christian, *Letters,* 1:84.
38 Quoted in Knowles, *Tolstoy,* 74. Unsigned review from *Saturday Review,* 29 March, 1862.
39 Tolstoi, *ПСС*, online edition, 3-4; 13-14.
40 Ibid., 1:11; 14.
41 Ibid., 1:12; 14.
42 Tolstoy would use this technique again, as, for example, in *War and Peace* in the scene in chapter twelve of Book VII when Sonya interprets the signs in the wax for Natasha and says she sees Prince Andrei, although she "had not seen anything." She tells Natasha that, although Andrei was lying down, "'his face was cheerful, and he turned to me.' And when saying this she herself fancied she had really seen what she described" (471).
43 Eikhenbaum writes of Tolstoy's futile struggles to create a "second" day after this first one. See *The Young Tolstoi,* 56-60. Perhaps because the day is so completely archetypal, it cannot be represented as one in a sequence.
44 Tolstoi, *ПСС*, online edition, 1:15; 18.
45 Ibid., 1:17; 19.
46 Ibid.
47 Ibid., 1:17; 22.
48 Ibid., 1:32; 33-34.
49 See Miller, "Tolstoy's Peaceable Kingdom," 58-59. The reader familiar with Tolstoy's oeuvre senses the looming of *War and Peace* with its massive exploration of the intersections, collaborations, and clashes of individual free choice and the inexorable workings of contingency on a global scale.
50 Tolstoi, *ПСС*, online edition, 1:33; 34-35.
51 Ibid., 1:34-35; 36.
52 Ibid., 1:35; 36-37.
53 Ibid., 1:69; 69.
54 Ibid., 1:70-71; 70. Tolstoy's sheltering under Gogol's "Overcoat" ["Шинель"] at this moment is evident. Hruska trenchantly analyzes the

significance of this passage at some length, pointing out its Biblical parallels (and the connection in Tolstoy's work between Jesus and the victim), as well as those to Gogol. She points out that Nikolai himself echoes Grap in chapter 22 when he asks, "Oh Lord, why dost Thou punish me so dreadfully?" See Hruska, 77.

55 Ibid., 1:72; 71.
56 Ibid., 1:72; 71; my italics.
57 Ibid., 1:38; 40.
58 Ibid.
59 Ibid.
60 See Miller, "Tolstoy's Peaceable Kingdom," 57-62.
61 Tolstoi, *ПСС*, online edition, 30:65. These quotations of *What is Art?* come from the translation by Aylmer Maude, 50-51.
62 Ibid., 1:39; 40. Numerous readers have noted this early expression of Tolstoy's later deep ambivalence about music and his responsiveness to it mingled with his disgust. See, for example, the excellent essay by Caryl Emerson, "Tolstoy and Music," 16-17, and Weir, 64-65. Christian cites a lengthy deletion from the final version of *Childhood* that sheds important and fascinating light on the young Tolstoy's thoughts about music and art in general. The young hero's mother is playing Beethoven, and the narrator regards his childhood response as affected: "In a certain French novel, the author describes the impression made on him by a Beethoven sonata [Christian points out that it is Balzac in *Cesar Birotteau* (1837)] and says that he can see angels with azure wings, palaces with golden columns... in short, strains every fiber of his French imagination in order to draw a fantastic picture of something beautiful...." In another version of this same "discarded chapter," Christian points out another even more significant passage about music:

> Music does not affect the mind or the imagination. While I am listening to music, I don't think about anything and don't imagine anything, but a strange delightful feeling so fills my soul that I lose all awareness of my existence: and this feeling is –recollection. But recollection of what? Although the sensation is acute, the recollection is obscure. It seems as if you are recollecting something which never happened. Is not recollection the basis of the feeling which any art

arouses in you? Does not the delight afforded by painting and sculpture come from the recollection of images? Does not the feeling inspired by music come from the recollection of feelings and the transitions from one feeling to another? Is not the feeling inspired by poetry the recollection of images, feelings and thoughts? (quoted in *Critical Introduction*, 25-26).

As Christian reminds us, Tolstoy retains very little of this passage. Tolstoy's creative processes of deletion are as fascinating in this early work as they are in the many drafts of *War and Peace* and *Anna Karenina*.

63   Tolstoi, *ПСС*, online edition, 1:40; 42.
64   Ibid., 1:46; 47.
65   Tolstoi, *ПСС*, Chertkov edition, 61:122, quoted in Christian, *Letters*, 1:202. Readers are urged to read this extraordinary letter in its entirety.
66   This is one of dozens of sharp correspondences—direct borrowings—by Tolstoy from a novel he continued to cherish all his life. See Charles Dickens, *David Copperfield*, chapter 2. In both novels the beloved mother and the adored servant who is also a mother figure share the same first name. For more on this subject, see note 83 on Dickens below.
67   Tolstoi, *ПСС*, online edition, 1:51; 52.
68   Ibid., 1:52; 53.
69   Ibid., 1:52; 53. Compare the fictional Nikolai's dreamy idyll of his mother to the following note, which Daniel Rancour-Laferriere highlights: "On 10 March 1906 the aging Tolstoy wrote the following note to himself on a stray piece of paper:

> A dull melancholic state all day. Toward evening this state changed into a tender feeling, a desire for affection, for love. As in childhood I longed to cling to a being who loved me, who took pity on me, and to weep tenderly and be consoled. . . . To whom can I cling? I'd like to make myself small and cling to mother as I imagine her to myself. Yes, yes, mommy [маменька], whom I had not even yet called by that name since I couldn't speak. . . . That's what my better but tired soul yearns for. Yes, mommy, come cuddle me [Ты, маменька, ты приласкай меня]. All this is insane [безумно], but it is all true (quoted in Rancour-Laferriere, 46-47).

See also Richard Gustafson, 14-15. Gustafson too highlights this passage; his reading of *Childhood* eloquently elaborates the importance of the garden to Nikolai's feelings of belonging and his love for his mother.
70 Tolstoi, *ПСС*, online edition, 1:52-53; 54.
71 Ibid., 1:54; 55.
72 Ibid.
73 Ibid., 1:55; 56.
74 Ibid.
75 Ibid, italics mine.
76 Ibid., 1:58; 59; italics Tolstoy's.
77 Ibid.
78 Ibid., 1:79; 78.
79 Ibid.
80 Christian, *Letters*, 1:11.
81 For the reference to the dog Dora, see Christian, *Critical Introduction*, 28.
82 For many astute and carefully observed insights into Tolstoy's reading of Dickens, see the outstanding essay by Philip Rogers. Rogers is here citing the semi-reliable memoir of Tatyana Tolstoy. But the textual comparisons he makes between the two works are completely compelling. See also Tom Cain, "Tolstoy's Use of *David Copperfield*," and Henry Gifford, "Dickens in Russia." For more commentary on the list of books that Tolstoy made late in life to chronicle what literary works shaped his sensibility, see Christian, *Critical Introduction*, 26-28. For the actual list, see Christian, *Letters*, 2: 484-486. On October 25, 1891, Tolstoy wrote to M.M. Lederle, a Petersburg publisher, who had written to many other well-known people for a list of the one hundred books that had most influenced them. Warning that his list was incomplete and not ready for publication, he sent it on nevertheless. Tolstoy divided his list (not even close to a hundred books) according to the age of reading (childhood to 14, 14-20, 20-35, 35-50, 50-63) and degree of influence—enormous, very great, and great. For the ages of 14-20 (this does not quite correspond to the year in which he read *David Copperfield*, for he was 22), he lists 17 books, 5 of which receive the designation "enormous": "Matthew's Gospel: The Sermon on the Mount," Rousseau's *Confessions* and *Emile*, Gogol's "Viy," and *David Copperfield*.
83 Shklovsky, "Art as Technique," 16.

84 Tolstoi, *ПСС*, online edition, 1:94; 92-93.

85 David describes Peggotty bringing him to his mother's body as a "time of confusion": "I only recollect that underneath some white covering on the bed, with a beautiful cleanliness and freshness all around it, there seemed to me to lie embodied the solemn stillness that was in the house, and that when she would have turned the cover gently back, I cried, 'Oh, no! Oh, no!'" His mother's familiar beloved body becomes unfamiliar—an embodied solemn stillness from which he draws back crying aloud (see Dickens, *David Copperfield*, 124-125). It is interesting that George Steiner, rather than noting the powerful echo of *David Copperfield* in this passage, instead links this scene to the affinities he discovers between Tolstoy and Homer: "But in the unflinching clarity of the Homeric and Tolstoyan attitude there is far more than resignation. There is joy, the joy that burns in the 'ancient glittering eyes' of the sages in Yeats' "Lapis Lazuli" (77). It is curious to note that Tolstoy himself had already linked the work of writing *Childhood* to Homer. In 1852, describing his many revisions of the text he wrote (in French) to his beloved Aunt T. A. Ergolskaia, the model for Natalya Savishna, "Perhaps this will be like the labor of Penelope; but I don't find that distasteful. I don't write from ambition but from taste. I find my pleasure and my usefulness in working, and I work" (translation from Christian, *Letters*, 1, 26).

86 Tolstoy, *ПСС*, online edition, 1:96; 94.

87 The fine, close reading offered by Rogers enumerates these many affinities between the two works. He quotes in full many of the passages I allude to in this essay. Any reader who reads these two novels in tandem will be struck by the close parallels between them, yet each text remains quintessentially of its own author.

88 Thoughts for an essay on *Childhood* have been percolating in my mind for decades. Since *Childhood* is dominated by Nikolai's lost mother, it does not seem inappropriate to cite here a letter from my late mother, Kathryn B. Feuer, a scholar of Tolstoy. Readers who dislike personal intrusions are urged to skip this note. I found this letter as I was working on this essay; it fell out of a copy of Tolstoy's novel that I keep at my summer house. Dostoevsky might say it was a recollection that appeared at the needed time. It is dated Sunday, January 4, 1981.

Dearest Robin,

This is a thank you letter. Thank you for a lovely Christmas visit.... I'll never forget Christmas Eve put-together time. I still have a few bloody knuckles, yet I accomplished nothing.

... I play the Bette Midler record a lot, am learning to love it. For me, she'll never match "Songs for a New Depression," every single one of which I love. But this is a good one.

I wish I knew your schedule. Mine this term is T-W-Th (What a pleasure!), but I'd love to give you a day off and take your *Childhood* session....

Poor Folk—right at the beginning Makar writes of the dear little birds tweet-tweeting and then quotes (roughly), "I wish I were a bird, *a bird of prey* [italics hers]. I consider this important, that the factor of will, aggression, is there from the start. Like Golyadkin Jr's "annihilating look" about which, if I remember correctly, he even consults his doctor....

Childhood. Here I do a 3-tiered thing which you may or may not approve of, but I offer it as something to fall back on. First, it's about art—T's lifelong dilemma—can beauty which is created=artifice=falsity be good? Here you get it in various isolated moments. It's possible to draw a "blue hare" (in art) but none exists in life (in Truth). N's father's ability to tell any story so well that what was good came out foolish, what was bad was affectionately laughable. And others.

Second tier—games. When his older brother won't "pretend" to play, the Swiss Family Robinson game flops. The game of cops and robbers—episode with Ilinka Grap (this episode and the one with Natalya Savishna and the tablecloth I consider the 2 fulcrums of the work) (fulcra?)

Third tier—games are another form of art—artifice—but what makes the book good is that T. offers no easy answer—sincerity or love as the solution. On the contrary, he shows the insidious double-facedness of love, pure innocent love. Nikolinka's love for Seriozha makes him cruel to Ilinka. His true innocent love for Sonechka leads him to betray Karl Ivanych—making fun of his gloves.

Here in this last point I think T comes to grips with Sterne. The chapter titles and method come from *Sentimental Journey*, but the message, I think, queries the assumption in *SJ* that natural feeling will always result in virtue. You're not doing *WP*. If you were I'd make a point of the author's digressions beginning here. Anyway, along with your own ideas on *Childhood*, which I know are numerous and very different [they clearly aren't, RFM] I hope the above will give you an easy class. [The letter continues on with more personal matters.]

Works Cited

Browne, Janet. *Charles Darwin: Voyaging*. Princeton, NJ: Princeton University Press, 1995.

Cain, Tom. "Tolstoy's Use of *David Copperfield*." In *Tolstoy and Britain*, edited by W. Gareth Jones, 67-78. Oxford: Berg, 1995.

Campbell, Mary Baine. *Wonder and Science: Imagining Worlds in Early Modern Europe*. Ithaca, NY: Cornell University Press, 1999.

Christian, R. F. *Tolstoy: A Critical Introduction*. Cambridge: Cambridge University Press, 1969.

____., ed. and trans. *Tolstoy's Letters*. 2 vols. New York: Charles Scribner's Sons, 1978.

Coleridge, Samuel Taylor *Biographia Literaria or Biographical Sketches of My Literary Life and Opinions*. Vol. 7. Edited by James Engell and W. Jackson Bate. Princeton: Princeton University Press, 1985.

Dickens, Charles. *David Copperfield*. New York: Pocket Library, 1958.

____. *Great Expectations*. Harmondsworth, UK: Penguin Books, 1965.

Dillard, Annie. *The Writing Life*. New York: Harper Collins, 1989.

Dostoevsky, F. M. *Полное собрание сочинений*. 30 vols. Leningrad: Nauka, 1972-90.

____. *A Writer's Diary*. Translated by Kenneth Lanz. 2 vols. Evanston: Northwestern University Press, 1994.

Dyson, Freeman. "The Information Flood." Review of *The Information: A History, a Theory, a Flood*, by James Gleick. *The New York Review of Books*, (March 2011).

Eikhenbaum, Boris. *The Young Tolstoi*. Translated and edited by Gary Kern. Ann Arbor: Ardis, 1972.

Emerson, Caryl. "Tolstoy and Music." *Anniversary Essays on Tolstoy*, edited by Donna Tussing Orwin, 8-25. New York: Cambridge University Press, 2010.

Feuer, Lewis S. *The Scientific Intellectual: The Psychological and Sociological Origins of Modern Science*. New Brunswick: Transaction Publishers, 1992.

Feynman, Richard. "The Dignified Professor." In *Creators on Creating: Awakening and Cultivating the Imaginative Mind*, edited by Frank Barron, Alfonson Montuori, and Anthea Barron, 63-67. New York: Penguin, 1997.

Gifford, Henry. "Dickens in Russia: The Initial Phase." In *Tolstoy and Britain*, edited by W. Gareth Jones, 61-67. Oxford: Berg, 1995.

Gleick, James. *Chaos: Making a New Science*. New York: Penguin Books, 1988.

Gustafson, Richard. *Tolstoy: Resident and Stranger. A Study in Fiction and Theology*. Princeton, NJ: Princeton University Press, 1986.

Hruska, Anne. "Loneliness and Social Class in Tolstoy's Trilogy." *Slavic and East European Journal* 44, no 1 (Spring 2000): 64-78.

Knowles, A.V., ed. *Tolstoy: The Critical Heritage*. London: Routledge & Kegan Paul, Ltd., 1978.

McEwan, Ian. "On John Updike." *New York Review of Books*. March 12, 2009.

McLean, Hugh. "Claws on the Behind: Tolstoy and Darwin." In *In Quest of Tolstoy*, 59-81. Boston: Academic Studies Press, 2008.

Miller, Robin Feuer. *Dostoevsky's Unfinished Journey*. New Haven, CT: Yale University Press, 2008.

____. "Tolstoy's Peaceable Kingdom." *Anniversary Essays on Tolstoy*, edited by Donna Tussing Orwin, 52-76. New York: Cambridge University Press, 2010.

Newlin, Thomas. "'Swarm Life' and the Biology of *War and Peace*." *Slavic Review* 71, no. 2 (Summer 2012): 359-385.

Orwin, Donna Tussing. *The Consequences of Consciousness: Turgenev, Dostoevsky, Tolstoy*. Stanford: Stanford University Press, 2007.

Rancour-Laferriere, Daniel. *Tolstoy on the Couch: Misogyny, Masochism and the Absent Mother*. New York: New York University Press, 1998.

Rogers, Philip. "A Tolstoyan Reading of *David Copperfield*." *Comparative Literature* 42, no. 1 (Winter 1990): 1-28.

Shklovsky, Viktor. "Art as Technique." In *Russian Formalist Criticism: Four Essays*, translated by Lee T. Lemon and Marion J. Reis, 13-21. Lincoln: University of Nebraska Press, 1965.

Simmons, Ernest J. *Leo Tolstoy*. 2 vols. New York: Vintage Books, 1960.

Steiner, George. *Tolstoy or Dostoevsky: An Essay in the Old Criticism*. New York: E.P. Dutton & Co., 1971.

Stoppard, Tom. *Arcadia*. London: Faber and Faber, 1993.

Tolstoi, Lev. *Полное собрание сочинений*. 90 vols. Edited by V. G. Chertkov et al. Moscow: Gosudarstvennoe izdatel'stvo "Khudozhestvennaia literatura," 1928-1958.

———. *Полное собрание сочинений в 100 томах*. Moscow: Nauka, 2000-.

Детство: http://feb-web.ru/feb/tolstoy/texts/pss100/t01/t01-011-.htm

Отрочество: http://feb-web.ru/feb/tolstoy/texts/pss100/t01/t01-091-.htm

Юность: http://feb-web.ru/feb/tolstoy/texts/pss100/t01/t01-154-.htm

Tolstoy, Leo. *Childhood, Boyhood, Youth*. Translated by Rosemary Edmonds. Harmondsworth, UK: Penguin, 1961.

———. *War and Peace*. Edited with revised translation by George Gibian. Translated by Louise and Aylmer Maude, second edition. New York: Norton Critical Edition, 1996.

———. *What is Art?* Translated by Aylmer Maude. New York: Bobbs-Merrill, 1960.

Wachtel, Andrew Baruch. *The Battle for Childhood: Creation of a Russian Myth*. Stanford: Stanford University Press, 1990.

———., and Ilya Vinitsky. *Russian Literature*. Cambridge, UK: Polity Press, 2010.

Weir, Justin. *Leo Tolstoy & the Alibi of Narrative*. New Haven, CT: Yale University Press, 2011.

Wilson, Edward O. *Consilience: The Unity of Knowledge*. New York: Random House, 1998.

VII

Fear and Loathing in the Caucasus: Tolstoy's "The Raid" and Russian Journalism

William Mills Todd III and Justin Weir

Lev Tolstoy's short work "The Raid: A Volunteer's Story" ["Набег: рассказ волонтера," 1853] marks a key moment in his early career. The story implicitly compares a young man's first experience in battle with the challenges of writing literature, riffing on Tolstoy's own autobiographical methods and underscoring his caustic view of journalism. Although "The Raid" was immediately recognized by his fellow soldiers as a barely concealed autobiographical retelling of Tolstoy's own military experience, modern readers may be puzzled by the apparent flurry of genres in its twelve short chapters—nature descriptions, *conte philosophique*, and war journalism, in addition to fiction and autobiography. Tolstoy summarizes the simple action of "The Raid" in its main title: the volunteer, a first-person narrator, cannot be dissuaded by his captain, named Khlopov, from joining a raiding party against a Chechen village.[1] The large, well-armed Russian party takes the village with no resistance, but as the Russians return to the fortress, the Chechens ambush them, fatally wounding a boyish, sentimental Russian officer, Ensign Alanin. Lieutenant Rozenkrantz, a parodically Romantic figure, proves ineffectual, both in battle and in comforting his dying comrade. The remaining Russian officers, except for Captain Khlopov, are remarkable only for their frivolously gallant French phrase-making.

When viewed in light of Tolstoy's long career, the story is more like an initial foray against the methods and subjects of contemporary literature that would occupy him for many years. Indeed, the real genius of the story lies in its remarkable account of the gestation of an artistic consciousness developing in response to both philosophical and narrative challenges. The subtitle, "A Volunteer's Story," captures these dimensions as deftly as the main title summarizes what one would conventionally call its action. Taken together, the titles suggest a work neither naïve nor experimental, despite its seeming simplicity and its set pieces (framing nature descriptions, parodies, meditations on abstract themes).

Tolstoy began writing "The Raid" just after he completed *Childhood* [*Детство, 1852*], and found himself at the proverbial crossroads of an authorial career. Down one well-trod path was military service and a familiar life; should he choose that path, it would be difficult to extract himself from the military commission he had only recently obtained.[2] Down the other path was the potential recognition, and possible fame, he might achieve as an author. Here he feared somewhat vainly that he would become just another *littérateur*, one of the professional journalists whom Tolstoy increasingly despised for their narrow-mindedness and petty squabbles. Today's readers know which path he ultimately chose, of course, but as we reread "The Raid" we can still discern some of the exciting chaos of these early inextricable aesthetic and professional decisions.[3]

The first draft of "The Raid" was written in 1852, while Tolstoy eagerly awaited word that his first publication *Childhood* had appeared in the prestigious thick journal *The Contemporary* [*Современник*]. With *Childhood* in print, Tolstoy's professional literary ambitions grew, and he resolved to add what would ultimately become "The Raid" to a larger series of sketches of military life in the Caucasus.[4] The diversity of literary genres one finds in "The Raid" itself is reflected in his plans for this series, which never materialized.

Tolstoy was incensed that Nikolai Nekrasov, the editor of *The Contemporary*, and the government censor had made changes to *Childhood*. The experience deepened his disgust for the world of thick journals and made him wary, even as he was thrilled to submit another story. On November 27, 1852, he spelled this out in a frank letter to Nekrasov:

> Although I have written something, I cannot send it to you now, first, because a certain success of my first work has developed my authorial vanity and I want my next works to be no worse than the previous one, and second because the cuts made by the censor in *Childhood* have made me rework many words to avoid similar incidents.... I will ask you, dear sir, to promise me with respect to my future writing that, if it pleases you to take it for your journal, you will not change anything at all. I hope that you will not refuse me this. As for me, I repeat my promise to send you the first piece I consider worthy of publication.[5]

Tolstoy was understandably quite proud of the warm reception that greeted *Childhood*, but he was troubled that his freedom as an author could be impinged upon so recklessly by the censor. And censorship was just one of the exigencies of publication in the major journals.

We speak of "fear and loathing" in part to recognize that Tolstoy was both overly preoccupied with and overly dismissive of the censor and entrepreneurial journalists who were implicated in his early efforts at authorship. He felt the call of journalism no less than other writers of the time, but he felt it differently. We recall that Tolstoy soon resolved to start his own military journal, *The Military Gazette* [*Военный листок*, 1855] but the government denied him permission.[6] He would later start a pedagogical journal, *Iasnaia Poliana* [*Ясная Поляна*], named after his estate, in 1861, drawing on his experience of teaching peasants in the school he set up on the subsequently famous estate. Tolstoy wrote pedagogical articles for this journal and he published twelve issues.[7] Those early years, then, witnessed the beginning of Tolstoy's perennially fraught relationship with publishing institutions. His founding of the *Intermediary* [*Посредник*] publishing house toward the end of the nineteenth century shows that his obsession did not diminish over time. "The Raid" must be read in this expansive context; otherwise much of the story loses layers of potential meaning. Questions of identity, independence, bravery, friendship, and so forth, that appear early in the story are broadly philosophical, but they are also grounded in this institutional environment. Gestures toward parody in the story echo Tolstoy's extensive metafictional consideration of the authorial process.

The very subtitle, "A Volunteer's Story," underscores the notion that freedom, including the author's freedom, if sacrificed, will be sacrificed only for a distinct (and temporary?) purpose. The notion of "volunteer" carries this charge. Indeed, the first chapter of the "The Raid" is consumed by this question and sets up the rest of the story. Although Tolstoy had more first-hand experience of the dangers of war than most, if not all, major nineteenth-century writers, he wrote relatively rarely about war: the Caucasian stories, the three Sevastopol Tales [*Севастопольские рассказы*, 1855], *The Cossacks* [*Казаки*, 1863], *War and Peace* [*Война и мир*, 1869], and *Hadji Murad* [*Хаджи Мурат*, completed 1904; published 1912]. In these works, especially the second and third, one finds certain common elements emphasized in varying degrees: the "spirit of the army" ["дух войска"] as the phenomenon that decides victory and directs the army, a narrator's or character's disapproving or sarcastic appreciation of any officer with romantic pretensions, the helplessness of the officers in determining the tide of battle, the unostentatious valor of the lower ranks or the exceptional unpretentious officer, the *leitmotifs* of pain (the wounded on stretchers, missing limbs) and disarray (dirt, dust), the blissful ignorance of the society back in the capital cities, and the limited viewpoint of an often inexperienced observer. To a certain extent, these elements are present in "The Raid." To an even greater extent, they are present in the drafts of the story but not in the final version, which may suggest that this is much less a war story about a "raid" and much more a narrative about "the story" and "the volunteer."

The elements of war in the story are quickly dispensed with. In revising the story, Tolstoy cut an introduction in which the anonymous first-person narrator expresses his interest in war and a childhood desire for heroism, removed from the end of chapter VI a long impassioned refutation of Russia's *casus belli* and condemnation of adventurers and career-making officers, eliminated an analysis of the "spirit of the army" from the end of chapter IV, and took out a last view of the officers in the conclusion. The effects attained by several of these changes were brevity and lack of artless repetition—the essence of the discarded introduction, for instance, emerges in the conversation with Captain Khlopov in chapter I. In other instances, ideas were cut that probably could not have been inferred by the volunteer from his contact with man and nature. And the removal of a discussion of the larger Caucasian conflict increases the absurdity of the raid, leaving one to assume that it was conducted to further careers, satisfy curiosity, and gain plunder. What little mention of fighting there is reads as a parody of the Caucasian war story, as in the explanation of Rozenkranz's exploits, or functions ironically, as in the looting of the village and the death of Alanin. All in all, these two passages constitute perhaps a fifth of the story.

Etymologically, parody is derived from the Greek words "to sing alongside." Such commentary on the works of fellow writers was a constant feature of European literature throughout the century and a quarter leading up to "The Raid," as works of fiction often competed with each other in being "realistic" by showing their predecessors to have been somehow naïve illusions, as Harry Levin has amply documented.[8] On the Russian scene, for example, Aleksandr Pushkin's author-narrator "sang along side of" the sentimental Lensky in *Eugene Onegin* [*Евгений Онегин*, 1823-31][9] and Mikhail Lermontov's hero Pechorin "sang alongside of" the would-be romantic hero Grushnitsky in *A Hero of Our Time* [*Герой нашего времени*, 1840], in which Pechorin boasts: "In me there live two men: one lives in the full sense of that word, the other thinks and judges him."[10] Pechorin, however, fails to apply the same ruthlessness to himself that he applies to Grushnitsky and, like the Byronic romantic outcast, demands more sympathy for himself than many later readers and parodying writers were willing to grant. Thus Rozenkranz, whose actions in society parallel both Pechorin's (showing off before young ladies) and Grushnitsky's (believing one has enemies), is "sung alongside of" as he is contrasted with Khlopov and deflatingly analyzed by both the volunteer and his own Circassian ("natural") mistress, a case of hoisting Lermontov's hero with Lermontov's petard, the multiple viewpoint. Here the volunteer looks beneath the mask and sees inner contradiction and dim-witted uncertainty (reflected in the terms "something" ["что-то"] and "as if" ["как бы"]):

> He often went out at night into the mountains with two or three Tatar allies, in order to lie in wait along the road and kill hostile Tatars who happened to be passing by. Although his heart told him more than once that there was nothing daring in this, he considered himself obliged to make people suffer, people in whom he was disenchanted for something, and whom it was as if he despised or hated.[11]

Rozenkranz's mistress describes him as someone much smaller than his pretentions: "He was the nicest and most humble person... and every evening he wrote his gloomy notes, kept accounts on graph paper, and prayed to God on his knees."[12] As Eikhenbaum points out, this is hardly the awe in which the paradigmatic romantic heroine holds the romantic hero.[13]

The two little episodes in which Rozenkranz manifests his futility are mock heroic masterpieces: skeleton plots with a central hero and situational clichés, a rescue in the nick of time, and the chivalrous treatment of an enemy. Rozenkranz is punctured, literally, in the latter instance, by a bullet "below the back."[14]

The main military action of the novel—the taking of the village—unfolds ironically: there is little resistance; the sole captive taken is a helpless old man; and the loot consists of a rag, a tin basin, two hens, and a white goat. The brief discussion of the skirmish is a prototype of Tolstoy's subsequent battle descriptions: the enemy is unseen from the narrator's viewpoint, the narrator describes the sounds of battle, shells fall impersonally out of the sky, the vain officer strikes poses, the inexperienced officer glows with enthusiasm, the wise officer keeps calm and does not get in his soldiers' way, the soldiers return toward the narrator, bearing the dead and wounded. Amongst the latter in this story is Alanin, the naïve youth who led an unnecessary charge. Neither his fatal wound, nor Rozenkranz's inept remark, nor the doctor's cruel probing produces an epiphany for Alanin—he just feels "surprise and reproach." Northrop Frye provides the perfect nomenclature for such plot development: "irony with little satire is the non-heroic residue of tragedy, centering on a theme of puzzled defeat."[15]

It is important to draw this distinction between irony and satire in "The Raid," for satire was what Tolstoy tried to eliminate from the story during the seven months that he was writing it. In other words, Tolstoy edited the story to focus more on literature itself and less on social behavior. One of his final comments on the story was: "I wrote a lot. It seems it will be good, and without satire.... It is even unpleasant for me to describe the bad sides of a whole class of people."[16] The satiric remainder is the parody of a Caucasian romantic hero, which is quite brief, and various comments, briefer still, on the officers, almost Gogolian in inspiration, if not in cleverness: "The battalion commander, expressing his rank on his fat face, set to eating."[17] The volunteer's negative evaluation of a German officer was cut, as was a passage in which Khlopov becomes a typical *raisonneur* of satire: "The captain said that the general's appearance was not merely not majestic but somehow stupid and drunken, and that it was fitting for a Russian general or colonel to be like a Russian soldier, not an English huntsman."[18]

"The Raid" is, then, less a work of anti-Romanticism than something else, emerging from a reportorial context. The parallels Eikhenbaum draws with the contemporary genre of the Caucasian military sketch are relevant. They show some of the materials the 1851 issues of *The Contemporary* set before Tolstoy: "notes," dates, geographical and ethnographical details, a wealth of Caucasian vocabulary, and parodies of romantic descriptions of the Caucasus.[19] Nevertheless, what Tolstoy finally presents is "The Raid: A Volunteer's Story," not "A Letter from the Caucasus," which was the story's first title. What the change of titles emphasizes is that we are dealing not so much with a bit of factual reportage mixed with various generalizations and comments on the inadequacy of past representations of the subject, as with a story—one that, as we shall see, examines the effects of fellow men and nature on a first-person narrator, who is seen in one magnified stage in the process of maturing. The facets of the Caucasian sketch that enter the story become not the objects of a report but the materials that contribute to this process.

Tolstoy treats the authorial or metaliterary aspect of the narrator's development philosophically. To become a successful author is entwined with becoming a mature and autonomous man. Chapter I introduces the volunteer, who is the first-person narrator, and Captain Khlopov, who informs him about the impending raid and tries to convince him not to participate. The volunteer's character development is opposed to that of Rozenkranz, the romantic hero whose autonomy is undermined by his clichéd behavior and whose masculinity is perhaps cast into doubt by his injury and his Circassian mistress' belittlement. Khlopov serves as both a better model of manhood and a philosophical foil for the volunteer. As we learn later in the chapter, the volunteer's estate is not far from Khlopov's childhood home, and so he is able to describe a visit to Khlopov's mother, who, when learning of the volunteer's destination, asks him to deliver an icon to her son. The simplicity of mother and son and the authenticity of their relationship contrast sharply with the other male-female relationships in the story.

There are both explicit and implicit signs that the volunteer has been dwelling on notions of choice and free will. As in other digressions in early works by Tolstoy, such as the one on *"comme il faut"* in *Boyhood* [*Отрочество*, 1854] and the one on "truth" in "Sevastopol in December" ["Севастополь в декабре месяце," 1855], in "The Raid," the narrator reflects on the definition of "bravery." Having recalled Plato's definition that bravery distinguishes between what is necessary and what is unnecessary to fear (in the Socratic dialogue the *Laches*), the narrator inscribes "choice" into the Platonic notion: "Yes, I said, it seems to me that in every danger there is choice, and a choice made under the influence, for example, of duty is bravery, but a choice made under the influence of a base feeling—that is cowardice."[20] We have here both the young man's callow need to philosophize about everything and his obsession with "measuring up" to his fellow soldiers. He overtly cites free will in his ruminations on bravery. Less overt is his implicit comparison of himself with Khlopov. As a "volunteer" he chooses freely whether or not to put himself in harm's way.

In fact, throughout the entire first chapter, the volunteer works to substantiate both his free will and his difference from others. By contrast, Khlopov repeatedly attempts to categorize the narrator in a way that limits his freedom, by comparing him to other people:

> Well, what then? You simply wish, evidently, to see how people are killed? . . . In 1832 there was also someone who wasn't serving, Spanish, it seems. He went on two campaigns with us, in some sort of blue cloak . . . still they did the lad in. Here, old fellow, you won't surprise anyone.[21]

Instead of serving in some capacity, the narrator is accused of merely wanting to watch, a physically passive role but one that is morally reprehensible. (The morality of vision is also the subject of "Sevastopol in December," written just two years after "The Raid.") Note, too, how "volunteer" becomes "one who doesn't serve." In the first paragraphs, the narrator was worried that he would "miss" ["пропустить"] the action. He feared his own absence. Now Khlopov threatens to define him by a similar negativity, by what he does not do—literally "one who does not serve." The narrator takes this attempt to define him and reverses it: rather than one who serves, he becomes one who *chooses* to serve. He makes an active choice, and a "brave" one, defining himself in the process.

Nothing would seem to be out of the ordinary with a first-person narrator distinguishing himself in this fashion. By creating a unique voice and telling a unique story, first-person narratives in the modern era almost always forge a singular identity. Unusual but significant for "The Raid," the like/unlike binary introduced by Captain Khlopov is tied by Tolstoy to the authorial dynamics of the story. After listening to the volunteer describe his choice as the very definition of bravery, Khlopov replies: "Well, I can't prove it to you . . . but we have a cadet who also likes to philosophize. You should talk with him. He even writes poetry."[22] Rather than the brave and free hero the narrator implies he is, he is likened to a philosophizer and verse writer. Khlopov does not necessarily mean to make a positive comparison, though he plainly deals with the narrator in a sympathetic way. The comparison to a poetry writer is the give-away that we are dealing with a metaliterary passage—Tolstoy reflected on the literary process even in his earliest experiments (e.g., "A History of Yesterday" ["История вчерашнего дня," 1851].

The narrator's first response to Khlopov's attempt to categorize him is in fact to philosophize about bravery. Now he chooses to "write verse" or, rather, to do what prose writers do instead: he tells a story. The remainder of Chapter I is devoted to the narrator's memory of visiting Khlopov's mother. A key moment in this enclosed story is, unsurprisingly, that Khlopov does not write his mother as often as he should. Although the narrator may or may not correctly celebrate Khlopov's bravery, Tolstoy underscores the point that Khlopov would make a bad author.

The authorial themes in the first chapter of the story are implicit, not hidden per se but not obvious either. Whereas Khlopov serves in the army, the narrator is a freely participating volunteer. Whereas Khlopov refuses to respect philosophizing and writing a means of individuation, the narrator endeavors to individuate himself in precisely those ways. The much larger and more obvious literary background created by Lermontov, who is not mentioned, and the military historian Aleksandr Mikhailovsky-Danilov, who is mentioned, sets up the entire chapter, in which the narrator distinguishes his ideas and his authorship as original. Khlopov is a figure against whom the narrator asserts his independence and his irreplaceability. Of course, Khlopov himself is also a model of authenticity in the story, but he is neither the "hero of our time" Pechorin figure of "The Raid" (that would be Rozenkrantz), nor even a typical "hero," since he acts and speaks more modestly. If anything, Khlopov plays the role of Lermontov's Maksim Maksimych, who pointedly fails to comprehend the writer-hero Pechorin and who avoids literary and philosophical discussions.

The philosophical questions of choice and free will discussed by the narrator and characters and suggested by the metafiction of the first chapter are closely entwined with Tolstoy's authorial concerns in this early period. And authorship at this time generally meant publication in a journal. Tolstoy thought a lot about these matters, even in his earliest fiction. For example, the penultimate chapter in an early draft of *Childhood*, "To Those Gentlemen Critics Who Care to Consider It," and the final chapter of that manuscript, "To Readers," sketch out Tolstoy's early ideas about authorial process and reader reception.[23] These chapters were hypothetical for Tolstoy—since he had not yet been published—and he removed them in the final version. His defensive address to the "critics" is thus itself a kind of fiction, and echoes attacks on critics in Nikolai Gogol's *Dead Souls* [*Мертвые души*, 1842] and Lermontov's *A Hero of Our Time*. The difference is that Tolstoy's metafiction is literally separated from its fiction.

In "To Those Critics," the context of the journal is unmistakable. Tolstoy writes:

> I embark on a literary career with great reservation and distaste.... Why? Because you, Dear Gentlemen, are for me those from whom in my literary career I am afraid to receive offense. The word offense I speak here not at all in a metaphoric sense, but in a direct one.... When you write criticism... of all readers you have most in mind the author, and sometimes him alone.[24]

Tolstoy insists on the singular, autonomous activity of the author and the critic and on the personal nature of their relationship. Tolstoy suggests, moreover, that were he to be attacked by critics, there should be no distinction between himself—Count Tolstoy, a nobleman with legal rights and privileges—and his authorial identity. Thus in his peculiar request to eliminate from reviews the use of the editorial first-person plural, "we," Tolstoy hopes, however naïvely, to individualize the critics and to force them each to assume a single responsible identity. A barely submerged threat is contained in Tolstoy's reference to "libel": "To write or say such things about a person that you would not say to his face nor write him means to say offensive things... means that you are writing libel."[25] The concept of libel reveals a relationship between the publishing institution and individual action. If it appears that we are digging too deeply for allusions to contemporary journalism in "The Raid," it is only because Tolstoy himself was intent on forcing an institutional relationship into an interpersonal one.

As is well known, Tolstoy's vision of readership is similarly individuated. In "To Readers," he says: "Any author—in the broadest sense of that word—when writing whatever, invariably imagines what effect his writing will have. When the entire work pleases one person, then that work, in my opinion, is perfect in some sense."[26] The idea of writing for a single reader stuck with Tolstoy—one can even imagine that the idea of aesthetic "infection" from his late essay *What is Art?* [*Что такое искусство?*, 1897] derives, in part, from his notions of the intimacy of aesthetic reception. With *What is Art?* in mind, G. N. Ishchuk cleverly remarks: "By the way, it is not difficult to guess that [Tolstoy's] 'imaginary reader' looks very much like the young Tolstoy himself."[27] Tolstoy is not the first, as we have said, to address critics and readers. Most important is that in his literary attempts to define himself he uses (real or imagined) institutional resistance in the creative appropriation of his authorial identity.

Despite the obvious differences between *Childhood* and "The Raid," they share a number of common structural elements and share them with much of Tolstoy's subsequent writings: contact with a preceptor, with society, with nature perceived by almost all the senses and in great detail; presentation of characters and scenes in contrasting pairs; the journey to link episodes, and provide different viewpoints for the narrator. This similarity of Tolstoy's narratives throughout his sixty-year writing career can hardly escape notice. Most of these structural elements are invariably present, even if only as underdeveloped nuclei. The major character undergoes a mental journey from stage to stage; in the novels or in *Confession* [*Исповедь*, 1880], that journey has many such stages. Sometimes this mental journey occurs on an ironic plane, as in *The Cossacks*. In most of the works, the intellectual journey is accomplished on a path (in all seasons, in lines or circles, by coach, horse, train, raft, or foot) along which or at the end of which the traveler changes his opinions, beliefs, or understanding. Such a path is a device Tolstoy probably learned from Laurence Sterne's *A Sentimental Journey* [1768], but also one which is perfectly melded to his conception of his protagonists as intellectually restless seekers. Indeed, with reference to "The Raid," Tolstoy's statement that he learned all about war from Stendhal is something of a red herring. The sort of mind that would pay articulate attention to its own sensations in the midst of a battle is less that of the ironically treated Fabrice del Dongo at Waterloo and more that of Yorick, who did not give the war between France and England much consideration in *A Sentimental Journey*.[28]

The volunteer's journey in "The Raid" is intellectual, as he goes through at least a dozen definitions of bravery. He offers the first six in chapter I, a dialogue (somewhat Socratic, although Khlopov's midwifery is passive).²⁹ The volunteer seems to start from the usual dictionary definition of "bravery" ["храбрость"] —"the absence of fear when in danger."³⁰ This is discernable from the fact that he has been waiting a month to see some action and regards as brave a Spaniard who rushed into the thick of battle in bright apparel³¹ From here the volunteer takes two of the captain's definitions (it is not brave to push in where one is not ordered, and bravery consists in behaving as one should), reconciles them with Plato's definition (bravery is the knowledge of what one should and should not fear), and arrives eventually at the following synthesis, which is not at all close to his implied definition from the story's previous page:

> It seems to me that in any dangerous situation there is a choice, and a choice made under the influence, for example, of a sense of duty shows bravery, while a choice made under the influence of a base feeling shows cowardice. A man, therefore, who risks his life out of vanity, or curiosity, or cupidity cannot be called brave, and, conversely, a man who turns away from danger under the influence of an honorable feeling of family obligation or simply conviction cannot be called a coward.³²

A fascinating psychological process is taking place here. The speed with which the volunteer changes definitions reveals the extent to which he feels guilty about his initial attitude, wanting to see people killed, as the captain puts it, and realizes his similarity to the Spaniard. The volunteer barely mentions his discomfort: "No matter how ashamed I felt that the captain had so stupidly interpreted my intentions, I did not try to dissuade him." Consequently this long definition becomes another generalization motivated by the emotional state of the narrator.³³

It is motivated as well by the volunteer's admiration for Captain Khlopov, which emerges from the first two chapters. He depicts Khlopov as a low mimetic saint in the mold of *Childhood*'s Natalya Savishna. The hagiography isolates them from the normal activities of earthly existence: Natalya gives up marriage to serve her masters while Khlopov does not play cards, carouses rarely, and smokes only cheap tobacco. Khlopov's saintly image is drawn to the needs of "The Raid"; the volunteer attributes to him a "simple, calm, Russian physiognomy" and little that is military or beautiful.³⁴ His values match his unprepossessing appearance when he shows indifference to the thrill of the campaign or of the hunt. He links these two activities, the hunt and military pursuits, by suggesting that the volunteer go hunting instead of taking part in a raid.[35] The volunteer's *vita* includes a passage in which Khlopov ignores a rising pheasant that would have gladdened the heart of any hunter.[36]

Next encountered along the volunteer's journey are Alanin and his implicit mentor Rozenkranz, presented in contrast to the volunteer-Khlopov pair. Alanin, like the volunteer at the beginning of the story, is "young," as the gruff captain says. The whole episode of Alanin's death within the thematic structure of the story is subordinate to the discussion of bravery, which is concluded at the end of Chapter X, and to the contrast between Khlopov and Rozenkranz. The description of Rozenkranz at the beginning of chapter IV is almost an exact antithesis to that of Khlopov at the beginning of chapter II: Rozenkranz lives with his dagger on, has four kinds of braid, five weapons, a large white horse, and a most un-Russian name (despite his protestations of ancient Varangian descent). Its Shakespearean reverberations reinforce Rozenkranz's fatuous foppery. Just as Alanin will follow Rozenkranz in mock heroism, rescuing a goat instead of two pigeons in the nick of time, and in excited behavior before battle, so will the volunteer come to imitate Khlopov's views on military enthusiasm, calling an adjutant who wants to go to battle in chapter V a "child," and professing to understand nothing, thus forgetting that enthusiasm and curiosity had been his own attitudes of the day before, just as he makes no comparison between the scribbling Rozenkranz and himself.

The definitions and examples of bravery in chapter II are those of the regiment: officers who abuse their horses on a hot, dusty day and Rozenkranz's posturing.

The subsequent important treatment of bravery occurs in chapter X—it marks the zenith of the volunteer's imitation of Khlopov, who is called "truly brave" for being himself, as always, before the skirmish. Next comes the final definition of bravery, whose seed was sewn in the captain's disapproval of the Spaniard in chapter I. That seed grew in the comparison of the two villages—the fort with its French-speaking officers and German music, both of which distress the volunteer; and the clean, lovely Caucasian village, which the greedy (*ergo* uncourageous) soldiers destroy. Then comes the ostentatious conversation in French between the two officers in chapter IX. All of this inspires the last definition of bravery: Russian bravery requires performing great deeds without lofty phrases. Echoing Khlopov's theme of "youth," the volunteer adds sententiously: "How can a Russian heart not feel pain when it hears vulgar French phrases from our young warriors, who have pretentions of imitating antiquated French knights?"[37]

It even turns out that the truly brave captain was afraid during battle, and thus was the dictionary definition completely reversed, as so often happens in Tolstoy, who in an ultimate *tour de force* would define away death in *On Life* [*O жизни*, 1887.]

"Vulgar French phrases" is a formulation that suggests an antithesis of Tolstoy's aesthetics, which aim for communicative efficiency and reject the superfluous and needlessly ornate. Like other early stories by Tolstoy, the narrative of "The Raid" meanders (à la Sterne) but does not dwell on the superfluous. After the village is destroyed, for example, the volunteer remarks:

> The sight was truly magnificent. However, for me as one who had not taken part in the action and was unaccustomed, the impression was in general spoiled. Something seemed superfluous to me—that movement and the animation and the shouting. A comparison involuntarily occurred to me of a man swinging his arms as though to cut the air with an axe.[38]

While describing the superfluous behavior, however, the narrator still makes use of a striking metaphor, the axe, which occurs to him against his will—so perhaps the episode is not entirely without utility. The image of the writer revealed in "The Raid" rests on similar balancing acts of irony, as the narrator cites authorial or journalistic conventions only in order to announce how he will overcome them.

"The Raid" ends not, as was originally intended, with the various officers striking characteristic poses, but with the volunteer engrossed in perceiving nature and hearing the strong, sensitive voice of the regimental tenor, just as he had been engrossed in perception two days before he set out. This is a fitting last example of how "The Raid" is less a parody, a war story, or a Caucasian sketch, than a story of a mind undergoing a stage in its development in reaction to a variety of phenomena—contrasting characters, contrasting surroundings, contradictory definitions, and the disharmony of war and nature. Tolstoy's writerly mind dwelled irrationally on the fear of having his independent motives wrongly interpreted, but simultaneously loathed being beholden to a journalistic institution that could give him a public voice. This insistence on the perceptions of a mind in action concludes not only the ostensible plot of the story, but also the plot of authorial development.

Endnotes

1. On the autobiographical material in "The Raid" and on its contemporary reception, see N. I. Burnasheva, 303-308, 310-14. Quotations of Tolstoy's works in this essay, unless otherwise noted, come from one of two sources: the as yet incomplete online *Полное собрание сочинений* [*Complete Collected Works*] in 100 volumes, hereafter cited by volume and page number in parentheses, or the older *Полное собрание сочинений* in 90 volumes, hereafter cited as Chertkov edition, followed by volume and page number in parentheses. All translations are William Mills Todd III's.
2. Burnasheva, "Произведения," 288-89.
3. Orwin, *Consequences of Consciousness*, 60-61.
4. Burnasheva, "Произведения," 287-88.
5. Quoted in Burnasheva, "Произведения," 288.
6. See N. N. Gusev, 47. In an 1858 letter to V. B. Botkin Tolstoy proposed a journal devoted to purely artistic, versus political, works and subjects. The journal was never realized. See Šilbajoris, 21-22.
7. Gusev, *Летопись жизни*, 129; Biriukov, *Биография Л. Н. Толстого*, I:241-68.
8. Levin, *Gates of Horn*, 39-48.
9. Pushkin, *Eugene Onegin*, VI:21-22.
10. Lermontov, *A Hero of our Time*, "Princess Mary," June 16.
11. Tolstoi, *ПСС*, online edition, 2:13.
12. Ibid.
13. Eikhenbaum, *Молодой Толстой*, 94.
14. Tolstoi, *ПСС*, online edition, 2:14.
15. Frye, *Anatomy of Criticism*, 224.
16. Tolstoi, *ПСС*, Chertkov edition, 3:292.
17. Tolstoi, *ПСС*, online edition, 2:14. E. N. Kupreianova notes that both "The Raid" and the incipient "Novel About a Russian Landowner" included satire of a Gogolian nature, but that Tolstoy pruned the satire for the final

versions (66). Nevertheless, a few Natural School touches do remain: the ludicrous icon of Khlopov's mother, the various "homunculi" (Nabokov's, not Sterne's, meaning) in chapter V, the non-heroic activities of the officers in chapter IV, the characterization of dress as extravagant throughout.

18 Tolstoi, *ПСС*, Chertkov edition, 3:219-20.
19 Eikhenbaum, *Лев Толстой*, 131-36.
20 Tolstoi, *ПСС*, online edition, 2:8.
21 Ibid.
22 Ibid., 2:9.
23 These essays are treated more fully in Weir, 42-49.
24 Tolstoi, *ПСС*, online edition, 19:137, ellipses ours.
25 Tolstoi, *ПСС*, online edition, 19:137.
26 Ibid., 19:141.
27 Ishchuk, *Проблема читателя*, 20.
28 The treatment of Tolstoy and Stendhal in Eikhenbaum, *Молодой Толстой*, 95-100, is in general more useful for later descriptions of war, since the volunteer has ceased to be an enthusiastic novice from the second page of "The Raid." Furthermore Eikhenbaum's equation of their "business-like, inelegant styles" ignores the difference between Tolstoy's frequently rhetorical, all-inclusive sentences and Stendhal's generally jerky "Code Napoléon" style.
29 Bursov notes that Tolstoy had been reading Plato just before writing "The Raid" (180).
30 Standard nineteenth-century (Dal') and twentieth-century (Ushakov, Ozhegov) offer this as a primary definition. The English "bravery," which usually translates "храбрость," is broader in meaning, incorporating appearance and bravado, as the Russian term does not.
31 Tolstoi, *ПСС*, online edition, 2:8.
32 Ibid., 2:9.
33 Ibid., 2:8.
34 Ibid., 2:10.
35 Ibid., 2:8.
36 Ibid., 2:11.
37 Ibid., 2:28.
38 Ibid., 2:23.

Works Cited

Biriukov, Pavel. *Биография Л. Н. Толстого: В двух книгах*. 2 Vols. Moscow: Algoritm, 2000.

Burnasheva, N. I. "Произведения 1852-1856 гг." In L. N. Tolstoi, *Полное собрание сочинений в 100 томах*, 283-567. Moscow: Nauka, 2000-.

Bursov, B. I. *Лев Толстой. Идейные искания и творческий метод, 1847-1862*. Moscow: Goslitizdat, 1960.

Eikhenbaum, Boris. *Молодой Толстой*. Petersburg/Berlin: Izdatel'stvo Z. I. Grzhebina, 1922.

———. *Лев Толстой*. Vol. 1. Moscow-Leningrad: 1928.

Frye, Northrop. *Anatomy of Criticism*. New York: Atheneum, 1966.

Gusev, N. N. *Летопись жизни и творчества Л. Н. Толстого*. Moscow: Academia, 1936.

Ishchuk, G. N. *Проблема читателя в творческом сознании Л. Н. Толстого*. Kalinin: Kalininskii gosudarstvennii universitet, 1975.

Kupreianova, E. N. *Молодой Толстой*. Tula: Tulskoe knizhnoe izdatel'stvo, 1956.

Levin, Harry. *The Gates of Horn: A Study of Five French Realists*. London: Oxford University Press, 1966.

Orwin, Donna Tussing. *Consequences of Consciousness: Turgenev, Dostoevsky, Tolstoy*. Stanford: Stanford University Press, 2007.

Šilbajoris, Rimvydas. *Tolstoy's Aesthetics and his Art*. Columbus: Slavica, 1990.

Tolstoi, Lev. *Полное собрание сочинений*. 90 vols. Edited by V. G. Chertkov et al. Moscow: Gosudarstvennoe izdatel'stvo "Khudozhestvennaia literatura," 1928-1958.

———. *Полное собрание сочинений в 100 томах*. Moscow: Nauka, 2000-.

Weir, Justin. *Leo Tolstoy and the Alibi of Narrative*. New Haven: Yale University Press, 2011.

VIII

Tolstoy's *Sevastopol Tales*: Pathos, Sermon, Protest, and Stowe[1]

Liza Knapp

> You will see terrible spectacles that will rend your soul; you will see war not in its correct, beautiful, and glittering ranks, with music and beating drums, with waving banners and generals prancing on horseback; rather, you will see war in its real expression—in blood, in suffering, in death . . .
>
> Lev Tolstoy, "Sevastopol in December"

Regarding the Pain of Others in Sevastopol

Early in "Sevastopol in December" ["Севастополь в декабре месяце"], the first of three tales Lev Tolstoy wrote about the siege of the city of Sevastopol (1854-55) during the Crimean War, the narrator announces that *this* representation of war shows us war "in its real expression—in blood, in suffering, in death" without sparing us.[2] The premise is one that readers and viewers are used to today, but Tolstoy, as he wrote about blood, suffering, and death in the Crimean War (1853-57), was among the first to give a truly modern representation of war. When Tolstoy's narrator tells us what we will *see*, as he ushers us through the besieged city, through the makeshift hospital, and into the ward where amputations are being performed, he puts us in the position of "regarding the pain of others." As Susan Sontag reminds us in her book with this title, the public's vicarious experience of the suffering caused by distant wars has become a "distinguishing feature" of our "modern life," as have the moral questions that arise from our awareness of "the horrors taking place throughout the world."[3]

The Crimean War, when armies of the Russian Empire fought the allied English, French, and Ottoman armies, is often referred to as the first modern war, in part because for the first time war was brought home from the distant front in a graphic, authentic, and timely way.[4] In London, Paris, St. Petersburg, and elsewhere, the public was made newly aware of the horrors of the war being fought. With varying degrees of freedom, the press published news of the war. Those at home responded. In England, the public was exposed to representations of suffering and death in various media. In dispatches from Crimea published in the London *Times*, William Russell and other war correspondents broke with the tradition of war writing, with its tendency to glorify and valorize the subject, to reveal the truth about the miserable conditions ("the filth and starvation, and deadly stagnation of the camp"), thus refusing to "tell lies to 'make things pleasant'" to the authorities.[5] In response to Russell's report in the *Times* about the slaughter of British cavalry at Balaklava, Alfred Tennyson, the Poet Laureate, composed "The Charge of the Light Brigade." The message of this poem is mixed: the poet honors the dead ("When can their glory fade?"), but notes that "someone had blunder'd" in ordering the charge. The soldiers ride "into the valley of Death" without "reason[ing] why": "theirs but to do and die."[6] The new medium of photography was also used to document this war: Roger Fenton became one of the first war photographers when he was sent to the Crimea by Prince Albert. Fenton, however, was under instructions from the War Office not to photograph "the dead, the maimed, or the ill." In his iconic image of this war, called "The Valley of the Shadow of Death," Fenton had to leave blood, suffering, and death to the imagination of the viewer and show us the empty, cannon-ball-ridden site of the slaughter memorialized by Tennyson.[7] The work of Russell, Tennyson, Fenton, and others, not to mention the private letters that made it home from the Crimea, fixed the war and its pain in the imagination of the British public, rousing pathos and protest, while also inspiring action to remedy the situation—from the dispatches of supplies paid for by the Crimean War Fund of the London *Times*, to the medical missions of Florence Nightingale and others, to the efforts (joined by Charles Dickens) to form an Administration Reform Association, to the resignation of the prime minister, Lord Aberdeen.[8]

In Russia, the young Tolstoy emerged as a major voice among those who bore witness to the pain and suffering of this same Crimean War. As a Russian subject, Tolstoy wrote in a different political and cultural context, under a system of censorship that was especially strict at the time.[9] Nevertheless, his tales had an enormous impact on the Russian reading public (including the recently crowned Tsar Alexander II). The first two tales, "Sevastopol in December" and "Sevastopol in May" ["Севастополь в мае"] appeared while Sevastopol was still under siege and were read, despite their elements of fictionality, as dispatches from the front.[10] Contemporary readers welcomed these reports, which were such a radical departure from what was published in *The Invalid* [*Инвалид*], the official organ of military news. (The year before, Tolstoy had in fact been involved in a proposal, squelched by Tsar Nicholas I, to publish an alternative journal for and about the military.[11]) Tolstoy's tales roused patriotic feeling and compassion for the defenders of Sevastopol. They also contributed to the soul-searching that Russians underwent when the war ended in a defeat that made it clear reform was necessary if Russia was going to take part in the modern world.

Tolstoy's tales, like the work of Russell and Fenton, were part of what may be seen as a new, modern mode of representation that flourished under the conditions of the Crimean War, the first "modern war." But the tales also bear the imprint of the intense literary apprenticeship in which Tolstoy was engaged during the early 1850s. While serving as an officer in the Russian army (first in the Caucasus, then briefly at Bucharest, before being transferred to the vicinity of Sevastopol), Tolstoy also devoted himself to literary pursuits: it is clear that his reading and writing during this period were part of the training through which Tolstoy, an autodidact from an early age, put himself. As the metaliterary comments within the Sevastopol tales suggest (and his diaries corroborate), the young Tolstoy thought hard about the craft of fiction and studied other novelists' practice of this craft intently as he read their work.[12]

The works known as "Sevastopol in December," "Sevastopol in May," and "Sevastopol in August, 1855" ["Севастополь в августе, 1855 г."] have been difficult to classify. They fit squarely in the tradition of Russian prose, as understood by Tolstoy: in his often-quoted "A Few Words Apropos of the Book *War and Peace"* ["Несколько слов по поводу книги *Война и мир*"], he declared that the works of Russian prose-writers never fit neatly into European generic molds.¹³ Are "Sevastopol in December," "Sevastopol in May," and "Sevastopol in August, 1855" dispatches from the front, sketches, tales, or, if read together, a proto-novel? Tolstoy's Sevastopol tales are often classified with Ivan Turgenev's *Notes of a Hunter* [*Записки охотника*, 1852] and Fyodor Dostoevsky's *Notes from the House of the Dead* [*Записки из мертвого дома*, 1862] as works on the boundary between fiction and non-fiction, with ties to the literary sketch. These authors, as they introduced the reading public to some facet of Russian reality usually ignored in print, worked their sketches into extended narratives, or framed tales, on their way to becoming a novel. (Mikhail Lermontov's earlier *A Hero of Our Time* [*Герой нашего времени*, 1840], with its description of life in the Caucasus, is a familiar forerunner of these works.) Viktor Shklovsky declared that these works of Lermontov, Turgenev, Tolstoy, and Dostoevsky constituted a native Russian alternative to the European novel. Shklovsky characterizes the latter as being a novel of family or the life of one individual, while suggesting that the new Russian form transcends this narrow focus.¹⁴ Tolstoy's Sevastopol tales are clearly rooted in the Russian literary genealogy that Shklovsky describes. For example, Tolstoy records in his diary that he (re)read Lermontov's *A Hero of Our Time* on July 11, 1854.¹⁵ He acknowledged his debt to Turgenev's *Notes of a Hunter* both privately, in his diary on July 22, 1853, where he complained that it was hard to sit down to write after reading Turgenev's *Notes*, and publicly in the dedication of "The Woodfelling" ["Рубка леса"] to Turgenev in 1855.¹⁶ As a developing novelist, Tolstoy also drew on sources outside the Russian tradition. Jean-Jacques Rousseau and Laurence Sterne are usually cited as formative influences; Tolstoy was inspired by Charles Dickens as he wrote *Childhood* [*Детство*, 1852] and the rest of his trilogy; and, like Homer, Stendhal was an important model as Tolstoy started to write about war. Tolstoy discovered William Makepeace Thackeray when he was at work on the Sevastopol tales: Tolstoy read him after composing the first tale and worked references to him into the second. In what follows, I will focus on Harriet Beecher Stowe as another formative influence on Tolstoy. Tolstoy would champion Stowe in his late *What Is Art?* [*Что такое искусство?*, 1897],¹⁷ but she has barely appeared among the pantheon of novelists cited as influences on the young Tolstoy.¹⁸ How did Stowe figure in Tolstoy's literary consciousness as he wrote his Sevastopol tales?

On August 28, 1854, a few months before he arrived in Sevastopol, Tolstoy records in his diary that he bought "OTH," his shorthand for *Onkel Toms Hütte*, the German translation of *Uncle Tom's Cabin*. He then reports reading it on August 29, 30, and 31, while sick, without further comment.[19] This novel, which was enormously popular in Europe, as well as in America, held particular interest for Russian readers since comparisons of slavery and serfdom were inevitable.[20] Serfdom was a topic that occupied Tolstoy, like so many of his peers, during this period, both because he was a serf-owner and because the Russian military depended so heavily on serf conscription.[21] (As Anne Hruska has shown in "Love and Slavery: Serfdom, Emancipation, and Family in Tolstoy's Fiction," serfdom was so enmeshed in Tolstoy's conception of love and family life that it would figure in the depths, if not on the surface, of all the fiction he went on to write.) It is likely that *Uncle Tom's Cabin* affected Tolstoy on a number of levels, as serf-owner, as a Russian subject, as a man seeking God and trying to come to terms with Christian teaching, as a motherless child, and—of most interest to me here—as a writer.

Stowe's goal in writing *Uncle Tom's Cabin* was to make her readers "bethink themselves," to use a term Tolstoy would popularize years later, when he commanded his readers to do just that in a work with that title ("Одумайтесь").[22] To this end, Stowe presents her readers with pathos, sermonizes, and stirs protest against slavery as she strives to bring about a conversion of the spirit. As Jane Tompkins has argued, Stowe wanted slavery to come to an end, but "the true goal of Stowe's rhetorical undertaking is nothing less than the institution of the kingdom of heaven on earth."[23] Tompkins explains that, as an alternative to the social order that has supported slavery, whether actively or by looking the other way, Stowe presents a vision of a realm ruled harmoniously by "motherly loving kindness," as embodied by Rachel Halliday in the Quaker settlement that helps Eliza, George, and their son escape.[24] Stowe writes *Uncle Tom's Cabin* from a point of view that is unabashedly maternal: she often addresses herself directly to mothers, and her icon of the tragedy of slavery is the separation of children from their mothers.[25]

As will be seen below, Tolstoy develops his own mix of pathos, sermon, and protest in what he called his "epic of Sevastopol."[26] These features had already started to manifest themselves in *Childhood* and *Boyhood* [*Отрочество*, 1854], concerned as they are with the death of the narrator's mother and his longing for her. However, the treatment of pathos, sermon, and protest reaches a new stage in the Sevastopol tales as Tolstoy shifted from a personal sorrow, the death of the child's mother, to a national (or international) sorrow, the pain of others at Sevastopol. Since Harriet Beecher Stowe used maternal pathos, sentimental technique, and sermonic poetics so powerfully in her national protest novel, it would have been natural for Tolstoy—who remained, as Richard Gustafson has noted, subject to longings for "a mother's embrace"—to take note of how she went about it.[27]

Tolstoy, as a devotee of Rousseau and Sterne, was very much attuned to the potential and the versatility of sentimental style.[28] "The power of the Russian nineteenth-century novel," in the words of Robert Belknap, "depends in part on earlier techniques of novel-writing which most Western novelists had abandoned."[29] Tolstoy and other Russians did not write well-made French novels, nor did they practice the craft of fiction that would later be prescribed by the guild of Henry James and his disciples. Often in the novels of Tolstoy, the author intrudes; the poetics are didactic (Morson); the tactics may even be sentimental. But, as Belknap suggests, these techniques can be a source of power. Philip Fisher has observed that many great nineteenth-century novelists, Tolstoy and Dostoevsky among them, relied on sentimentality to bring about "radical revision" within "accepted patterns of feeling and representation."[30] Stowe's *Uncle Tom's Cabin* provided the young Tolstoy with an immediate model of how to derive power from sentimental techniques.[31]

In what follows, I use Stowe as point of reference as I examine Tolstoy's strategies for incorporating pathos, sermon, bitter truth, and a spirit of protest into the Sevastopol tales. The features at stake in this discussion remain a constant of Tolstoy's writing. They became notoriously dominant in his late works. In the early Sevastopol tales, as in his great novels, *War and Peace* [Война и мир, 1869] and *Anna Karenina* [Анна Каренина, 1877], Tolstoy used these features in a more reserved, muted, and mysterious way, sometimes nearly, but never completely, canceling them out. Thus, he subjects pathos to withering analysis, he ironizes over the sermon, or he undercuts protest by pointing to the futility of trying to change. But even after Tolstoy performs these operations, the pathos, sermon, and protest are never fully suppressed. They remain unmistakable features of Tolstoy's writing and a source of its enduring power.

Tolstoy, "Uncle Tim," and Stowe's Devices

"Reading the story of some English lady [рассказ какой-то Английской барыни], I was struck by the ease of her devices [непринужденность ее приемов], which I lack, and which I must work to acquire and pay attention to."[32] This excerpt from Tolstoy's diary of November 1, 1853, shows how his literary apprenticeship worked: as he read the fiction of others, he concerned himself with his own development as a novelist—what could he learn from the style of others? Boris Eikhenbaum raised the possibility that Harriet Beecher Stowe's early story "Uncle Tim," which appeared in the journal *The Contemporary* [*Современник*] in Russian translation in 1853, prompted Tolstoy to record this comment in his diary.[33] Whereas Eikhenbaum states that it is "possible" Tolstoy had this story in mind, the compilers of the notes to Tolstoy's diary in the Chertkov edition of Tolstoy's *Complete Works* are more certain: they write that the story by "some English lady" was "evidently" "Uncle Tim" by the American Stowe, especially since the journals of the period contained no other stories by "an English lady."[34] Since *The Contemporary* was regular reading for him, it is extremely likely that Tolstoy read "Uncle Tim" in 1853, even if it was not the story that prompted the reflections on his craft in his diary.

In Eikhenbaum's view, Stowe's story is characterized by the very ease of narration that Tolstoy found lacking in his early work. Eikhenbaum quotes the opening lines and several other lines culled from Stowe's "Uncle Tim" as demonstrations (without comment).[35] In the Russian translation, which omits a preamble in the first person, "Uncle Tim" opens with the narrator's address to the reader: "Did you ever see the little village of Newbury in New England? I dare say you never did . . ."[36] Stowe's narrator thus takes the narratee under her wing in a confident manner. Later in the story, the narrator uses "you" for a whole paragraph, in which she describes "your" recognition of a certain place, including what "you surely remember," what "you may have admired," what "you haven't forgotten . . ."[37] Not only does she usher "you" into the story, she tells you what is going on in your mind. The other examples Eikhenbaum cites to illustrate Stowe's natural, unforced narration are cases of transitions that are made by the means of narrative intrusions. In all cases, the narrator wields authority in a natural, confident, reassuring—and maternal—way.[38] (Tolstoy may have admired her style and "devices," but they were not naturally suited to *his* narrative voice.) In content, "Uncle Tim," a "New England sketch," offers, aside from regional color, a heart-warming story of family life and Christian community, with good resulting from the friendship between a young minister, George Griswold, who is about to die, and his sister's suitor, James Benton, who is so moved by George's first sermon that he becomes a kind of disciple and then, after George's death, a minister himself.[39]

As the diary entry cited by Eikhenbaum and several others like it attest, during this period of literary apprenticeship Tolstoy was consciously working on his "devices" and other features of narration. Not satisfied with some aspects of his own style, he noted how others practiced the craft he was trying to master. Tolstoy's reading habits thus make it very likely that when he read the bestseller *Uncle Tom's Cabin* in 1854, he read it attentively, paying attention not just to the message but to the poetics of the novel—all the more so since he was already attuned to Stowe's poetics from his reading of "Uncle Tim" the year before. I suggest that Stowe be numbered among the novelists, such as Stendhal, Thackeray, Turgenev, and Nikolai Gogol, who figured in Tolstoy's creative consciousness as he wrote the Sevastopol tales.

Uncle Tom's Cabin in Sevastopol: "Do not be ashamed . . ."

Whereas Viktor Shklovsky places Tolstoy's Sevastopol tales along with Turgenev's *Notes of a Hunter* in a Russian literary movement out of which rose a new Russian novel, Philip Fisher, in the context of his discussion of American realism, places these two Russian works together with Stowe's *Uncle Tom's Cabin* in a larger mid-nineteenth-century movement that "put onto the map of representation what had until then been overlooked or unmentioned worlds of people."[40] Fisher credits Tolstoy with writing "the first realistic account of ordinary men in war," suggesting that Tolstoy did for war what Turgenev did for serfdom and Stowe did for slavery.[41] (In fact, Turgenev's *Notes of a Hunter* had, from early on, been compared to Stowe's novel and was often even called the Russian *Uncle Tom's Cabin*.)[42] Tolstoy, following in the mode of both Turgenev and Stowe, sought to "confer visibility" on aspects of life that were hitherto largely ignored in art.[43] In fact, much like Stowe, he focused on conferring visibility on *the pain of others*.

Stowe's goal in *Uncle Tom's Cabin*, as she explains in her "Concluding Remarks," was "to exhibit [slavery] in a *living dramatic reality*."[44] She wrote to make what she saw as the evil and pain of slavery real, live, and dramatic to her readers. She does so in the sentimentalist mode, which had historically been, in Fisher's words, "a crucial tactic of politically radical representation."[45] But Stowe herself draws attention to the limits of the novel as she reminds us of the real world beyond: "Nothing of tragedy can be written, can be spoken, can be conceived, that equals the frightful reality of scenes daily and hourly acting on our shores, beneath the shadow of American law, and the shadow of the cross of Christ."[46] Stowe sought to use "sentimental power" to enact change, although, as Jane Tompkins has argued, in answer to the question of what is to be done, Stowe envisioned not only "specific alterations in the current political and economic arrangements," which she believed fell short because they do not change "the moral conditions that produced slavery in the first place."[47] Stowe also had her sights on something more radical, "a change of heart" or a "conversion in the spirit."[48]

Tolstoy, similarly, sought "to exhibit" his subject, the war, "in a *living dramatic reality*," as Stowe had done for slavery. In his effort to make the siege of Sevastopol real, live, and dramatic, Tolstoy takes extreme measures to involve the reader. Eikhenbaum observes that in the first Sevastopol tale, Tolstoy puts the reader in the position of "an inquisitive correspondent," in a comment that recalls the work of Russell and others.[49] There is, in fact, overlap in the English journalist's and the Russian novelist's accounts, in both substance and style. But Tolstoy went further in involving the reader.[50] He uses, most famously, second person narration in "Sevastopol in December," discussed by Gary Saul Morson in his essay "The Reader as Voyeur: Tolstoi and the Poetics of Didactic Fiction." Tolstoy's purpose, according to Morson, is to eliminate the aesthetic distance normally assumed in reading, to "frame" the reader, and to make the reader feel responsible for the pain seen in Sevastopol.[51]

Tolstoy begins the tale with a lyrical description of an approach to the besieged Sevastopol, then interjects descriptions of what "you" (the narratee, as I will call the referent of the second person pronoun used in this tale) see, do, and feel, as you are ferried into Sevastopol and led through the town, into the hospital, where you visit with the wounded, the amputees, and the dying, and then to the fourth bastion where you witness a death.

The use of "you" in "Sevastopol in May" is certainly overdetermined. Sermons, editorials, dispatches from war correspondents, sentimental fiction, regional sketches, and—as Morson argues—guidebooks all come to mind as genres where this device thrives. That said, Stowe's "devices" provided Tolstoy with further specific models for this form. As mentioned above, Stowe starts off "Uncle Tim" using the second person and then returns to it later in the story. When Stowe uses the same device in *Uncle Tom's Cabin*, more is at stake. Stowe wants to "frame" (to borrow Morson's term) the "you" she addresses.[52] In *Gendered Interventions: Narrative Discourse in the Victorian Novel*, Robyn Warhol shows how Stowe uses direct address to her readers both to engage them in the action of the novel and to remind them of the reality out there, the reality in which the readers live and feel and for which the readers bear, as Stowe reminds them, real responsibility.[53] Stowe uses forms of address and appeal to the reader, with varying degrees of immediacy. For example, early on, her narrator ushers the reader into the action as an observer in her first description of Uncle Tom's cabin, modulating between an inclusive first person plural and second person: "Let us enter the dwelling. The evening meal at the house. . . . Therefore, doubt not that it is her [Aunt Chloe] you see by the fire . . ."[54] Here the narrator of *Uncle Tom's Cabin* uses the device of second person address to the reader casually, as she did in "Uncle Tim." But at other points in *Uncle Tom's Cabin*, Stowe uses the second person not simply to usher her reader in as an observer, but to put her reader in the protagonist's shoes, as in the question "how fast could *you* walk?" if you were trying to save *your* child, as Eliza is as she escapes.[55] Stowe wrote *Uncle Tom's Cabin* in order to engage readers in the pain and sorrow of others, but she also reminds readers that the pain represented in the novel is "nothing," however, compared to the "frightful reality of scenes daily and hourly acting on our shores."[56]

By asking us how fast *we* could walk, Stowe draws overt attention to, and encourages, a process of identification between her readers and her subjects. She often does so by appealing to the readers' experiences of maternal love, evidently relying on the assumption that the hearts of mothers will be pierced by another's pain, especially if they have undergone the loss of a child of their own. These operations are fundamental to the sentimental novel, as Fisher explains: "The sentimental novel creates the extension of feeling on which the restitution of humanity is based by means of equations between the deep common feelings of the reader and the exotic but analogous situations of the characters."[57] Stowe's algebra of sentimentalism in *Uncle Tom's Cabin* has raised resistance: it strikes many critics as naïve, narcissistic, and dangerous.[58] Can one person really fathom the pain of another? Does Stowe not overlook differences? Is, for example, a shared experience of maternal bereavement enough of a common denominator to prompt any real understanding of others? However, other scholars have reminded us that Stowe's "equations of feeling" are an act of faith, rooted in a particular vision of Christian love and love of neighbor that eradicates earthly differences as it looks toward heaven. How Tolstoy responded to this feature in Stowe's work is impossible to say, but his Sevastopol tales suggest that he himself was, on the one hand, drawn to "equations of feeling" (and the sentiments of brotherly love that they create), but, on the other hand, wary of these very equations.

In "Sevastopol in December," as Morson argues, Tolstoy attempts to put "you" into relationship with others and their pain.[59] The greatest concentration of pain is met in the makeshift military hospital where "you are suddenly struck by the sight and the smell of forty or fifty amputees and other severely wounded patients."[60] The narrator coaxes "you" into the room, saying: "Do not trust the feeling that holds you back on the threshold of the hall—it is a wrong feeling— go on, do not be ashamed that you have come as if *to look* at the sufferers, don't be ashamed to approach them and talk to them: the unfortunate like to see a compassionate human face, they like to tell about their sufferings and hear words of love and sympathy."[61] Tolstoy's emphasis on "to look" in this passage anticipates Susan Sontag's vexed questions about the ethics of *regarding* the pain of others.[62] Whereas not being willing to look could be a matter of cowardice—of wanting to spare oneself the pain—the narrator's repetition of "do not be ashamed to . . ." suggests that the narratee may be held back by more complicated feelings.[63] The narrator assures "you" that your compassion will be comforting to the sufferer, *but how convincing is this assurance?* Shame lingers in the reader, even if the narratee is finally coaxed in. Tolstoy complicates the "extension of feeling" (to apply Fisher's term[64]) by airing this shame in an unsettling way.[65]

As the narratee converses with one of the wounded, an amputee, the narrator explains that "suffering somehow inspires, in addition to deep feelings of compassion, a fear of causing offense and a lofty respect for the one who undergoes it."[66] Tolstoy here shows his trademark technique, detected by Nikolai Chernyshevsky already in these early works, of presenting the "dialectics of the soul."⁶⁷ Another early critic, Dmitry Pisarev, wrote that Tolstoy managed to bring out "the mysterious, unclear movements of the soul that have not reached consciousness and are not completely understood even by the person who experiences them."⁶⁸ The sophistication with which Tolstoy tracks these movements of the soul threatens to frustrate the compassionate leap required for "equations of feeling." A soul too bogged down in "dialectics" may have trouble responding to the pain of another.

Soon, "you" are approached by the wife of this amputee, who is there caring for her husband. After she has chattered away about how her husband was wounded, showing her pride in his heroic sacrifice, her husband responds dismissively: "That's my missus, your honor! You'll have to excuse her, you know, that's a woman's way [бабье дело]—she says silly things."⁶⁹ At this point, Tolstoy shifts abruptly from this suggestion, made by her husband, of her feminine inadequacy, to the real point, which is the narratee's realization of his own inadequacy as he regards the pain of this amputee and others like him: "You start to understand the defenders of Sevastopol; you become for some reason ashamed of yourself in front of this man. You want to say too much to him to express your compassion and your bewilderment to him; but you can't find the words or are dissatisfied with the ones that do come to mind,—and you silently bow before this taciturn, unconscious grandeur and strength of spirit, this modesty in the face of its own worth."⁷⁰ In this synopsis of what "you," the narratee, are feeling, the narrator confirms that you *feel* compassion for the amputee in pain, but explains that you are unable to *express* it adequately. Tolstoy affirms but subverts the impulse of sentimentalism.

"So what if he's a stranger, you still have to have pity"

As "you" approach another sufferer, who is on the verge of death, the amputee's wife takes on the role of guide—the narrator signals that he cedes that role to her when he refers to her as "your [female] guide" ["ваша путеводительница"].⁷¹ She hovers over you, "as if you were kin."⁷² The narrator uses a fixed expression, but on the literal level it suggests that she, for her part, feels a sense of relatedness to you, a stranger, with whom under normal circumstances, outside of this site of suffering, she would have nothing in common. But now you are in the zone of her sentimental motherly embrace. When "you" ask whether another sufferer is too far gone to even hear you, she responds that he still hears, although barely, and tells of how that morning she had fed him tea, explaining her actions by adding: "So what if he's a stranger, you still have to have pity" ["Что ж, хоть и чужой, все надо жалость иметь"].[73] Of course, the wife's words could be dismissed by menfolk as womanish sentiment (her husband had in fact just declared saying silly things to be what women do, in Russian, "бабье дело"). But Tolstoy is challenging the narratee and, ultimately, the reader to penetrate to the heart of this sentimental message.

The amputee's wife sets forth in her simple, expressive, and difficult-to-translate idiomatic statement the law of love for one's neighbor— "So what if he's a stranger, you still have to have pity" ["Что ж, хоть и чужой, все надо жалость иметь"]. Part of the difficulty in rendering this statement in English stems from the way the Russian grammar encodes a moral understanding of the way God and his creation work. The amputee's wife's words do *not* suggest that this kind of compassion for strangers comes naturally or instinctively. The word "надо" ["must," "have to"] means that an external law, an external authority, is being imposed, even if it is one that she also feels deeply in her maternal heart. She uses "надо," a modal predicate (even if not strictly a verb) that is *deontic*, in the sense that it attempts to "bind" people to perform an action. Without any overt dative (to identify the person[s] bound to perform this action) the deontic modal has a universal force: any and all must perform the activity, in this case, all must fulfill God's will and have compassion on a dying man, even though he may be a stranger.[74] This message of compassion as a deontic modal, which is articulated by the amputee's wife, is not what comes naturally, even though it is often embedded in childhood as the spiritual equivalent of a mother's—or wet nurse's—milk; this view will resurface in Tolstoy's work as the core of his religious message.[75]

In his novels, Tolstoy will continue to feature heroes who, like "you" the narratee in "Sevastopol in May," do not know what to do or say when faced with the pain of others. Thus, for example, in *Anna Karenina* as he reflects on Kitty's loving care for his dying brother Nikolai, Levin notes his own inadequacy in the face of suffering and death, even that of his own near and dear one. Tolstoy's Levin is thus a lot like the "you" that Tolstoy envisions in the Sevastopol tales: both Tolstoyan constructs are left anxious, churning in the dialectics of their souls, as they regard the pain of others. By contrast, Kitty, like the amputee's wife in Sevastopol, acts on the compassion she feels. Levin concludes that Kitty learned something about nursing and comforting the sick and dying in Soden (when she, in imitation of Varenka, tried to act as a sister of mercy to suffering Russians), but he is impressed by—and perhaps on some profound level envious of—something more than her nursing skills: her faith. Although he remembers that Agafya Mikhailovna, his peasant nurse, was also able to care for the dying, Levin determines that their response was *not* animal or instinctual, but rooted in their faith. What Tolstoy has Levin spell out in *Anna Karenina* is contained, in seed form, in the amputee's wife's words: "So what if he's a stranger, you still have to have pity."

The acts of the amputee's wife, as she shows compassion for this dying man by feeding him tea, evoke the Gospel pericopes in which a woman anoints Jesus—and, in Luke, weeping, also bathes his feet with her tears—in anticipation of his death.[76] To the chagrin of the disciples, who complain about the waste of the "very expensive" ointment, Jesus approves the woman's expression of love—tears and all—even in Mark and Matthew, declaring that wheresoever the gospel will be preached, the woman's deed will be told. As he chides the male disciples for not grasping the significance of this woman's compassion, Jesus implicitly criticizes their own inadequate response to a body (soon to be) in pain. Certainly, anointing bodies for death was woman's work in that context. But Jesus transcends divisions of labor to intimate that these male disciples should respond to the suffering and the dying. It is a deontic modal; it is God's law. In the Sevastopol tales, Tolstoy evokes this Gospel precedent, putting the reader in the position of these disciples.[77]

In her expression of compassion, "so what if he's a stranger, you still have to have pity," the amputee's wife—"your" guide in this zone of blood, suffering, and death—clearly makes the "equations of feeling" at the heart of sentimentalism, but she does so without making them overt. As she comforts and cares for the stranger, she is both obeying God's law and extending to the stranger the love she feels for her own husband. The message the amputee's wife expresses is one that is often iterated in *Uncle Tom's Cabin* and is central to its ethics, plot, and poetics. In the action of the novel, Stowe's heroes and heroines model this extension of familial love to non-family members, often fulfilling the commandment to love your neighbor explicitly. If, for example, members of the Quaker household who shelter Eliza during her escape show her compassion, it is because, as Stowe makes explicit, they are extrapolating from love of their own kin to love of neighbors who are strangers.⁷⁸ (Tolstoy tends to compress this step.) Or when Eliza attempts to get Mrs. Bird to help her along her way, she tries to *move* her into action. She suddenly asks Mrs. Bird "Ma'am . . . have you ever lost a child?" When she gets an affirmative answer, Eliza says: "Then you will feel for me." Eliza proceeds to explain to Mrs. Bird that she has buried two of her children and is running away with the child in her arms because her master was going to sell him, "a baby that had never been away from his mother in his life."⁷⁹ Stowe uses the same dynamic that Eliza orchestrates with Mrs. Bird to activate in her readers compassion for the slaves who suffer in the novel.⁸⁰ (Whether these two experiences of losing a child are commensurable or not is open to debate; Stowe, for better or for worse, uses the common denominator as a source of compassion.)⁸¹

In the finale of the novel, Stowe addresses mothers, saying: "And you, mothers of America, —you, who have learned, by the cradles of your own children, to love and feel for all mankind, —by the sacred love you bear your child . . . by the desolation of the empty cradle, that silent nursery, —I beseech you, pity those mothers that are constantly made childless by the American slave-trade!"⁸² Although Stowe often specifically played on maternal heartstrings, her sentimental techniques had wider applications. In fact, Stowe was recycling an old tactic, which dates back to Homer: the denouement of the *Iliad* hangs on Achilles actually making the equation of feeling that the grief-stricken Priam prompts when he asks Achilles to imagine what his own father will feel when he, soon, will grieve for the dead Achilles. This equation of sentiment plays on paternal love, so important in Homer's context. This (along with the will of the gods) works: Achilles takes pity on Priam and surrenders the body. Stowe puts this strategy, tried and true in the *Iliad*, to her own use throughout *Uncle Tom's Cabin*, as part of a sentimental feminization of culture.

Tolstoy, like Stowe, understood that to act on the reader's conscience, he should move the reader. To get the job done, he relies on the amputee's wife, making her "our guide" in the hospital and having her articulate the message. But can the reader adopt her credo—"so what if he is a stranger, you still have to have pity"? Although Tolstoy does not present it as instinctive, natural behavior, the context suggests that somehow what this (presumably) illiterate soldier's wife feels and expresses is probably harder for the reader to express and maybe even to feel (gender, class, education, and faith may all figure in). Yet Tolstoy is not dismissing the amputee's wife's compassion for the dying stranger as "бабье дело" or something only fit for women. This compassion is possibly what the reader has been taught, and may even feel, even if the reader does not and cannot express it. What has been revealed to the soldier's wife has remained hidden from the wise and prudent reader. But here in the hospital in Sevastopol Tolstoy offers the reader a glimpse of compassion in action.

The amputee's wife, our "(female) guide" in the hospital ward, is soon left behind in this tale, as the tour of Sevastopol continues. In each of the two subsequent tales, however, Tolstoy includes sisters of mercy, who also serve as the reader's "(female) guides" to regarding the pain of Sevastopol.[83] When the narrator praises the sisters of mercy in "Sevastopol in May" for their "active, practical engagement," he contrasts it to "empty, feminine, morbidly weepy compassion" in a move that shows him clearly dismissing certain forms of feminine response to the pain of others.[84] What distinguishes these sisters of mercy is that they *act* on the credo of: "So what if he's a stranger, you still have to have pity."

Tolstoy's Sevastopol tales reflect—and contribute to—the redefinition of heroism for the modern age that began during the Crimean War. The time was ripe. One manifestation of this new heroism was the way Russian, French, and English sisters of mercy came to constitute a new kind of war hero. Florence Nightingale towered as the English icon of this new heroism, gendered feminine, but contributing to the reconsideration of masculine heroism that this "modern" war brought about.[85] Lytton Strachey commented on the lack of sentimentality in Florence Nightingale, noting that her "heroism was of sterner stuff."[86] In his depiction of the amputee's wife and in his tributes to Russian sisters of mercy, Tolstoy adds his Russian perspective. In contrast to the image of Florence Nightingale during and after the Crimean War, Tolstoy's Russian sisters of mercy (even if they do converse in French[87]) and wives of amputees are characterized by a sentimental ethos and a sentimental power, which figures into the reconsideration of masculine heroism that Tolstoy begins at Sevastopol and then develops in *War and Peace* and beyond. (Platon Karataev acts on the same principles as the amputee's wife, considering every neighbor his kin and showing compassion for strangers.)

"The death and sufferings of such a worthless worm as me": Equations of Feeling in Sevastopol and at Borodino

In "Sevastopol in December," the reader finds himself on the threshold of the inner sanctum of a makeshift hospital, without feminine guidance. The narrator tells "you" to enter only if your nerves are strong. Here is where the doctors are engaged in the "repulsive but beneficent business of amputation."[88] As this description makes clear, war "in its real expression—in blood, in suffering, in death . . ." is to be found not on the battlefield, but here in this zone that, as Eikhenbaum has reminded us, had previously been out of bounds for art.[89] As "you" witness an amputation, watching as "a sharp curved knife enters into the white, healthy body" and see an amputated arm tossed by a *feldsher* into the corner, Tolstoy's narrator draws attention to another wounded man who watches his comrade's operation: he suffers "not as much from physical pain, as from the psychic pain of anticipation."[90] Tolstoy shows one man regarding the pain of another, his "fellow soldier" ["товарищ"] who is his neighbor, both literally and in the Christian sense. Whether intentionally or not, Tolstoy recreates Pascal's "image of the human condition," which Pascal describes as a cell where men, all condemned to death, watch their fellows be executed, one by one, waiting their own turn "in suffering and without hope."[91] The enumeration of the particular sights the reader will face in this room ends abruptly with a dash, after the mention of the moans of the man who is watching, waiting for his limb to be amputated. After the dash, the narrator summarizes what you will see (soul-rending sights, war in its true expression) and what you will not see (war as it is ordinarily depicted, in glorified mode).

The narrator then turns back to "you." What does this sight of the blood, suffering, and death of others do to you? Tolstoy suggests that you are changed by the experience, so that you ask: "What do the death and sufferings of such a worthless worm as I am mean in comparison to all these deaths and all these sufferings?"[92] The sight of the pain of others has reminded you of your own mortality, which seems to have brought about a change in you: you now cease to see yourself as all that matters, or even what matters most. What you feel at this point may be the seeds of brotherly love. Tolstoy gives you only an intimation of these feelings before bringing you back to your "normal state of superficiality, petty concerns and engagement only in the present."[93] Outside, in the sunshine, you are next met with the sight of an officer's funeral procession exiting from a church; even though you might still hear shots being fired, the narrator announces that what you see and hear "will not take you back to your former thoughts [those experienced in the amputation room]: the funeral will strike you as a supremely beautiful military spectacle, the sounds as supremely beautiful military sounds, and you will connect neither with this spectacle, nor with these sounds, the clear thought, transferred to yourself, of suffering and death, as you did in the dressing station."[94] The Russian syntax is dense, but Tolstoy indicates that the suffering and death of others no longer signify what they did in the amputation room, when you "transferred" the suffering and death you beheld there—or at least the thought of it—to yourself and felt inklings of a transcendent brotherly love. Back in the amputation room "you" performed an equation of sentiment as you responded to the blood, suffering, and death of others.

The love in the face of blood, suffering, and death felt briefly in the amputation chamber of "Sevastopol in December" is made explicit in *War and Peace*. During the battle of Borodino, Tolstoy represents war, as he did in Sevastopol, "in its true expression," "in blood, in suffering, and in death," when the severely wounded Andrei Bolkonsky finds himself in a dressing station. He experiences both a horror that, true to his earlier presentiment, human beings in this war are *chair à canon* [cannon fodder] and an outburst of love, brought on by his own suffering, the care of the doctors, and what he himself feels as he watches the doctors amputate the leg of the man lying next to him. This man turns out to be Anatole Kuragin, his personal enemy, now his neighbor in this site of blood, suffering, and death. Tolstoy thus reprises the amputation scene in the Sevastopol tales, substituting Andrei and Anatole, with their personal connections, for you the reader and the nameless amputee. Prince Andrei behaves very sentimentally as he bursts into "tender, loving tears for people, for himself and for their and his errors."[95]

The chapter ends with his inner monologue, as Andrei haltingly, ecstatically, tearfully, and sentimentally invokes Jesus's sermons about love: "Compassion, love for our brothers, for those who love us, love for those who hate us, love for our enemies—yes, that love which Christ preached on earth, which Princess Marya tried to teach me, and which I didn't understand; this is why I was sorry to lose life, this is what is still left for me if I was to live. But now it's too late. I know it!"[96] His identification of this love as something that "Princess Marya tried to teach [him] and which [he] didn't understand" reminds us that he had earlier dismissed it as womanish sentiment or "бабье дело." (As he lay wounded on the battlefield at Austerlitz, contemplating the amulet his sister had given him, he longed for faith to be as simple as it seemed to be for his sister, but he was still dismissive of her feminine piety and her Jesus; he may have felt a softening of the heart when his wife was giving birth and dying, but after Natasha's betrayal he dismissed Christ's teachings about forgiveness and loving your enemies as womanish sentiment, not fit for a man.)[97]

This scene of Andrei watching as his neighbor's leg is amputated echoes, with variations, what happened in the amputation room in "Sevastopol in December" as "you" watched and as you transferred to yourself the suffering and death. What Tolstoy revealed there only in part is expressed more fully—and more sentimentally—in *War and Peace* when Andrei weeps and feels a transcendent brotherly love as he reacts to his own pain and responds to his neighbor's. The wounded Andrei obeys, invokes, and echoes the sermons of Jesus, which were evoked more mutedly in the original scenes in "Sevastopol in December."

In the very next chapter of *War and Peace*, Tolstoy shifts the action to Napoleon as he, weakened by a cold, looks out on the battlefield of Borodino, depressed and not his usual self-satisfied self.[98] We are told that for the first time he "transferred to himself [на себя переносил] the sufferings and death he had seen on the battlefield."[99] Tolstoy reinforces the point in the next sentence: "The heaviness in his head and chest reminded him of the possibility of even his own suffering and death." Tolstoy again provides a variation on what happened to "you" in "Sevastopol in December." Napoleon does what "you" did as you "transferred to yourself" the "thought of the suffering and death" of others. Tolstoy splits the original scene into two halves—Andrei witnessing the amputation and Napoleon "transferring suffering and death"—and then develops each into its own episode. The two adjacent episodes in *War and Peace* are complementary and together hark back to their common source in "Sevastopol in December."

Much as "you" did in the first Sevastopol tale, Napoleon transfers to himself the suffering and death of others—to which he is ordinarily impervious. For this brief moment, Napoleon performs an equation of feeling, which is an entirely new emotional operation for him. As characterized by Aleksandr Pushkin in Chapter 2, Canto 14 of *Eugene Onegin* [*Евгений Онегин*], Napoleon and his imitators "regard all others as zeroes and themselves as the only integer, ... the millions of two-legged creatures are just tools."[100] Tolstoy even echoes this view of Napoleon in "Sevastopol in May" when he notes that each of the officers he describes is "a little Napoleon," "a little monster, ready to start a conflict, even now, and to kill a hundred or so men simply in order to get an extra star or a third more pay."[101] To be (like) Napoleon for Tolstoy, as for Pushkin, meant being willing to *dis*regard the death and pain of others in order to achieve your goals. But here, for this one moment in *War and Peace*, Tolstoy's Napoleon himself starts to take stock of his own mortality and ceases to care about the goals he has been selfishly striving for and the war he had been waging (we are told that at this moment Napoleon does not care about his goals of Moscow, victory, or glory). He feels, for the first time, the equality and brotherhood without which these equations of feeling cannot be made. The rationale is that you have to acknowledge the other as your equal in order to respond to his pain.[102] The vulnerability Napoleon feels, as he is moved for the first time by the pain and death of others, humanizes him for this moment. The next step would have been for Napoleon, the epitome of selfish behavior, to feel brotherly love for these men.

Tolstoy's Napoleon in *War and Peace*, however, reverts back to being his Napoleonic—selfish and often sappy—self.[103] Tolstoy's narratee in "Sevastopol in December," when he steps out of the amputation chamber into the sunshine, ceases to transfer to himself the suffering and death of others. He will go on to witness, toward the end of "Sevastopol in December," the death of a sailor, which, like the scene in the amputation room, will rend his soul. He will be moved to patriotic feeling, as Tolstoy's narrator praises the heroes of this "epic of Sevastopol," the "Russian people," for their sacrifice. But, as the tale ends, the military band is playing a waltz on the boulevard, with the sounds of war from the bastions echoing and possibly harmonizing with the music.[104] As Morson argues, the story sets about disturbing the reader's sense of "aesthetic joy," which it does.[105] And yet, as Tolstoy illustrates time and time again, human beings are all too prone to surrender to music and other diversions. "Sevastopol in December" thus stirs in the reader discordant messages about regarding the pain of others.

The Sun Also Rises on Sevastopol

"Sevastopol in May," Tolstoy's second tale, written shortly after completion of the first, follows a handful of officers as they move in and out of danger over two days and especially on a starlit spring night of heavy casualties. It also presents, at the beginning, at the end, and at critical points throughout, monologues from the narrator. Thus, recalling the preacher in Ecclesiastes, Tolstoy's narrator comments on the vanity of the officers' concerns—they strive for earthly rewards in the form of "Annas and Vladimirs" (Russian medals of honor)—while "the angel of death ceaselessly hovers" above them, while the sun rises again and then sets.[106] Tolstoy's narrator bemoans the loss of life, but adds a disturbing note to his lament about all human toil being for naught when, after reminding us that "the question not resolved by diplomats is being resolved even less by powder and blood." Then, announcing that he wants to share a "strange thought" that has often occurred to him about war, he asks, why not just dismiss the armies and have the matter decided by one-on-one combat between two men?[107]

Boris Eikhenbaum observes that these monologues sound like sermons and argues that the new sermonic mode that Tolstoy developed in "Sevastopol in May" was "an artistic discovery" critical to the development of Tolstoy's style.[108] In the words of Eikhenbaum, the author "holds forth as an orator, as a sermonist—he does not narrate, nor does he even describe, but rather he declaims, he sermonizes." Tolstoy sermonizes on subject matter that has been popular with preachers from Ecclesiastes on.[109] According to Eikhenbaum, when Tolstoy's narrator is in this sermonizing mode, he "does not identify with any of his characters and does not participate in the events," "nor is he an observer any longer"; he is rather "a sermonist, a judge, whose voice does not mingle in, but overpowers [покрывает] [the voices of the characters], and sounds in the silence like the voice not even of an outsider, but of a being from another world."[110] The sermonic narrative voice, which emerges in "Sevastopol in May" "as if from another world," will return to haunt Tolstoy's fiction.

Eikhenbaum mentions in a footnote to his observation about the sermonic narration in "Sevastopol in May" that Tolstoy had tried his own hand at writing sermons in 1851.[111] Tolstoy's attempts, composed during an Easter week in which he also prepared for communion, have not survived.[112] Tolstoy's diary indicates that he continued to be interested in the sermon as a form of literary persuasion: on November 22, 1853, he comments on the potential of the sermon as a means of "religious education of our lower class"—provided the sermonist is able to "sacrifice his authorial self-love."[113] Tolstoy's composition of sermons in 1851 and his remarks about sermons in 1853 indicate his keen interest in the genre. Orthodoxy offered many models, from the sermons of Byzantine greats, like John Chrysostom, to those of Filaret (1782-1867), the Metropolitan of Moscow, author of the catechism, and a renowned sermonist. Furthermore, as Dmitry Likhachev has observed, Russian literature in its early stages, from the eleventh through the sixteenth centuries, tended to be sermonic and in the seventeenth century the archpriest Avvakum made the narrative of his life into a sermon.[114] Tolstoy admired Karamzin for his interest in moral education, and was familiar with Gogol's preaching in his *Selected Passages from Correspondence with Friends* [Выбранные места из переписки с друзьями, 1847], as well as the sermonic elements that Gogol incorporated into his fiction.[115] Tolstoy also had non-Orthodox inspiration for sermon-writing: Sterne, referred to by the young Tolstoy as his "favorite writer," incorporated sermons into his fiction (and was himself a published author of sermons, a fact Tolstoy probably would not have known).[116] William Makepeace Thackeray, whose works are mentioned in "Sevastopol in May," sermonized periodically in his novels, despite his insistence that sermons do not belong in novels, and he appealed in *Vanity Fair* not just to John Bunyan's *Pilgrim's Progress*, but directly to the book of Ecclesiastes (the mood and style of the preacher of Ecclesiastes leaves its mark on Tolstoy's "epic of Sevastopol").

To this list of possible inspirations for Tolstoy's sermonizing in "Sevastopol in May" should be added Harriet Beecher Stowe. As she wrote to Frederick Douglass in 1851, "I am a ministers [sic] daughter—a ministers [sic] wife & I have had six brothers in the ministry ... & I certainly ought to know something of the feelings of ministers."[117] Robyn Warhol has observed that Stowe had "internalized" "the rhetorical techniques of sermons," and used these "strategies" "to bring home her message to her readers."[118] Stowe appropriated from her sermonic heritage a number of strategies, but she showed a particular genius for denouncing, as if from the pulpit, the perversions and contradictions in the world she inhabited, "beneath the shadow of the American law, and the shadow of the cross of Christ."[119] One of her most effective tactics was to reveal truths that culture covers up. She writes: "Scenes of blood and cruelty are shocking to our ear and heart. What man has nerve to do, man has not nerve to hear. What brother-man and brother-Christian must suffer, cannot be told us, even in our secret chamber, it so harrows up the soul! And yet, oh my country! These things are done under the shadow of thy laws! O, Christ! Thy church sees them, almost in silence!"[120] Her mission is to draw attention to the disturbing, shameful truth about slavery, which institutions (church, country) and individuals (her readers) do their best to ignore. Not only would hearing these truths "harrow up the soul," but it would, or should, make it impossible to carry on according to custom and routine. In *Uncle Tom's Cabin*, Stowe aimed to defamiliarize slavery in the hope that her readers would not be able to revert back to their former, more comfortable perception.

Whereas Stowe had clear goals as she sermonized about slavery, Tolstoy's program is less clear when he sermonizes in "Sevastopol in May." He too, however, tells people what they may not want to hear and he too tries to root out the contradictions in the world he describes. Sevastopol is, to be sure, a special environment, but many of its truths also apply to the public back home. At the start of "Sevastopol in May," the narrator reminds us that the angel of death has been hovering ceaselessly over Sevastopol for months; the tale ends with us contemplating a pile of decaying corpses. In the tale, Tolstoy shows those depicted in relationship to this angel and this pile of corpses: the officers, for the most part, when they are out of danger and not in the trenches or on the bastions, go about Sevastopol as if it were Nevsky Prospect, ignoring the angel of death and the corpses amassing—until they themselves face imminent danger.

To draw the reader's attention to this angel of death and pile of corpses, Tolstoy uses the rhetoric of the sermon, in a pair of linked passages that describe, in a collective way, what has been happening in Sevastopol: Tolstoy offers metonymic indications of human endeavors in what are essentially lists. The first of these occurs at the start of "Sevastopol in May"; the second, which is a reprise of the first, occurs toward the end (Chapter 14). (In the interim, between these chapters, the narration follows individual officers through a night of heavy enemy fire.) Eikhenbaum considers these two passages to be especially sermonic. He observes that Tolstoy repeats words and whole phrases, condensing and introducing new material to intensify their pathos.[121] Whereas in Chapter 1 the narrator mentions the angel of death hovering over Sevastopol and all its activities, in Chapter 14 the angel of death has been replaced by a graphic representation of the (barely) living among the dead: hundreds of people, "with curses and prayers on their parched lips, crawl, toss, turn, and moan" among the corpses strewn over a field—and against the backdrop of the rhythms of nature and the beauty of God's creation. Chapter 14, only a paragraph long, ends with a lyrical description of the sun rising, "promising joy, love, and happiness to all the awakening world."[122] In the next chapter, Tolstoy cuts back to his main participants, the surviving officers, who, out of danger again, revert back to their futile behavior, causing the narrator to call them "little Napoleons."

"Why do they not embrace like brothers in tears of joy and happiness?"

In the next and final chapter (16) of "Sevastopol in May," a ceasefire has been declared. Tolstoy writes: "On our bastion and on the French trench white flags are displayed and between them in the flowering valley in clumps lie, without shoes, in gray and in blue clothing, mangled corpses, which workers are carrying away and laying on stretchers. The horrible, heavy smell of dead flesh fills the air. From Sevastopol and from the French camp crowds of people have poured out to look at this spectacle [of the corpses] and with eager and benevolent curiosity they stream toward each other..."[123] In his description of the Russians and French during the ceasefire, Tolstoy alternately refers to them as *separate and opposed categories*, as befits enemies whose differences explain the war (they come from two separate camps; some corpses wear gray uniforms, whereas others wear blue) and as *united,* as part of the same group (the corpses lie helter-skelter in mixed clumps; the men all mingle and fraternize in the no-man's land where the corpses are strewn). Although the Russians and the French come out of their separate camps in order "to look at the spectacle," they end up drawn not to the spectacle of the corpses but to each other. They exchange words, with the Russians showing off their French; they light each other's pipes and cigarettes; and, in an echo of Homer, two of them exchange cigarette cases.[124] At this point, during the ceasefire, the opposition between French and Russians is drawn into question in an ostensive way.

Earlier in "Sevastopol in May" Tolstoy had begun to deconstruct the differences between Russian and French, friend and foe, differences that provide the structure necessary to animate and support war.¹²⁵ The narrator, in preacher mode in Chapter 1, ends his sermonic opening by questioning war itself as an institution when he shares his "strange thought" with us (Why have whole armies fight? Would it not be more humane and more logical just to have two people fight?), and concludes by raising the possibility that war is madness [сумасшествие] and that human beings are not as rational as they are purported to be.¹²⁶

Lyrical references to the sun rising at the beginning of Chapter 2, with their possible evocations of Ecclesiastes and a general sense of all human toil being for naught, also contain veiled questions about oppositions between enemies and possible intimations of war being in violation of God's law.¹²⁷ Tolstoy writes that the sun rises and shines "with equal joy for all," right after mentioning that the sun rises over the *English* entrenchments and then over the bastions, Sevastopol itself, and the Nikolaevsky barracks.¹²⁸ This description accurately tracks the course of the sun over Sevastopol in relation to the cardinal points, but it also evokes Jesus's words in the Sermon on the Mount that God the Father "maketh his sun to rise on the evil and on the good."¹²⁹ Jesus makes his point that people should strive to be like God, and thus to love, rather than hate, their enemies.¹³⁰ Tolstoy's declaration that the sun shines "with equal joy for all" has the effect of unifying both camps, English and Russian, in warm embrace. But if we take into account the veiled allusion to Jesus's sermons about loving your enemy, then the young Tolstoy's reference to the sun rising and shining "with equal joy for all" also reminds us that war violates the heart of Christ's teaching.

Tolstoy, evocatively but forcefully, prompts his readers to see the arbitrary nature of war and to regard enemies as modal brothers. At some points, his sermonic narration does not seem to distinguish between French and Russian and, as it shines equally on both, achieves a divine omniscience. At other points, the narrator expresses patriotic sentiments and disdain for the enemy. But "Sevastopol in May" does not contain the kind of celebration of the Russians found in "Sevastopol in December," where Tolstoy praises the simple soldiers and sailors for their humble heroism and their sacrifice.¹³¹ In this second tale, with its focus on vainglorious Russian officers, none of whom merits the title of hero and some of whom deserve to be called monsters or even little Napoleons, Tolstoy's narrator repeatedly puts the Russians and French on equal footing, as if to prepare for the scene of fraternization while the white flags are flying.

In the final chapter of "Sevastopol in May," just as the French and the Russians, in a mix of soldiers and officers, have moved from discussing the relative merits of Turkish, Russian, and French tobacco to acknowledging the corpses—"Isn't it terrible, this sad duty that we are carrying out?" ["N'est-ce pas terrible la triste besogne, que nous faisons?"] says a Russian cavalry member, "motioning to the corpses"—Tolstoy's narrator cuts them off. "Enough," says the narrator.[132] He then returns us to the horror of war (using a transition like in Stowe's "Uncle Tim" that Eikhenbaum commented on): "Let us look instead at this ten-year-old boy . . . " This boy walks by the piles of corpses, pokes at one of the bodies, and screams.[133] Tolstoy uses this defamiliarizing response to the corpses as his transition into full sermon mode.[134] The boy is the only one to really look at the corpses. The sight fills him with horror.

This prompts Tolstoy's narrator to ask why "these people—Christians professing the same one great law of love and self-sacrifice—looking at what they have done [the carnage in front of them that they have caused], do not suddenly fall repentant to their knees before him who, having given them life, placed in the soul of each, along with the fear of death, love of the good and the beautiful?" Why "do they not embrace like brothers in tears of joy and happiness?"[135]

As he asks these questions, Tolstoy's narrator sheds the ironic tone that he assumes elsewhere and that will return. His mode of sermonizing recalls what Stowe does throughout *Uncle Tom's Cabin* and especially in the "Concluding Remarks." Both Tolstoy and Stowe point out the inconsistency between what people practice—war for Tolstoy, slavery for Stowe—and what they preach or profess—Christian love, in both cases.[136] In this passage, Tolstoy's message is like Stowe's throughout *Uncle Tom's Cabin*: it could be summarized as, "Christians, bethink yourselves." Stowe asks: "And now, men and women of America, is this a thing to be trifled with, apologized for, and passed over in silence? . . . — is this a thing for you to countenance and encourage?"[137] Tolstoy's refrain from *Uncle Tom's Cabin* in the Sevastopol tales is the question: can you justify killing "in the shadow of the cross of Christ"?

Stowe's message is more single-minded and more pointed: she draws repeated attention to the fact that slavery violates Christian belief. Thus, for example, she complains that Christ's "church sees . . . scenes of blood and cruelty . . . almost in silence."[138] As for Tolstoy, in the Sevastopol tales, his convictions had not yet become fixed; he is still searching. But he does (through his preacher-narrator) address the reader in an earnest way to raise the vexed question of whether killing each other in war is what "Christians professing the same one great law of love and self-sacrifice" should do. As the narrator asks: would embracing tearfully like brothers not be more in keeping with what they profess?[139] After all, the Russians and French have just been fraternizing; the sun has been shining equally joyfully over all. At this point, Tolstoy's prose takes on a sermonic and sentimental quality. Even at this young age, Tolstoy felt the bitter truths that would haunt him later. He already had intimations of the kingdom of God, or of a higher truth, for which a sermonic tone was necessary: ordinary prose would not do.

The Sevastopol tales have been subjected to various forms of editing, revision, and censorship, from initial publication through to the present; censors, editors, scholars, translators, disciples, and Tolstoy himself are responsible for the changes.[140] Thus, when "Sevastopol in May" was first published, the editors of *The Contemporary* felt compelled to add a jingoistic line depicting Russia as a victim of aggression. Tolstoy saw to it that this line was omitted from subsequent editions. Burnasheva and Layton have noted, however, that some Russian editions and English translations have edited out some of Tolstoy's original passages, possibly on the grounds that their content was judged incompatible with Tolstoy's later pacifism. (Also edited out of some editions were some of Tolstoy's most searing condemnations of war.) Tolstoy's readers now have available a text that is true to Tolstoy's original vision. In this version, Tolstoy's narrator praises the defenders of Sevastopol and shows them bent on destroying the enemy, but he also, in sermonic mode, shares his "strange thoughts" about war and asks *why* men who profess the law of love do not embrace like brothers? As he wrote the Sevastopol tales, Second Lieutenant Tolstoy himself was not ready to beat swords into ploughshares. But the seeds of his later pacifism may be found in the Sevastopol tales, in his representation of "war in its true expression"— "in blood, in suffering, and in death"—and also in questions such as those he poses at the end of "Sevastopol in May." Tolstoy would repeat these questions elsewhere in his later fiction, such as in *War and Peace*, when, just as a prayerful Natasha takes to heart Christ's message about loving and forgiving your enemies, the priest reads proclamations of war, which contain orders to kill enemies, or when Levin, with his characteristic Tolstoyan drive for consistency, fixes on the contradiction that arises when a church that preaches love promotes war.[141]

"Sevastopol in May" ends with an announcement that the fighting goes on, as the "white flags" that promised peace are defamiliarized into "white rags" that signify nothing: "No! The white rags have been hidden away—and again the engines of death and suffering sound, again innocent blood flows and moans and curses are heard."[142] Tolstoy's preacher-narrator then proceeds to ask whether what he has just said belongs to a category of bitter truth better left unuttered, lest it make life unbearable. But, of course, the question he has posed—"Why do they not embrace like brothers in tears of joy and happiness?"— continues to echo in the reader's consciousness, even if the fervent sentiment gives way to bitter irony as the fighting continues.

"My God, my God! When will it all end!"

Composed after the surrender of Sevastopol, the third, final tale, "Sevastopol in August, 1855," follows a young officer, Vladimir Kozeltsov, fresh out of military school, as he arrives at Sevastopol. He is fueled by patriotic feeling and ambition, and inspired by fantasies of dying a glorious, heroic death by the side of his older brother Mikhail, an experienced officer who has just recovered from a wound and is returning to action. Tolstoy uses the contrast between the two brothers' perceptions, one naïve and hopeful, the other experienced and disillusioned, as he narrates the younger Kozeltsov's *Bildung* [education] and baptism by fire in Sevastopol. Once separated from his older brother, young Kozeltsov takes his place among the soldiers of whom he is (nominally) in charge; he experiences danger; he feels affection for this band of brothers, which helps him stop nursing disappointment over the reunion with his older brother; and he starts to grow up. But, before the end of "Sevastopol in August, 1855," both Kozeltsov brothers will be dead.[143] The tale ends with a pervasive sense of futility. As the Russians abandon Sevastopol and reach land, the retreating soldiers cross themselves, but then curse the enemy with bitterness.

Tolstoy grants to a sister of mercy, who appears briefly in this final Sevastopol tale, what may be its resounding line: "My God, my God! When will it all end!" ["Боже мой, боже мой! Когда это все кончится!"][144] This sister, identified as young and pretty, guides the two Kozeltsov brothers through the hospital where they have come to visit an amputee, in what the reader recognizes as a reprise, in third person narration, of the reader's tour of the amputation ward in the first tale, in which the amputee's wife acted as guide. Watching the younger Kozeltsov gaping, sighing, and groaning at the pain of others, the sister asks whether he has just arrived in Sevastopol. She then looks at him and bursts into tears. Though she weeps as she says this, the tears do not represent the "empty, feminine, morbidly weepy compassion" that the narrator dismisses in the second tale.[145] Her feminine sentiment is active and powerful. She is soon lifting the head of the suffering amputee they are visiting onto the pillow and easing his pain. At this point young Kozeltsov notices her wedding ring.[146] This young sister of mercy's husband is presumably dead; she thus transfers the love she felt for him to others, in a living "equation of feeling," under the same principle of: "So what if he's a stranger, you still have to have pity."

In young Kozeltsov's soul that night, his first in the shelter among his men, with heavy fire exploding outside, troubled images of the wounded and blood are mixed with fantasies of this pretty young sister nursing him as he lies dying, and then with memories of his mother seeing him off and blessing him as she wept and prayed in front of a wonder-working icon.[147] These two feminine figures, full of tears but active (nursing or blessing), comfort him, but they also turn his soul toward God. He suddenly starts praying to almighty God, who hears all prayers. At this point, young Kozeltsov grows up.[148] After surrendering himself to the will of God in prayer, the "childish, fearful, hemmed in" soul of Vladimir Kozeltsov "suddenly becomes manly, enlightened, and sees new, vast, and bright horizons."[149] The transformation of Vladimir Kozeltsov takes place through prayer to the almighty God, but the pathos of the sister of mercy and of his mother prepared his soul for this change. Without their tears, would his soul have sought God?

The young Kozeltsov, in the absence of his mother and the sister of mercy, finds comfort in the band of brothers of his battalion. On the night before his death, as he huddles with them in the shelter, he experiences that special Tolstoyan brotherly love that the young Tolstoy and his biological brothers fantasized about in their game of "ant brothers," when they would huddle together in a hideout made by draping shawls between chairs and over boxes and dream of universal brotherly love (this dream may have fed the question "Why do they not embrace like brothers?").[150] At one point, Tolstoy notes that young Kozeltsov felt, among these men in the shelter, "that feeling of comfort he had as a child, playing hide-and-seek, when he would crawl into a cupboard or under his mother's skirt."[151] Young Kozeltsov has been forever exiled from his mother's protective embrace (womb, arms, skirt, shawl, etc.), even though she may have blessed him with wonder-working icons before departure. But what he now has, instead, is the brotherly love of the men in this shelter, which offers him the same comfort and exaltation on the eve of his death.[152]

Young Kozeltsov grows into manhood and brotherly love only to die. He does not die the glorious death of his earlier fantasies. As the Russians retreat from Sevastopol, he is mourned by the young *junker* [military volunteer] who had been looking after him, hoping to protect him from the death that occurs anyway. This junker, Vlang or Vlanga—the narrator explains that he was known by this feminized form to "all the soldiers" who "for some reason declined his last name in the feminine gender"[153]—becomes the surrogate for the sister of mercy and the mother of young Kozeltsov's fantasies as he suddenly remembers Kozeltsov and begins to weep while he and others, crammed onto a boat, retreat from Sevastopol, as the stars shine above, "just the same as yesterday."[154]

Tolstoy ends the tale with the Russians cursing and threatening the enemy after having made signs of the cross as they arrived safely on the shore across from Sevastopol. And yet it is the sister of mercy's tearful "My God, my God! When will it all end!"—uttered mid-tale—that resounds long after the tales are over.[155] The siege itself did in fact end shortly thereafter, as did, eventually, the Crimean War, but Tolstoy leaves the reader haunted by the bitter truth that "it" will not really end. What began as a question becomes an exclamation. The exclamation point introduces an element of despair and futility. What could have become a lament Tolstoy makes into a cry of protest.[156] As a war widow and as a sister of mercy, this woman speaks not from the "otherworldly" perspective of Tolstoy's sermonist-narrator, but from the womb, to protest against the blood, the sufferings, and the death.

As he composed his "epic of Sevastopol," the young Tolstoy mastered—and made uniquely Tolstoyan in the process—techniques akin to those used by Stowe in *Uncle Tom's Cabin*, as she sermonized in the name of maternal love and used sentimental power as a form of protest. Tolstoy's perspective, however, was very different: whereas Stowe narrates from a maternal point of view, Tolstoy's was the point of view of a motherless child. This mode of narration came naturally to him in his trilogy *Childhood, Boyhood, Youth* as he focused on the death of the hero's mother and wrote in the first person. But, as he responded to the blood, suffering, and death of others in the siege of Sevastopol, he had to develop new modes of narration and master new devices. With Stowe's motherly example in the background, Tolstoy imbued his epic of Sevastopol with elements of pathos, sermon, and protest. His narrative voice may be manly, as it modulates between irony and sentiment, but Tolstoy would never leave behind the perspective of the motherless child.

Throughout much of the Sevastopol tales, Tolstoy keeps the pathos in check, threatening to dismiss it as womanish sentiment, and subjecting it to bitter irony. And yet the pathos, sermon, and protest surface forcefully: in the credo of the amputee's wife, "He may be a stranger, but you still must have compassion" ("Sevastopol in December"); in the narrator's question "Why do they not embrace like brothers?" followed by his reminder that such questions are usually not uttered aloud, lest they make life untenable ("Sevastopol in May"); and in the young sister of mercy's question that becomes a cry of despair and protest, "My God, my God, when will it all end!" ("Sevastopol in August, 1855"). Emerging from the words of Tolstoy's sermonist-narrator, of the amputee's wife, and of the tearful sister of mercy is the ethic of brotherly love in the face of death that would become the holy of holies in Tolstoy's life and art, the expression of both the longing and the consolation of the motherless child.

Endnotes

1 An earlier version of this paper was presented at the national conference of the American Association for the Advancement of Slavic Studies in November, 2010. I am very grateful to Hugh McLean both for the illuminating insights he offered in his role as discussant and for the valuable comments he made on this essay.

2 Tolstoi, *ПСС*, online edition, 2:87. Quotations from the Sevastopol tales are from volume 2 (1852-1856) of the online *Complete Collected Works* [*Полное собрание сочинений*] in 100 volumes, hereafter cited by volume and page numbers. The text of these works is more complete in this edition than in the earlier Chertkov edition. The translations are mostly my own; I consulted and sometimes adapted the Aylmer and Louise Maude translation in Leo Tolstoy, *Collected Shorter Fiction*.

Quotations from *War and Peace* come from the translation by Richard Pevear and Larissa Volokhonsky (with slight changes), cited by page number, along with the part, volume, and chapter number. Unless otherwise noted, quotations from and references to other works by Tolstoy (e.g., other works, diaries, letters, etc.), cited as Chertkov edition by volume and page number refer to the *Полное собрание сочинений* in 90 volumes.

3 Phrases cited are from the dustjacket of *Regarding the Pain of Others.* Sontag cites a journal entry of Charles Baudelaire from the early 1860s: "It is impossible to glance through any newspaper, no matter what the day, the month or the year, without finding on every line the most frightful traces of human perversity. . . . Every newspaper, from the first line to the last, is nothing but a tissue of horrors. . . . And it is with this loathsome appetizer that civilized man daily washes down his morning repast" (Sontag, 107).

4 Trudi Tate writes of the war from the English perspective: "The Crimean War was the first war to be reported first hand in the newspapers, the first to be photographed, the first to be painted by official war artists, and the first to make use of the new technology of the telegraph. It was the first modern war in the sense that it took place partly at the level of representation. More than this: representations of the war had a tangible effect upon the conduct of the conflict and the politics which surrounded it" (162). For further discussion of the Crimean War as the first modern war, see Peck; Markovits.

5 Russell, *Dispatches from the Crimea,* 163. See John Peck (26-34) on Russell's break with the tradition of war writing, which depicted the events of war "as an epic struggle, a play, where opposing forces led by exemplary generals engage in dramatic confrontations" (30). Peck explains that Russell was writing for a novel-reading public and that his sensibility and style were influenced by contemporary novelists.

In an early review of Tolstoy, Aleksandr Druzhinin compares Russell's and Tolstoy's accounts of the Crimean War, declaring the latter to be superior in terms of artistic talent. Druzhinin is right that Russell was no Tolstoy; the two also wrote within very different political and publishing contexts. But Russell and Tolstoy still approached the material with many of the same attitudes and under many of the same influences.

6 Tennyson, "Charge of the Light Brigade," 222. These lines read: "Was there a man dismay'd? / Not tho' the soldier knew / Someone had blunder'd: / Theirs not to make reply, / Theirs not to reason why, / Theirs but to do and die: / Into the valley of Death /Rode the six hundred." The events in question occurred on October 25, 1854, at Balaklava. Russell's "The Cavalry Action at Balaklava" appeared in the *Times* on November 14, 1854; Tennyson's poem was published on December 9, 1854, in the *Examiner*. For discussion, see Tate.

Tolstoy wrote a ballad, said to have circulated widely, "Song about the battle at the Chernaia River on August 4, 1855" ["Песня про сражение на г. Черной 4 августа 1855 г."] (Chertkov edition, 4:307-308), in which military leaders and their blunders are treated with bitter, but more jocular, irony. Tolstoy participated in the affair described although, as he wrote to his brother, he did not fire his weapon (Chertkov edition, 4:421). Although the ballad is more unofficial and irreverent than the Poet Laureate Tennyson's "Charge," it conveys much of the same spirit.

7 See Sontag (48-51) for a discussion of Fenton's role as "first war photographer." For a reproduction of the photograph, see http://graphics8.nytimes.com/images/blogs/morris/match1-large.jpg. Fenton rearranged the cannonballs for his photograph. For discussion of this, see http://opinionator.blogs.nytimes.com/2007/09/25/which-came-first-the-chicken-or-the-egg-part-one/ (thanks to Steven Shaklan for drawing this to my attention).

8 Markovits, *Crimean War,* 1-62.

9 For discussion of the censorship and editing of Tolstoy's Sevastopol tales, see N. I. Burnasheva and Susan Layton.

10 "Sevastopol in December" was published in *The Contemporary* [*Современник*] in June 1855 to great acclaim, with Tsar Alexander ordering a French translation to be printed in *Le Nord* [*The North*], an official Russian publication that came out in Brussels (Burnasheva, notes, 2:395). It roused readers in Russia to patriotic heights and riveted their attention to the pain of others in Sevastopol. Ivan Aksakov wrote to his father that reading it made him want to head off to Sevastopol (Burnasheva, 2:396). And Turgenev reported to Ivan Panaev that the first sketch

was a "miracle," that "tears came to [his] eyes as [he] read it, and [he] cheered 'Hurrah!'" (Burnasheva, 2:396).

11 Before writing the Sevastopol tales, Tolstoy collaborated on a proposal, turned down by Tsar Nicholas I (in the months before his death), to publish a journal with the mission of being accessible both "in cost and in content" to all people in the military world. (For the text of related materials, see Chertkov edition, 4:281-284). The new journal would express the "spirit" of the military. The plan was, as Tolstoy described it, to create and disseminate a new kind of military literature, different from the official military literature, such as had appeared in the official organ, *The Invalid* [*Инвалид*]. (In the second tale, one of the protagonists imagines his sweetheart getting news of his heroic exploits and the medals he receives from *The Invalid*. Tolstoy makes it clear that what finds its way into *The Invalid* is not "war in its real expression," but rather a heroized version.) Tolstoy's interest in this venture shows his commitment to a new approach to writing for and about the military and his desire to escape official constraints.

According to Markovits (19-20), the London *Times* reached the Russians in Sevastopol around the same time that it reached the English in their encampments in the area, a fact that the English learned from a captured Russian. (Some English expressed concern over the enemy Russians learning too much from Russell's reports and advocated censorship or the elimination of war correspondents; Russell responded to this criticism in some of his dispatches.) In addition to commissioning and printing dispatches from the front by Russell, Thomas Chenery (whose reports on conditions in the hospitals in Scutari had an important effect on public opinion), and others, the London *Times* editorialized and published letters from readers. In editorials and letters, the editors and public went through a variety of responses to reports of distant pain and suffering and analyzed this phenomenon.

12 For discussion of the young Tolstoy's concern with his craft and other writers' practices, as documented in his diary and elsewhere, see Boris Eikhenbaum, *Young Tolstoy* [*Молодой Толстой*] and *Lev Tolstoi* [*Лев Толстой*].

In "Sevastopol in May," Tolstoy's narrator makes comments about the contemporary state of literature, regretting that Homer and Shakespeare have been replaced by "an endless tale of Vanity and Snobs," in a reference to William Thackeray, whom Tolstoy had read recently.

13 Tolstoy, "Apropos of the Book War and Peace," 1217-24.
14 Viktor Shklovsky, *Pro and contra* [*За и против*], 96-7. Shklovsky writes of a "new type of novel," but then explains parenthetically that "we do not have a name for a work of this genre." Shklovsky notes that Tolstoy's new novel, with its search for a hero and devastating analysis of reality, harks back to Lermontov's *A Hero of Our Time*. Shklovsky cites Engels's "Origin of the Family, Private Property, and the State" ["Der Ursprung der Familie, des Privateigenthums und des Staats," 1884] on the novel being a "mirror" of the European family, along with Mikhail Saltykov-Shchedrin's comments on the novel being "primarily a work about familiness" ("по преимуществу произведение семейственности") (97).
15 Tolstoi, *ПСС*, Chertkov edition, 47:11.
16 Ibid., 46:170.
17 In *What Is Art?* [*Что такое искусство?*, 1897], Tolstoy champions Stowe's *Uncle Tom's Cabin* as an example of "good art," a work that promotes love of God and love of one's neighbor, that draws human beings together, that furthers their sense of brotherhood by "evok[ing] in them those feelings that show they are already united in the joys and sorrows of life." Not many novelists do this, according to Tolstoy; he places Stowe in the company of Dostoevsky, Victor Hugo, Dickens, and George Eliot (*What Is Art?*, 151-2).
18 Eikhenbaum is the exception. For discussion of his comments on Tolstoy's (possible) response to Stowe's "Uncle Tim," see below. For discussion of the influence of *Uncle Tom's Cabin* on Tolstoy's *late* novel, see Karen Smith.
19 Tolstoi, *ПСС*, Chertkov edition, 46:24; 46:266.
20 For discussion of the reception of Stowe's *Uncle Tom's Cabin* in Russia, see John MacKay, "The First Years of *Uncle Tom's Cabin* in Russian," and *True Songs of Freedom: Uncle Tom's Cabin in Russian Culture and Society*. As MacKay explains, the publication of Russian versions was not allowed until late 1857. But many Russian readers, like Tolstoy, read the novel earlier in translation.

In *True Songs of Freedom*, MacKay analyzes a number of different assessments Tolstoy made of *Uncle Tom's Cabin*, including, in addition to the lavish praise of later years (*What Is Art?* and elsewhere), a couple of negative comments in letters in 1858 (to Nikolai Nekrasov) and in 1863 (to Afanasy Fet) (39-51). Tolstoy's disparaging remarks, as MacKay notes, need to be understood within the context of Tolstoy's relations with his correspondents, his changing political stances, and many other factors. They are very much in keeping with Tolstoy's mode of responding to other writers, even ones whose works he took very seriously. (The ultimate case of this would be the mixed messages he emitted about Dostoevsky).

21   Tolstoy's diaries of the early 1850s (before and after he read *Uncle Tom's Cabin* in August, 1854) contain a number of references to serfdom, to being a serf-owner, and to interactions with his serfs. He mentions a conversation "about our Russian slavery" (then remarking in his diary on June 24, 1854, that slavery is "an evil, but an extremely nice [милое] one" (Chertkov edition, 47:4). But on July 8, 1855, Tolstoy mentions in his diary wanting money to arrange for freeing his serfs. Then on August 1, 1855, he mentions another conversation about slavery and then that his story "A Russian Landowner" would have as its main idea the impossibility of slavery for an educated, "correct" landowner of the day (Chertkov edition 47:58). For further discussion of this story, see Anne Lounsbery, "On Cultivating One's Own Garden with Other People's Labor: Serfdom in 'A Landowner's Morning,'" included in this volume.

In 1856, after Tsar Alexander II's speech announcing that serfdom would be abolished "from above," Tolstoy came up with a plan for offering his serfs their freedom (for discussion, see Feuer, 138-140). The plan backfired, when his serfs refused his offer. As Feuer explains, they thought that he was trying to swindle them because he expected compensation, whereas they thought the tsar would give them the land for nothing. Tolstoy was wounded by their response and disavowed his liberal tendencies.

Perhaps Tolstoy, as he tried to execute this plan for liberating his serfs, expected his life to imitate the happy ending of Stowe's novel: in the chapter called "The Liberator," young George Shelby gathers his slaves and offers them their freedom. At first they are bewildered and say they do not want their freedom, but then they agree, with hymns and thanksgiving, as George explains that he resolved on the grave of Uncle Tom, "before God," that he would never own another slave (380).

22 "Bethink Yourselves" is the title used by Chertkov in the English translation of "Одумайтесь," Tolstoy's treatise against the Russo-Japanese War and war in general, which was published in the London *Times*. "Bethink Yourselves" may be seen as the culmination of the thinking about war that began in the Sevastopol tales, in response to the Crimean War. This made the *Times* an especially fitting place to publish it; he added, fifty years later, his response to the seminal discussion that took place in the *Times* during the Crimean War.

23 Tompkins, *Sensational Designs*, 141. The later Tolstoy would also be known for plans for instituting the Kingdom of Heaven on earth by finding it within each individual (see his *The Kingdom of God Is Within You* [*Царство божие внутри вас*, 1894]).

24 Tompkins, *Sensational Designs*, 141; Stowe, *Uncle Tom's Cabin*, 117.

25 Stowe addresses mothers at various points within the novel, in authorial intrusions and again in her "Concluding Remarks." Incidents that hinge on the separation of children from their mothers are the mainstay of the plot of *Uncle Tom's Cabin*; one of its miraculous moments reunites a mother and child after many years.

26 Tolstoi, *ПСС*, online edition, 2:93.

27 Gustafson, *Leo Tolstoy*, 14-15.

28 In his diary in December of 1853, Tolstoy praises the Russian sentimentalist Nikolai Karamzin for his efforts, back in 1777, to use literature for purposes of moral education [нравоучение] and complains that nowadays "if you start to talk about it being necessary for literature to further moral education, nobody understands you" [Chertkov edition, 46:213-14]. Stowe would have understood.

29 Belknap, "Novelistic Technique," 233.

30 Fisher, *Hard Facts*, 91-93.

31 In my book-in-progress, *Dostoevsky and the Novel of the Accidental Family*, I argue that Stowe, similarly, was a model of "sentimental power" (Tompkins) for Dostoevsky, starting with *Notes from the House of the Dead* [*Записки из мертвого дома*, 1861], a work that, like the Sevastopol tales, has its genesis in the sketch and makes visible the pain of others, which was hitherto out of bounds of fiction. Dostoevsky uses many of the same sentimental techniques, especially in a web of invocations of maternal

love. I take Dostoevsky's decision to publish a translation of Hildreth's early anti-slavery novel in his journal *Time* [*Время*] not only as evidence of Dostoevsky's acute interest in abolitionist literature, but also a form of indirect tribute to Stowe's novel, which other Russian journals had already made available.

32 Tolstoi, *ПСС*, Chertkov edition, 46:189.

33 Eikhenbaum, *Лев Толстой*, 157. Given the prohibition against translating Stowe during this period (see MacKay; Orlova), it is interesting that *The Contemporary* went ahead with another work by Stowe (even such a benign one). *Uncle Tom's Cabin* was causing a sensation in Europe at the time (see Denise Kohn et al., eds., *Transatlantic Stowe.*).

34 Tolstoi, *ПСС*, Chertkov edition, 46:441.

35 Eikhenbaum, *Лев Толстой*, 157. Tolstoy wrote in his diary a month later, on December, 1853: "I have a big shortcoming—the inability to relate simply and lightly the circumstances of the novel, which link together the poetic scenes" (Chertkov edition, 46:208). According to Eikhenbaum, Tolstoy is following up on the concern about his own craft that he first voiced after reading "Uncle Tim" (*Лев Толстой*, 157).

36 Stowe, "Дядя Тим," 30.

37 Ibid., 33.

38 Among the other "devices" that may have caught Tolstoy's attention are her similes. For example, a young teacher acts on his pupils "as a small but strong spring brings into motion a whole factory"; this same young teacher bounds out of his schoolroom "with the speed of seltzer water bubbling out of a pitcher" (these are translations from the Russian version, which shortened and took other liberties with Stowe's originals). Tolstoy himself became known for his similes, especially those in *War and Peace*. To the list of his many masters as he learned the art of simile, from Homer to Gogol, Stowe might be added, especially in view of his remark about her "devices."

39 As mentioned above, in December 1853 Tolstoy, reflecting on Karamzin, expressed his desire for literature to go back to teaching morals. Stowe's story, which he had read a month earlier, does just that.

40 Fisher, *Still the New World*, 198. Like Turgenev's *Notes of a Hunter* and Tolstoy's Sevastopol tales, *Uncle Tom's Cabin* was published serially at first;

it is also genealogically related to the literary sketch. Stowe began as an author of regional sketches: "Uncle Tim" (also known as "Uncle Lot"), her first published work, belongs to this genre.

41 Ibid.
42 Henry James comments thus on the parallels between Turgenev's *Notes of a Hunter* and Stowe's *Uncle Tom's Cabin*: "Incontestably, at any rate, Turgenev's rustic studies sounded, like *Uncle Tom's Cabin*, a particular hour: with the difference, however, of not having at the time produced an agitation—of having rather presented the case with an art too insidious for instant recognition, an art that stirred the depths more than the surface" ("Turgenev and Tolstoy," 126). See MacKay, *Song of Freedom*, for discussion of the pairing of Turgenev's *Notes of a Hunter* and Stowe's *Uncle Tom's Cabin*.
43 Fisher, *Still the New World*, 197.
44 Stowe, *Uncle Tom's Cabin*, 383 (italics Stowe's).
45 Fisher, *Hard Facts*, 92.
46 Stowe, *Uncle Tom's Cabin*, 384.
47 Tompkins, *Sensational Designs*, 132.
48 Ibid., 132, 133.
49 Eikhenbaum, *Молодой Толстой*, 120.
50 Aside from the way both Russell (occasionally) and Tolstoy (throughout "Sevastopol in December") manipulate pronouns and use what Morson sees as "guidebook" style ("you" and the iterative present tense), they both describe the ceasefire in similar terms. Obviously, they are describing the same phenomenon, so one would expect some overlap. But Russell and Tolstoy also share a desire, no doubt fanned by the particulars of the Crimean War, to offer a true account of war. They both do this by presenting narratives without heroes, without clear causality, without an Aristotelian plot arc.
51 Morson, "Reader as Voyeur," 388-92.
52 Ibid., 392.
53 Warhol, *Gendered Interventions*, 102-103.
54 Stowe, *Uncle Tom's Cabin*, 17.
55 Ibid., 43-44. Stowe writes: "If it were *your* Harry, mother, or your Willie, that were going to be torn from you by a brutal trader, to-morrow morning, — if

you had seen the man, and heard that the papers were signed and delivered, and you had only from twelve o'clock till morning to make good your escape—how fast could *you* walk? How many miles could you make in those few brief hours, with the darling at your bosom,—the little sleepy head on your shoulders,—the small, soft arms trustingly holding on to your neck?" (43-44).

56 Ibid., 384.

57 Fisher, *Hard Facts*, 118-19.

58 Elizabeth Barnes observes: "Stowe's novel perpetuates a tradition of constructing sympathy as a narcissistic model of projection and rejection: claiming that individuals are all alike under the skin, *Uncle Tom's Cabin* makes diversity virtually unrepresentable, reinforcing the idea of humanity as dependent upon familiarity" (92).

59 Elizabeth Cheresh Allen draws attention to Turgenev's narrator's occasional shifts into second person narration in *Notes of a Hunter* to "impart immediacy and intimacy to his presentation" (150). His strategy is more similar to Stowe's in "Uncle Tim" than in *Uncle Tom's Cabin*, where Stowe tries to make the reader feel responsible for the pain.

60 Tolstoi, *ПСС*, online edition, 2:84. Eikhenbaum observes that Tolstoy's focus on the hospital, usually "outside of art," "destroys the romantics' canon of battle" (*Молодой Толстой*, 118). He sees this as part of the influence of Stendhal on Tolstoy's depiction of war. (Tolstoy himself, later in life, acknowledged that he read Stendhal's descriptions of battles before his own baptism by fire and found that Stendhal was right about the confusion among the participants about what is going on.) In *The Charterhouse of Parma* [*La Chartreuse de Parme*, 1839] Fabrice, seeking a safe haven, enters what he thinks will be a canteen wagon only to find an amputation is taking place. Tolstoy outdoes Stendhal by having the amputations take place on a much greater scale in this modern war.

Tolstoy's focus on the hospital reflects, above all, the reality of the Crimean War, in which so many deaths occurred not on the battlefield, but in (makeshift) hospitals, often from disease and infection. Thus, whereas so many of the features of Tolstoy's "epic of Sevastopol" date back to Homer, this aspect is something new.

61 Ibid., Tolstoy's italics.

62 In *Regarding the Pain of Others* Sontag focuses mostly on images, especially photographs, of others in pain, whereas Tolstoy creates a fictional situation where a hypothetical reader views the (fictional) sufferer directly. But many of the ethical questions are the same.

63 Sontag writes (in regard to viewing photographs of something like the scene that Tolstoy depicts) that "there is shame as well as shock in looking at the close-up of a real horror. Perhaps the only people with the right to look at images of suffering of this extreme order are those who could do something to alleviate it—say, the surgeons at the military hospital where the photography was taken—or those who could learn from it. The rest of us are voyeurs, whether or not we mean to be." Sontag argues that sympathy, alone, does not do any good. The situation Tolstoy creates is, of course, different, because he is bringing "you" (his hypothetical reader) face to face with "actual" suffering and into human contact.

64 Fisher, *Hard Facts*, 118.

65 Writing from a twentieth-century perspective, Sontag is suspicious of sentimentality, for "sentimentality, notoriously, is entirely compatible with a taste for brutality and worse." Sontag also points out that sympathy can have the effect of absolving the viewer: "Our sympathy proclaims our innocence as well as our impotence. To that extent, it can be (for all our good intentions) an impertinent—if not an inappropriate—response" (102-3). Tolstoy, from his own perspective, is skeptical of certain expressions of sympathy, dismissing "empty, feminine, morbidly weepy compassion" (Chertkov edition, 2:110), so different from the active compassion embodied by the sisters of mercy.

James Baldwin raises objections to Stowe's sentimentality in *Uncle Tom's Cabin*: "Sentimentality, the ostentatious parading of excessive and spurious emotion, is the mark of dishonesty, the inability to feel; the wet eyes of the sentimentalist betray his aversion to experience, his fear of life, his arid heart; and it is always, therefore, the signal of secret and violent inhumanity, the mask of cruelty" ("Everyone's Protest Novel," 496).

66 Tolstoi, *ПСС*, online edition, 2:85. Tolstoy shows that in this zone of pain social differences are deconstructed. Adding to the tension of the "relation" of the reader to the "other" in pain is the social inequality, which is encoded in the forms of address: the reader addresses the soldier-amputee

using the second person singular, appropriate for a social inferior, whereas the soldier-amputee addresses the reader using the polite form, appropriate for a superior, adding "your honor" for good measure. This inequality is reversed in the face of suffering, as the socially superior reader finds himself in awe of a mere soldier. This kind of reversal was one of Tolstoy's trademarks.

67 Chernyshevsky, "Детство и отрочество," 97.
68 Pisarev, "Три смерти," 133.
69 Tolstoi, *ПСС*, online edition, 2:85.
70 Ibid., 2:85-6.
71 Ibid., 2:86.
72 Ibid.
73 Ibid.
74 The amputee's wife is providing, in a new form, the message that Jesus conveys through the parable of the Samaritan (Luke 10:30-37).
75 Knapp, "Tue-la!" 13.
76 See Matthew 26:3-13; Mark 14:3-9; Luke 7:36-50; John 12:1-8; the woman is unnamed in Matthew, Mark, and Luke, but identified as Mary, the sister of Lazarus, in John.
77 As Jane Tompkins has argued (134-139), Stowe relies on Christian plots and symbolism in her novel where both little Eva and Uncle Tom are figured, especially at their deaths, as sacrificial lambs and Christ figures. Tolstoy does the same, in a more muted way, in the scene under discussion, as well as later in "Sevastopol in December," when we witness the death of a soldier, which evokes the passion of Christ.
78 In *Uncle Tom's Cabin*, Stowe shows one member of the Quaker household who takes in the runaway Eliza and her family reasoning, as she decides how to respond to Eliza: "Why, now, suppose 'twas my John, how should I feel?" Simeon, her interlocutor, then lays bare the "equation of feeling" by responding: "Thee uses thyself only to learn how to love their neighbor, Ruth." Ruth then replies, "To be sure. Isn't it what we are made for? If I didn't love John and the baby, I should not know how to feel for her" (120).

In his later years, contrary to Stowe, Tolstoy would regard love of family as an impediment to love of neighbor. In "Sevastopol in December," however, the amputee's wife is capable of both kinds of love.

79 Stowe, *Uncle Tom's Cabin*, 72.
80 Thus, Stowe's narrator addresses the reader: "And oh! mother that reads this, has there never been in your house a drawer, or a closet, the opening of which has been to you like the opening again of a little grave? Ah! Happy mother that you are, if it has not been so" (75).
81 In a letter of December 16, 1852, to Eliza Cabot Follen, Harriet Beecher Stowe writes that *Uncle Tom's Cabin* "had its root in the awful scenes and sorrow" she had experienced at the death of her child. She makes a very direct "equation of feeling" when she writes: "It was at his dying bed and at his grave that I learned what a poor slave mother may feel when her child is torn away from her" (*Uncle Tom's Cabin*, 413).

(Her use of the epistemic modal "may" at least allows for some difference; she does not claim absolute knowledge of the other's pain or an actual equivalence.)
82 Stowe, *Uncle Tom's Cabin*, 384.
83 The sister of mercy in "Sevastopol in August" will be discussed below. Tolstoy refers to sisters of mercy in his last two tales, but not in "Sevastopol in December." This fits the scenario outlined by Curtiss, according to which the Russian sisters of mercy were not in action until 1855.
84 Tolstoi, *ПСС*, online edition, 2:110.
85 See Markovits (98-122) for the development of this feminine heroism in England and Nightingale's part in it. Nightingale was known for her administrative talents more than for her bedside manner. Her compassionate care was not sentimental, in the sense that it was *not* obviously rooted in the "equations of feeling" that Tolstoy presents. For her, the family was not the point of reference and inspiration. (She appears to have had no interest in family life personally, but also seems to have seen it as less central than many. Nightingale, for example, believed that children were better off brought up in crèches.) On Russian sisters of mercy, see Curtiss.
86 Quoted in Markovits, *Crimean War*, 106.
87 Tolstoi, *ПСС*, online edition, 2:151.
88 Ibid., 2:86.
89 Eikhenbaum, *Молодой Толстой*, 118.
90 Tolstoi, *ПСС*, online edition, 2:87.

91 Pascal, *Pensées*, 130. Pascal writes: "Imagine a number of men in chains, all condemned to death, among whom each day a few are slaughtered [*égorgés*] in sight of the others; those who remain see their own condition in that of their likes, and looking at each other in suffering and without hope, wait their turn. This is the image of the condition of men" (130, #199).

92 Tolstoi, *ПСС*, online edition, 2:87.

93 Ibid.

94 Ibid. The Russian reads as follows: "похороны покажутся вам весьма красивым воинственным зрелищем, звуки—весьма красивыми воинственными звуками, и вы не соедините ни с этим зрелищем, ни с этими звуками мысли ясной, перенесенной на себя, о страданиях и смерти, как вы это сделали на перевязочном пункте."

95 Tolstoy, *War and Peace*, 3:2:37; 814.

96 Ibid.

97 When Pierre reminds him that Christ forgave the woman taken in adultery, Andrei says that may be good for others, but he could not do it (2:5:21; 597). And when Marya begs him to forgive those who have wronged him (Natasha; Kuragin), in accordance with Christ's law, Andrei responds: "If I were a woman, Marie, I would be doing that. It's a woman's virtue. But a man must not and cannot forget and forgive" (3:1:8; 631).

98 On April 11, 1855, writing in his diary in the Fourth Bastion of Sevastopol, Tolstoy complained of a cold and fever, then wrote: "And furthermore I'm annoyed, especially now that I'm sick, that it doesn't even enter anyone's mind that I could be good for something more than *chair à canon*, and the most useless, at that" (*ПСС*, Chertkov edition, 47:41). For Tolstoy, as for his fictional Napoleon a decade later, having a cold makes him more prone to think about dying. (Napoleon's cold at Borodino is a historical fact; Tolstoy refuses to let this have an effect on the war, but, drawing on his own experience in 1855, does imagine that a cold could affect Napoleon's personal response to what was happening—and to the threat of death.)

99 Tolstoy, *War and Peace*, 3:2:38; 815.

100 Pushkin, *Евгений Онегин*, *ПСС*, 5:36.

101 Tolstoi, *ПСС*, online edition, 2:124. In the context of the Crimean War, reference to a "little Napoleon" would also bring to mind Napoleon's nephew,

Napoleon III, who, after a coup d'état, had become emperor of France in 1851. This Napoleon was dubbed *"Napoléon le petit"* by Victor Hugo.

102 Stowe adheres to this same view and makes it explicit at various points: for example, Eva's mother denies the fact that a slave's maternal feelings are equal or equivalent to her own (151).

103 Tolstoy writes that Napoleon, "like all Frenchmen," "could not imagine anything sentimental without mentioning *ma chère, ma tendre, ma pauvre mère*" ["my dear, my tender, my poor mother"] (3:3:19; 873). Tolstoy is very aware of uses and abuses of "sentimental power," and careful to distinguish between Napoleon's sentimentality and that, for example, of Platon Karataev.

104 Tolstoi, *ПСС*, online edition, 2:93.

105 Morson, "Reader as Voyeur," 387.

106 Tolstoi, *ПСС*, online edition, 2:94.

107 Ibid., 2:94-95. The idea of solving the matter by one-on-one combat appears in folklore, in epic, and in the *Tale of Bygone Years* [*Повесть временных лет*].

108 Eikhenbaum, *Лев Толстой*, 170-77. Eikhenbaum draws attention to the presence of, and the contrast between, the two "styles," two "tones," and two modes of narration in "Sevastopol in May" (*Лев Толстой,* 171).

109 *Vanity Fair* was fresh in Tolstoy's mind and an important subtext for "Sevastopol in May." But some of the references to vanity, coupled with those to the sun rising and setting, while humans strive for naught, seem to evoke Ecclesiastes directly.

110 Eikhenbaum, *Лев Толстой*, 175

111 Eikhenbaum, *Молодой Толстой*, 123.

112 Tolstoi, *ПСС*, Chertkov edition, 46:58; 46:60; 46:301.

113 Ibid., 46:204.

114 Likhachev, *Человек в литературе*, 133-134; 144.

115 See Richard Peace (10-11) for commentary on Gogol's sermonizing as it relates to the "strong homiletic element" that Likhachev has found at play in the medieval Russian literary tradition.

116 Tolstoi, *ПСС*, Chertkov edition, 46:82.

117 Quoted in Weinstein, *Cambridge Companion*, 1.

118 Warhol, *Gendered Interventions*, 106-8. In Stowe's early "Uncle Tim," the narrator herself moves into sermonic mode at various points; furthermore, at the heart of the tale is the first sermon preached by Uncle Tim's son upon his return home from Divinity School. (The Russian translation cuts and compresses Stowe's description of his style of preaching.)

119 Stowe, *Uncle Tom's Cabin*, 384.

120 Ibid., 358.

121 Eikhenbaum, *Лев Толстой*, 173.

122 Tolstoi, *ПСС*, online edition, 2:123.

123 Ibid., 2:126.

124 In Book 12 of Homer's *Iliad*, the two enemies, Glaucus and Sarpedon, find their ancestors had been "guest-friends," exchange armor, and agree not to kill each other. The ceasefire at the end of "Sevastopol in May" also brings to mind the halt in the fighting at the end of the *Iliad* for the burial of Hector (Book 24). But it is clear that the fighting here, as in Sevastopol, will start up again and will soon leave Achilles dead.

125 As David Hume explains in "A Treatise on Human Nature" [1740], "When our nation is at war with any other, we detest them under the character of cruel, perfidious, unjust, and violent: But always esteem ourselves and allies equitable, moderate, and merciful" [quoted in Hedges, 19]. This kind of binary thinking is often used to fuel war.

126 Tolstoi, *ПСС*, online edition, 2:94-5.

127 Tolstoy evokes Ecclesiastes in the way he combines his indications of the sun rising with a message about the ultimate futility of human endeavors. Evocations of Ecclesiastes of this kind are likely to make war, like other human endeavors, seem pointless.

128 Tolstoi, *ПСС*, online edition, 2:95. Tolstoy based this on his own diary entry, adding, however, the "shining just as joyfully for all," which, with its biblical resonance, changes everything.

129 Matthew 5:45.

130 Ibid., 5:44.

131 Konstantin Leont'ev complained that Tolstoy was unfair in his depiction of the educated classes, as he drew attention to their "vanity and self-love," qualities that Tolstoy's simple soldiers and мужики [peasants] in Sevastopol seemed to lack. For discussion see Burnasheva's commentary, 2:440-441.

132 Tolstoi, *ПСС*, online edition, 2:127.

133 Ibid.

134 For discussion of this, see Knapp, "Development of Style and Theme." In *Uncle Tom's Cabin* Stowe also uses the child's perspective on slavery, young George Shelby's and especially little Eva's, to highlight the evil that the "civilized" adults cease to notice or manage to ignore. In the case of Eva, she offers an estranged—and otherworldly—perspective. Stowe uses her naïve point of view to draw attention to contradictions between the teachings of the Bible and the ways of the world.

135 Tolstoi, *ПСС*, online edition, 2:128.

136 Stowe and Tolstoy share a desire for consistency in the application of Christian teaching. The following exchange, typical of Stowe, shows little Eva taking to heart and acting on Christ's teaching, whereas the community that surrounds her assumes that these teachings cannot or should not be taken seriously. When challenged about her love for the servants, Eva says, "Don't the Bible say we must love everybody?" to which her cousin replies: "O, the Bible! To be sure, it says a great many such things; but, then nobody ever thinks of doing them,—you know, Eva, nobody does" (237).

137 Stowe, *Uncle Tom's Cabin*, 384.

138 Ibid., 358. Stowe not only sermonizes about this question in the voice of the narrator; many of her subplots show her characters coming to similar realizations, especially Augustine St. Clare, who, after Eva's death, professes: "My view of Christianity is such ... that I think no man can consistently profess it without throwing the whole weight of his being against this monstrous system of injustice that lies at the foundation of all society, and, if need be, sacrificing himself in the battle" (272). Stowe's irony is that St. Clare himself is not strong enough to act on this conviction. He complains about the "apathy of religious people on this subject, their want of perception of wrongs that filled me with horror," but then admits that he himself had "only that kind of benevolence which consists in lying on a sofa, and cursing the church and clergy for not being martyrs and confessors" (272). Whereas Miss Ophelia, his cousin from the North, declares: "It seems to me I would cut off my right hand sooner than keep on, from day to day, doing what I thought was wrong," although even she admits that this is easier said than done (192). (Later in his life, Tolstoy would appeal to similar arguments.)

St. Clare, as he makes "excuses" for going along with slavery, sounds like many Tolstoyan heroes as they reason that they, as individuals, cannot change systems or institutions. The only solution they see is to ignore the evil or divert themselves from it. "Of course, in a community so organized, what can a man of honorable and humane feelings do, but shut his eyes all he can, and harden his heart." It is thus that St. Clare explains his situation to his Northern cousin, Miss Ophelia, who keeps asking him: "How can you shut your eyes and ears? How can you let such things alone?" (191).

139 Although historians suggest that the real issues at stake in the Crimean War had more to do with political and territorial tensions than the keys to churches or the protection of the rights of Orthodox in the Turkish Empire in Jerusalem, the fact that this war was (ostensibly) in part over these matters of faith, and thus vaguely reminiscent of the Crusades, adds an edge of irony to the killing: Tolstoy wants to know whether one should be killing in the name of Christ. As he asks *why* these men do not embrace, he emphasizes the fact that, differences of Christian confession aside, these Catholics, Anglicans, and Orthodox all profess "the same one great law of love."

140 See Burnasheva's commentary on the Sevastopol tales and Layton for discussion.

141 Very late in life, Tolstoy would return to this same point in his correspondence with Gandhi, where he illustrates the contradiction at the heart of this passage in "Sevastopol in May." For example, he tells the story of a priest in a Russian school interrogating a girl on the catechism, asking her whether it is *always* true that "thou shalt not kill." The "correct" answer would be for her to cite the two exceptions outlined in Filaret's catechism, war and capital punishment. But the girl gives what Tolstoy considers the right answer: there are no exceptions. The authorities, however, tell her she is wrong.

142 Tolstoi, *ПСС*, online edition, 2:128. In a characteristic verbal move (and a complex example of "defamiliarization" in action), Tolstoy now substitutes the word rags [тряпки] for what he had been calling flags [флаги] earlier. When the flags were flying and signifying a truce, Tolstoy was willing to call them flags, but as they are taken down and hidden away (and the

fighting starts again), Tolstoy calls them what they are (from a "defamiliarized" point of view): nothing but simple rags.

143 The root of their family name "Kozeltsov" means "goat" in Russian, a detail that invites us to regard them as sacrificial animals.

144 Tolstoi, *ПСС*, online edition, 2:151.

145 Ibid., 2:110.

146 As Tolstoy first introduces this sister of mercy, she is following an older one who speaks to her in French, as she also gives orders to a *feldsher*. As Curtiss notes, the delegations of Russian Sisters of Mercy, sponsored by the Grand Duchess Elena Pavlovna, "ranged from illiterates of humble background to members of the upper nobility" (84).

147 Writing in his diary on April 11, 1855, Tolstoy regretted that he might end up as "*chair à canon*" and that nobody seemed to mind the thought of that. Then in the next sentence he announces, as a reason for living on: "I want to fall in love with the sister of mercy I saw at the dressing station" (Chertkov edition, 47:41).

148 Dostoevsky's Alyosha Karamazov undergoes an analogous transformative moment when, as his "soul longed for freedom, for space, for vastness," he prays. Dostoevsky then announces: "He fell to the earth a weak youth, but rose a warrior [боец], steadfast for the rest of his life . . ." (Dostoevsky, *PSS*, 14:328).

149 Tolstoi, *ПСС*, online edition, 2:157.

150 In "Reminiscences" ("Воспоминания") recorded late in life (1903-1906), Tolstoy wrote fondly of the feeling of love and tenderness he felt when he would huddle together with his brothers as they pretended to be "ant brothers" in the hope of unlocking a mystery that would make everyone happy, eliminate anger, and make everyone love one another. Tolstoy speculates that his oldest brother Nikolai, who made up this game of "ant brothers," had heard the grownups talking about the Moravian brothers and the brotherly love, inspired by the gospels, that they practiced and preached. (The Russian word for "ant" is close to the word for "Moravian.") Tolstoy notes that he himself made it the mission of his life to bring the love that he and his brothers yearned for, as they clung together in their hide-out between chairs draped with shawls, out into the open, to include all the people of the world (Chertkov edition, 34:385-86).

As Tolstoy's young hero Kozeltsov, yearning for his mother's protective embrace on his last night, disappointed in his reunion with his biological brother, and fantasizing about the sister of mercy, experiences, in the presence of "the angel of death," intimations of a form of transcendent brotherly love felt for all those who happen to be near him, Tolstoy follows a paradigm he would often repeat in his fiction. Tolstoy's testimony suggests that it also had deep personal resonance.

151 Tolstoi, *ПСС*, online edition, 2:170.

152 In *Resident and Stranger* Richard Gustafson discusses the tension felt by Tolstoy—and Tolstoyan heroes—as they long for their "mother's arms" and a divine love that is motherly, but reconcile themselves with sonship to the Father and residence in his Kingdom (see esp. 14-15). This mindset, as I suggest below, would have come into play as Tolstoy read Stowe, since maternal pathos figures so prominently in *Uncle Tom's Cabin*.

153 Tolstoi, *ПСС*, online edition, 2:163.

154 Ibid., 2:180.

155 The exclamation may echo Jesus's "My God, my God! Why hast thou forsaken me?" (Matthew 27:46). Like Jesus, the sister of mercy asks her God why his plan requires so much suffering. Certainly, her words are not directed only to God but also to humans in earshot, but God still should be taken into account as her addressee. Tolstoy's hero Nikolai Irtenev echoes this same line in *Childhood* when he declares: "Lord! Why do you punish me so terribly!" (1:72). The context there is a boy's humiliation as he flubs the steps of a mazurka, which is very upsetting to him, but, obviously, of a different order of magnitude from the blood, suffering, and death at Sevastopol. For discussion of Tolstoy's echoes of Christ's words in the trilogy, see Hruska, "Loneliness," 73.

156 Tolstoy sets it up so that echoing in the sister of mercy's "When will it all end!" are the laments of widows, sisters, and mothers, from Andromache, Hekabe, and Helen on down through the ages. Tolstoy praises the Russian people for their willingness to die for the motherland in "Sevastopol in December," but, for all the common ground between him and Homer, he may, in his "epic of Sevastopol," ultimately move toward a more sentimental, feminized ethos, if only because of his Crimean focus on regarding the pain of others.

Works Cited

Allen, Elizabeth Cheresh. *Beyond Realism: Turgenev's Poetics of Secular Salvation.* Stanford: Stanford University Press, 1992.

Baldwin, James. "Everybody's Protest Novel." In *Uncle Tom's Cabin. Norton Critical Edition*, edited by Elizabeth Ammons, 495-500. New York and London: W. W. Norton & Co., 2010.

Barnes, Elizabeth. *States of Sympathy: Seduction and Democracy in the American Novel.* New York: Columbia University Press, 1997.

Belknap, Robert. "Novelistic Technique." *Cambridge Companion to the Classic Russian Novel*, edited by Malcolm V. Jones and Robin Feuer Miller, 233-50. Cambridge and New York: Cambridge University Press, 1998.

Burnasheva, N. I. "Комментарии." L. N. Tolstoi. *Полное собрание сочинений в 100 томах.* Vol. 2. Moscow: Nauka, 2002.

http://feb-web.ru/feb/tolstoy/texts/pss100/t02/t02-081-.htm; ... pss100/t02/t02-094-.htm; ... pss100/t02/t02-131-.htm.

Chernyshevsky, Nikolai. "Детство и отрочество. Сочинение графа Л. Н. Толстого." In *Л. Н. Толстой в русской критике. Сборник статей*, edited by S. P. Bychkov, 91-104. Moscow: Gosudarstvennoe izdatel'stvo "Khudozhestvennaia literatura," 1952.

Curtiss, John Shelton. "Russian Sisters of Mercy in the Crimea, 1854-1855." *Slavic Review* 25 (1966): 84-100.

____. *Russia's Crimean War.* Durham, NC: Duke University Press, 1979.

Druzhinin, Aleksandr Vasil'evich. "'Метель', 'Два гусара': Повести графа Л. Н. Толстого." In *Литературная критика*, edited by N. N. Skatov. Moscow: Sovetskaia Rossiia, 1983. http://az.lib/ru/d/druzhinin_a_2/test_0140.shtml.

Dostoevskii, Fedor Mikhailovich. *Полное собрание сочинений в тридцати томах.* 30 vols. Leningrad: Nauka, 1972-1990.

Eikhenbaum, Boris. *Лев Толстой.* Leningrad: 1928-1931. Reprinted by Slavische Propyläen, Bd. 54. Munich: Wilhelm Fink, 1968. Page references are to the 1968 edition.

____. *Молодой Толстой.* Petersburg and Berlin: Z. I. Grzhebin, 1922.

[Fenton, Roger] http://graphics8.nytimes.com/images/blogs/morris/match1-large.jpg.

Feuer, Kathryn B. *Tolstoy and the Genesis of* War and Peace. Edited by Robin Feuer Miller and Donna Tussing Orwin. Ithaca, NY: Cornell University Press, 1996.

Fisher, Philip. *Hard Facts. Setting and Form in the American Novel*. New York and Oxford: Oxford University Press, 1987.

____. *Still the New World: American Literature in a Culture of Creative Destruction*. Cambridge, MA: Harvard University Press, 1999.

Fleming, Angelea Michelli, and John Maxwell Hamilton, eds. *The Crimean War as Seen by Those Who Reported It. William Howard Russell and Others*. Baton Rouge: Louisiana State University Press, 2009.

Gustafson, Richard. *Leo Tolstoy: Resident and Stranger*. Princeton, NJ: Princeton University Press, 1986.

Hedges, Chris. *War is a Force that Gives Us Meaning*. New York: Random House, 2002.

Hruska, Anne. "Loneliness and Social Class in Tolstoy's Trilogy *Childhood, Boyhood, Youth*." *Slavic and East European Journal* 44 (2000): 64-78.

____. "Love and Slavery: Serfdom, Emancipation, and Family in Tolstoy's Fiction." *The Russian Review* 66 (2007): 627-46.

James, Henry. "Turgenev and Tolstoy, 1897." In *Theory of Fiction: Henry James*, edited by James E. Miller, Jr., 262-64. Lincoln: University of Nebraska Press, 1972.

Knapp, Liza. "The Development of Style and Theme in Tolstoy." In *Cambridge Companion to Tolstoy*, edited by Donna Tussing Orwin, 161-75. Cambridge and New York: Cambridge University Press, 2002.

____. "'Tue-la! Tue-le!': Tolstoy's *Anna Karenina* and Three More Deaths," *Tolstoy Studies Journal* 11 (1999): 1-19.

Kohn, Denise, Sarah Meer, Emily B. Todd, eds. *Transatlantic Stowe: Harriet Beecher Stowe and European Culture*. Iowa City: University of Iowa Press, 2006.

Layton, Susan. "The Maude Translation of the *Sevastopol Tales*." *Tolstoy Studies Journal* 20 (2008): 14-26.

Likhachev, Dmitry. *Человек в литературе древней Руси*. Moscow: Nauka, 1970.

Markovits, Stefanie. *The Crimean War in the British Imagination*. Cambridge and New York: Cambridge University Press, 2009.

MacKay, John. "The First Years of *Uncle Tom's Cabin* in Russia." In *Transatlantic Stowe: Harriet Beecher Stowe and European Culture*, edited by Denise Kohn, Sarah Meer, and Emily B. Todd, 67-88. Iowa City: University of Iowa Press, 2006.

―――. *True Songs of Freedom*: Uncle Tom's Cabin *in Russian Culture and Society*. Madison: University of Wisconsin Press, 2013.

Morris, Errol. "Which Came First, the Chicken or the Egg? (Part One)." *New York Times*, September 25, 2007. http://opinionator.blogs.nytimes.com/2007/09/25/.

Morson, Gary Saul. "The Reader as Voyeur: Tolstoi and the Poetics of Didactic Fiction." In *Tolstoy's Short Fiction*, edited by Michael R. Katz, 379-93. New York and London: W. W. Norton & Co., 1991.

Orlova, R. D. *Хижина, устоявшая столетие*. Moscow: Kniga, 1975.

Pascal, Blaise. *Pensées*. Edited by Ch.-M. des Granges. Paris: Garnier, 1964.

Peace, Richard. *The Enigma of Gogol: an Examination of the Writings of N. V. Gogol and Their Place in the Russian Literary Tradition*. Cambridge and New York: Cambridge University Press, 1981.

Peck, John. *War, the Army and Victorian Literature*. New York: St. Martin's, 1998.

Pisarev, Dmitry. "Три смерти. Рассказ графа Л. Н. Толстого." *Л. Н. Толстой в русской критике. Сборник статей*. Edited by S. P. Bychkov, 132-44. Moscow: Gosudarstvennoe izdatel'stvo "Khudozhestvennaia literatura," 1952.

Pryse, Marjorie. "Stowe and Regionalism." *Cambridge Companion to Harriet Beecher Stowe*, edited by Cindy Weinstein, 131-53. Cambridge and New York: Cambridge University Press, 2004.

Pushkin, Aleksandr. *Полное собрание сочинений в десяти томах*. Leningrad: Nauka, 1977-79.

Russell, William Howard. *Dispatches from the Crimea*. London: Frontline Books, 2008.

Shklovsky, Viktor. *За и против: заметки о Достоевском*. Moscow: Sovetskii pisatel', 1957.

Smith, Karen R. "*Resurrection*, *Uncle Tom's Cabin*, and the Reader in Crisis." *Comparative Literature Studies* 33 (1996): 350-71.

Sontag, Susan. *Regarding the Pain of Others*. New York: Farrar, Straus and Giroux, 2003.

Stendhal [Marie-Henri Beyle]. *La Chartreuse de Parme*. Paris: Pocket classiques, 1989.

Stowe, Harriet Beecher. *Uncle Tom's Cabin*. In *Norton Critical Edition*, edited by Elizabeth Ammons, 2010. New York and London: W. W. Norton & Co., 2010.

____. "Дядя Тим. Рассказ г-жи Бичер-Стоу." *Современник* 41 no. 9 (1853): 30-50.

Tate, Trudi. "On Not Knowing Why; Memorializing the Light Brigade." *Literature, Science, Psychoanalysis, 1830-1970: Essays in Honour of Gillian Beer*. Edited by Helen Small and Trudi Tate, 160-80. Oxford: Oxford University Press, 2003.

Tennnyson, Alfred. "The Charge of the Light Brigade." In *The Works of Alfred Lord Tennyson, Poet Laureate*, 223-224. New York and London. MacMillan and Co., 1894.

Tolstoi, Lev. *Полное собрание сочинений в 100 томах*. Moscow: Nauka, 2000-.
"Севастополь в декабре месяце":
http://feb-web.ru/feb/tolstoy/texts/pss100/t02/t02-081-.htm
"Севастополь в мае":
http://feb-web.ru/feb/tolstoy/texts/pss100/t02/t02-094-.htm
"Севастополь в августе 1855 года":
http://feb-web.ru/feb/tolstoy/texts/pss100/t02/t02-131-.htm

____. *Полное собрание сочинений*. 90 vols. Edited by V. G. Chertkov. Moscow: Gosudarstvennoe izdatel'stvo "Khudozhestvennaia literatura," 1928-1958.

Tolstoy, Leo. *Collected Shorter Fiction*. 2 vols. Translated by Louise and Aylmer Maude and Nigel J. Cooper. New York: Knopf, 2001.

____. *What is Art?* Translated by Aylmer Maude. New York: Macmillan, 1986.

____. "A Few Words Apropos of the Book War and Peace." In *War and Peace*, translated by Richard Pevear and Larissa Volokhonsky, 1217-24. New York: Alfred A. Knopf, 2007.

____. *War and Peace*. Translated by Richard Pevear and Larissa Volokhonsky. New York: Alfred A. Knopf, 2007.

Tompkins, Jane. *Sensational Designs: The Cultural Work of American Fiction, 1790-1860*. New York and Oxford: Oxford University Press, 1985.

Turgenev, Ivan. *Записки охотника. Собрание сочинений в десяти томах*. Vol. 1. Moscow: Gosudarstvennoe izdatel'stvo "Khudozhestvennaia literatura," 1961.

Warhol, Robyn R. *Gendered Interventions: Narrative Discourse in the Victorian Novel*. New Brunswick, NJ: Rutgers University Press, 1989.

Weinstein, Cindy. Editor's Introduction to *Cambridge Companion to Harriet Beecher Stowe*, 1-14. Cambridge and New York: Cambridge University Press, 2004.

IX

On Cultivating One's Own Garden with Other People's Labor: Serfdom in "A Landowner's Morning"

Anne Lounsbery

"It is true that slavery is an evil, but it is an extremely loveable evil." With these memorable words the young Lev Tolstoy characterized the institution of Russian serfdom.[1] Yet at the time that he wrote this cryptic, off-hand, and rather appalling diary entry in 1854, Tolstoy was also in the process of writing what was to become "A Landowner's Morning" ["Утро помещика"]—a story that depicts serfdom as anything but loveable. How can we make sense of the diary entry (an apologia, if equivocal, for human bondage?) alongside a text that represents this same system of bondage as an insurmountable barrier to living a good life? It may be that the best way to approach the profound contradiction apparent here is to think about genre, or more specifically, to think about what different genres aim to accomplish.

"A Landowner's Morning" describes a day in the life of a young nobleman who is trying, with little success, to communicate with and to help his serfs. The action is set in a countryside village [деревня], but the story is not an idyll; this village is the protagonist's ancestral home, but the story is not about a family. In fact, understanding what this text is *not*, particularly in generic terms, is crucial to understanding what it *is*. These distinctions come into focus when we consider "A Landowner's Morning" alongside Childhood [Детство], a novella written in roughly the same period (1851-52) and set in the same environment. But unlike "A Landowner's Morning," *Childhood* is an idyll, and it *is* about family.[2] And these generic distinctions, as it turns out, make all the difference when it comes to the significance that each text implicitly ascribes to the institution of serfdom.

In *Childhood*, quite unlike in "A Landowner's Morning," we hear echoes of the diary's assessment of serfdom as "an extremely loveable evil." At this point in his life, as Anne Hruska has explained, Tolstoy was sometimes capable of seeing serfdom as loveable precisely because he could see it as being inextricably entwined with a stable social order that had at its center family love. If one conceived of serfdom in this way, emancipation was still a moral necessity, but it was also a threat, since it brought with it the "adulteration of social customs and traditional forms of life."[3] *Childhood*'s main focus is a certain "traditional form of life," the life of an extended family with an organic tie to a particular rural place. In Mikhail Bakhtin's terms, *Childhood* is a "family novel" or perhaps a "provincial novel," genres that have their roots in idyll and in folkloric temporality.[4] Such forms place the clan (the family as it stretches across time, over generations) in an absolutely central role in both life and literature, fostering a cycle-of-life view of the world. As Bakhtin puts it: "Idyllic life and its events are inseparable from this . . . corner of the world where the fathers and grandfathers lived and where one's children and their children will live"; "the cyclical repetition of the life process [is] of crucial importance."[5]

In large part because idyllic time emphasizes what is iterative, cyclical, and (therefore seemingly) inevitable, the idyll's chronotope tends toward naturalizing the social order—representing the way things *are* as the way things *must be*—rather than toward critiquing it.[6] And the "cyclic rhythmicalness" that "renders less distinct all the temporal boundaries between individual lives" invites us to believe that we are all somehow *in this together* ("this" being a system that is both organic and immutable), no matter what our positions in the social hierarchy happen to be.[7] All of which, of course, proves helpful when it comes to construing serfdom as a relationship of love.

Furthermore, the fact that *Childhood*'s narrative stance is strongly informed by the point of view of a small boy helps to justify its naturalizing impulse, because for small children, what is—especially within the family—is the only thing that can be.[8] Yes, this narrative point of view is intended to create—and does create—the "estranging" effect that has been much emphasized in Tolstoy criticism, the estrangement that conveys social criticism by using the figure of the naïf (whether a child, a peasant, or a horse) to notice what others accept or ignore. Nonetheless, I would argue that the reader's experience of seeing through little Nikolenka's eyes is ultimately more naturalizing than estranging in its *overall* effect, because while the child's point of view highlights local instances of injustice, in the end this point of view also helps to keep the narrative lodged more or less within the genre of the idyll. And since idyll is a genre suited to the placid representation of what "naturally" is and what has always been, it is not a genre that makes social criticism one of its chief goals.

But in "A Landowner's Morning," instead of an idyll's celebration of rural ways or patriarchal family ties, we encounter something like an adaptation of the eighteenth-century *conte philosophique* [philosophical tale], a genre designed not to meditate on the rhythms of a life in tune with some version of nature, but rather to *test ideas against hard facts*, thereby subjecting our assumptions about the existing social order to radical, rational critique. In direct contrast to the idyll, the philosophical tale is well adapted to social criticism and even political propaganda, particularly under a government determined to censor subversive ideas (a fact that was clear to Louis XIV at the moment of the genre's birth, when he banned François Fénelon's *Les Aventures de Télémaque* [*The Adventures of Telemachus*] in 1699 for its allegorically-expressed attack on absolutism).[9]

A standard reference work explains that the *conte philosophique* aims to subject "everything that [has] been taken for granted . . . to a kind of radical positivist (analytical and empirical) critique:"[10]

> The philosophical tale may be defined as an episodic narrative, more imaginary than realistic, structured by frequent changes of scene resulting from travel, and controlled by a central theme—optimism, destiny, progress, relativism, natural law—that involves the problem of evil. The unfolding of the plot confirms, undermines, or otherwise qualifies the idea under consideration by testing it against a series of concrete experiences and observations in the world at large.[11]

At the center of the philosophical tale, then, is a quest for truth, or more narrowly, for a correct and clear-sighted relationship between theory and practice, both in an individual's life and in the organization of society.

At the center of "A Landowner's Morning" is the young protagonist's quest for "the ideal of happiness and justice" as Tolstoy saw it.[12] Indeed, as Boris Eikhenbaum notes, the story serves as clear evidence that even in his youth Tolstoy had little patience for art that lacked "a clear, practical aim."[13] Tolstoy's intentions are clear in his notebooks: the text that ultimately became "A Landowner's Morning" was to be not only "dogmatic" and "instructive," he declared, but also "serious and useful," a "useful and good book," a "good and useful thing." This is indeed a work of literature "with a goal": "in my novel I will lay out the evil of the Russian government."[14]

When we think about how the *conte philosophique* seeks truth by posing philosophical and political questions in the form of a story, we realize that much of "A Landowner's Morning" is written in what we might call the interrogative mode: the narrative is largely taken up by the many queries the landlord poses to his serfs (and by the serfs' predictably evasive replies, which are often questions as well). These endless little questions help explain why it makes sense to read the story in light of its engagement with the big question that dominated Russian intellectual life in the decade leading up to 1861, i.e., the "peasant question" ["крестьянский вопрос"]. Clearly, even though Tolstoy eschews open ideological polemics, "A Landowner's Morning" is an intervention in the debate over serfdom; more specifically (as I will discuss below), it is in dialogue with two other texts that played crucial roles in this debate, Gogol's *Selected Passages from Correspondence with Friends* [Выбранные места из переписки с друзьями, 1847] and Turgenev's *Notes of a Hunter* [Записки охотника, 1852].

After a brief account of the composition and publication history of "A Landowner's Morning" and an overview of its contents, I will analyze the techniques Tolstoy uses to dramatize the estrangement that is built into the noble/peasant relationship: the shifting and evocative vocabulary used to designate social positions, the main character's scripted but ultimately desultory circuit through the village, the weird question-and-answer format that structures much of the narrative, and the symbolic geography of the space it depicts. The unnamed village of "A Landowner's Morning," which is never clearly situated on the map of Russia, is presented to us as repellently alien—a broken, crooked, fragmented, *illegible* space that reflects less the peasants' reality than the landlord's despairing sense of "his" people's impenetrability.

Tolstoy worked on what would finally appear (in part) as "A Landowner's Morning" on and off for several years, from 1852 until its publication in *Notes of the Fatherland* [*Отечественные записки*] in December 1856. The range of his activities during this period can only be described as astounding: he fought in the Caucasus and the Crimea (including, of course, at the Battle of Sevastopol), gambled, womanized, and read voraciously; he wrote *The Cossacks* [*Казаки*, 1863], "The Raid" ["Набег," 1852], "Notes of a Billiard Marker" ["Записки маркера," 1855], *The Sevastopol Tales* [*Севастопольские рассказы*, 1855–56], *Childhood* (1852), *Boyhood* [*Отрочество*, 1854], *Youth* [*Юность*, 1857], and other important works; he sold the main house at Iasnaia Poliana to pay gambling debts, gambled away the proceeds of the sale, and devised plans to found a new religion; he participated in Moscow and Petersburg literary circles, enjoyed his fame, argued and reconciled with Turgenev, made friends with the poets Fyodor Tiutchev and Afanasy Fet, drank with gypsies, mourned his brother's death, and almost fought a duel.[15] Through it all he was continually adding to the diaries and correspondence that recently inspired the organizers of a conference devoted to Tolstoy's work to call their event "The Over-Examined Life."[16]

"A Landowner's Morning" has its origins in the unfinished *Novel of a Russian Landowner* [*Роман русского помещика*, 1851-57], a work conceived by Tolstoy to be a full-scale novel that would address large issues and be populated by characters of many different social strata.[17] By the time "A Landowner's Morning" came out, Tolstoy had essentially abandoned the longer project, and he did not see the published story as a fragment of a work that remained in progress.[18] But, of course, "A Landowner's Morning" shares many features with *Novel of a Russian Landowner*, most notably, perhaps, what Tolstoy consistently described as the "goals" that motivated his writing on this topic, as noted above.[19]

"A Landowner's Morning" opens with a letter from nineteen-year-old Prince Nekhliudov, who is attempting to explain to his skeptical aunt why he has abandoned his university studies in Moscow to devote himself to the management of his estate and the good of his peasants.[20] Nekhliudov's letter is written in the fall, a few months after his arrival in the village and eight or nine months before the June morning on which the entirety of the story's action will take place. In "childish handwriting" (and originally, we are told, in French),

Nekhliudov recounts that he arrived to find his estate in terrible shape and his peasants living in destitution—and what responsibility could be more pressing or more "sacred," he asks, than his duty to "these seven hundred human beings for whom I must answer before God?"[21] Nekhliudov tells his aunt that he is quite sure he was "born for" this life; it is his "calling"; on his estate he will be able "to do good and to love the good." The aunt, writing in response, attempts to dissuade him, diagnosing not only her nephew's "desire to appear original" but also the futility of his plans for remedying the serfs' misery: "The poverty of few peasants is an unavoidable evil, or an evil which may be addressed without forgetting all one's own obligations to society, to one's family, and to oneself."[22] The two letters serve as an introduction to the main body of the story, which is devoted almost entirely to Nekhliudov's Sunday-morning village tour and his "interviews" with peasants who have, for the most part, petitioned the master for some kind of charity.

Page after page bristles with question marks as the landlord tries to extract information from his serfs (Why did you sell your only calf? Why do you refuse the new hut I am offering you? Why did you not tell me earlier that you need wood for repairs? Why do you lie to me?). And as often as not, the serfs answer with questions of their own (With what am I to feed a calf? How could I possibly live in that strange new hut? Why would I think it permissible to ask the master for everything? Would I dare lie to you?). Sometimes Nekhliudov's endless questions strike us as simultaneously rhetorical and desperately sincere, as when he tries to get a dissolute peasant to see that the charity he is requesting of the master comes out of other peasants' labor: "But where does the master's grain come from? . . . Who has ploughed the field? Who has harrowed it? Who has sowed it, harvested it? The peasants, yes? . . . Why then should I give it to you, and not to others?"[23]

As these endless interrogations suggest, clearly what interests Tolstoy is not the protagonist as an individual, but rather the large questions that underlie all these smaller ones, the most important of which seems to be: "How can a landowner live a good life given current social arrangements?" The answer is that he cannot. The story itself makes this abundantly clear, but if we need further confirmation we can refer to a notebook entry of 1855: "The main idea of the novel must be that it is impossible for an educated landowner of our time to live a just life with [i.e., while relying on] slavery." Not only did Tolstoy intend his narrative to serve as an exposé of rural poverty and its causes, but as late as August 1855 he wanted it to "demonstrate the means for correcting" these problems: he wanted to *answer* the questions he was posing.[24] Clearly, when Tolstoy was writing, goals were never in short supply (as another diary entry of this period asserts, "Writing without aim or hope of utility [is something] I definitely cannot do.")[25]

All the more interesting, then, that "A Landowner's Morning" is emphatically inconclusive. One of the most telling moments in the story is when Nekhliudov, having just been confronted with new evidence of his serfs' seemingly immitigable poverty, asks abruptly and reflexively, "But why are you so poor?"[26] The hapless peasant stares back in silence until the master elicits from him an account of the *"cercle vicieux,"* or "vicious circle," as Nekhliudov labels it in his mind, that has led this peasant and his family to such extremes of material want.[27] The peasant's explanation of his indigence—his land is not fertilized because he has no livestock because he cannot grow enough grain to feed livestock because his land is not fertilized—is both watertight and vaguely reminiscent of Samuel Beckett. The remedies suggested by the peasants themselves (e.g., please stop requiring my child to attend school, give me some timbers to prop up my rotting hut for one more winter, and find my useless widower son another wife to work to death) offer no more promise of solving the real problems than do the landowner's futile acts of ad hoc charity (secretly passing a few coins to an abused old woman, donating a bit of grain to those on the brink of starvation). Here we find ourselves trapped along with landowner and peasants in a world where an understanding of causality, when causality can be established at all, offers no way out.

The structure of "A Landowner's Morning," such as it is, reflects a similar sense of confinement and pointless repetition. As I noted above, the story's title signals to us that it will be organized not around plot but instead around a simple unit of time. Tolstoy takes a similar tack in other early works: "A History of Yesterday" ["История вчерашнего дня," 1851], *Childhood*, "Sevastopol in December" ["Севастополь в декабре месяце," 1855]. All these texts, by taking as their organizational principle a temporal unit, "[challenge] conventional views of what constitutes an event worth narrating," exploring "the significance of everyday events that usually escape attention."[28] But in "A Landowner's Morning" the almost ostentatiously arbitrary nature of such a structure serves another purpose as well: the morning-like-any-other evokes the strong possibility of repetition without resolution. The story's spatial semiotics reinforce this impression as Nekhliudov makes a circuit of his village (a circuit he makes every Sunday morning, we are told), tracing a path from his house to the various peasants' huts and back again. Though Nekhliudov refers to notes he has jotted down to remind himself which households he must visit, his movements strike us as quite desultory, less a trajectory than a rambling circular tour that might well be repeated on any other Sunday. What was supposed to have been a life built on teleology—"to do good and to love the good"—seems to have devolved into the landowner's own version of a *cercle vicieux*.

This does not bode well for Tolstoy's protagonist, because Nekhliudov, I would argue, is trying above all to figure out *how to be a landowner*. It is as if he has just finished reading Gogol's *Selected Passages from Correspondence with Friends* and has made the ill-advised decision to take its exhortations to heart—which was precisely what Tolstoy's own brother Dmitry did in his youth: he tried (with predictably bad results) to apply the precepts laid out in Gogol's 1847 how-to handbook for serf owners, a tract so reactionary that it bordered on the delusional.[29] By declaring literacy among peasants to be useless, for example, and urging masters to explain to serfs that it is simply the masters' duty to compel serfs to labor ("because it has been commanded by God that man must earn his bread by the sweat of his brow"[30]), Gogol had managed to infuriate people on virtually every point of the political spectrum; in fact, *Selected Passages* was bizarre enough to cause a considerable scandal.

"A Landowner's Morning" certainly does not endorse Gogol's reactionary politics; rather, it undermines them. But what Tolstoy's text shares with Gogol's is a certain uncomfortable assumption that informs both—a sense that the relationship between a landowner and his peasants is probably not going to be "natural" at all, no matter how much one might wish it to be. In *Selected Passages* Gogol's response to this unnaturalness is a strenuous and truly fantastic denial of modernity itself—and especially modernity's complex social arrangements, hybrid class categories, and mobility—in favor of a patriarchal wonderland characterized by unchanging and unmediated social relations. (For example Gogol rejects both law and money, two prime examples of the lamentably artificial structures that interpose themselves between people in modern times.) The avowed aim of *Selected Passages* is "the destruction of complex and worldly relations such as the present ones" and a return to "simple custom" and the "simple, uncomplicated social mainsprings" of antiquity.³¹

In a chapter called "The Russian Landowner" (the section of *Selected Passages* that provoked the most ire in contemporary readers), Gogol imagines an estate-world embodying his ideals of permanence and stasis, a world where (as he says elsewhere) "everything can be returned to its place."³² But in order to "return everything to its place," one must first know where these places are and what they are called. Thus the opening sentence of this chapter assumes that the first challenge facing the landowner [помещик] who has recently arrived at his estate is in effect to believe himself to be something called a помещик: "The most important thing is that you have arrived in the countryside and that you set yourself to being a помещик."³³ With this goal in mind, Gogol instructs the landowner to make absolutely sure that everyone has his categories straight: "Gather the peasants together and explain to them *what you are and what they are*," he writes, and while you are at it, be sure to teach the village priest, too, "what a landowner is [and] what a peasant is."³⁴

Tolstoy shares Gogol's preference for traditional, clear, *unadulterated* categories, a preference that goes along with a strong distaste for social hybridity and mixing. Nekhliudov shares this taste as well: he frowns in displeasure, for example, when he notices what he takes to be modernity's incursions, such as a flashy framed portrait of a general or a young wife's peasant bling (beads and a spangled head covering), into his serfs' lives.³⁵ Peasants are supposed to *stay peasants* (in fact, staying the same is a large part of what defines them, in Tolstoy's and Nekhliudov's view), which means that there is nothing less appropriate to the timeless essence of peasant-ness than following "fashions" of any sort.³⁶ Indeed, Tolstoy's various paeans to traditional class hierarchy (most notably in *Childhood* and *War and Peace* [*Война и мир*, 1869]) seem to be motivated as much by revulsion at the adulterated nature of modern social categories as they are by simple nostalgia for the past. Even in the post-emancipation world of *Anna Karenina* [*Анна Каренина*, 1877], when Levin expresses disgust at the smarmy upstart-merchant type who capitalizes on Stepan Oblonsky's aristocratic profligacy by paying bottom dollar for Oblonsky's forest, it is above all the social *indeterminateness* of this buyer-person (what exactly *is* he?) that repulses Levin.

In *Anna Karenina* Levin's self-consciously noble identity recalls that of the author himself. Viktor Shklovsky notes the assiduous and rather anxious attention paid to "genuine" nobility and genealogical distinction in Tolstoy's family of origin. (Shklovsky's descriptions of the writer's early years—and the stately, archaic, deeply patriarchal sensibility that shaped his upbringing—are among the most evocative passages in his biography.)[37] Levin echoes this noble self-consciousness in his proud retort to the accusation that he is a "reactionary": "I've never really thought about who I am. *I am Konstantin Levin, that's all.*"[38] In Gogol's terms, Levin is saying *I am what a landlord is*.[39] In other words, Levin naturalizes his class position, presenting it as an immutable fact that he does not even have to think about (not true, of course—Levin thinks about his class position all the time). For Tolstoy, it seems, peasants are fine, noblemen are fine, even priests are fine, but mixtures are not so fine. And mixtures are the stuff that modernity is made of.

But here one should note that Tolstoy, unlike Gogol, does not seem to have convinced himself that the past was perfect, or even that it was all that great. Even Levin, who is not a serf owner but merely a landlord, "[cannot] help noticing" that his whole life is based on "an unpleasant relation to [his] laborers"![40] Thus while Gogol's moralism, apophatic leanings, and nostalgia for the organic society of an imaginary lost era are all discernible in Tolstoy's work and thought, in the end what distinguishes Tolstoy's politics from his predecessor's is a strong empiricist impulse. As we see in "A Landowner's Morning," Tolstoy tests his own ideas against reality—a verification process that held no interest at all for Gogol. So even though "A Landowner's Morning" is informed by an interest in rigid social classifications that recalls Gogol's in *Selected Passages*, Tolstoy's empiricism requires him to pursue this interest in a considerably more nuanced way.

With the title of "A Landowner's Morning," Tolstoy immediately directs our attention not to an individual or an event but to a class label, and the narrative's first word is "prince": "Prince Nekhliudov was nineteen years old when he left his third year of study at the university and arrived at his village to pass the summer vacation there by himself."[41] But the categories that Gogol wants to see as self-evident and immutable—"what a landowner is and what a peasant is"—are the categories that Tolstoy interrogates. He does this by first having his protagonist embrace these categories wholeheartedly and then laying out the consequences of this decision. Nekhliudov seeks to found his life on the belief that "master" is indeed *what he is*, and he wants the peasants to see what they are as well, or what they should be. As he patiently explains to the hopeless reprobate Iukhvanka, "If you want to be a good peasant, then change your life," because a "good peasant" will not lie, beat his elderly mother, drink, or steal timber.[42]

In "A Landowner's Morning" we continually encounter the key words that designate characters' places in the social order, the words that Gogol presents as perfectly (almost magically) sufficient to the task of organizing how people should live. But in Tolstoy's text we read these terms so many times that the repetition begins to have a vaguely estranging effect that causes us to wonder what they might really mean. "Помещик" ("landowner," derived from the word for an estate originally given to a member of the nobility by the tsar), "барин" ("master," related to "бояр" ["boyar"], a word used in pre-Petrine times to designate noblemen), "крестьянин" ("peasant," related to the word for Christian), and "мужик" (also "peasant," from the word for man)—all appear over and over. More often than not the narrator refers to Nekhliudov simply as "the young помещик"; when the peasants address him they generally call him "барин" ("master"), unless they are using a folksy term like "батюшка" or "отец" (both "father") or a more formal one like "кормилец" ("benefactor") or "ваше сиательство" ("your excellency"). "Барин" suggests the physical presence of an individual ("here comes the master"), and is spoken from a peasant's point of view; it also calls up the opposition between master and peasant and thus a very specific power relation. "Помещик" instead calls to mind the estate owner's relationship to his land and thus perhaps to the state; it can imply not only an opposition to "peasant" but also to "merchant" or "city-dwelling courtier." The term "господа" ("lords") occurs once in the story, spoken by Nekhliudov's old nurse when she urges him to stop spoiling the peasants by going too easy on them: "Is that how lords are supposed to act?" she asks.[43] Interestingly, the word designating legal membership in the nobility—"дворянин," related to the word for court—never occurs at all, which perhaps tells us something about the way Tolstoy would have preferred to define nobility: that is, not primarily as a relationship to state power, but as a relationship among people. Censorship did not permit the use of the words "раб" or "рабство" ("slave," "slavery") in printed references to serfdom, but Tolstoy used both in his diaries.

When the peasants call Nekhliudov "батюшка" and "отец," they are invoking a whole set of patriarchal social arrangements (one might in theory call them "agreements") that the peasants will of course try to use to their own advantage. Thus the moment when one impoverished serf, begging not to be required to move to a new house, utters the emotionally-charged words "батюшка ваше сиятельство!"—roughly, "Papa your Excellency!"—is the moment when his wife chooses to throw herself at the master's feet, a dramatic display of abjection that succeeds in getting the couple what they want ("Benefactor!" the wife cries, "you are our father, you are our mother!"[44]).

In fact, the peasants seem to be able to make more effective use of the vocabulary available to them than their master does, despite Nekhliudov's hope that by looking into Iukhvanka's face and speaking the right words, he will "touch the peasant and by persuasion bring him back to the true path"[45]—as though the right words were all the situation required. Behind Nekhliudov's repeated attempts at heart-to-heart talks with peasants we hear Gogol's recurring advice to landlords and officials: "All your dealings should be personal."[46] ("Personal" here translates Gogol's "лично" and "самолично," implying face-to-face, unmediated interaction.)[47] Nekhliudov thinks that by personally issuing a correctly-worded remonstrance, he is being what a master is, and for him, this is what counts. When the peasants fail to be "touched" by his speeches, when they remain vacant-eyed and evasive, Nekhliudov castigates himself for having chosen the wrong words: "It seemed to him that everything he said was not what should be said"; "he felt he was not saying what he ought to be saying."[48] Here once again we recall Gogol's admonitions, particularly the memorably weird parts of *Selected Passages* that attempt to explain precisely what sorts of vocabulary a landowner must adopt in speaking to peasants: "Keep in reserve a supply of synonyms for 'brave fellow' and . . . 'mollycoddle,'" Gogol advises; "dig up still more similar words" and try always to use only "powerful words."[49]

In the end, Nekhliudov's failed attempts to communicate personally [самолично] as Landlord to Peasant suggest that these labels alone will not allow him to understand and address the phenomena he encounters in his circuit of the village—sights that are sometimes so unfathomably alien that Nekhliudov cannot even bring himself to remember, from one visit to the next, how his peasants actually live:

> Nekhliudov had long known, not by hearsay or by believing what others said but by his own direct experience, that his peasants lived in a state of extreme wretchedness; but this whole reality was so incompatible with his upbringing,

On Cultivating One's Own Garden with Other People's Labor

his manner of thinking and his way of life that he kept involuntarily forgetting the truth, and every time he was reminded of it as he was now, in a vivid and palpable way, his heart became unbearably heavy and sad.[50]

The extreme poverty and disorder of the peasants' environment strike the landowner as incomprehensible, and the long passages devoted to describing their conditions seem intended to represent not only the physical facts that Nekhliudov confronts, but also his difficulty in absorbing this information.

At every dwelling he must first pass through the yard, from which he looks at the hut from outside:

> Churis's house consisted of a half-rotten log square, musty at the corners and bent over to one side, so sunken into the ground that right over the dung heap could be seen one red-framed window with a broken shutter and another, smaller window stuffed up with flax. . . . [The hut and lean-tos] had at one time been covered with one thatch roof, but now the black rotting straw hung only over the eaves so that overhead in some places the framework and rafters were visible.[51]

The passage continues in the same manner for nearly a page: the trees are broken and their leaves scanty, remnants of a post and wheel are lying about, tools have been tossed onto a pile of blackened manure, and a cart without wheels stands next to "a confused pile of empty useless beehives."[52] And after he enters the dwelling, things only get worse:

> Nekhliudov walked into the hut. The uneven, stained walls of the kitchen corner were hung with all kinds of rags and clothes, and the icon corner was literally covered with reddish cockroaches swarming over the images and the benches. In the middle of this black, stinking, fifteen-foot hut there was a big crack in the ceiling, and even though there were two supports propping it up, the ceiling was so bent that it threatened to cave in at any moment.[53]

Similar scenes recur at other houses:

> Davydka's hut stood crooked and alone at the edge of the village. Around it was no yard, no hut, no barn, just a few dirty stalls . . . There was no living creature near the hut except for a pig, which lay in the mud by the threshold and squealed.[54]

In the passage describing this structure's interior, it seems as though virtually every noun is preceded by an adjective indicating some variant of "broken."

Chickens are flying about inside; there is no furniture, not even beds; so complete is the impression of "desolation and disorder" that Nekhliudov finds it "hard to believe that this place is inhabited" at all.[55]

But it seems that Nekhliudov's idea of what constitutes an inhabited place—a home—does not coincide with the peasants' idea of such a place, a fact made clear to Nekhliudov, if only briefly and temporarily, in a moment of painful revelation. Having just offered the destitute Churis the chance to leave his disintegrating house and move into a brand new one—brick, solid, and warm—Nekhliudov is preparing to bask in the well-deserved gratitude he thinks is about to come his way. Instead, Churis and his wife offer frantic objections to the suggestion their landlord deems so reasonable and generous: "But what kind of a life would we have there?...it's an uninhabited place...barren!...it's a new place, an unknown place."[56] By contrast, they insist, their current home—with its rotting roof, desolate yard, and tumbledown shacks—is "a cheery place, a familiar place"; for Churis, the hut signifies "all our peasant surroundings" ["все наше заведение мужицкое"], the place where his forefathers lived and died.[57] Only at this moment (and only, it seems, briefly) "did the young landowner understand *what all this meant* to Churis and his wife—the collapsing hut, the broken well with the dirty puddle, the rotting stables and barns, the cracked willows that could be seen through the crooked windows."[58]

In passages like this one, the story directs our attention as much to the landowner's futile attempts at understanding the peasants' relationship to their environment as it does to the environment itself. Even when Nekhliudov finds himself at the home of a prosperous peasant family (the last stop on his tour), his appreciation of the orderly household—thriving apiaries, abundant livestock, strapping women—does not translate into an understanding of the people themselves. Nekhliudov is entirely unsuccessful in his attempt to convince the family patriarch, Dutlov, to invest in farmland with him, once again for reasons that the landowner finds mystifying. The old man simply answers Nekhliudov's questions with more questions, refusing to divulge any information and pursuing an agenda of his own that remains opaque to the master.[59] While Dutlov professes to have no money and claims not even to count his beehives ("as many as God has given! One must not count them, the bees do not like it"[60]), his only request to the master is that his sons be permitted to pay their rent in kind rather than in labor hours, so that they can work as teamers and thus make money—clearly the old peasant has analyzed the economics of his situation, whether or not the bees approve.⁶¹ Throughout most of the conversation with his master, Dutlov occupies himself with his bees (which do not sting him but do sting Nekhliudov), and when the landowner offers apiary advice gleaned from a nineteenth-century version of *Country Living* magazine (*Maison Rustique* [*The Rustic House*], a decidedly amusing title in the context of a crumbling Russian village), the old man replies, "Well, yes, батюшка . . . they may write things like that in books, but maybe they write them out of malice," because really, "who can teach the bees where to build their combs?"⁶²

Dutlov is skillful when it comes to deflecting Nekhliudov's questions, but the master has as much right to enter this old man's house as he does to enter the home of any serf. Surveillance is a fact of peasant life ("I've come to take a look at your household," Nekhliudov says to Churis⁶³); peasant space cannot protect itself against such intrusions.⁶⁴ Peasant culture, however, evolved mechanisms for doing just that, and Nekhliudov's constant frustration attests to the effectiveness of his serfs' evasions. In fact, Nekhliudov's greatest complaint about his serfs would seem to be their incomprehensibility, since that is what thwarts his plans: "What am I to do with [Iukhvanka]? I can't see him in this situation, but how can I get him out of it? He's wrecking all my best plans."⁶⁵ What appears to bother Nekhliudov most about this incorrigible peasant is that his behavior is *inexplicably* bad; thus the young landowner asks his steward over and over: but *why* is this man so intractable? What has made him this way?⁶⁶ In this passage as in others, "A Landowner's Morning" evokes not so much the peasant's labor—all the hard physical work that sustains the master's way of life, work that is never once represented in the story—but rather the master's labor, the thankless work of trying to make sense of senseless people. Only in Nekhliudov's recurring but inchoate feelings of "embarrassment," "shame," and "conscience" does Tolstoy hint at the underlying problem, which is both moral and structural: people who own other people and thus the fruits of other people's labor are not well positioned to take an honest account of either their own lives or others' motives.⁶⁷

The nobleman's blindness ensures that peasants will remain an enigma, a problem demanding study—hence the peasant *question*. The years when Tolstoy was working on "A Landowner's Morning" coincided with Russian literature's most influential intervention in the debates over serfdom, Turgenev's *Notes of a Hunter*. In 1847 Turgenev began to publish his stories (or notes—"записки," as he called them) in the journal *The Contemporary* [*Современник*] before bringing them together in one volume in 1852. Tolstoy was, of course, well aware of Turgenev's work (in fact he was intimidated by it to some degree), and certainly no reader who came across Tolstoy's story would have failed to think of Turgenev.[68]

Yet the differences between *Notes of a Hunter* and "A Landowner's Morning" are more illuminating than the parallels. For one thing, Tolstoy is not concerned to let us know exactly where the action of "A Landowner's Morning" takes place. Toward the story's conclusion Dutlov's sons (seeking permission to work as teamers) refer briefly to Odessa and Romen, thus suggesting a location in or near Ukraine, but this lone geographic fact is of little import and in the end the village is not situated on the map, or even named. "A Landowner's Morning" entirely lacks the striking geographic specificity of Turgenev's stories, the first of which (in the 1852 volume) opens with the following sentence: "Whoever has happened to travel from Bolkhov County into the Zhizdra region will no doubt have been struck by the sharp differences between the nature of the people in the Orel province and those in Kaluga." After comparing "the Orel peasant" and "the Kaluga peasant," Turgenev opts for an even greater degree of specificity: "An Orel village (I am talking about the eastern part of the Orel province) is usually situated among ploughed fields and close to a ravine . . . A Kaluga village, on the other hand, will be surrounded for the most part by woodland. . . ."[69] The insistent attention to subtle distinctions (e.g., reminding us that we are dealing not with *western* Orel but with *eastern* Orel) signals Turgenev's ethnographic approach, an approach that assumes that close study of a certain well-defined milieu will yield the insights one seeks.

But neither Tolstoy nor Turgenev spends much time describing what a typical peasant actually does—that is, the repetitive and often crushing physical labor of working the land. In "A Landowner's Morning" we never witness this work being performed; instead, we see it as traces left on peasants' bodies. Iukhvanka's mother, for instance, represents "the last limit of old age and ruin that is possible in a living person": bony frame, drooping head, hands deformed by heavy toil, and a face bearing "the most monstrous marks of wretchedness and old age."[70] Davydka's mother, too, "had long ceased to be a woman and was only a laborer"; for now, she says, she is strong enough to bear up under this burden, but she tells Nekhliudov, "My daughter-in-law died from work, and I will too." When Nekhliudov expresses shock at this statement—the woman's matter-of-fact acknowledgement that peasant labor can be *lethal*—she explains that her son's young wife died under the horrible strain [натуга] of constant work combined with hunger and grief over the loss of a newborn child whom she could not feed.[71]

Labor that marks the body in this way does not, it seems, lend itself to artistic representation. If there are virtually no well-known nineteenth-century Russian novels that are primarily about peasant life, this is largely because the kind of work peasants most often do—hour upon hour of backbreaking, monotonous tasks performed alongside others who are engaged in the same work—is not well suited to a narrative form that evolved to represent an individual's progress in life and the compromise this individual must reach with society in order to *develop*.[72] Peasants are rarely the heroes of novels because personal development is not thought to be the peasant's concern, and because the conditions of peasant life are not ideal for generating the more or less teleological narrative that novels generally require.

This fact is implicitly acknowledged in the *form* of Tolstoy's and Turgenev's texts: neither attempts to tell the story of one peasant's life in a long narrative (instead they write sketches about various peasants); both are told from the point of view of the landowner, whose attempts at understanding constitute much of what the sketches are about (especially in Tolstoy); and perhaps most important, both are structured around the master's mobility and the serfs' immobility. The master comes and goes as he wishes, while the serfs generally stay put—the reflection, of course, of a particular power relation. The landowner makes rounds, moving through a landscape (Turgenev) or a village (Tolstoy), and in both cases taking advantage of his right to cross lines that would constitute impassable boundaries to peasants, but that are not boundaries at all to him. Thus the peasant comes to be seen as the product of a "milieu" in a way that the landowner is not, and the landowner comes to serve as a traveling lens rather than a character who interests us in his own right.

While Tolstoy's peasants are presented to us as entirely immobile—we see them at home in their huts, sometimes even in their beds—Turgenev manages to depict peasants who enjoy (or endure) some degree of mobility. In order to do so, he must focus on exceptional peasants, those whose circumstances permit (or require) them to do something other than work eighteen hours a day in a field alongside others who do the same. In *Notes of a Hunter* we sometimes read about serfs who are foresters and huntsmen, who have fallen through cracks in the system and are wandering about the countryside, who live by gathering herbs in the woods, and who are young enough to be sent to spend summer nights outdoors guarding livestock in the meadows. In other words, despite Turgenev's ethnographic impulse, his focus is not on agricultural labor—which is to say, it is not on the circumstances under which the great majority of peasants actually made their living.

Tolstoy's focus is on more typical peasants, those who stay in one place in order to work fields owned by the master—and yet, quite strikingly, "A Landowner's Morning" concludes with a lyrical fantasy of peasant mobility and freedom. After his frustrating morning in the village Nekhliudov returns to the manor house, where Tolstoy surrounds him with accoutrements signaling the landowner's vast distance from his serfs (not only luxurious furniture and a piano but papers, accounts, books, and *Maison Rustique*). Fearing that he is "wasting the best years of [his] life" and feeling himself to be anything but free, Nekhliudov gives himself over to a vision of Dutlov's vigorous teenage son Ilyusha driving a fast *troika* along a highway.[73] Picturing Ilyusha's evident joy in his own movement, Nekhliudov imagines the young peasant arriving at a crowded inn, crossing himself, eating with his companions, saying his prayers, and lying down to sleep under the sky.[74] And at this point in the narrative, Nekhliudov seems to enter into Ilyusha's mind:

> And in his dream he sees Kiev with its saints and its crowds of pilgrims, Romen with its merchants and goods, he sees Odest [Odessa] and the distant dark blue sea with white sails, and Tsargrad [Constantinople] with its golden houses and white-breasted, black-browed Turkish girls, and he is flying there, rising on some kind of invisible wings. He flies freely and easily, further and further, seeing below him the golden cities glowing brightly and the dark blue skies with stars and the dark blue seas with white sails—and it feels sweet and joyful to him to fly further and further . . . "Wonderful!" whispered Nekhliudov to himself, and the thought came to him, "Why am I not Ilyusha?"[75]

These are the last words of "A Landowner's Morning": the nobleman who feels trapped by the nature of his relations with the peasants projects onto them a freedom that they have never in fact enjoyed.[76]

By contrast, our last glimpse of actual peasants (in the penultimate chapter, a few pages before the Ilyusha fantasy) shows Nekhliudov approaching the manor house and confronting the ragged petitioners—in varying states of drunkenness, ill-health, grief, and rage—whose quarrels he must adjudicate and whose problems he must untangle.[77] No wonder he would prefer to be Ilyusha. And here, in this contrast, we see one key way in which "A Landowner's Morning" points unmistakably toward ideas that would shape Tolstoy's entire life and work. In Richard Gustafson's words: "Count Leo Tolstoy was fated by his noble origins to a life separated from the vast majority of the people, the peasants, among whom he lived. Despite his sense of mission to the world, there was no way he could participate in the life of the very people, who, he saw, made his or any life possible. Every effort he made—teaching their children, joining in their work, dressing like them, writing for them—turned out to be but a symbolic gesture void of effective content."[78]

"A Landowner's Morning" can avoid issuing explicit commentary on the most horrific injustices of serfdom because Nekhliudov is a good master who is trying to do the right thing. These injustices—not only the economic exploitation built into the system but also the abuses that inevitably attend this basic one, such as forced marriages, starvation, beatings, the buying and selling of human beings, and other violence—form a large part of what occupies Turgenev in *Notes of a Hunter*. Tolstoy more or less ignores these social facts, as Hruska points out: "While Tolstoy sometimes complained in his diary about the 'impossibility of a correct life' under serfdom . . . his complaints tend to be abstract, with considerably less concern for the brutality inherent to serfdom than was shown by, for example, Turgenev or Dostoevsky."[79]

In fact, recent criticism has come quite close to describing at least one other Tolstoy text as a defense of serfdom: in *Childhood* Georgii Lesskis sees Tolstoy's tendency "calmly to accept the idea of serfdom as a reality, and not to consider the position of house-serfs and peasants to be unfair."[80] Lesskis argues that contemporary readers would have recognized the life of the saintly old serf nanny Natalya Savishna in *Childhood* to be a rewriting of a famous story in *Notes of a Hunter*, "Ermolai and the Miller's Wife" ["Ермолай и мельничиха"].

In Turgenev's sketch, a young woman's life is ruined by her owner's interference in her love for another serf; in *Childhood*, the same plot becomes a vaguely amusing episode in Natalya Savishna's past, a long-ago event, briefly and blithely narrated, that caused her to surrender her right to marry—and to surrender, in effect, her very subjectivity—in favor of service to the master's family.[81] In Tolstoy's comic rewriting of Turgenev's peasant tragedy, Natalya Savishna is perfectly content with her fate—a re-construing of Turgenev's story that is particularly disturbing to anyone who has ever read the odious pro-slavery novels written in response to *Uncle Tom's Cabin* in mid-nineteenth-century America, novels in which happy slaves (especially "mammies" like Natalya Savishna, women whose lives are devoted to raising their masters' offspring) confirm for us how very pleased they are with their place in the social order.

But "A Landowner's Morning" allows for no such whitewashing, not even the most subtle or implicit. Even if the story is less concerned with indicting serfdom as an institution than it is with exploring the futility of good intentions, the text's very structure works to debunk any argument Nekhliudov might marshal to justify the existing social arrangements. The story insists so strongly on the ways in which the landowner's social position *blinds* him that nothing he might say or think in defense of this position could ever be convincing (and since the entire narrative is told from Nekhliudov's point of view, no position other than his is available to us). The constant emphasis on Nekhliudov's incomprehension and his inability to offer meaningful help to the peasants combines with the text's plotlessness and its unspecified setting to create a sense of bewilderment, isolation, and pointless repetition, a movement that feels anti-teleological and even entropic.

Childhood, too, is loosely structured around an arbitrary and potentially repeatable unit of time and a series of *tableau*-like scenes that do not serve to move the narrative forward, but instead describe phenomena that are supposed to be recurring or vaguely typical.[82] But the effect here is entirely different than it is in "A Landowner's Morning." As I noted above, in *Childhood* the explicit focus on family life aims at making this life meaningful by naturalizing it (by suggesting that things cannot be any way but the way that they always already are), and it does so in large part by situating the clan in a kind of time that emphasizes what is iterative, cyclical, and (thus) "natural"—the temporality of idyll and of the family novel. Idyllic time is anti-teleological, but it is not at all entropic. Although it moves in circles/cycles and is cut off from larger temporal systems where linear "progress" is happening, this does not mean that the idyll represents its world as pointless; rather, it predictably creates and recreates its own predictable (but genuine) meaning through closed cycles of repetition.[83]

The generic underpinnings of *Childhood*—its roots in idyll—help make it possible for Tolstoy to imply an intimate connection between serfdom and family, and thus to construe serfdom as a relationship of love. And an idyll-inflected text is likely to work to encompass in its view of "family" everyone who is in the home—including those like Natalya Savishna, whose individual interests are effectively denied by being subsumed under the interests of a putatively organic unity. This tendency is reinforced by a narrative point of view that acknowledges virtually no separation, for example, between the child nobleman and his serf nanny, as when Nikolenka says: "For as long as I remember myself, I remember Natal'ia Savishna" (words that recall Bakhtin's remarks on how idyll "renders less distinct all the temporal boundaries between individual lives").[84] *Childhood*'s implicit argument is that it might well be worth it for the Natalya Savishnas of the world to be forced to sacrifice themselves for the common good, which in the end turns out to be their own good as well: this really is a text about the loveable side of slavery.

Such an argument can only be made (or implied) in a family story—and "A Landowner's Morning" is not a family story. Nekhliudov is an orphan; his teenage fantasy of domestic and conjugal bliss—a pretty, saintly wife who will devote her entire being to him and to his peasants—is obviously self-serving and unrealistic. Lacking the family context of *Childhood* (or *War and Peace* or *Anna Karenina*, for that matter), "A Landowner's Morning" cannot argue that the bitter sacrifices required of individual peasants are ultimately in the service of some greater good, and it cannot redeem Nekhliudov's repetitive circuit through the village by implicating it in the natural cycles of idyll. Thus even though writing about a *good* landowner allows Tolstoy to avoid looking at the shocking brutalities on which other critics of serfdom lavished their attention, Tolstoy in no way avoids the most basic fact about the institution: that serfdom is above all a relation of *economic* inequality and injustice. As early reviewers of "A Landowner's Morning" noted, while Turgenev's emphasis in *Notes of a Hunter* had been on the serf's basic (and still contested) humanity, Tolstoy's was on the economic arrangements that kept the peasants, as Nekhliudov remarks in naïve amazement, "so poor."[85]

By choosing to write a story about serfdom that was *not* also a story about family, *not* an idyll in any sense, Tolstoy required himself to explore the considerably less loveable side of this institution, a decision that again attests to the empiricist drive that sets Tolstoy apart from many other ideological writers (including Gogol). This choice also points to what one might call Tolstoy's submerged Enlightenment sensibility: actually, as I suggested in the introduction to this paper, "A Landowner's Morning" can be read as a kind of philosophical tale. The paradigm of this genre is often taken to be Voltaire's *Candide* [1759], a narrative structured around the travels of a naïf whose wanderings allow him to observe and interrogate the social arrangements he encounters in various locales. The protagonist of a philosophical tale starts out with an idea (in the case of *Candide*, the conviction that "all is for the best in this best of all possible worlds"), an idea that "the unfolding of the plot [then] confirms, undermines, or otherwise qualifies . . . by testing it against a series of concrete experiences and observations in the world at large."[86]

Nekhliudov's experience in the countryside tests a theory—the theory that a landowner [помещик] can cause his serfs to lead good (virtuous, prosperous) lives in the absence of any fundamental change to the existing social and economic order. The naïve young landowner, convinced that it is his duty to "act upon" his peasants ("this simple, receptive, uncorrupted class of people"), sets out to "save them from poverty," to "reform their vices, which are the result of ignorance and superstition, to develop their morality, [and] to cause them to love the good."[87] As we have seen, Nekhliudov discovers these beliefs to be inadequate when tested against real life in the village. "Have my peasants gotten richer?" he asks himself, "Have they been morally educated and developed? Not in the least."[88] Like Candide, then, he must reassess.

Voltaire closes his tale with the famous (and famously ambiguous) injunction to "cultivate one's own garden," an idea communicated to Candide in his exchange with a virtuous and prosperous old farmer: "You must possess an enormous and splendid property," says Candide; but no, the farmer replies, "I have only twenty acres . . . all of which I cultivate myself with the help of my children; and our labor keeps us from three great evils—idleness, vice, and poverty."[89] *Candide* ends with the main character's reiteration of the old farmer's cultivate-our-garden maxim, but in "A Landowner's Morning" such an injunction could not constitute an *ending*, because it is in effect where the protagonist *began*. Nekhliudov set out to cultivate his garden, and the garden turned out to be an estate requiring oppressed laborers to work it. In "A Landowner's Morning" the closest we come to *Candide*'s vision of a good life—twenty acres cultivated by one modest, hard-working family who profess to avoid all involvement in the larger world—is the family of the old bee-keeping peasant Dutlov. Indeed, Dutlov sounds a lot like Voltaire's farmer, who insists on his own ignorance of all "public affairs" ("I never listen to the news from Constantinople; I am content with sending the fruits of my garden to be sold there").[90] Dutlov says the same: "I'm busy enough feeding my own family."[91]

Dutlov, however, is a serf who can own no land at all. In fact, Tolstoy's peasant "farmer" refuses to go in with Nekhliudov to buy land ("it's not for me to buy groves"[92]), knowing very well that he would run the risk of being cheated by the барин and left without legal recourse.[93] This peasant understands that his best option is to cultivate his garden; too bad, then, that the garden is not actually his. In the end, what Tolstoy's story suggests is that Voltaire's essentially middle-class model of virtue is unlikely to be available to Russians, whether noblemen or peasants. What, then, is our Everyman Landowner to do? Where is he to go? This, it seems, is the dilemma that leads the protagonist, at the conclusion of "A Landowner's Morning," to imagine himself as a truly free version of Dutlov's son, a young man who simply flies away, soaring first over the highway and then through the sky, his gaze directed not ahead at the intractable problems of the village but down at the golden rooftops and up at the shining stars.

Endnotes

1 Tolstoi, *ПСС*, Chertkov edition, 47:4. My attention was drawn to this diary entry by Anne Hruska's article. Unless otherwise marked, all quotations of Tolstoy are from the Chertkov edition of *Полное собрание сочинений* [*Complete Collected Works*] in 90 volumes, hereafter cited by volume and page number. All translations are mine, but I have also referred to Leo Wiener's English version of "Утро помещика," titled "A Morning of A Landed Proprietor."

2 The focus of idyll or pastoral (terms that are often used interchangeably, and are certainly interchangeable for my purposes) is "the peace and

simplicity of the life of shepherds and other rural folk in an idealized natural setting"; more broadly, it can be defined as "any [literary] work that opposes simple to complicated life, to the advantage of the former," with the simple life being not necessarily that of shepherds, but also, say, that of children or the lower classes (Abrams, 202-3).

3 Hruska, "Love and Slavery," 628. Of course, Tolstoy was not alone in representing serfdom as "a patriarchal system that mirrored family structure, with the serf-owner as father and the serfs as dependent children"; in this he was joined by the Slavophiles. However, Tolstoy differed from the Slavophiles "in his willingness to see serfdom as connected to love, rather than as a violation of the bonds between gentry and peasantry" (Hruska, 628, 628n7).

4 Bakhtin, "Forms of Time," 226-29.

5 Ibid., 225, 229. Bakhtin also remarks on the important role that children play in these genres (227).

6 This is not to say, however, that the idyll can never accommodate social criticism; celebrating the purity and simplicity of the past can imply a strong critique of the present (impure, hierarchical) social order. On this see Empson, as well as Bakhtin, 231.

7 Bakhtin, "Forms of Time," 225.

8 Technically, *Childhood* is not narrated from Nikolenka's point of view, since the narrator speaks as a young adult recalling his past. However, the prevalence of *style indirect libre* leads the reader to experience the text as if it were being recounted from the child's perspective.

9 The philosophical tale issues "a veiled imperative to bring about change in the established sociopolitical system" by revealing a "tension between theory and actuality [that] arouses a feeling that things ought to be other than they are" (Hollier, 468). I am indebted to Ilya Kliger for first suggesting to me the parallel between this genre and "A Landowner's Morning."

10 Hollier, *A New History*, 488. While Tolstoy's social criticism (in "A Landowner's Morning" and elsewhere) cannot be described as positivist, it is certainly analytical and empirical.

11 Ibid., 471.

12 Tolstoi, *ПСС*, Chertkov edition, 4:399.

13 Eikhenbaum, *Young Tolstoi*, 69. For Eikhenbaum, "A Landowner's Morning" serves as "an étude of sorts for the 'landowner' chapters of Tolstoy's future novels" (71). In fact, Eikhenbaum repeatedly uses the word "embryo" to describe the relationship between Tolstoy's mature works and his earliest writings, including not only stories and fragments of stories but also diary entries, notes, plans for self-improvement, etc. (45, 46, 69). Indeed, one can readily list the ways in which "A Landowner's Morning" forecasts Tolstoy's later techniques and ideas: its refusal of conventional plotting in favor of a structure based only on a unit of time; its rejection of (auto)biography as *form* combined with the inclusion of considerable autobiographical *content*; a protagonist whose goal is to figure out the right way to live; the fraught relationship between landowner and peasant; the use of dreams and near-dream states to explore consciousness; the careful, almost bloodless analysis of how selflessness and selfishness come together in every individual, etc. As such a list suggests, this particular story yields itself easily to what one might describe as the always-already approach ("Look, there he is—it's Tolstoy! He's already *himself!*"). In this paper I try to strike a balance by acknowledging how "A Landowner's Morning" reflects what would later reveal themselves to be enduring Tolstoyan preoccupations, while also focusing on the story's relationship to the particular historical moment that produced it.

14 Tolstoi, *ПСС*, Chertkov edition, 4:398-400. At times here Tolstoy is referring to the "Novel of a Russian Landowner," the unfinished work from which "A Landowner's Morning" was ultimately excerpted and adapted. Tolstoy's relentless insistence on this work's didactic intent might put one off from reading it altogether.

15 Orwin, *Cambridge Companion*, 3-7.

16 The conference was "The Over-Examined Life: New Perspectives on Tolstoy," Harvard University, Davis Center for Russian Studies, April 19 – 20, 2002.

17 Here Tolstoy's use of the word "novel"—роман—is deliberate, as well as somewhat eccentric when compared to the typical usage of the period. For Tolstoy at this time, роман designated a long work (longer than повесть, which meant basically a long story), and specifically one that did *not* have love intrigue as its main plot element (Tolstoi 2007, 3:397).

18 Tolstoi, *ПСС*, Chertkov edition, 3:434. For a detailed account of both works' composition and their complicated interrelationship, see the commentary in 4:397-405. After the publication of "A Landowner's Morning," Tolstoy makes only two very brief mentions of *Novel of a Russian Landowner* in his notebooks (4:406).
19 Ibid., 4:400.
20 Tolstoy used the surname Nekhliudov in other works as well, most notably in the early story *Lucerne* (in which a nobleman called Nekhliudov asks fundamental ethical questions about human unity) and in the late novel *Resurrection* [*Воскресение*, 1899] (in which another Nekhliudov is transformed—eventually—after confronting the devastating consequences of his own mistreatment of a fellow human being). The name also appears in *Boyhood, Youth,* and *Notes of a Billiard Maker*. Hugh McLean has argued that it is "a thinly disguised autobiographical signal . . . a 'softened' variant of нехлюдой, 'not thin,' a synonym of толстый, 'fat,' of which Tolstoy is a variant" (McLean, "Resurrection," 100). While one might counter that a great many of Tolstoy's characters who are *not* named Nekhliudov incorporate aspects of the author's own traits and experiences (and that McLean's etymology feels a bit stretched), it is true that these Nekhliudovs reflect with particular directness one of Tolstoy's most enduring concerns: how to live in a manner that takes full and honest account of one's responsibility to other people.
21 Tolstoi, *ПСС*, Chertkov edition, 4:123.
22 Ibid., 4:124-5.
23 Ibid., 4:149.
24 Ibid., 4:403 (italics mine).
25 Quoted in Eikhenbaum, *Young Tolstoi*, 69.
26 Tolstoi, *ПСС*, Chertkov edition, 4:134.
27 Ibid., 4:136.
28 Knapp, "Development of Style," 162. When Knapp points out that Tolstoy prided himself on demonstrating how such seemingly unimportant events were in fact "more significant, more serious" than "the facts usually printed in newspapers and histories" (Tolstoy's own words, quoted by Knapp, 162), I am struck by the dramatic contrast between Tolstoy's and Dostoevsky's views of print culture and the meanings of "news." For Dostoevsky,

who worked much of his life as a professional journalist, newspapers not only provided a crucial source for his art, they also could be taken as a reflection of what was really happening—and thus what was truly important—at a given moment. In other words, Dostoevsky believed in something called "public opinion," and he believed that this phenomenon could be accurately represented by printed texts. Tolstoy, by contrast, devoted a fair amount of time to debunking such views, as in Book VIII of *Anna Karenina* when Levin argues that the "people's voice" calling for Russia to go to war against the Turks is in fact *merely* the voice of a few newspapers in the capitals (733). One can only imagine what Dostoevsky would have made of Tolstoy's remark in a letter to his brother, "There's nothing I fear more than turning myself into a journalist-scribbler"! (4:400).

29 Shklovsky discusses Dmitry's effort in his biography of Tolstoy (86-97). McLean writes that Dmitry, inspired by *Selected Passages*, "attempted to follow the principles [Gogol] set forth": "he wanted to do his moral duty to his peasants, sitting in judgment on them and trying to raise their standards of behavior"—but without questioning the institution of serfdom (McLean, *Quest of Tolstoy*, 39). See also Medzhibovskaya, 42.

30 Gogol, *Selected Passages*, 138.

31 Ibid., 192, 40.

32 Ibid., 191.

33 Ibid., 137. The Russian is "Главное то, что, ты приехал в деревнию и положил себе непременно быть помещиком" (Gogol, *ПСС*, 8:321).

34 Gogol, *Selected Passages*, 137, 143 (italics mine).

35 Tolstoi, *ПСС*, Chertkov edition, 4:140, 139.

36 By 1890 the French sociologist Gabriel de Tarde, for example, was already elaborating on the relationship between following fashions and *being modern* (358, 226).

37 See, for example, Shklovsky, 65, 87; on Tolstoy's early childhood generally, see 26-54.

38 Tolstoy, *Anna Karenina*, 155 (italics mine).

39 Levin makes the point more explicitly a little later in the same chapter: "I consider the [real] aristocrats to be myself and people like me: people who can point back in their family history to three or four honorable

generations... who never depended on anyone, but who lived as my father and my grandfather did... I value what is mine by birth and labor" (*Anna Karenina*, 157). Compare here what Tolstoy wrote of his own father: "He did not serve anywhere in the reign of Nicholas, and all his friends were also as free as himself, they held no offices... Father never groveled before anyone" (quoted in Shklovsky, 49).

40 Tolstoy, *Anna Karenina*, 292.
41 Tolstoi, *ПСС*, Chertkov edition, 4:123.
42 Ibid., 4:144.
43 Ibid., 4:168.
44 Ibid., 4:132.
45 Ibid., 4:144.
46 Gogol, *ПСС*, 8:358.
47 Zeldin translates this as "Do not be in touch with anyone other than personally" (185). See also his alternate rendering: "All your dealings with the officials will be personal" (185).
48 Tolstoi, *ПСС*, Chertkov edition, 4:144, 132.
49 Gogol, *Selected Passages*, 141.
50 Tolstoi, *ПСС*, Chertkov edition, 4:134.
51 Ibid., 4:126.
52 Ibid., 4:126-7.
53 Ibid., 4:129.
54 Ibid., 4:147.
55 Ibid.
56 Ibid., 4:131-2.
57 Ibid., 4:132.
58 Ibid., 4:133 (italics mine).
59 Ibid., 4:158-164.
60 Ibid., 4:160.
61 Ibid., 4:161.
62 Ibid., 4:160.
63 Ibid., 4:128.
64 In Foucauldian terms, we might see Nekhliudov as a kind of walking panopticon peering around corners and through windows, keeping the peasants in line—or trying to—by *seeing* them. This reminds us of

what might be described as modernizing rather than archaizing or "organicist" about Tolstoy's worldview (again, modern as in the Enlightenment sense of what is modern, as we see in the *conte philosophique*): his insistence on clear categories and systematic ways of thinking.

65 Tolstoi, *ПСС*, Chertkov edition, 4:154.
66 Ibid., 4:145-6.
67 Ibid., e.g., 4:128, 133, 137, 138.
68 See Eikhenbaum, 72 as well as 35, 77.
69 Turgenev, *ПСС*, 3:7.
70 Tolstoi, *ПСС*, Chertkov edition, 4:139.
71 Ibid., 4:151.
72 *Anna Karenina*'s famously powerful scene of Levin mowing alongside his peasants represents a touristic kind of labor: a certain meaning accrues to the landlord's work in this passage precisely because Levin does it once, and by choice. This has little to do with what work represents in a peasant's life. In the last decades of the nineteenth century, however, populism did inspire a number of Russian novels about peasants; see, for example, Goriachkina.
73 Tolstoi, *ПСС*, Chertkov edition, 4:166.
74 Ibid., 4:169-70. Medzhibovskaya, whose interest is in Tolstoy's religious thought, remarks of this passage, "The landowner's dreaming his peasant's dreams is a special kind of religious envy indeed" (64). Medzhibovskaya's view is that Tolstoy has Nekhliudov *recognize* in his peasants "a form of primordial unity"; I would lean more toward the conclusion that Tolstoy has his protagonist *imagine* such a unity.
75 Tolstoi, *ПСС*, Chertkov edition, 4:170-1.
76 Nekhliudov's fantasy of joyful, bracing motion recalls the famous scene at the end of Gogol's *Dead Souls*, when a *troika* carries Chichikov and Russia off into an unknown future.
77 Tolstoi, *ПСС*, Chertkov edition, 4:167.
78 Gustafson, *Leo Tolstoy*, 16.
79 Hruska, "Love and Slavery," 627, n3.
80 Quoted in Hruska, "Love and Slavery," 630, n14.
81 Quoted in Hruska, "Love and Slavery," 630.

82 "*Childhood* is linked together not by a movement of events which form a plot, but by a sequence of diverse scenes... which succeed each other in the course of one day—from morning until evening by the hands of the clock" (Eikhenbaum, 56); for more on the structure of *Childhood*, see 48-67.

83 The idyll, Bakhtin writes, is set in "a little spatially limited world ... sufficient unto itself, not linked in any intrinsic way with other places, with the rest of the world" (225). At one point near the end of "A Landowner's Morning," Tolstoy's protagonist bitterly regrets having withdrawn from progressive, modern, linear time, the kind of time that is, in Bakhtin's terms, "linked ... with the rest of the world": Nekhliudov recalls that in his student days, "the future looked altogether different! Then the future was full of enjoyment, various activities, and glittering success, undoubtedly *leading ... to the greatest good in the world*" (167, emphasis mine). And since Nekhliudov's renunciation of this kind of "progress time" is not even rewarded with an idyll, the disappointment proves all the more galling.

84 Bakhtin, "Forms of Time," 225.

85 For nineteenth- and early twentieth-century responses to "A Landowner's Morning," see Tolstoi 2007 3:435-440.

86 Hollier, *A New History*, 471.

87 Tolstoi, *ПСС*, Chertkov edition, 4:165.

88 Ibid., 4:166.

89 Voltaire, *Candide*, 74. Of course, one should not assume that Candide's complacent formula represents Voltaire's own "solution": it is unlikely that Voltaire himself saw the cultivation of one's own garden as an adequate response to the myriad sufferings and injustices described in his tale.

90 Ibid., 74.

91 Tolstoi, *ПСС*, Chertkov edition, 4:163.

92 Ibid.

93 Ibid., 4:156.

Works Cited

Abrams, M. H. *A Glossary of Literary Terms*. New York: Harcourt Brace, 1999.

Bakhtin, Mikhail. "Forms of Time and Chronotope in the Novel." In *The Dialogic Imagination: Four Essays by M. M. Bakhtin*. Edited by Michael Holquist, translated by Caryl Emerson and Michael Holquist, 84-258. Austin: University of Texas Press, 1981.

Eikhenbaum, Boris. *The Young Tolstoi*. Translated by Gary Kern. Ann Arbor, MI: Ardis Press, 1972. First published 1922 by Slavische Propylaen Press.

Empson, William. *Some Versions of Pastoral*. New York: W.W. Norton and Co., 1974. First published 1935 by Chatto & Windus Press.

Gogol, Nikolai. *Selected Passages from Correspondence with Friends*. Translated by Jesse Zeldin. Nashville, TN: Vanderbilt University Press, 1969.

———. *Полное собрание сочинений*. 14 vols. Edited by N. L. Meshcheriakov. Moscow: Akademii nauk, 1937-1952.

Goriachkina, M. S. "Своеобразие реализма народнической прозы." In *Проблемы типологии русского реализма*, edited by N. L. Stepanov and U.R. Fokht, 379-407. Nauka: Moscow, 1969.

Gustafson, Richard F. *Leo Tolstoy: Resident and Stranger*. Princeton, NJ: Princeton University Press, 1986.

Hollier, Denis, ed. *A New History of French Literature*. Cambridge, MA.: Harvard University Press, 1994.

Hruska, Anne. "Love and Slavery: Serfdom, Emancipation, and Family in Tolstoy's Fiction." *The Russian Review* 66 (October 2007): 627-646.

Knapp, Liza. "The Development of Style and Theme in Tolstoy." In *The Cambridge Companion to Tolstoy*, edited by Donna Tussing Orwin, 161-175. Cambridge, UK: Cambridge University Press, 2002.

Lesskis, Georgii. *Лев Толстой, 1852-1869*. Moscow: OGI, 2000.

McLean, Hugh. *In Quest of Tolstoy*. Boston: Academic Studies Press, 2008.

———. "Resurrection." In *The Cambridge Companion to Tolstoy*, edited by Donna Tussing Orwin, 96-110. Cambridge, UK: Cambridge University Press.

Medzhibovskaya, Inessa. *Tolstoy and the Religious Culture of his Time: A Biography of a Long Conversion*. Lanham, MD: Rowman and Littlefield, 2008.

Orwin, Donna Tussing, ed. *The Cambridge Companion to Tolstoy*. Cambridge, UK: Cambridge University Press, 2002.

Shklovsky, Viktor. *Lev Tolstoy*. USSR: Progress Publishers, 1978. First published 1963 by Molodaia Gvardiia Press.

de Tarde, Gabriel. *The Laws of Imitation*. Translated by Elsie Clews Parsons. New York: Henry Holt and Co., 1903.

Tolstoi, Lev. *Полное собрание сочинений*. 90 vols. Edited by V. G. Chertkov. Moscow: Gosudarstvennoe izdatel'stvo "Khudozhestvennaia literatura," 1928-1958.

Tolstoy, Leo. *Anna Karenina*. Edited by George Gibian, translated by Aylmer and Louise Maude. New York: W. W. Norton and Co., 1995.

———. "A Morning of a Landed Proprietor." In *A Landed Proprietor, The Cossacks, Sevastopol*, translated by Leo Wiener, 3-78. Boston: Dana Estes & Co., 1904.

Turgenev, Ivan. *Полное собрание сочинений и писем*. 30 vols. Moscow: Nauka, 1979.

Voltaire. *Candide, or Optimism*. Translated and edited by Robert M. Adams. New York and London: W. W. Norton and Co., 1991.

Tolstoy's Lessons: Pedagogy as Salvation[1]

Ilya Vinitsky

> Thou shall not try to tempt me vainly
> By means of frog of thy device.
> As teacher I take rather strangely
> All works conceived in days of vice.
>
> Lev Tolstoy, Letter to I. P. Borisov and A. A. Fet[2]
>
> And if you're not willing, then I will use force.
>
> Johann von Goethe, "The Erlking"

This essay will address not the lessons of Lev Tolstoy the author but of Lev Tolstoy the teacher—that is, not the moral messages embedded in the renowned novels and stories that Tolstoy wrote, but the pedagogical activities connected to the school for peasant children that Tolstoy founded and ran on his rural familial estate, Iasnaia Poliana, between 1859 and 1862. Polemics about pedagogy were being waged in government circles and intellectual journals throughout the 1850s and 1860s, and with particular intensity on the eve of and immediately following the emancipation of the serfs in 1861. Questions of whether and how members of the peasantry should be educated gave rise to much debate during this time. Having announced his abandonment of a literary career, fleeing the intellectual superficiality and corruption of city life to Iasnaia Poliana, Tolstoy provided his answers to those questions by establishing the school, along with a journal of pedagogy, both named after the estate. To be sure, the school and journal gave Tolstoy what literature could not—an opportunity to creatively realize ideas useful to the common people. But arguably they do more. I will argue in this essay that they disclose not only the young Tolstoy's public policy views but also his private concerns, not only his social beliefs but his psychological conflicts, not only his philosophical convictions but his spiritual struggles. Ultimately, I will suggest, Tolstoy undertook his pedagogical activities as a means to achieve salvation for himself.

In 1860, Tolstoy set forth the social and cultural reasons for which he had founded his school: "In the matter of Russia's progress," he wrote to an influential acquaintance in government affairs,

> it seems to me that however useful may be telegraphs, roads, steamers, guns, culture (with all its charity foundations, theaters, Academies of the Arts, and so forth)—all of this is premature and to no purpose until such time . . . as it will be evident that, in Russia, of all potential students only one percent of the population goes to school. . . . Popular education is a vital need for the Russian people. There is *no such* education. It has not yet begun and will never begin as long as the government is in charge of it. . . . In order for popular education to take place it must be placed into the hands of society. . . . For *me* this issue has been decided. In a half year my school begot three others just like it nearby, and they have had equal success everywhere.[3]

Tolstoy did not envision just any member of society educating the peasants. On the contrary, he was convinced that the upper classes, which claimed cultural leadership of Russia, posed a serious danger to healthier, wiser, and more moral peasants, especially peasant children, who had no need for the technological innovations or aesthetic refinements extolled by the upper classes. He had even less use for professional educators and government-sponsored educational programs with which he had become disenchanted during his "pedagogical travels" of 1860-1861, when he toured Europe, visiting various educational institutions.

But even before those travels Tolstoy had rejected the traditional understanding of the task of pedagogy. Real pedagogy, he declared, did not entail merely writing and fulfilling lesson plans but seeking "to learn the general paths of education and its rules" on the basis of direct experimentation, through trial and error. In other words, the task of Tolstoy's school was to discover a *practical philosophy* of pedagogy. So strongly did he perceive the need for a system of public education that he declared, "whether it is permitted or not, even if I am all by myself, I will found a *secret society of public education*."⁴ This society was never formally established, but the readership of the pedagogical journal Tolstoy founded and published functioned as one in some ways.

This journal, *Iasnaia Poliana* [*Ясная Поляна*], was, in its own way, Tolstoy's equivalent of Dostoevsky's *Diary of a Writer* [*Дневник писателя*, 1873-76, 1877, 1881].⁵ The first issue of the journal (together with a literary appendix, in which literary works for peasants and the best compositions of the schoolchildren were printed) came out in January of 1862. The ostensible task of this journal, which Tolstoy declared to be nonliterary and nonpolitical, was to describe and explain the school he had founded. In fact, under the pretext of discussing pedagogical questions, Tolstoy boldly and provocatively articulated many of his most radical ideas—the very ideas that, with variations here and there, eventually became major tenets of his philosophy and were crystallized in his later fictional and non-fictional works.

For example, on the subject of education Tolstoy maintained the following: *all* pedagogical doctrines and methods are rooted in deceit or vanity; *all* modern educational institutions from the village school to the university are based on compulsion and lies, and therefore the entire system of education must be changed, starting with its keystone, the parochial school; the *only* criterion for true education should be the natural development of children, which gives birth to a free system that does not require force to maintain; the ideal education, as Rousseau correctly stated, can be found not ahead of us but behind us, and for this reason children—especially peasant children and especially boys (here Tolstoy is Russifying Rousseau)—are closer to an innocent and happy state of human existence than educated adults because they are healthier, wiser, and more moral; adults—especially aristocratic adults—that is, already-corrupted human beings around fourteen years or older *should not* educate children on the basis of their own views and experience because they will corrupt the children.⁶

But Tolstoy also held forth on such subjects as social and technological progress—which, he said, the upper classes glorify, often with religious enthusiasm—claiming that it was *not needed by the peasants* (at least not now), and in fact constituted dangerous ideological fetishism. By contrast, he insisted, everything essential in the world has always been as it is now, and therefore will always be the same. He also took up the subject of art, declaring it no less than abominable to inflict aristocratic, intellectual, narrow, and arbitrary aesthetic values on healthy peasants, to whom a Beethoven quartet is unpleasant noise, the best verses of Pushkin are an assortment of sounds, and the *Venus de Milo* is just a naked girl; they would develop for themselves appropriate—that is, is natural—aesthetic sensibilities.[7]

Tolstoy himself actively thrust his journal into the public arena by announcing it in well-known publications and making a polemical call for powerful journalists to enter the discussions about education, among other activities.[8]

In 1861 Tolstoy described the school he had founded at Iasnaia Poliana in a programmatic article entitled "The Iasnaia Poliana School in November and December" ["Ясно-полянская школа за ноябрь и декабрь месяцы"] (evoking one of his Crimean war chronicles, "Sevastopol in December" ["Севастополь в декабре месяце"]). Tolstoy reported that the school

> resides in a two-story stone building. Two rooms are occupied by the school, another by the lab, and two by the teachers' offices. On the porch under an awning hangs a little bell with a string tied to the clapper, on the porch below there are parallel bars and a rack [of weights]. On the porch above there is a bench. The staircase and porch are covered in snowy or muddy footprints; on the porch hangs a schedule. The instructional day is organized as follows: around eight in the morning, a teacher who lives at the school, an administrator of the school and a lover of outward order, sends one of the boys, who almost always sleeps in [the teacher's] lodgings, to ring the bell.[9]

Tolstoy goes on to say that lessons start at eight in the morning, continue until noon, and then resume from three until five in the afternoon, although the children often stay until late at night "because you can't chase them out of the school—they ask for more."[10] Sometimes, Tolstoy noted, lessons take place in the fields, in the garden, or in the nearby forest. In the evenings, there are readings of literary works and discussions of moral themes. On occasion Tolstoy would play the piano for the students.

In the school, boys and girls from five to fifteen years of age studied together. The students were divided into two classes that were in turn divided into two groups according to age and level of education. Instruction was provided at no cost. The main courses offered were reading, writing, grammar, religious history and theology, Russian history, mathematics, basic natural sciences, land-surveying (geodesy), drawing, draftsmanship, and singing. Lessons in manual labor and gymnastics were considered especially important. The school had its own library, a small museum, a laboratory, a workshop, and athletic grounds.[11]

Tolstoy recruited a group of young teachers to staff the school. By the beginning of 1861 there were twelve teachers, mostly former students who shared Tolstoy's pedagogical ideas and, in Tolstoy's opinion, would be cured through contact with morally healthy peasant children of the delusions inherent in the Western socialism favored by radical university students at the time.[12] Although he chose the teachers himself, Tolstoy was often dissatisfied with them: "The teachers are bad. Alexandr Ivanovich is stupid. Alexandr Pavlovich is morally unwell. Ivan Ilyich is the most reliable of all. Every teacher has some kind of nasty secret. At best it's women [ежели это бабы, то хорошо]."[13]

Tolstoy dubbed the school's overarching principles the "Criteria of Freedom."[14] These criteria comprised:

- voluntary attendance (and, as Tolstoy noted, everyone attended);
- the freedom to come and go at will if a lesson is uninteresting (and no one misses a lesson);
- the absence of textbooks and homework; one brings only oneself to school as a result of "one's receptive nature and the confidence that the day at school today will be as joyous as it was yesterday"[15];
- a variable schedule, depending on the interests of the students;
- the repudiation of corporal punishment and coercive disciplinary measures (no one ever breaks the rules);
- freedom of expression on the part of students and teachers, and in general *unconstrained* conversations between teachers (first and foremost Tolstoy himself) and students, about all things of interest to children, are greatly valued.[16]

Overall, according to Tolstoy, the school was governed by simplicity, unity, love, and collaboration.[17] It was, again according to the plans of its founder, not only an educational institution, but in its own way a glade of happiness and freedom in the gloomy forest of pedagogical establishments in Russia and the West, establishments with which Tolstoy had become disenchanted during his "pedagogical travels" of 1860-1861.[18]

Tolstoy's school and the pedagogical principles behind it engendered opposition from a wide array of liberals and conservatives, as well as professional educators, and even some parents. Objections ranged from the philosophical—members of the upper classes have no right to educate children—to the political—Tolstoy was "endeavoring to overturn the entire system of public education in Russia and the whole world," running a veritable "school of depravity"—to the personal—Tolstoy was not a trained educator, Tolstoy was too idealistic, Tolstoy knew nothing about peasant children.[19]

But, undaunted by opposition, Tolstoy persevered, inspired in part by an ideal vision of the school of the future that "perhaps will not be a school as we understand it—with chalkboards, benches, podia for teachers or professors. Perhaps it will be a gallery, a theater, a library, a museum...."[20] This ideal might not be realized any time soon, Tolstoy acknowledged:

> Only a hundred years from now the concepts that I perhaps unclearly, awkwardly, unpersuasively, am trying to articulate may become commonplace; only a hundred years from now all established institutions—academies, gymnasia, universities—may become obsolete; then freely forming institutions will be founded on the principle of freedom of a generation of learners.[21]

Tolstoy conceived of the school at Iasnaia Poliana as a prototype of that school of the future.

Ironically, this prototype, designed to embody the "criteria of freedom," was ruled over by Tolstoy like an autocrat. Not only did he choose the students, determine the curriculum, and select who would teach it, he wielded exceptional emotional influence over his students. Like Goethe's Erlking ["Der Erlkönig," 1782], he could produce strong anxieties in his students. In contrast to Goethe's character, however, he could also inspire their love. Accordingly, Tolstoy's diaries and journal of pedagogical activities record multiple instances in which the children displayed the warmest of feelings toward him, looked at him with loving eyes, placed their hands on his, and so forth. Tolstoy attempted to explain his unquestionable spiritual leadership and absolute control over every aspect of the school by claiming that it was better for him to influence the children and young teachers than for corrupt society to do so.

A staff member of the journal sought to illustrate the extent of Tolstoy's influence with an anecdote. Late one night Tolstoy, surrounded by children and teachers, was playing Schubert's ballad version of Goethe's poem "The Erlking." In the poem, a gray demon-king attracts a child's soul with enchanting words about his wealth and his daughter's beauty, and then forcibly seizes the soul. Reaching the finale, Tolstoy, "himself swept up by the power of the images depicted, struck the piano keys with all the strength in his muscular hands, the music ended with a heart-rending chord, and the final words of the ballad—'the dead child lay in his arms'—groaned in the nighttime hush." His audience was shaken. Then Tolstoy, like an experienced performer, sharply altered the emotional mood: he began a Mendelssohn-like lyrical melody. The frightened children, not knowing what he would play next, asked him not to play "Leshii" [a forest spirit in Russian folklore who "exhausted [a] child to the point of death"], preferring instead a romance or "The Cherub Song." Tolstoy played on until the evening was over, at which point "students, teachers, and the Iasnaia Poliana peasant children, full of 'sweet sounds and prayers,' dispersed." This scene demonstrates the vast power of Tolstoy to manipulate the emotions of the students at Iasnaia Poliana.[22] In essence, Tolstoy reigned as the absolute authority in his "free" realm.[23]

Here I should stipulate that, at least for many of the students, Tolstoy's authority was imperceptible or pleasant, even arguably beneficial. Some student essays preserved in the archives of the Tolstoy museum portray the unconstrained familial atmosphere that flourished under Tolstoy's paternalistic control.[24] In fact, in the article "The Iasnaia Poliana School in November and December" Tolstoy describes his relationship with the school's students not as one of parent and children but as one of equals taking nighttime walks while discussing abstract subjects like the nature of evil and the uses and abuses of art.[25]

Indeed, despite his insistence on his superior judgment in pedagogical matters large and small, Tolstoy at times represented students as his superiors, at least in creative potential. In an article entitled "Who Teaches Whom to Write, Do Peasant Children Teach Us or Do We Teach Peasant Children?"

["Кому у кого учиться писать, крестьянским ребятам у нас или нам у крестьянских ребят"], which appeared in the September 1862 issue of *Iasnaia Poliana* and became one of the most well-known and provocative articles the journal was to publish, Tolstoy depicts his experience of this superiority.[26] The putative subject of the pedagogical article is methods of teaching composition to peasant children. In it Tolstoy recommends assigning as themes for student compositions folk proverbs expressing the ethical wisdom of peasants that children instinctively recognize. He also recommends promoting as compositional models not the artistic works of professional writers but the compositions of the students themselves, for "children's compositions are more just, more elegant, and more moral than the compositions of adults."[27] He argues that educated people in general "should not teach reading and writing, especially poetic writing, at all to children and especially peasant children," and he reports that, as soon as he gave his peasant students free rein in their compositions, they wrote "such poetic works as have never existed before in Russian literature."[28]

Tolstoy then describes the germination of true artistic creation in the hearts of two peasant boys, Fedka and Semka, who had only recently learned to read and write.[29] These two boys, in creating together with him a story derived from a Russian proverb, surpassed him in everything: in their choice of details, their sense of proportion, their instinctive perception of the whole, and the truthfulness and beauty of their descriptions. At the same time each of the boys had his own strikingly pronounced authorial method.

According to Tolstoy, the story they composed was unprecedentedly good (better than anything Goethe could write!), but, alas, the paper manuscript of this story was inadvertently used by the other children for fireworks. Tolstoy was distraught, but Fedka and Semka calmed him: they would sit down and write it again. They worked all night in Tolstoy's house. Tolstoy, enchanted, watched as the spirit of the peasants' (childish) collective consciousness gave birth to true art. The next morning the story was again finished—in a version as good as, if not better than, the first.[30] Thus, Tolstoy found, art was blossoming in the pure souls of peasant children, art that was not only qualitatively superior to his own but that could seemingly endure forever. (From here one can find a direct path to Tolstoy's later tract *What is Art?* [*Что такое искусство?*, 1897].)

Tolstoy's own artistic sensibilities informed what I would call the mystical conclusion of the article on teaching composition to peasant students. Having observed the creative efforts of the boys, he felt that he had found the philosopher's stone of art:

> I cannot convey the feeling of restlessness, joy, fear, and almost remorse that I experienced in the course of that night. I felt that from this day onward a new world of delight and misery—the world of art—had opened up for [Fedka]; it seemed to me that I had glimpsed what no one ever has the right to see—the germination of the mysterious flower of poetry. It was both frightening and joyful for me, as for a treasure hunter.... I was joyful because, suddenly, completely unexpectedly, the philosopher's stone for which I had searched in vain for two years was revealed to me—*the art of teaching the expression of thoughts*. I was frightened because this art evoked new demands, a whole world of desires, incompatible with the environment in which the students lived, as it seemed to me at first. It was impossible to be mistaken. This was no accident, but conscious creation.[31]

At the same time, this *revelation* aroused in him a certain holy terror, tinged with a strange feeling of shame:

> It vaguely seemed to me that I was unlawfully peering through a glass hive at the work of bees, hidden to the gaze of mortals; it seemed that I had corrupted the pure, pristine soul of a peasant child. I vaguely felt in myself remorse at some sacrilege. *I thought of children whom idle and lecherous old men force to act out erotic scenes to fuel their tired, worn-out imaginations,* and at the same time I was as elated as someone who has seen something he has never seen before should be.[32]

I would suggest that Tolstoy's strange confession here contains the key to his pedagogical outlook at this time. Joy and shame for Tolstoy-the-pedagogue are intertwined with his unique religious feeling. Tolstoy's exaltation of the peasant boys' creative activity points not only to Jean-Jacques Rousseau and his worship of natural man—the obvious reference—but also directly to Tolstoy's religious views, specifically to his interpretation of Christ's homily about the kingdom of heaven as rendered in the gospel of Matthew, Chapter 18:

1. At the same time came the disciples unto Jesus, saying, Who is the greatest in the kingdom of heaven?

2. And Jesus called a little child unto him, and set him in the midst of them,
3. And said, Verily I say unto you, Except ye be converted, and become as little children, ye shall not enter into the kingdom of heaven.
4. Whosoever therefore shall humble himself as this little child, the same is greatest in the kingdom of heaven.
5. And whosoever shall receive one such little child in my name receiveth me.
6. But whosoever shall offend one of these little ones which believe in me, it were better for him that a millstone were hanged about his neck, and that he were drowned in the depth of the sea.

This lesson of Christ about the danger of offending the little children, who are greater than all others in the kingdom of heaven, is incorporated by Tolstoy into his pedagogical theories on the relationship the upper classes should have with the lower, the connections between the world of adults and the world of children, and his own pedagogical practices while teaching the Iasnaia Poliana students. It seems to me that Tolstoy is articulating his awareness of what he deems the frightful ethical responsibility assumed by teachers. The better the teacher, Tolstoy suggests, the more strongly and tortuously he must feel this responsibility. This is not Christian pedagogy (that is, teaching in accordance with Christian principles), but rather a socially-colored "pedagogical Christianity" centered on children of lower social classes.[33] Thus, he maintains, the kingdom of heaven, the source of salvation, may be discovered in the soul of a peasant boy, where the culturally corrupt adult Tolstoy looks, hoping to "humble himself" enough to enter that kingdom, and fearing that he no longer can. Moreover, he was afraid that he might—because of his corruptness as an adult and member of the upper classes—destroy the potential source of salvation and, consequently, doom himself.[34]

I would note that for Tolstoy pedagogy and Christianity were intricately interwoven, a connection that was manifested in a number of ways. For example, he devoted a great deal of his time to reading the Bible to the students, and numerous Christian allusions appear in his articles and letters during his three "pedagogical years." In "The Iasnaia Poliana School in November and December," discussing some boys who go to school united by a single aim—to learn—Tolstoy unexpectedly recalls more words of Christ from the passage where the "little children" are mentioned: "For where two or three gather in my name, there am I with them."[35] Tolstoy often referred to pedagogy as a new religion, comparing his school to a church and monastery.[36] And in a letter commenting on his experiment in education at Iasnaia Poliana, Tolstoy remarked, with a symbolic allusion to Christ's disciples, that, of his twelve teachers, one had turned out unworthy (it was a follower of socialism that Tolstoy did not like).[37] Most tellingly, Tolstoy wrote to his relative and confidante Aleksandra Tolstoy in August of 1862, "You know what the school was for me since I opened it. It was my entire life, *my monastery, the church in which I was saved and am being saved from all of the anxieties, doubts, and temptations of life*."[38]

Many years later, Tolstoy included an entire section on the religious and moral value of the child, beginning with the above-mentioned verses about the little children from the Gospel of Matthew, in his didactic "Circle of Reading" ["Круг чтения," 1904], a collection of wise sayings for every day of the year. After these verses Tolstoy cites two more verses from Matthew: "I praise you, Father, Lord of heaven and earth, because you have hidden these things from the wise and learned, and revealed them to little children. Yes, Father, for this is what you were pleased to do."[39] Then follows commentary from Tolstoy himself:

> Why are children morally higher than the majority of people? Because their reason is not perverted by deception, nor temptation, nor sin. Nothing lies before them on the path to perfection. Meanwhile before adults lie sin, temptation, and deception.[40]

Pedagogical activities for Tolstoy represented an intermediate realm between sin and innocence, enabling the penitent to return to a lost paradise, the doors of which have been locked. For him, Iasnaia Poliana was distinguished from traditional schools as Law in the Old Testament is distinguished from Freedom in the New Testament, offering a path to salvation for its creator, although that path is narrow and its edges are steep. Thus I conclude that Tolstoy engaged in his pedagogical activities in pursuit of his own personal salvation, aside from the salvation of his students or his country.

At the end of 1862 Tolstoy closed the school and abandoned teaching. Why? Tolstoy himself and his biographers suggest various reasons: he was offended by government authorities, who carried out a search of the premises in his absence and consequently "slandered" him in the eyes of the peasants; old students grew up and new ones were not added; the journal attracted too few subscribers (Tolstoy had hoped for two hundred) and spent too much (accruing a debt of three thousand rubles); he had gotten married; his passion had cooled; he had overcome his literary crisis; and so forth. In a letter written in the autumn of 1863 Tolstoy declared that his views of life, peasants, and society had entirely changed and that he now looked with astonishment at his enthusiastic pedagogical activity, "as souls look from above on their discarded bodies"[41]:

> I love children and pedagogy, but it is difficult for me to understand myself as I was a year ago. Children come to me in the evenings and bring with them recollections about the teacher that I was and will no longer be. I am now a writer with all the strength of my soul, and I write and think like I have never written and thought before. I am a happy and calm husband and father, and I have no secrets from anyone and no wishes other than that everything should go on as it did before.[42]

However, Tolstoy professed himself glad to have "attended that school," treating the Iasnaia Poliana experiment as a school of life.

All of these reasons undoubtedly played a role in his decision to leave the realm of pedagogy. But even if these were not the reasons, the outcome of the experiment would have been the same. I would explain Tolstoy's departure from pedagogy as part of the quest that would shape his life, the quest for personal, as well as national, salvation. Tolstoy created his school like a work of religious art in which he sought his own salvation, and moved away from the creation when it was finished. Yet he remained unsaved. His new religious-artistic project became *War and Peace* [*Война и мир*, 1869], the vast novel about past Russian aristocracy (which included in its historical orbit his own family), the exposure of whose falsehood and hypocrisy, rampant among Russia's military and political leaders, would enable both Russia and Tolstoy to save themselves, or so he hoped.

In a sense, Tolstoy's life and works may be viewed as explorations of a series of *scenarios of salvation*, which featured a variety of contents, but always followed more or less the same form. He went from one to another, never satisfied. Yet each new scenario, including the school at Iasnaia Poliana, astonishes us by its brilliant, innovative potential as a path to salvation, issuing from Tolstoy's indomitable, militant, searching, suffering, shameful, rejoicing, and eternally youthful spirit.

Endnotes

1 I am indebted to James M. Tonn for translating an earlier version of this essay from Russian into English.
2 The letter is dated February 15, 1860. The original reads: "Не искушай меня без нужды, / Лягушкой выдумки твоей. / Мне как учителю уж чужды / Все сочиненья прежних дней" (60:322; the translation is mine).
3 60:328-330 (italics mine). Quotations of Tolstoy are from the 90 volume edition of his *Complete Collected Works* [*Полное собрание сочинений*], cited by volume and page number. All translations are mine. Schools modeled on Tolstoy's, built with his assistance, began appearing in neighboring villages. They anticipated in some ways the Tolstoyan movement of the 1880s to the 1900s, centered on Iasnaia Poliana, that regarded "civilized" society as misguidedly believing itself to be making progress when it was actually heading toward self-destruction.
4 Tolstoi, *ПСС*, Chertkov edition, 60:330-31.
5 The use of the name of his estate—the village of Iasnaia Poliana in Tula Province—as the title of the journal was a matter of principle for Tolstoy: the truth about education (and, for that matter, life) could not be discovered in large cities, not in Petersburg and Moscow institutions and journals, but in the countryside, and especially in Tolstoy's native countryside. The epithet "clear" ["ясная"] was also possibly intended as a subtle jab at the misguided, obscure, or false philosophizing of contemporary theorists of pedagogy, whose ideas, divorced from practice, were, according to Tolstoy, ruining the most important activity of the era (though one of Tolstoy's more acrimonious critics noted that Tolstoy's school turned out not "clear" but "heavily clouded.") (E-g-m-t [Chumakov], Педагогические парадоксы, 174).
6 These ideas are formulated in the following articles by Tolstoy: "О народном образовании" (8:4-25)," Ясно-полянская школа за ноябрь и декабрь месяцы" (8:23-75, 8:110-125), "Воспитание и образование" (8:211-246), "Прогресс и определение образования" (8:325-355). On Tolstoy's pedagogical theories, see Cohen; Murphy; *Mossman*; and Pinch.

7   Tolstoy believed the most important pedagogical task was to give a generation of peasant children an opportunity to develop—or at least not to prevent from developing—an understanding of art and of the world that "that is just as new in form as it is in content" (8:116).
8   Tolstoi, *ПСС*, Chertkov edition, 8:496-504. For the epigraph to his journal Tolstoy chose a line from Goethe's *Faust*: "You believe that you push, but in reality it is you who are being pushed" ["Glaubst zu schieben und wirst geschoben"]. Tolstoy's epigraph was intended for those contemporary theorists and practitioners of pedagogy who arrogantly believed that they knew how and what to teach to peasant children even while ignoring the "secret laws" of the pedagogical process, which could only be discovered during the practice of teaching those children.

   Mephistopheles says these words to Faust during the mad, hellish dance they attend on Walpurgis Night. The choice of a Mephistophelean quotation as an epigraph might have been inspired by Goethe's devil's biting satire of contemporary educational institutions (first and foremost the university) in *Faust*. In the beginning of the tragedy Mephistopheles, donning Faust's professorial gown, gives murderous "lessons" to a beginning student (later he re-encounters this student, who has by then received his baccalaureate degree, and continues to ridicule "dead" pedagogy).
9   Tolstoi, *ПСС*, Chertkov edition, 8:30.
10 Ibid.
11 I would note that Tolstoy did not care what happened to his students once they left the school; hence we know almost nothing about them as adults (see 8:623-25).
12 However, in the spring of 1862, in Tolstoy's absence, teachers at Iasnaia Poliana were placed under arrest for two days for unconfirmed suspicions of anti-government activity, namely, the establishment of a secret press.
13 Tolstoi, *ПСС*, Chertkov edition, 8:602.
14 Ibid., 8:25.
15 Ibid., 8:30.
16 The resemblance of the Iasnaia Poliana pedagogical experiment to a utopian commune was evident to Tolstoy's contemporaries. According to the memoirs of a German writer and acquaintance, Tolstoy would boast that on the doors of his school hung a sign saying "Enter and exit freely."

According to other memoirs, in one of the classrooms hung another favored slogan: "Do what you want!" Tolstoy's biographers have suggested that the first sign was a polemical response to the inscription on the doors to Dante's hell ("Abandon all hope, ye who enter here" ["Lasciate ogni speranza voi ch'intrate"]; Tolstoy thought of all modern systems of education as a "hell"). The second was undoubtedly a quotation from the famous pedagogical (anti-scholastic) utopia of the French humanist François Rabelais. These very words ["fais ce que tu voudras"] were the rule in Brother Jean's joyful Abbey of Theleme, the inhabitants of which freely expressed their individual wills, enjoyed society, the arts, reading, played sports, and were most happy and virtuous because they were free. It is notable that Tolstoy reread Rabelais's novel in the month when he decided to begin his "new profession" as an educator.

17 Tolstoi, *ПСС*, Chertkov edition, 8:31-40.
18 See Eikhenbaum, part 1, 371-392; part 2, 37-55.
19 Tolstoi, *ПСС*, Chertkov edition, 8:556.
20 Ibid., 8:246.
21 Ibid.
22 In this case, Tolstoy marshals the power of music, which he would, many years later, depict as subversive in "The Kreutzer Sonata" ["Крейцерова соната," 1889].
23 On the eve of his turn to pedagogy, Tolstoy is said to have lamented that he was as "unloved" as the hero of his short novel *The Cossacks* [*Казаки*, 1863]. In this light, Iasnaia Poliana can be viewed as a place where he created and cultivated children's love (and even adoration) for himself.
24 One student, Vaska Morozov (whom Tolstoy said he held in higher regard than Goethe) recorded the informality that characterized the relationship between Tolstoy and his students. He reports that, one day, to the delight of the children, Tolstoy returned home after his year-long voyage around Europe and went to freshen up: "Lev Nikolaevich came out [undressed] with two brushes, combing his hair. We just gasped when we saw how old he was, and I couldn't help but say: 'Lev Nikolaevich! How old you look!' Lev Nikolaevich said: 'Yes, *the sand is already pouring out of my ass*' ['уж из жопы песок сыпется']. Then Lev Nikolaevich got dressed and we went to exercise" (171).

25 I think that Tolstoy is here polemicizing not only with Nikolai Chernyshevsky, as Eikhenbaum claims (part 2, 100-103), but also with Turgenev's well-known story "Bezhin Meadow" ["Бежин луг," 1852], a classic depiction of peasant children in Russian literature. This story features an enlightened but obviously superior gentleman [барин] who eavesdrops on the conversations of serf boys about evil forces and is touched by their poetry. Tolstoy the teacher converses with children as with equals.

26 Tolstoi, *ПСС*, Chertkov edition, 8:301-324. In this article Tolstoy puts forth a rare—for him positive—even enthusiastic appraisal of someone else's work. (Of course, we should not forget that he himself prompted this work, participated in its creation, and published it in his journal.)

27 Ibid., 8:323.

28 Ibid. For a structural analysis of the compositions of Tolstoy's schoolchildren, see Thomas Winner.

29 Fedka is the pseudonym Tolstoy gave to Vaska Morozov. Fedka and his comrade Semka ("a morally and physically healthy lad of about twelve years, nicknamed Vavilo" (8:624)), appear in a few of Tolstoy's articles and in his diaries they—especially the former—are mentioned repeatedly. As Eikhenbaum notes, Fedka and Semka in some way personify for Tolstoy two major tendencies of his own work (115).

30 I am deliberately avoiding the question of what the contents of this story actually were, since they have no bearing on Tolstoy's reaction to the story. It seems that, for him, it would have been better if this story, resurrected phoenix-like from the ashes, had not been preserved at all but had existed only in his "pale" paraphrase, like a simulacrum of some higher creation. In fact, in his account, the boys' story is like a myth engendered from peasant nature itself; it is some mystical type of folklore, wholly undermining the concept of literature as an individual or professional performance.

31 Tolstoi, *ПСС*, Chertkov edition, 8:305.

32 Ibid., 8:307. Scholars of Tolstoy have long been abashed by the strange sexual (pedophilic) metaphor used by Tolstoy in his description of his pedagogic triumph/defeat: he indirectly compares himself with depraved old men who spy on children. Eikhenbaum explains that the use of sexual terminology, which "attaches to the entire experiment an especially

profound and somewhat sinister meaning," reflects a "historical trauma of the era," which is revealed in Tolstoy's letters of the 1860s, in which he refers to the composition of stories as "an obscene business."

33 Tolstoy began planning to develop his own version of Christianity in the early 1850s.
34 It is interesting to note the parallel to Gogol, also the creator of a religious and pedagogical utopia (but not a school). In general, it reminds us that the idea of personal salvation of the artist through useful activity far from the petty world is Romantic in origin.
35 Matthew 18:20; 8:34.
36 Tolstoi, *ПСС*, Chertkov edition, 60:436.
37 Ibid., 8:503.
38 Ibid., 8:496 (italics mine).
39 Matthew 11:25-26.
40 Tolstoi, *ПСС*, Chertkov edition, 43:72.
41 Tiutchev, *Лирика*, 1:174.
42 Tolstoi, *ПСС*, Chertkov edtion, 61:24.

Works Cited

Cohen, Adir. "The Educational Philosophy of Tolstoy." *Oxford Review of Education* VII, no. 3 (1981): 241-251.

E-g-m-t (Chumakov, A.). "Педагогические парадоксы (по поводу статьи Льва Толстого 'Воспитание и образование')." *Воспоминание* 12 (1862): 169-177.

Eikhenbaum, Boris. *Лев Толстой*. Leningrad: Priboi, 1928.

Morozov, V. "Сочинение." In *Неизвестный Толстой в архивах России и США*, edited by I. P. Borisova, 171-74. Moscow: AO TEXHA-2, 1994.

Mossman, Eliott. "Tolstoy and Peasant Learning in the Era of the Great Reforms." In *School and Society in Tsarist and Soviet Russia*, edited by Ben Eklof, 36-69. New York: St. Martin Press, 1993.

Murphy, Daniel. *Tolstoy and Education*. Dublin: Irish Academic Press, 1992.

Pinch, Alan. "The historical background." In *Tolstoy on Education: Tolstoy's Educational Writings 1861-62*, selected and edited by Alan Pinch and Michael Armstrong and translated by Alan Pinch, 9-28. London: The Athlone Press, 1982.

Tolstoi, Lev. *Полное собрание сочинений*. 90 vols. Edited by V. G. Chertkov. Moscow: Gosudarstvennoe izdatel'stvo "Khudozhestvennaia literatura," 1928-1958.

Tiutchev, Fyodor. *Лирика*. 2 vols. Moscow: Nauka, 1966.

Winner, Thomas. "'*Glaubst zu schieben und wirst geschoben*': Some observations about Tolstoj's experiments with children's writing." In *Slavic Poetics. Essays in Honor of Kiril Taranovsky*, edited by Roman Jakobson, Cornelis H. van Schooneveld, and Dean S. Worth, 507-524. The Hague: Mouton, 1973.

An Afterword on the Wondrous Thickness of First Things

Caryl Emerson

Do Titans also have helpless childhoods, awkward adolescences, and false starts that would noiselessly fall by the wayside, were it not for the masterpieces that followed? Or are bits of later genius somehow extractable from everything a Titan writes, at any stage, and thus worthy of our reverent recuperation? So deep are the shadows cast by masterpieces that the work that precedes them can be dismissed as a mere preliminary and at the same time—paradoxically—enhanced, hyper-scrutinized for hints of later, larger themes. Reading the first works of famous authors, the temptation to live in the shadows is great.

Placing greatness in its proper context is a delicate task with Dostoevsky and Tolstoy. One important reason has been the global reach of their spiritual and intellectual legacy—like Shakespeare, the Bible, the Buddha, the Koran, these two titanic Russian authors belong to the world (and have been translated into most of its languages). Another is the mesmerizing weight of their work within the Russian tradition, the perennial fascination exercised by their two biographies and the competition between them. It has long been routine among literary critics to contrast their life-trajectories, usually seen as a case of deprivation versus abundance. Dostoevsky was assailed by disasters and crises imposed from without (poverty, arrest, exile, epilepsy, all conditions of loss), whereas Tolstoy, born into privilege, wealth, talent, health, and conditions of plenty, generated his crises from within, creating an event for himself by voluntarily *taking something away* (denouncing it, urging us not to do it). In her Introduction, Elizabeth Cheresh Allen bends this familiar contrast the other way, noting parallels between these two writers. Each had an orphaned childhood punctuated by painful deaths, uncertain first steps, a full-stop and then a significant gap, followed (after ten years in Dostoevsky's case, three years in Tolstoy's) with works of qualitatively different genius. In time, each would lose half of his children (Dostoevsky two out of four, Tolstoy six out of thirteen). Allen notes that the early works of both men were raved over as well as panned. At the time, neither readers nor critics knew with whom they had to deal; greatness did not yet exist. But it was incubating in both of them—and as several essays in this volume attest, much in the mature value systems of each was in place from a very early age, even in their maiden works. So the trial decade (for Dostoevsky the 1840s, for Tolstoy the 1850s) cannot quite be called a laboratory, nor the routine quest of a beginning author in search of identity. Backshadowing too must be avoided, that is, the temptation to take greatness as a predestined given and read it back into the early works. These were years when an apprentice writer's raw talent could develop, or could collapse and die. Success could fuel it—but (as Dostoevsky's career eloquently shows) so could crisis and trauma. Potentials everywhere exceeded actualities. As Tolstoy went on to ask in *War and Peace*, do "causes" or "laws" exist that might explain why things tip one way rather than the other?

After Tolstoy himself (and perhaps Aristotle), the contributor to this volume who has most closely pondered the theory behind such questions, and provided the framework for their discussion, is Gary Saul Morson. He opens his 2013 collection of essays *Prosaics and Other Provocations* with a conviction that has shaped his career: that "time is open, the present moment makes a difference, and whatever does happen, something else could have."[1] Morson lays out this idea in his *Narrative and Freedom: The Shadows of Time*, where the creativity of these two Russian novelists comes to sanctify, with a sort of secular grace, the idea of uninterrupted potency across a temporal continuum.[2] Tolstoy is examined for his commitment to contingency, Dostoevsky for his commitment to human freedom. Linking the two is Mikhail Bakhtin—for whom novels in general, and novels by these two Titans in particular—were "forms of thought" that liberated the tied-down, boxed-in world of epic, and of lyric and tragic drama as well, into a world of possibility. But as Morson (together with Bakhtin) never tires of arguing, to say things could have happened otherwise is not to say that the world is wholly open, arbitrary, or relative. Some early drafts and apprenticeship works are indispensable for a writer's development, and some are not. At times, working over a story (or an idea, or a personality) ruins it, at other times improves it. Details might mean sublimely, or might mean nothing, or might even mean negatively, cluttering and obscuring the scene. According to scholarly convention, to read a work of art closely means to justify all its details within the designed frame. But why, Morson asks, need structure be taken as the most necessary virtue of a work of verbal art? Equally virtuous can be situations where "the actual process of writing provided not a predetermined design but a series of provocations."[3] In life, whether inside the novel or outside of it, the very idea of a structured past is an empirical fallacy. This insight might be applied not only to the works of a writer, but also to the writer's biography. Can the creative history of Tolstoy and Dostoevsky be approached processually? Is it possible, from our present vantage point, to read potentials in the early works "on their own," not as part of a scaffolding that conceals masterpieces? The essays here suggest various ways of "reading but not reading *in*," that is, of being alert to particulars but not linear in their projection, not backshadowed (which is "foreshadowing after the fact").[4]

Literary commentary that comes a century or so after its subject matter was created cannot avoid some sort of shadow, however. One productive use of this volume's after-shadow might be to identify clusters of themes, or gravitational force fields, that appear to have organized the energies of both our Titans in their apprenticeship. In this afterword I discuss two such pivotal clusters, taking my cue from categories provided by Bakhtin.[5] One field belongs to the fictive "hero" (as a created, living personality), and is thus necessarily a view from the inside outward; the other is the field of the "author" (that consciousness at work on the formal craft of creating a world), a synoptic and coordinating view constructed from the outside in. In the realm of the hero, our focus will be the interlocking anxieties of shame and the creative imagination. In the realm of the author, it is experimentation at the literary edge: the attempt by these two fledgling writers to force literary forms into new service (what Morson called, three decades ago, work on the "boundaries of genre," those liminal domains that the great Russian writers so love to disrupt, suspend, and reconstruct). For each cluster we will identify territory shared by our two writers, and note where the scholars represented here see the most significant points of divergence.

First, the disconcerting issue of creativity and shame. At the center of the volume, Elizabeth Cheresh Allen (for Dostoevsky's *Netochka Nezvanova*) and Robin Feuer Miller (for Tolstoy's *Childhood*) overlap on an excruciating moment in the lives of children: an orphaned young person in search of love pursues a self-affirming fantasy—and discovers the thrill of creative writing. In this pursuit Allen distinguishes the moral imagination, which is capable of assessing the potential effects of one's actions on others, from the creative imagination proper, a more free-wheeling force that in Dostoevsky's desperately deprived children provides an alternative, an escape, literally a lifeline for the threatened self. Netochka saves herself (or buys time for herself) by bonding with the amoral storyteller, outside and inside her own consciousness. It is difficult to censure the orphan for this. Although ashamed of her indulgence in fantasy, she is very young, helpless, and alone. Dostoevsky and Tolstoy are far less patient with motivations for creativity in grown-ups. When Dale Peterson pursues the same theme but with an older protagonist in *White Nights*, the solitary walker of St. Petersburg, one feels that Dostoevsky is indeed censuring both the Dreamer and Rousseau. This is a faked *flâneur*, who pretends an intimacy of interaction with houses but cannot manage any actual contact. The story is told fifteen years after the fact and its only real encounter, as Peterson points out, is solipsistic, with the Dreamer's earlier self: during those distant white nights, he had preferred to be a "phantom lover."[6] All the more amazing, then, that Peterson seems to assume that the fantasy-object Nastenka really existed, that the Dreamer had actually met this divine, trembling, bereft creature that first evening on the bridge. That need not have been so. Peterson properly sees chronic dreaming as a pathology. But he does not take the final step, which would be to view the Dreamer as a writer with (in Allen's terms) a mature "creative imagination," a person who knows full well how to tell life from fantasy (the narrator is brutally honest with his "dear reader" on this score) but chooses not to do so, for tantalizingly long stretches of narrative.[7] The dreamer is no shameful self-punishing coward, no merely timid suitor, no victim of idle circumstance or bad luck when he "loses" his Nastenka. In his dream-story, the lodger *must* return at some point and snatch his love away—deep down the Dreamer knows this must happen—because she was herself dreamed up. The denouement to the tale must be written in such a way that he does not wake up with her in real life, within his four drab walls. He postpones that moment as long as possible, because these fantasies are his only spiritual nourishment. But only nothing can come of nothing.

Dreaming up Nastenka—the wise, passionate, vulnerable young woman of his most intense desire—is not the same, of course, as the paranoid Goliadkin dreaming up his double. Gary Saul Morson, in his explication of the dark sides of thinking empathetically, hammers home the difficult truth that we don't bother to torture a stone. If it's alive, it is worth poking with a stick, prodding into a reaction. But, Morson asks, when I cannot accept what I see of myself, when I create an alternate to myself, from what perspective can I know I am real? The shameful horror and mystery of a "misidentification of a subjectivity *from the inside*" leads Morson to suggest something more awful than Bakhtin had permitted himself in his ruminations over Dostoevsky.[8] We are humanized not by thought but by feeling—but pain alone is insufficient to humanize us. Only humiliation can do that. Here Lewis Bagby provides a complementary insight into Dostoevsky's psychic economy when he notes the peculiar form that shame takes in Makar Devushkin's letters to his far more pragmatic, resilient correspondent, Varvara Dobroselova, in *Poor Folk*. Everything in this text is stripped down: no omniscient narrator, no frame, no epilogue, only the slow unstoppable loss of Makar's one intimate interlocutor, and his frantic scrambling to replace the intimate company of his Varenka's letters with a literary style of his own. As the humiliated Makar intuits, it will become his only autonomous capital. Among the most startling aspects of this fledgling epistolary novel, which is also central to its early companion piece *A Faint Heart*, is the unexpected kindness of the poor clerk's superior, who generously slips him a hundred rubles (unlike Tolstoy, Dostoevsky allows people in power to be generous). But this humanitarian gesture eventually feeds into the shame. Susanne Fusso's discussion of the early Dostoevsky and vaudeville provides valuable counterpoint to these horrific no-exit scenes. Only in those genres where inner shame and pain are registered as comic, almost circus routine and not as deep psychic realities, namely in commedia dell'arte and its descendent, the vaudeville stage, can the audience laugh at humiliating situations. The faithless wife in "Another Man's Wife" is a hero and a winner; only the men under the bed are fools. Fast forward to that 1870 masterpiece, *The Eternal Husband*, to see this erotic triangle played out in the crookedly cruel talent of Dostoevsky's novelistic prose, with the addition of the sacrificed child.

What about the early Tolstoy on creativity and shame? Miller provides the topic sentence for comparing our two writers on the creative impulse: "For Tolstoy, from his earliest fiction this impulse was marked with ambivalence—euphoria and moral guilt—whereas for Dostoevsky the creative impulse and the process ensuing from that impulse were affirmative, even when the undertones were dark."[9] Indeed: as crookedly as his creations might grow toward the light, Dostoevsky *must* affirm, his words must create, for his scenarios (especially in his early period) are sunk in poverty. His impoverished characters dream, double themselves, create loopholes in order to survive; they create epistolary novels and memoirs out of desperation and fantasize by the book. Since they are proud, there can be shame when others catch them at these activities. By contrast, Tolstoy's scenarios, for all that they share the grievous loss of a parent, are sunk in security and wealth. They are the rosy well-fed children behind the window through which Dostoevsky's ragged orphans timidly peek and fantasize a better life. In order to survive, Tolstoy's siblings in *Childhood* do not need to create art. They take up poetry and drawing as part of their noble-class upbringing, and even the days that begin in humiliation (a dead fly falls on Nikolenka's nose) end in delighted self-expression and love. Miller emphasizes this healthy, well-endowed child's honesty and sense of wonder. And then she cites the astonishing letter from Tolstoy in 1865, in which he insists that children are not fooled by adult cleverness or cover-up, that what impresses the child is the "flush of shame appearing on my face against my will," the sure sign of what is "secret and best in my soul."[10] Shame, for the pre-Titan Tolstoy, was confessional and purifying. For the pre-Titan Dostoevsky, operating almost all the time dangerously close to starvation, violence, and the irreversible violation of innocence, shame could quickly become unbearable. Unless dramatized in a vaudeville skit, it drove one not into wisdom, but into madness.

Let us now consider our second cluster: an author's experimentation with the boundaries of received literary form. Both Dostoevsky and Tolstoy set vigorously to this task, the former in his brilliant re-castings of the Gogolian "poor clerk," the latter in his overall rejection of romanticism in favor of sterner, more analytic and didactic eighteenth-century genres. But as the contributors to Part II demonstrate, Tolstoy experimented with more vanity and self-loathing, and with bitterer vengeance. "Euphoria and moral guilt"[11] accompany his every move from pen to paper, from his very earliest publications. In Tolstoy's quasi-journalistic dispatches from the Caucasus discussed by William Mills Todd and Justin Weir, the bitterness, anxiety, and anger have multiple causes. The first is simple aristocratic disdain at any interference in his work, whether by government censor or the discretion of an editor: if it pleases you to take this piece, writes the young count, "you will not change anything at all."[12] But the deeper cause is revealed later: Tolstoy bears a grudge against the very institution of journalism, with its presumption of a general public treated to a journalist's generalized voice. My honor as author admits of no collective critical reception, Tolstoy seems to suggest. This is not class war or social war but a duel. Thus it must be conducted eye to eye, my personal word against your personal word. He does, of course, have an "imaginary reader" in mind for his work, but as always with Tolstoy, that reader is modeled on himself.[13] Thus the shame and anxiety of not getting it right, of having words (or life) fail him once again, can never be alleviated or supplemented by someone else's take on the matter. In the self-proliferating dynamics of this sort of confession, any audience worthy of Tolstoy's trust can only echo his narrator's failure and thereby reinforce it. Liza Knapp further explores Tolstoy's arsenal of discomfiting, sure-to-fail devices in her juxtaposition of Tolstoy's Sevastopol Tales to the sermonizing of Harriet Beecher Stowe. Tolstoy surely learned from the hortatory second-person address of this earnest sentimental novelist, the "daughter, wife, and sibling of ministers," but one suspects that he feared Stowe's method did not hurt enough, that it was too easy on the reader (which is to say, on the author-surrogate, which was himself). "Affirming but subverting sentimentalism," Tolstoy complicates any easy identification the reader might make with bereft mothers and motherless children.[14] With that situation he had long been familiar; in his mature writing, it would be transformed into nostalgia for the purity of childhood grieving, untainted by the fantasies and drives of adolescence. Tolstoy needed a new boundary to disturb, a new shock to administer. So he stretched the sermonic mode to its absolute outer limit, to incorporate cosmic irony, even a cosmic void. Tolstoy claims (in "Sevastopol in May") that the hero of his story, "which is and will always be beautiful and magnificent," is Truth—but he feels no obligation to spell out its content, as a preacher might at the end of a sermon. Let the reader gaze at the dead bodies strewn across the meadow. In the final Sevastopol story, "Sevastopol in August," both brothers die in a battle that was already lost.

In the volume's final two essays, all these themes figure in: the dependence and pathos of children; the shame of writing and perhaps even of language (together with its creative benefits); the attempts to break new literary ground by estranging genre conventions or juxtaposing types of narrative. Both Anne Lounsbery and Ilya Vinitsky approach these themes through Tolstoy and the peasantry. Lounsbery, a scholar of Russian geographical space, notes that Tolstoy's tales of the rural gentry belong to different genres depending on whom he wants to shame, or whom to spare shame. Seen from the gentry child's innocent perspective (as in *Childhood*), serfdom is automatized, gently patriarchal, loveable even, an indispensable part of the security of the idyll. From the point of view of unhappy well-intentioned Nekhliudov, the landowner who would discuss civic reform and justice with his serfs, it is a communication nightmare. For Nekhliudov's experience that morning, the correct genre is the philosophical tale of Voltaire, designed to "test ideas against hard facts" and watch the ideas fall apart.[15] In "A Landowner's Morning" Tolstoy looks back both to *Candide* and to the tendentious slave owner's apology offered by Nikolai Gogol. But what inevitably flies to mind for us are the later embedments of these nightmares in the great novels: Konstantin Levin trying to grasp the logic of his peasant laborers in *Anna Karenina*, and those painful chapters on the discontent and rebellion of the Bogucharovo peasants in *War and Peace* (Princess Marya Bolkonskaya wants only to help them, but they stonewall her utterly; what the peasants trust and respect are Nikolai Rostov's fists). If we eschew all backshadowing and ignore the rich human contexts that inform those later "scenes from peasant life," the indeterminate early story that Lounsbery analyzes becomes as damning as the final Sevastopol tale. People who own other people and live off their labors are corrupt in *all* their faculties, creative as well as perceptual and communicative; they cannot take "an honest account of either their own lives or others' motives."[16] The whole person is held accountable for sins that come with the epoch. Again, we would be kinder to a helpless and capricious child.

In his treatment of Tolstoy as pedagogue to peasant boys, Vinitsky shows us the landlord of Iasnaya Poliana mixing (or dissolving) genres in a stubborn, even tyrannical way. The same irritated tone toward journalism that Todd and Weir registered on behalf of Tolstoy in "Fear and Loathing in the Caucasus" is present in Tolstoy's insistence on the non-political nature of his educational ideas, and thus the innocence of his publications. But Tolstoy's intent to found a "secret society of public education" gives him away.[17] If a secret society is required, then its principles are probably subversive. At stake is not only Tolstoy's word, anchored in Rousseau, against everyone else's. Also constantly on display is the force of Tolstoy's own personality, playing piano, planning and animating the lessons, mesmerizing the young boys, insuring that no punishments are inflicted and no disciplinary rules laid down (since no one disobeys, both are unnecessary), while not failing to notice where the teaching staff falls short of duplicating Tolstoy. The creativity of these young pupils fed into Tolstoy's own creative writings on pedagogy. But with this one large difference: that the boys wrote for themselves, whereas Tolstoy generalized on them for the sake of a doctrine intended to castigate grown-ups. The terrifying emotional honesty that Tolstoy brought to his three-year pedagogical passion, his need to "save" his corrupt adult self through these activities, adds yet another genre to the primer, confession, philosophical tale, and sermonette that served Tolstoy the writer: the temporary "scenario of salvation."[18] He could not, of course, pretend that the peasant lads Fedka and Semka were as much under his grip as were Natasha Rostova, Pierre Bezukhov, or even that model peasant entity, Platon Karataev. But the peasant pupils did one thing to perfection: with their spontaneous intelligence, keen eye for fakery, and straight-as-an-arrow moral judgment, they could humiliate the civilized adult. For Tolstoy, this reproach was irresistible. Dostoevsky—who knew humiliation in infinitely finer detail than Tolstoy—did not crave this psychological condition.

"Before they were Titans": let me close on the title of this volume. Recall that the Titans were the first offspring of Gaia and Uranus (Mother Earth and Father Sky), six sons and six daughters. Only the youngest, Cronus, was courageous enough to rebel against his father (at Gaia's request) for casting their brothers, the Cyclops, into Tartarus. But Cronus, ascending to rule, proved himself a dishonorable Titan. So that no child of his could repeat his patricidal act, Cronus swallowed each newborn infant until his wife Rhea (goddesses put up with the barbaric ways of their menfolk for only so long) hid the newborn Zeus in a cave and tricked her husband into swallowing a swaddled stone. Zeus survived to launch a massive war against Cronus, after which Olympus could at last be built, the gods canonized, regularized, each given a human skill or need to protect.

There are periodic rebellions, in Russian culture, against the Titans. With that much greatness smothering the field, how can anyone born later draw a clean full breath, say a new word? Mayakovsky and the Futurists bragged about throwing some of the greats off the steamship of modernity; Nicolai Berdiaev, in his traumatized essay from 1919, "Specters of the Russian Revolution," held Gogol, Dostoevsky, and Tolstoy responsible for the degeneration and collapse of a civilization. Maxim Gorky demonized Dostoevsky both before his departure from Lenin's Russia and after his repatriation to Stalin's USSR; Bakhtin did battle against Tolstoy for decades. And of course our two mature Titans, while alive, struggled warily and at times mightily against one another. They were Russia's most famous contemporaries who refused to meet.

Before they were Titans, this wariness, territoriality, and antipathy was less pronounced. There was more "loose space" and "loose time" around each of them. Their writing was less well weeded, perhaps, thicker than it would be later on, when mastery of their medium would refine the details, perfect the lines, draw up more precise boundaries and ideologies. Tolstoy and Dostoevsky are so very great that, had they not chosen to become preachers or prophets, the world would have thrust that mantel upon them. The essays here are hardly bathed in sunshine, just because they try to avoid backshadowing. But they do alert us to an earlier texture for the voices of these two immortals, as their gifts are breaking out into the light.

Endnotes

1 Morson, *Prosaics*, 1.
2 See Morson, *Narrative and Freedom*, especially chapter 2 ("Foreshadowing") and chapter 4 ("Sideshadowing").
3 Morson, "Strange Synchronies," 486.
4 See Morson, *Narrative and Freedom*, chapter 6, "Backshadowing": "The past is viewed as having contained signs pointing to what happened after, to events known to the backshadowing observer. Visible now, those signs could have been seen then" (234). For the idea of the backshadow, Morson

is indebted to the late Michael André Bernstein, Foregone Conclusions: *Against Apocalyptic History* (Berkeley: University of California Press, 1994).

5 In Bakhtin's view, an author creating a hero works with the same two perspectives that orient any human being in the world, that of the "other" (the outside view that creates coherence) and the "I" (the inner view that generates free movement). The "otherly" perspective—from which authors must work—sees what Bakhtin calls "surroundings" ["окружение"]: it always includes within its purview the body of the character as a finalized object for others. The "I" or inner perspective has access solely to a "horizon" ["кругозор"]: modeled on what my own eyes see, it cannot therefore include the finished outer contour of my own body but only the bodies of others. A horizon is the sole perspective available to the consciousness of heroes. See Bakhtin, "Author and Hero," 13-15; 22-27.

6 Peterson, "Dostoevsky's *White Nights*," 105.
7 Ibid., 97.
8 Morson, "Me and my Double," 50.
9 Miller, "The Creative Impulse," 154.
10 L. N. Tolstoy, quoted in Miller, "The Creative Impulse," 173.
11 Miller, "The Creative Impulse," 154.
12 L. N. Tolstoy, quoted in Todd and Weir, "Fear and Loathing," 195.
13 Todd and Weir, "Fear and Loathing," 203.
14 Knapp, "Tolstoy's *Sevastopol Tales*," 222.
15 Lounsbery, "On Cultivating One's Own Garden," 269.
16 Ibid., 281.
17 Vinitsky, "Tolstoy's Lessons," 301.
18 Ibid., 310.

Works Cited

Allen, Elizabeth Cheresh, ed. *Before They Were Titans: Essays on the Early Works of Dostoevsky and Tolstoy*. Boston: Academic Studies Press, 2015.

Bakhtin, Mikhail. "Author and Hero in Aesthetic Activity." In *Art and Answerability: Early Philosophical Essays by M. M. Bakhtin*, translated by Vadim Liapunov, 4-256. Austin: University of Texas Press, 1990.

Berdiaev, Nikolai. "Specters of the Russian Revolution" ["Духи русской революции"]. In *Out of the Depths (De Profundis): A Collection of Essays on the Russian Revolution*, edited and translated by William E. Woerhlin, 33-64. Irvine, CA: Charles M. Schlacks, 1986.

Morson, Gary Saul. *Narrative and Freedom: The Shadows of Time*. New Haven, CT: Yale University Press, 1994.

____. *Prosaics and Other Provocations. Empathy, Open Time, and the Novel*. Boston: Academic Studies Press, 2013.

____. "Strange Synchronies and Surplus Possibilities: Bakhtin on Time." *Slavic Review* 52, no. 3 (Fall 1993): 477-93.

____. "Tempics and The Idiot." In *Celebrating Creativity. Essays in honour of Jostein Børtnes*, edited by Knut Andreas Grimstad and Ingunn Lunde, 108-34. University of Bergen, 1997.

Index

A

Abrams, M. H., 119, 140n14, 141n24, 148, 290n2
Adams, Robert, M., 298
Aksakov, Ivan, 243n10
Alexander II, 213, 243n10, 246n21
Allen, Elizabeth Cheresh, 1, 115, 119-120, 250n59, 261, 318, 320, 327
Altman, Janet G., 16
Andrew, Joe, 16, 110n23, 116, 124-125, 142n40, 143n53, 144n63-64,
Anisimov, I.I., 87n77
Andersen, Hans Christian, 182n19
Apollonio, Carol, 16, 34n13, 35n14
Aristotle (Aristotelian plot), 249n50, 318
Arndt, Walter, 110n35
Augustine, 139
Austerlitz, 229
Avvakum, 232

B

Babel, Isaac, 153
Bagby, Lewis, 6, 9, 15, 321

Bakhtin, Mikhail, 16, 18, 33n6, 34n11, 35n17, 39, 61, 268, 287, 290n4-7, 296n83-84, 318-319, 321, 326, 327n5, 328
Balaklava, 212, 243n6
Baldwin, James, 251n65, 261
Balzac, Honoré de, 5, 40, 87n68, 89, 112, 162, 185n62
    Cesar Birotteau, 185n62
    Eugenie Grandet, 5
    Père Goriot, 87n68, 89
Barnes, Elizabeth, 250n58, 261
Barran, Thomas, 108n2, 112
Baudelaire, Charles, 108n1, 112, 242
    Fleurs du Mal, Les, 108n1
Beethoven, Ludwig van, 171, 185n62, 302
    Sonata pathétique, 171
Belinsky, Vissarion, 6, 15-17, 33n4-6, 40, 62-63, 78, 82, 84n6, 84n11, 88n83, 89n102
Belknap, Robert, 16, 34n12, 38n55, 40, 216, 247n29, 261

Index

Bely, Andrei, 1, 11n1
Bem, Alfred L., 33n6, 40
Benjamin, Walter, 108n1, 112
Berdiaev, Nikolai, 327
Biriukov, Pavel, 183n32, 207, 209
Boltzmann, Ludwig, 159
Borisov, I. P., 299
Borisova, I.P., 315
Borodino, 227-229, 254n98,
Brant, L. B., 138
Brontë, Charlotte, 137n2, 148, 163
    Jane Eyre, 137, 145n90, 148, 163, 176
Browne, Janet, 158, 181n12, 190
Buddha, 317
Bulgakov, V., 163
Bunyan, John, 232
Burnasheva, N. I., 207n1-2, 207n4-5, 209, 237, 243n9-10, 256n131, 258n140, 261
Burton, Richard, 109n8, 112
Bursov, B. I., 208n29, 209
Butterworth, Charles, E., 109n5, 113
Buzina, Tatiana, 37n46, 40 Cain, Tom, 187n82, 190

C

Campbell, Mary Baine, 160, 182n23, 190
Caucasus, 7-8, 12, 164, 193-194, 199, 213-214, 271, 323, 325
Chekhov, Anton, 1, 86n49, 90
Chenery, Thomas, 244n11
Chernyshevsky, Nikolai, 45, 79-80, 88n94, 90, 138, 156, 164, 221, 252n67, 261, 314n25
Chertkov, V. G., xi, 11-12, 180n5-6, 217, 241n2, 243n6, 244n11, 246n21, 247n22, 247n28, 248n35, 251n65, 254n98, 259n147, 259n150, 289n1, 312n8
Christian, R. F., 180n5, 184n37, 185n62, 186n65, 187n81-82, 188n85, 190
Christianity, Christian, Christians, 55, 136, 141n36, 215, 218, 221, 227, 233, 236-237, 252n77, 257n136, n138, 258n139, 277, 308, 315n33
Chumikov, A. (E-g-m-t), 311n5, 315
Circle of Reading, 309
Cocking, J.M., 141n33, 141n36, 148, 149
Coleridge, Samuel Taylor, 157, 180n10, 190
    Biographia Literaria, 157, 180n10, 190
Cohen, Adir, 311n6, 315
Contemporary, The, 116, 155, 194, 199, 217, 237, 243n10, 248n33, 282
Crimean War, 8, 211-213, 226, 240, 242n4-5, 243n8, 247n22, 249n50, 250n60, 254n101, 258n139, 302
Curtis, James, 11n7
Curtiss, John Shelton, 253n83, 85, 259n146, 261

D

Danilov, S.S., 82, 84n7, 89n102
Dante, 181n14, 313n16
Darwin, Charles, 158, 181n14, 190, 191
Descartes, René, 50, 54
    Pensées, 52, 153, 254n91, 263
Derzhavin G. R., 175
Dickens, Charles, 112, 162-163, 166, 173, 176-178, 186n66, 187n82, 188n85, 190-191, 214, 245n17,
    David Copperfield, 163, 166, 173-174, 176-178, 186n66, 187n82, 188n85, 190-191,,
    Great Expectations, 162, 183n27
Dillard, Annie, 159, 181n18, 190
Dmitriev, Iu. A., 83n3, 84n7, 89n102, 175
Dmitriev I. I., 175
Dobroliubov, Nikolai A., 15, 40
Dostoevsky, Fyodor, xi, 1-12, 15-152, 153-156, 162, 164, 173, 179n1-2, n4, 188n88, 190-191, 214, 216, 245n17, 246n29, 247n31, 259n148, 285, 292n28, 301, 317-326
    "Another Man's Wife," 5-6, 9, 61-83, 84n4, 85n27, 86n45, 322

Brothers Karamazov, The, 44-45, 50-51, 55, 58n4, 59, 111n40, 115, 163
"Christmas Party and a Wedding. From the Notes of an Unknown Person, A," 62, 70-72, 86n45, 86n52
Devils, The, 54, 89
Diary of a Writer, 301
Double, The, 6, 9, 17, 41-42, 43-58, 58n5, 59n19, 85n27
"Dream of a Ridiculous Man, The," 108, 111n40, 153-154
Eternal Husband, The, 6, 59, 61-62, 74-83, 86n67, 87n63, 87n73, n76, 89n102, 90, 322
Faint Heart, A, 71-72, 86n53, 321
Gentle Creature, The, 142n44
Honest Thief, An, 36n36
Idiot, The, 35n14, 328
Insulted and Injured, The, 115
"Jealous Husband, A," 6, 9, 61, 66, 68-77, 83, 85n43, 86n45
Netochka Nezvanova, 5, 7, 9, 115-137, 137n1, n.3, 139n4-6, 142n36, n38, 144n62, 148n113, 320
Notes from the House of the Dead, 44, 214, 247n31
Notes from Underground, 17, 59n20, 107, 101 111n42, 136
Poor Folk, 5-6, 9, 15-42, 111n37, 137n2, 189, 321
"Uncle's Dream," 83n3, 89n101
White Nights, 6, 9, 93-112, 320
Druzhinin, Aleksandr V., 138, 242n5
Dunnigan, Ann, 58n3, 60, 139n6, 149
Dupeuty, Charles, 77, 90
Dyson, Freeman, 157, 180n8, 190

E

Eagle, Herbert, 39n57, 40
Eliot, George, 245n17
Eliot, T. S., 178

Edmonds, Rosemary, 181n15, 192
Eikhenbaum, Boris, 8, 11n16, 183n31-32, 184n43, 190, 198-199, 207n13, 208n19, 208n28, 209, 217-219, 227, 231, 233, 236, 244n12, 245n18, 248n33, 248n35, 250n60, 255n108, 261, 270, 291n13, 296n82, 297, 313n18, 314n25, 314n29, 314n32
Einstein, Albert, 162
Emerson, Caryl, ix, 1, 4, 11, 39, 185n62, 190, 297, 317
Empson, William, 290n6, 297
Engels, Friedrich, 245n14
Ergolskaia, T. A., 188n85
Etov, V. I., 16

F

Fanger, Donald, 109n8, 111n41, 112
Fénelon, François, 269
Fenton, Roger, 212-213, 243n7, 261
Fet, Afanasy, 246n20, 271, 299
Feuer, Kathryn B., 188n88, 246n21, 262
Feuer, Lewis S., 182n24, 190
Feynman, Richard, 161, 182n25, 191
Field, John, 171
Filaret (Metropolitan of Moscow), 232, 258n141
Fink, Hilary, 108n3, 112
Fisher, Philip, 216, 218-221, 247n30, 248n40, 262
Fleming, Angelea Michelli, 262
Follen, Eliza Cabot, 253n81
Frank, Joseph, 5, 11n13, 32n3, 33n6, 38n55, 39n56, 40, 61-62, 78, 83n3, 84n4, 88n81-82, 89, 109n6, 109n9, 111n41, 112, 130, 136, 137n1, 143-144n62, 145n86, 148
Fridlender, Georgii M., 16, 35n19, 38n55, 39n56, 40, 42, 138, 144n70, 148
Frye, Northrop, 198, 207n15, 209
Fusso, Susanne, 6, 9, 61, 89, 139n5, 149, 321

G

Gandhi, Mahatma, 258n141
Garnett, Constance, 58n4-5, 59
Gauss, Carl Friedrich, 162
Gifford, Henry, 187n82, 191
Girard, René, 32n2, 40
Gleick, James, 162, 183n29, 190-191
Goethe, Johann von, 299, 304-306, 312n8, 313n24
    Erlkönig, Der, 299, 304-305
    Faust, 312
Gogol, Nikolai, 1, 4, 16, 20, 30, 33n6, 33n9, 38n55, 51, 55, 106, 111n41, 112, 184n54, 187n82, 198, 202, 207, 218, 232, 248n38, 255n115, 263, 270, 274-278, 288, 293n29-34, 295n76, 297, 315n34, 322, 324, 326
    Dead Souls, 4, 202, 295n76
    Inspector General, The, 55
    "Nose, The," 51
    "Overcoat, The," 30, 38n55, 39n55, 184n54
    Selected Passages from Correspondence with Friends, 232, 270, 274-276, 278, 293n29, 294n49, 297
    Viy, 187n82
Goldenveizer, A.V., 164
Goncharov, Ivan, 1
Goriachkina, M. S., 72, 297
Gospel(s), 187, 224, 259n150, 307, 309
Gozenpud, A., 82, 83n3, 85n43, 88n101, 89n102
Grossman, Leonid, 16, 35n15, 40, 116, 137n1, 138n3, 145n86, 149
Gusev, N. N., 207n6-7, 209
Gustafson, Richard, 187n69, 191, 216, 247n27, 260n152, 262, 285

H

Hamilton, John Maxwell, 262
Harden, Evelyn, 59n19
Hazlitt, William, 118, 140n12, 149
Hedges, Chris, 256n125, 262

Hesiod, 120
Hildreth, Richard, 248n31
    Slave, The, 248n31
Hoffmann, E. T. A, 111n41, 113
Hollier, Denis, 290n9-10, 296n86, 297
Holquist, Michael, 111n42, 112, 296
Homer, 2, 120, 188n85, 214, 225, 234, 244n12, 248n38, 250n60, 256n124, 260n156
    Iliad, 225, 256n124
Hruska, Anne, 180n6, 184-185n54, 191, 215, 260n155, 262, 268, 285, 289n1, 290n3, 295n79-81, 297
Huet, Marie-Hélène, 108n4, 112
Hugo, Victor, 245n17, 255n101
Hume, David, 256n125

I

Iakubovich, I. D., 33, 41
Iasnaia Poliana, 154, 271, 299-300, 302, 304-305, 308-313
Iasnaia Poliana (journal), 195, 301, 306
Intermediary, 195
Invalid, The, 213, 244n11
Ibsen, Hendrik, 124,
    Wild Duck, The, 124
Ishchuk, G. N., 203, 208n27, 209

J

Jackson, Robert Louis, 33n6, 38n55, 39n61, 41, 71, 86n49, 90, 116, 120, 139, 141n35-36, 149
Jacobson, Roman, 316
James, Henry, 162, 216, 249n42, 262
Jencks, Charles, 86n57, 90

K

Karlinsky, Simon, 84, 90
Kaye, Danny, 181
Karamzin, Nikolai, 36n28, 37n44, 232, 247n28, 248n39
    Poor Liza, 36n28, 37n44
Kekes, John, 118, 140n16, 149

Kentish, Jane, 142, 148
Kirpotin, Valerii Ia., 16, 33n3, 41, 87n68, 90
Kliger, Ilya, 290n9
Knapp, Liza, 8-9, 139n4, 211, 252n75, 257n134, 262, 292n28, 323
Knowles, A.V., 180n7, 184n38, 191
Kohn, Denise, 248n33, 262, 263
Kock, Paul de, 77-78, 87n77-78, 90
Koni, F., 82
Krasnostchekova, Elena, 116, 122, 132, 142n42, 147n99, 149
Kupreianova, E. N., 207n17, 209

L

Lanz, Kenneth, 179, 190
Layton, Susan, 237, 243n9, 258n140, 262
La Rochefoucauld, François, 55
Le Carré, John, 153
Leatherbarrow, William, 16-17, 33n7, 37n43, 38n55, 41, 149
Lederle, M. M., 187n82
Lee, Desmond, 149
Lemon, Lee T., 191
Leontev, Konstantin, 256
Lermontov, Mikhail, 1, 39n57, 40, 197, 201-202, 207n10, 214, 245n14
    Hero of Our Time, A, 39n57, 40, 197, 201-202, 207n10, 214, 245n14
Lesskis, Georgii, 285, 297
Levin, Harry, 197, 207n8, 209
Liapunov, Vadim, 327
Likhachev, Dmitry S., 232, 255n114-115, 262
Locke, John, 48-49, 58n7-8, 60
Lord Aberdeen (George Hamilton-Gordon, 4th Earl of Aberdeen), 213
Louis XIV, 269
Lounsbery, Anne, 4, 8, 10, 11n11, 246, 267, 324
Lyles, John, 36n25, 41

M

MacKay, John, 245n20, 248n33, 249n42, 263
Magarshack, David, 59, 109n7, 110n20, 112
Markovits, Stefanie, 242n4, 243n8, 244n11, 253n85-86, 262
Marullo, Thomas, 116, 139, 149
Matveyev, Rebecca E., 41
Maude, Aylmer, 185n61, 192, 241n2, 262, 264, 298
Maude, Louise, 192, 241n2, 262, 264, 298
Mayr, Ernst, 158
Medzhibovskaya, Inessa, 293, 295n74, 297
Meer, Sarah, 262-263
McDuff, David, 35n16, 40
McEwan, Ian, 155, 179n3, 191
McLean, Hugh, 181, 191, 241n1, 292n20, 293n29, 297
McReynolds, Susan, 16
Merezhkovsky, Dmitrii, 2
Miller, Robin Feuer, ix, 7, 9, 40, 153, 179n1, 191, 261-262, 320
Mikhailovsky, N.K., 69-70, 84n4, 85n40, 90
Mikhaylovsky-Danilov, Aleksandr, 201
Mochulsky, Konstantin, 11n9, 12, 109n6, 112, 116, 138n3, 139n5, 145n86, 146n92, 149
Moleschott, Jacob, 45
Monahan, Michael A., 12, 112, 149
Morozov, V. (Vaska), 313n24, 314n29, 315
Morris, Errol, 263
Morson, Gary Saul, ix, 4, 6, 9, 11, 12, 36n22, 41, 43, 216, 219-221, 230, 249n50-51, 255n105, 263, 318-319, 321, 326n1-4, 328
Mossman, Eliott, 311n6, 315
Motidzuki, Tetsuo, 76-78, 87n70-71, 87n74, 88n82, 90
Murphy, Daniel, 311n6, 315
Murray, Penelope, 139n8, 149

N

Nagel, Thomas, 58n12, 60
Napoleon, 208n28, 229-230, 234-235, 254n98, 254n101, 255n103
Nechaeva, V.S., 72, 83n3, 86n53, 87n.55, 90
Nekrasov, Nikolai A., 15, 82, 88n.101, 155, 164-165, 182n22, 194-195, 246
Nestor, 48
Newlin, Thomas, 183n28, 191, \
Nicholas I, 6, 213, 244n11, 294n39
Nightingale, Florence, 212, 226, 253n85
Nietzsche, Friedrich, 181n14
Nikolaeva, S. Iu., 148n110, 149
Nora, Pierre, 111n44, 112
Notes of the Fatherland, 61, 83n1, 84n15, 86n45, 96, 115

O

Odoevsky, Vladimir, 33n9, 41
  Living Corpse, The, 33n9
Orlova, R. D., 248n33, 263
Orwin, Donna Tussing, 179n4, 190-191, 207n3, 209, 262, 291n15, 297

P

Panaev, Ivan, 243n10
Paperno, Irina, 88n94, 90
Parsons, Elsie Clews, 297
Parts, Lyudmila, 86n60, 87n69, 88n94, 90
Pascal, Blaise, 45, 52-54, 59n16, 60, 153, 227, 254n91
Passage, Charles E., 111n41, 113
Peace, Richard, 33n9, 34n10, 34n12, 41
Peck, John, 242n4-5, 263
Petersburg Almanac, The, 32n3
Petersburg Chronicle, The, 62, 70-72, 85n45, 95, 98
Peterson, Dale, 6, 9, 93, 320
Pevear, Richard, 242n2, 264
Plato, 119-120, 136, 141n24-25, 141n33-36, 200, 204, 208n29
  Republic, The, 119, 141n25-27, n20-34, 149

Pinch, Alan, 311n6, 315
Pisarev, Dmitry, 222, 252n68, 263
Poe, Edgar Allan, 108n1
  Man of the Crowd, The, 108n1
Pratt, Branwen E. B., 76, 87n69, 90
Price, Martin, 118, 140n19, 149
Prince Albert, 212
Proskurina, Iu. M., 109n6, 113
Pryse, Marjorie., 263
Pushkin, Aleksandr, 1, 4, 30-31, 35n21, 37n44, 38, 41, 52, 90, 103, 105, 110n35, 112, 136, 197, 207n9, 230, 254n100, 263, 302
  Boris Godunov, 6, 52
  Eugene Onegin, 4, 103, 105, 136, 197, 207n9, 230, 254n100
  Queen of Spades, The, 35n21, 37n44
  "Stationmaster, The," 30, 105

R

Rabelais, François, 313n16
Rancour-Laferriere, Daniel, 186n69, 191
Rapp, Emily, 37n46
Reis, Marion J., 191
Rogers, Philip, 187n82, 188n87, 191
Rosenshield, Gary, 16, 41, 111n43, 113
Rossini, 85n43, 102
  Barber of Seville, The, 102-103, 105
  Otello, 85n43
Rousseau, Jean-Jacques, 93-95, 107, 108n1-5, 109n5, 112-113, 163, 170, 176, 179n4, 187n82, 214, 216, 301, 307, 320, 325
  Confessions, 94, 108n3, 112, 187n82
  Emile, 187n82
  Julie, ou la nouvelle Héloïse, 94
  Rêveries du Promeneur Solitaire, Les, 93-95, 107, 108n1, 109n5, 113
Rowe, William, 116-117, 139n7, 143n47, 145n85, 149
Rozanov, Vasilii, 33
Russell, William, 212-213, 219, 242n5-6, 244n11, 249n50, 262- 263

S

Saint Petersburg Gazette, 95
Saint Petersburg News, 85n45
Saltykov-Shchedrin, Mikhail, 245n14,
Samoilov, V.V., 81-83, 88n101, 89n102
Sand, George, 137n2, 138
Scanlan, James, 136, 148n114, 149,
Scott, Walter, 102, 132-133, 135, 150
    St. Ronan's Well, 133, 147n101, 150
Scruton, Roger, 117, 140n10-11, 140n23, 150
Sechenov, Ivan, 45
Serman, I. Z., 87n76, 89n102, 90
Shakespeare, William, 2, 70, 118, 140n9, 162, 181n14, 205, 244, 317
    Hamlet, 140n9
    Othello, 70, 85n43
    Tempest, The, 118
Shaklan, Steven, 243n7
Shapiro, Fred, 58, 59n25, 60
Shapiro, Judith, 181n19
Shelley, Percy Bysshe, 119, 140n22, 150
Shklovsky, Viktor, 158, 177, 180n11, 187n83, 191, 214, 218, 245n14, 263, 275-276, 293n29, 293n37, 294n39, 297
Šilbajoris, Rimvydas, 207n6, 209
Simmons, Ernest J., 182n26, 191
Smith, Karen R., 245n18, 263
Socrates, 48,
Sontag, Susan, 212, 221, 242n3, 243n7, 251n62-63, 251n65, 263
Sophocles, 162
Stendhal (Marie-Henri Beyle), 203, 208n28, 214, 218, 250n60, 264
    Chartreuse de Parme, La, 250n60, 264
Steiner, George, 2, 11-12, 188n85, 191
Sterne, Laurence, 163, 176, 189, 203, 206, 208n17, 214, 216, 232
    Sentimental Journey, A, 189, 203
Stoppard, Tom, 159, 182n20, 191
    Arcadia, 159, 182n20, 191
Stowe, Harriet Beecher, 8, 10, 211, 214-225, 232-233, 236, 240-241, 245n17-18, 20, 246n21, 247n24-25, 28, 31, 248n33, 248n36-40, 248n41-42, 249n55, 250n58-59, 251n65, 252n77-78, 253n80-81, 255n102, 256n118, 257n134, 257n136-138, 260n152, 262-265, 323
    Uncle Tim, 217-218, 220, 236, 245n18, 248n35, 249n40, 256n118
    Uncle Tom's Cabin, 10, 215-216, 218, 220, 224-225, 233, 236, 240, 245n17-18, n20, 246n21, 247n24-25, 248n33, n40, 249n42, 250n58-59, 251n65, 252n77-78, 253n81, 257n134, 260n152, 262-263, 286
Strachey, Lytton, 226
Straus, Nina Pelikan, 117, 150
Sue, Eugène, 137
    Mathilde. Memoires d'une jeune femme, 137n2

T

de Tarde, Gabriel, 293n36, 297
Tate, Trudi, 242n4, 243n6, 264
Tennyson, Alfred, 212, 243n6, 264
    Charge of the Light Brigade, The, 212, 243n6, 264
Terni, Jennifer, 62-63, 78, 80-81, 84n8-9, 12, 88n80, 90
Terras, Victor, 33n6, 33n36, 38n53, 42, 83n3, 86n52, 91, 111n41, 113, 116, 139, 138, 143n50, 143n54, 150
Terry, G. M., 42
Tester, Keith, 108n1, 113
Thackeray, William Makepeace, 214, 218, 232, 245n12
    Vanity Fair, 232, 255n109
Time, 248n31
Times, 212, 243n6, 244n11, 247n22, 250n59
Tiutchev, Fyodor, 271, 315n41, 316

Todd, Emily B., 262-263
Todd, William Mills, III, ix, 4, 8, 9, 11n8, 12, 193, 207n1, 323, 325
Toepffer, Rodolphe, 163, 176,
Tolstoy, Lev, xi-xii, 1-10, 45, 58n3, 116, 121, 153-326
    Anna Karenina, 157, 171, 186n62, 216, 223-224, 262, 275, 287, 293n28, 293n38-39, 294n40, 295n72, 324
    Boyhood, 8, 121, 159, 163, 181n15, 199, 215, 240, 271, 292n20
    Childhood, 5, 7-9, 116, 121, 155-192, 194-195, 202-204, 214-215, 240, 260n155, 262, 267-268, 271, 273, 275, 285-287, 290n8, 296n82, 320, 322, 324,
    Confession, 157, 203
    Cossacks, The, 8, 196, 203, 271, 313n23,
    Death of Ivan Ilych, The, 157
    Hadji Murad, 196
    "History of Yesterday, The," 165, 201, 273
    Kreutzer Sonata, 313n22
    "Landowner's Morning, A," 5, 8, 10-11, 246n21, 267-289, 290n9-10, 291n13-14, 292n18, 296n83, n85, 324
    "Notes of a Billiard Marker," 271, 292n20
    On Life, 206
    "Raid: A Volunteer's Story, The," 4, 8-9, 193-208, 271
    Reminiscences, 183n32, 259n150
    Sevastopol Tales, The, 5, 8-9, 165, 196, 211-265, 271, 323-324
    "Sevastopol in August," 213-214, 238, 241, 253n83, 324
    "Sevastopol in May," 213-214, 219, 223, 226, 230-238, 241, 244n12, 255n108-109, 156n124, 158n141, 323
    "Sevastopol in December," 199-200, 211, 213-214, 219, 221, 228-230, 235, 241, 243n10, 249n50, 252n77-78, 253n83, 260n156, 273, 302
    Strider, 177
    "Summer in the Country," 154
    War and Peace, 4, 45, 58n3, 157, 163, 165, 184n42, n49, 186n62, 191-192, 196, 216, 226, 228-230, 237, 242n2, 245n13, 248n38, 262, 264, 275, 287, 310, 318, 324
    "Woodfelling, The," 214
    Youth, 8, 121, 163, 181n15, 240, 271, 296n82
Tolstaya, A. A., 173
Tompkins, Jane, 215, 219, 247n23-24, 247n31, 249n47, 252n77, 264
Tonn, James, M., 311n1
Trilling, Lionel, 118, 140n17, 150
Trubetskoi, Nikolai, 33n6, 42
Turgenev, Ivan S., 1, 78, 87n76, 89n102, 97, 110n11, 113, 164, 191, 209, 214, 218, 243n10, 248n40, 249n42, 250n59, 261-262, 265, 270-271, 282-287, 295n69, 297, 314n25
    "Bezhin Meadow," 314n25
    "Ermolai and the Miller's Wife," 285
    "Flower, The," 97
    Notes of a Hunter, 214, 218, 248n40, 249n42, 250n59, 270, 282, 284-285, 287
Turner, C. J. G., 87n76, 89n102, 91
Tynianov, Iurii, 33n6, 42

U

Updike, John, 155, 179n3, 191

V

Venturi, Robert, 73, 86n58, 90-91
Vetlovskaia, Valentina, 33n3, 33n6, 34n9-10, 42
Vinitsky, Ilya, 8, 10, 179n4, 192, 299, 324-325
Vinogradov, Viktor, 16, 34n10
Vladimirtsev, V. P., 16, 42

Volokhonsky, Larissa, 242n2, 264
Voltaire, 288-289, 296n89, 298, 324
    Candide, or Optimism, 288-289, 296n89, 324

W
Wachtel, Andrew, 7, 11n15, 12, 116, 138n4, 150, 164, 179n4, 182n22, 183n32-35
Warren, Joseph, 118
Warhol, Robyn, 220, 232, 249n53, 256n118, 265
Wasiolek, Edward, 150
Weinstein, Cindy, 255n117, 263, 265
Weir, Justin, 4, 8, 9, 180, 183n32, 185n62, 192, 193, 208n23, 209, 323, 325
West, Rebecca, 59n18, 60

Wiener, Leo, 298, 298
Wilson, E. O., 158-159, 181n16, 192
Winner, Thomas, 314n28, 316
Woerhlin, William, E., 328
Wordsworth, William, 119, 140n20-21, 150, 157, 180n9-10
Woodward, James B., 86n60, 87n73, 91
Wyss, Johann David, 168

Y
Yeats, W. B. 188n85

Z
Zeldin, Jesse, 294n47, 297
Zhiliakova, Emma, 16, 34n9, 36n35, 39n56, 42
Ziusudra of Sumer, 37n46

www.ingramcontent.com/pod-product-compliance
Lightning Source LLC
Chambersburg PA
CBHW051108230426
43667CB00014B/2496